W9-BLL-053

ADVANCE PRAISE

FOR

Imaginative Writing

The Elements of Craft

Second Edition

About the Author

Photo: Peter Ruppert

Janet Burroway is the author of plays, poetry, essays, children's books, and seven novels including *The Buzzards*, *Raw Silk* (runner up for the National Book Award), *Opening Nights*, and *Cutting Stone*. Her publications include a collection of personal essays, *Embalming Mom*, in addition to a volume of poetry, *Material Goods*, and two children's books in verse, *The Truck on the Track* and *The Giant Jam Sandwich*. Her most recent plays, *Medea With Child*, (The Reva Shiner Award), *Sweepstakes*, *Division of Property* (2001 Arts & Letters Award), and *Parts of Speech*, have received readings and productions in New York, London, San Francisco, Hollywood, and various regional theatres. Her textbook *Writing Fiction*, now in its seventh edition, is used in more than three hundred colleges and universities in the United States. She is Robert O. Lawton Distinguished Professor Emerita at the Florida State Universities in Tallahassee.

Imaginative Writing

The Elements of Craft

Second Edition

Janet Burroway
Florida State University

PENGUIN ACADEMICS

PEARSON
Longman

New York   San Francisco   Boston
London   Toronto   Sydney   Tokyo   Singapore   Madrid
Mexico City   Munich   Paris   Cape Town   Hong Kong   Montreal

Vice President and Editor in Chief: Joseph Terry
Acquisitions Editor: Erika Berg
Development Manager: Mary Ellen Curley
Development Editor: Adam Beroud
Executive Marketing Manager: Ann Stypuloski
Production Manager: Savoula Amanatidis
Project Coordination, Text Design, and Electronic Page Makeup: Elm Street Publishing
    Services, Inc.
Cover Designer/Manager: Nancy Danahy
Cover Photo: Miro, Joan (1893–1983). © ARS, NY. Dragonfly with Red Wings in Pursuit
    of a Serpent which Crawls Like a Spiral, etc. Photo Credit: Scala/Art Resource,
    NY, Fundacion Miro, Barcelona, Spain.
Photo Researcher: Ilene Bellovin
Manufacturing Buyer: Mary Fischer
Printer and Binder: R. R. Donnelley and Sons Company—Crawfordsville
Cover Printer: Phoenix Color Corporation

For more information about the Penguin Academics series, please contact us by mail at
Longman Publishers, attn. Marketing Department, 1185 Avenue of the Americas, 25th
Floor, New York, NY 10036, or by e-mail at 222.ablongman.com.

For permission to use copyrighted material, grateful acknowledgment is made to the
copyright holders on pp. 392–395, which are hereby made part of this copyright page.

Library of Congress Cataloging-in-Publication Data
Burroway, Janet.
    Imaginative writing: the elements of craft / Janet Burroway. —2nd ed.
        p. cm.—(Penguin academics)
    Includes bibliographical references and index.
    ISBN 0-321-35740-X
    1. English language—Rhetoric. 2. Creative writing (Higher education) 3. College
readers. I. Title. II. Series.

PE1408 .B8843 2007
808—dc22   2006006329

Please visit our website at http://www.ablongman.com

ISBN 0-321-35740-X

5 6 7 8 9 10—DOC—09 08

*For Neal, Eleanor, Holly, and Thyra
who inherit the language*

Contents

CHAPTER 3 CHARACTER 79

CHAPTER 4 SETTING 131

Preface to the Instructor

In the second edition of *Imaginative Writing* I have tried to refine and focus several features of the book without fundamentally changing its purpose, which is to provide a workable and energizing multigenre text for basic creative writing courses. Users and reviewers have been generous in their help, and have led me to add exercises in the early chapters that will help students to develop a draft, to add or alter some of the "Try This" exercises and a good many of the readings, to make exercises easier to identify and find in the text, and to expand the glossary. The revision narratives in Chapter 6, "Development and Revision," have been expanded; sample formats have been added to each genre chapter; and I have clarified, expanded, or simplified instances where reviewers pointed out muddle, sketchiness, or the goblins of jargon. Collaborative Exercises are now available as a separate supplement accompanying the text. The single greatest change in this edition is a shift from a general discussion of "the essay" to a focus on "creative nonfiction," particularly the personal essay and memoir. Although these were discussed in the first edition, many reviewers felt that the essay as such was adequately covered in standard courses, and that students needed a clearer notion of what "creative" or "literary" nonfiction offers in terms of freedom and stricture, demand and possibility.

The core organizing principle of *Imaginative Writing* remains the same, which is that students in a multigenre course can benefit from playing with various writing techniques before they settle into a particular form. Much, if not most, of the advice given to students is relevant to any sort of writing and to most of the genres: the need for significant detail, for example, applies equally to narrative scene, poetic line, and theatrical dialogue; voice is a concept that applies to a character, a narrator, a memoir, a lyric persona, and so forth. My expectation is that by discussing techniques and offering exercises that let students experiment with those techniques *before* they commit to a formal project will make the instruction less threatening and encourage a sense of adventure. Beginning this way will also make it possible to illustrate the extent to which *all* writing is imaginative (as well as autobiographical) and that different genres share similar sources and build on similar skills.

I have taken fiction and poetry as givens in a multigenre course. I have personally been convinced of drama's usefulness in developing a writer's facility (with characterization, dialogue, plot, pace, symbol). I have also wanted to acknowledge the growing popularity of creative nonfiction, the continuity of imaginative writing with the essay form students have inevitably studied, and the fact that emerging writers may find it easiest to begin with the material of their own lives.

The book is organized on the assumption that a college semester is fifteen or sixteen weeks long and that one or two weeks are always lost to administration, holidays, exams, and illness, so that material for fourteen weeks is about right. Roughly, the first five weeks are intended to cover five areas of imaginative technique (image, voice, character, setting, and story), the sixth the processes of development and revision, and two weeks each can then be devoted to creative nonfiction, fiction, poetry, and drama.

Each chapter begins with a graphic or photographic image accompanied by a "Warm-up" prompt, which may be assigned in class or as a journal entry or replaced by one of the instructor's invention.

Each of the technique chapters proceeds with a discussion of that technique, including illustrations from more than one genre (some invented and some taken from established writers); "Try This" exercises linked to particular aspects of the topic; then complete selections in the various genres. Like the "Warm-up" features, the "Try This" exercises can be used as in-class practice, assigned for journal entries, or left for the students to choose from. I think it's important, at least sometimes, to discuss resulting pieces in class, in order to get students used to a nonjudgmental discussion of roughs and written play. (This neutral way of workshopping is described at the end of the next section, "Invitation to the Writer.") Further comments and exercises among the selections at the end of each chapter link the readings to the techniques discussed and suggest *briefly*—there are no questions aimed at literary interpretation—how to read the selections for what can be taken away from them and made part of a repertoire of skills. But, of course, all the selections illustrate many things, and they can be assigned in any order or quantity that suits the individual instructor. The second edition, at the request of several reviewers, also contains development ideas at the end of each technique chapter, to aid those teachers who encourage students to be thinking toward a finished piece.

Chapter 6, "Development and Revision," suggests ways to use the material generated in the first five weeks toward the writing of finished pieces, and here too the workshop may prove a positive help to the writer through exploration rather than praise and critique. The "Try This" exercises in this chapter can be used in class or out, and if it feels right, students can be encouraged to exchange journal pieces and try developing and revising passages not their own. This chapter is followed by some examples, with discussion, of aspects of the rewriting process.

I've envisioned that for each of the final four chapters, dealing with creative nonfiction, fiction, poetry, and drama, one week will be spent discussing the genre and roughing out a draft, a second workshopping and working at revision. (Instructors will know what is comfortable and doable for their classes; my inclination would be to assign a short story and an essay of about 1,500 words each, three poems, and one ten-minute play.) Each of these final chapters outlines what is unique and defining about each of the genres in order to suggest ways of exploiting the particular nature of that genre and to help the students use what they have learned in the first six weeks. The chapters close with a sample format for the featured genre.

The exercises in these chapters are designed to promote development of some aspect of the genre under discussion or to aid revision in terms of focus, cutting, attention to language, originality, and so forth. At this point, the critical component of the workshop becomes relevant; students will no doubt be ready to talk about not only what sort of thing this piece of work *is* but whether and where it "works."

The order of presentation is always problematic in a writing text—everything really needs to be said at once—and many instructors will find that they would have chosen a different sequence for the techniques or the genres or both, so I'll say a little about my rationale. When I laid out the plan for the text *Writing Fiction* many years ago, I had, out of my classroom experience, a strong sense that students focusing on that form needed a sense of its structure and to face the question: What is a story? But for the more playful and process-oriented course for which *Imaginative Writing* is intended, it seems to me that the core need and the first skill is the one represented by the irreplaceable maxim: *Show; don't tell.* Again and again, I have seen an *aha!* moment in the classroom when a student suddenly grasps the principle of addressing the senses, a technique so simple and yet so elusive. It is also often revelatory that diction and point of view direct meaning, and I have addressed this issue second. From image and voice to character is a logical progression; then to the outside world of setting, and only then to a consideration of what it means to tell a story, whether in memoir, poetic, fictional, or dramatic form.

I put development and revision together, in the middle of the book, in the hope of suggesting that these are ongoing parts of the same process, rather than representing a beginning and an end.

When I came to ordering the genres, I reasoned that creative nonfiction offers beginning writers the easiest segue from the material of their own lives and from the essay writing they find most familiar. From the personal essay or memoir to fiction may prove a short imaginative step. Poetry leads them then to focus on density and the effects of language. Finally, drama in many ways asks that they distance themselves farthest from autobiography, that they externalize everything verbally or visually.

There is nothing sacred about this order, and I have tried to balance the chapters between self-containment and linkage, so that an instructor who prefers another sequence may shop around in the text and shape his or her course to fit. In practice, I think it may be most difficult to alter the sequence of the five techniques chapters, and no problem at all to switch—or omit—any of the genres.

The Appendix, "A Basic Prosody," offers more information about, and practice in, poetic form. A glossary of the terms covered in the text follows the appendix.

New to the second edition of *Imaginative Writing* is a supplement containing a revised version of the collaborative exercises that appeared as an appendix in the first edition. These have been recast for ease of use, and represent a *bricolage* of suggestions for in-class play. Some involve writing, but most are taken from theater, art, dance, meditation, and physical therapy. Some instructors will be eager to try them; others may recoil from them as disruptively boisterous or dreamily New Age. But if I have any proselytizing to do, it is at this pulpit. I say to my students, and also to teachers considering the supplement: *Don't worry about it, go with it, give it a shot.* Students are often resistant to getting out of their chairs, embarrassed to pick up a felt-tip, reluctant to make a nonverbal sound. Yet simple stretching and breathing can break down the rigidity of the classroom. Repeated improvisations such as the "word-at-a-time story" sometimes become the cohesive social force in a writing class. Mask making sometimes begins with the groans of the artistically challenged and leads to breakthrough on character. Mirroring can teach more about narrative than a lecture on conflict or connection. I have over several years become convinced of the useful energy generated by each one of these exercises, and I've tried to indicate the purpose of each one. In the meantime, however, they are separately presented in a supplement to take or leave.

It often seems pretty well impossible to teach a course across the genres—a semester to do everything, as if you were asked to teach "Intro to Human Nature" or "The History of Work" in sixteen weeks. My hope is that this book will make it feel a little more possible. What *Imaginative Writing* is *not*, however, is comprehensive. It tries to cover the basics in a way that is sound but brief, overwhelming to neither the student nor the personality and methods of the instructor. I will be interested to hear from anyone who teaches from the book how well I have succeeded in this, and how I might improve the book in future editions (jburroway@english.fsu.edu).

Meanwhile, I am grateful to numbers of people, especially my colleagues Elizabeth Dewberry, Robert Olen Butler, Jimmy Kimbrell, and Ned and Elizabeth Stucky-French; and always to my students and former students, of whom I would like to name especially Heather Sellers, Ann Turkle, Michael McClelland, Beth Watzke, Carissa Neff, Debbie Olander, Thom Mannarino, Pat Murphy, William Nesbitt, Tom Bligh, and Sara Pennington. Many of the readings, ideas, and exercises in this book are here thanks to their talent, invention, and spirited help. Creative writing exercises tend to be, like scientific information in a more generous time, freely offered, freely shared, and passed from hand to hand. I know that I have cadged, cobbled, and adapted my "Try This" exercises from Marta Mihalyi, Maria Irene Fornes, Aimee Beal, Margaret Rozga, Cheril Dumesnil, Laura-Gray Street, Mary Ann Lando, Gerald Shapiro, Matt Zambito, and Michael Kardos, many of them from the pedagogy panels of the Associated Writing Programs. Other ideas will have come to me third-hand, or I will have forgotten where I read or heard them; to those unacknowledged, equal thanks and apologies.

I have relied on the incisiveness and generosity of my reviewers: Dan Bentley-Baker, Florida International University; Michael Bertsch, Shasta College; Lawrence Coates, Southern Utah University; Jeffrey DeShell, University of Colorado at Boulder; David James, Oakland Community College; Bruce W. Jorgensen, Brigham Young University; Jeff Mann, North Dakota State University; Almeda Glenn Miller, Kootenay School of the Arts and Selkirk College; D. K. Peterson, Virginia Tech; Lauren Puccio, Columbia University; Shouhua Qi, Western Connecticut State University; Michael Ritterbrown, Glendale College; Porter Shreve, University of North Carolina—Greensboro; Sarah L. Stecher, Tulsa Community College; and Susan Swartout, Southeast Missouri State University; and on the insight and cheer of my editors, Adam Beroud and Erika Berg, to all of whom great thanks. My husband, Peter Ruppert, brings light to life and lit.

JANET BURROWAY

Invitation to the Writer

I just realize that we start out in these very awkward ways,
and we do look a little stupid as we draft, and that's all
right . . . You have to be willing to go into the chaos and
bring back the beauties.

Tess Gallagher

You . . .

You started learning to write—at the latest—as soon as you were born. You learned within hours to recognize an "audience," and within a few days that expressing yourself would elicit a response. Your basic desires created the fundamental form of story—I want, *I want*, I WANT!—with its end in gratification (comedy) or denial (tragedy). Within a year you had begun to understand the structure of sentences and to learn rules of immense subtlety and complexity, so that for no precisely understood reason you would always say "little red wagon" rather than "red little wagon." You responded to rhythm and rhyme (*One, two. Buckle my shoe*). You matched images and explained their meanings (*This is a giraffe. Dog is hungry*). You invented metaphors (*My toes are soldiers*). By the time you could speak you were putting together personal essays about what you had done and what had happened to you and forecasting fantasies of your future exploits. By the time you started school, you had (mostly thanks to television) watched more drama than the nobility of the Renaissance and you understood a good deal about how a character is developed, how a joke is structured, how a narrative expectation is met, and how dramatic exposition, recognition, and reversal are achieved. You understood the unspoken rules of specific traditions—that Bugs Bunny may change costume but the Road Runner may not, that the lovers will marry, that the villain must die.

You are, in fact, a literary sophisticate. You have every right to write.

This needs saying emphatically and often, because writing is one of those things—like public speaking, flying, and garden snakes—that often calls up unnecessary panic. Such fear is both normal (a high percentage of people feel it) and irrational (statistically, the chances of disaster are pretty low). It is true that some speakers do humiliate themselves, some planes do crash, some snakes are poisonous. Nevertheless, people do learn to speak, fly, and garden. And people learn to shrug at their dread and write.

. . . and writing . . .

All writing is imaginative. The translation of experience or thought into words is of itself an imaginative process. Although there is certainly such a thing as truth in writing, and we can spot falsity when we encounter it in print, these qualities are hard to define, hard to describe, and do not always depend on factual accuracy or inaccuracy. Often what is *most* original, that is, imaginative, is precisely what "rings true."

Aristotle said that when you change the form of a thing you change its purpose. For example, the purpose of an algebra class is to teach algebra. But if you take a photo of the class, the purpose of the photo *cannot* be to teach algebra. The picture would probably serve the purpose of commemorating the class and the people in it. On the other hand, if you wrote a short story about that class, its purpose might be (not to teach algebra or to commemorate the class, but) to reveal something about the emotional undertow, the conflict in or between students, the hidden relationships in that apparently staid atmosphere.

It's impossible to tell *the truth, the whole truth, and nothing but the truth* in words, because words are of a different form than experience, and their choice is determined by the vast array of cultural and personal influences. Writers learn very quickly that a written incident is not necessarily credible because it "really happened," and that convincing writing is in the writing and not in the facts. When you write about an experience, you put it in a new form and therefore furnish it with a new purpose. Part of the hard work and the pleasure of writing is discovering what that purpose is. You will never exactly "catch" an experience you have lived, but you may both discover and reveal new insights in the recasting of that experience.

All writing is autobiographical as well as invented. Just as it's impossible to write the whole and literal truth about any experience, so it's also impossible to invent without drawing on your own experience, which has furnished your brain. Your view of yourself, the place you live, the people you know, the institutions you live with, your view of nature and God or the gods will inform not only your dreams and daydreams, what you say, wear, think, and do, but also everything you write. What you write will inevitably reveal to a certain extent both what you think the world is like and what you think it *should* be like.

Between the two impossibilities—of perfectly capturing your experience in words and of avoiding it altogether—lies the territory that we call "creative." Begin by writing whatever comes to you, recording your observations, trying out your ideas, indulging your fantasies. *Then* figure out what you want to make of it, what its purpose is, and what it means. Then work toward making it "work"—that is, toward making it meaningful for the reader who is your partner in the imaginative act.

. . . and reading . . .

At the same time, you yourself need to become a reader of a writerly sort, reading greedily, not just for entertainment but also focusing on the craft, the choices, and techniques of the author; "reading the greats," in novelist Alan Cheuse's words, "in that peculiar way that writers read, attentive to the peculiarities of the language . . . soaking up numerous narrative strategies and studying various approaches to that cave in the deep woods where the human heart hibernates."

Reading as a writer involves not asking, *What does this mean?* so much as, *How does it work? Why has the author made this choice of imagery, voice, atmosphere? What techniques of language, pacing, character contribute to this effect?*

Reader/writers sometimes become impatient with this process. "How do you know the author didn't just want to do it that way?" The answer is: you don't. But everything on the page is there because the writer chose that it should be there, and the effectiveness of the piece depends on those choices. The British critic F. R. Leavis used to observe that a poem is not a frog. In order to understand the way a frog works you must kill it, then splay out the various respiratory, digestive, muscular systems, and so forth. But when you "take apart" a piece of literature to discover how it is made, and then put it back together by reading it again, it is more alive than before. It will resonate with all you have learned, and you as a writer will know a little better how to reproduce such vitality.

. . . and this book . . .

My creative writing workshop exchanged a few classes with a group of student choreographers. The first time we came into the dance theater, we writers sat politely down in our seats with our notebooks on our laps. The choreographer-dancers did stretches on the carpet, headstands on the steps; some sat backward on the chairs; one folded herself down into a seat like a teabag in a teacup. When they started to dance they were given a set of instructions: *Group A is rolling through, up and under; Group B is blue Tuesday; Group C is weather comes from the west.* The choreographers began to invent movement; each made up a "line" of dance. They repeated and altered it. They bumped into each other, laughed, repeated, rearranged, and danced it through. They did it again. They adjusted. They repeated. They danced it through. Nobody was embarrassed and nobody gave up. They tried it again. One of the young writers turned to me with a face of luminous discovery. "We don't *play* enough," she said.

That's the truth. Writing is such a solitary occupation, and we are so used to moiling at it until it's either perfect or *due*, that our first communal experience of our writing also tends to be awful judgment. Even alone, we internalize the criticism we anticipate and become harsh critics of ourselves. "The progress of any writer," said the great poet Ted Hughes, "is marked by those moments when he manages to outwit his own police system."

Imaginative Writing assumes that you will play before you work—dance before performing, doodle before fiddling with, fantasize before forming, *anything goes* before *finish something*. This is not an unusual idea among writers and teachers of writing. ("Indulge yourself in your first drafts," says novelist Jonathan Lethem, "and write against yourself in revisions.") But it is easier to preach than to practice.

Nevertheless, most of the techniques that writers use are relevant to most forms of imaginative writing and can be learned by playing around in any form. So the first five chapters of this book talk about some techniques that are useful in any sort of writing or relevant to more than one genre, and suggest ways to play with those techniques. The purpose of these chapters is to free the imagination. The sixth chapter talks about ways to develop and revise your experiments into a finished piece. The last four chapters discuss what is particular to each of four forms—creative nonfiction, fiction, poetry, and drama—and how you can mold some of what you have written toward each of them.

There is a lot of "do this" in the following pages, but a good deal more of "try this." The overriding idea of the book is *play*—serious, strenuous, dedicated, demanding, exhilarating, enthusiastic, repeated, perfected play. It is the kind of play that makes you a superior swimmer or singer, a first-rank guitar, pool, polo, piano, or chess player. As with any sport or musical skill, a writer's power grows by the practice of the moves and the mastering of the instrument.

Insofar as writing is a skill, it can only be learned by doing. Insofar as writing is "inspired," it may pour out of you obsessively, feverishly, without your seeming to have to make any effort or even without your seeming to have any responsibility for it. When that happens, it feels wonderful, as any writer will tell you. Yet over and over again, writers attest to the fact that the inspiration only comes with, and as a result of, the doing.

. . . and your journal . . .

While you use this book you will be writing one—a journal that should be, first of all, a physical object with which you feel comfortable. Some writers keep notes in a shoebox or under the bed, but your journal probably needs to be light enough to carry around easily, sturdy enough to stand up to serious play, large enough to operate as a capacious holdall for your thoughts. Think of it as a handbag, a backpack, a trunk, a cupboard, an attic, a warehouse of your mind. Everything can go into it: stuff you like and what you paid too much for, what Aunt Lou gave you and the thing you found in the road, this out-of-date whatsit and that high-tech ware. You never know what you're going to need; absolutely anything may prove useful later on.

TRY THIS 0.1

In other words, write any sort of thing in your journal, and write various kinds of things:
- An observation
- An overheard conversation
- Lists
- Longings
- Your response to a piece of music
- A rough draft of a letter
- Names for characters
- Quotations from what you are reading
- The piece of your mind you'd like to give so-and-so
- An idea for a story
- A memory
- A dream
- A few lines of a poem
- A fantasy conversation
- Titles of things you are never going to write
- Something else

Your journal is totally forgiving; it is 100 percent rough draft; it passes no judgments.

Throughout *Imaginative Writing* there will be prompts, trigger lines, and ideas for playing in your journal. Here are a few general suggestions:

- **Freewrite.** Gertrude Stein called this "automatic writing." Either on a regular schedule or at frequent intervals, sit down and write without any plan whatsoever of what you are going to write. Write anything that comes into your head. It doesn't matter what it is *at all*. This is the equivalent of volleying at tennis or improvisation at the piano; it puts you in touch with the instrument and limbers the verbal muscles.

- **Focused freewrite.** Pick a topic and focus on it. Write for five or ten minutes saying anything at all about it—*anything at all*—in any order.

- **Brainstorm.** Start with the question *"What if . . . ?"* Finish the question and then free-associate around it, absolutely anything that pops into your head—ideas, situations, connections, solutions, and images, no matter how bizarre. This is a problem-solving technique that can also generate energy for imaginative writing. If you need an idea, or if your character is facing a decision, or if you don't know what your setting looks like—whatever the problem, whatever idea might be struggling to surface—brainstorm it and let your mind run free.

- **Using the world.** Your journal may record your own feelings and problems, but make it more outer-directed than a diary, because training yourself to observe the outside world will help develop the skills of an imaginative writer. Make a daily habit of recording something you experienced or noticed. It may be an overheard remark, an unexpected sight, a person who caught your attention, even a news item or something you learned in a class. Knowing that you are going to write every day will give you a habit of listening and seeing with writing in mind. A writer is a kind of benevolent cannibal who eats the world—or at least, you'll experience the world with an eye and ear toward what use you can make of it.

Make a habit, rather than a chore, of writing in your journal. If you skip a day, it's not the end of the world, but it may well be that, as with a physical workout, you have to coax or cajole yourself into writing regularly before you get to the point when you look forward to that part of your life, can't wait for it, can't do without it. You will know some of the patterns that help you create a habit. Write first thing in the morning? At the same hour every day? After a shower? With a cup of coffee? Before you fall asleep? Use your self-discipline to make yourself sit down and write, but once you get there, tell your inner critic to hush, give yourself permission to write whatever you please, and *play*.

TRY THIS 0.2

Here is a list of lists:
- Things on which I am an expert
- Things I have lost
- Signs of winter
- What is inside my body
- Things people have said to me
- What to take on the journey
- Things I have forgotten
- Things to make lists of

Pick any one of these items to generate a list in your journal.

Pick a single word from your list and write a paragraph about it. Is this the germ of a memoir or a story?

Write a single line about each item on the list. Is this the start of a poem?

. . . and your workshop

Many of us think of the primary function of a writing workshop as being to criticize, in order to improve, whatever piece of writing is before us. This is, again, absolutely natural, not only because of the way the writing workshop has evolved over the years but because nothing is more natural than to judge art. We do it all the time and we do it out of a valid impulse. If you tell me you've just seen a movie, I don't ask the plot, I ask: *How was it?* Art *sets out to* affect us emotionally and intellectually, and whether it has achieved this is of the first interest. The poet and critic John Ciardi said of literature that "it is never only about ideas, but about the experience of ideas," and the first thing we want to know is, naturally, "how was the experience?"

But if the first thing you and your workshop expect is a writer at *play*, and if in order to play you banish your inner critic and give yourself permission to experiment, doodle, and dance, it doesn't make a lot of sense to subject that play to immediate assessment. I'm going to suggest that for most of the time this book is being used, you avoid the phrases, *I like, I don't like, This works, this doesn't work*—and all their equivalents. It may be harder to forgo praise than blame, but praise should be a controlled substance too. Instead, discipline yourself to explore whatever is in front of you. Not *What I like*, but *What this piece is like*. Interrogate it, suggest its context, explore its nature and its possibilities:

- *Is there a drama in this situation?*
- *I'm wondering what this word suggests.*
- *This reminds me of . . .*
- *It's like . . .*
- *I think this character wants . . .*
- *What if . . . ?*
- *The rhythm is . . .*
- *Could this be expanded to . . . ?*
- *Is the conflict between . . . ?*
- *Does this connect with . . . ?*
- *The atmosphere seems . . .* and so forth.

This kind of descriptive, inquisitive, and neutral discussion of writing is *hard*. It will pay off in the freedom that each writer feels to write and in the flexibility of critical response you're developing in the workshop. In the later part of the course, when everyone is writing in a particular form and revision is the legitimate focus of the work, there will be a time to discuss not only *what this piece is trying to do* but also where and whether it succeeds. At that point, critique will help.

Even when you arrive at the point that criticism is relevant and helpful, there are a few basic protocols for the workshop that should always be observed:

- The piece is under discussion. The author is not. Make sure your comments relate to the nature of the writing and not (even by implication) to the character of the writer. Separate the writer from the voice or character.

- Continue to interrogate the piece: *What kind is it? What does it suggest? What is its apparent aim?*

- The goal of the workshop is to make *this* piece the best that it can be. There's no place for dismissal or disregard. On the contrary, the obligation of the workshop is to identify and foster the promise in every story, essay, poem, or drama.

- As the writer, your obligation is to listen attentively, take everything in, and keep your natural defensiveness in check. Your workshop leader may (or may not) offer you a chance to speak. But this is the least important part of the workshop process for *you*. The most important part comes later, when you get back to work. Then (and only then) you will begin to sort out what's most useful.

TRY THIS 0.3
Make use of these prompts or trigger lines for easy freewrites. Pick one of them—quickly; don't think about it too much—write it down and keep writing. Anything at all. Whatever the prompt suggests. Keep going. A little bit more.
- This journal is
- My mother used to have
- There was something about the way he
- The house we lived in
- In this dream I was
- She got out of the car
- The first thing I want in the morning

More to Read

Bernays, Anne and Pamela Painter. *What If . . . ?* New York: Longman, 2003.

Friedman, Bonnie. *Writing Past Dark*. New York: HarperCollins, 1993.

Laurie Lipton, "Leashed Passion"

WARM-UP
Write a paragraph about a single small part of this picture (not the whole beast, but
its leash or feet, for example). Include the color, the smell, sound, texture, and taste of
the thing described. How does this focus on sensory detail create a particular feel or
emotional response? How does it differ from the impact of the picture as a whole?

CHAPTER ONE

IMAGE

Image and Imagination
Concrete, Significant Details
Figures of Speech

When I talk about pictures in my mind I am talking, quite
specifically, about images that shimmer round the edges . . .
You just lie low and let them develop.

Joan Didion

Image and Imagination

There is a simple trick at the heart of imaginative writing.

If I say, "Not everything that appears to be valuable is actually valuable," you
will understand me in a general kind of way, but you won't think I've said anything very interesting (and you might feel a little preached at). Whereas if I say,
"All that glistens is not gold," you literally "see" what I "mean."

The trick is that if you write in words that evoke the senses, if your language is full of things that can be seen, heard, smelled, tasted, and touched,
you create a world your reader can enter.

George Plimpton begins his account of a season as a rookie with the Detroit
Lions this way:

> I decided finally to pack the football. It was a slightly used Spalding ball, an
> expensive one, with the information printed on it that it was "tripled-lined and
> lock-stitched." Its sponsoring signature was that of Norman Van Brocklin, the
> ex-Phildelphia Eagle quarterback. It seemed a little deflated. I pressed it down
> hard against the shirts and was able to get the canvas suitcase cover zipped up
> around it.

Even if you're ignorant about triple-lining, lock-stitching, Norman Van Brocklin,
and the Philadelphia Eagles, because Plimpton begins by putting you in a scene
you can see and feel, he draws you immediately into his story.

It's no accident that the words *image* and *imagination* have the same root (Latin *imago*, a picture or portrayal), because what all imaginative writing has in common is that it calls up pictures in the mind. Any sort of writing—reports, treatises, theories, instructions—may be enlivened by examples. But the kinds of writing we group under the heading *imaginative*—poetry, song lyrics, play scripts, film scripts, personal essays, memoirs, stories, novels—exist fundamentally as representations. They portray people, places, and objects, as if physically present. Any particular piece of imaginative writing may or may not be "imaginary" in the sense of made-up; it may or may not have its origins in "real" people or what "really" happened. What all such pieces invariably have in common is that the writing calls up sense impressions in the mind—readers *see, hear, smell, taste,* and *feel* the scene by responding through their imaginations.

Novelist Robert Olen Butler points out that *all* art objects are sensuous and are produced by a process that is sensuous rather than logical. Artists in other media than literature are clear about the nature of their process, because they work with material that is fundamentally of the senses. The musician deals in sound, the painter in color and composition, the sculptor in texture, the dancer in bodily movement. But because as writers we deal in a medium of words, which are abstract symbols, we may find it harder to set logic and argument aside. Writing as an art begins when we surrender ourselves to the world of images.

An image is a word or series of words that evokes one or more of the five senses. *An image appeals to the senses.* This is the foundation of imaginative writing. If you can "grok" that fact (a useful word that means to understand in the gut as well as the head), you are on your way to being a writer.

Here is a thought that does not contain an image:

It is best to consider consequences before proceeding.

Here is an image that contains the same thought:

Look before you leap.

A thought without an image:

It's important to reassure your offspring of your affection.

An image that contains the thought:

Have you hugged your child today?

A thought without an image:

The situation is being manipulated by peripheral interests.

An image that contains the thought:

Wag the dog.

A thought without an image:

I will do everything in my power to overturn this unjust verdict.

An image that contains the thought:

I will fall like an ocean on that court! (Arthur Miller, *The Crucible*)

A thought without an image:

The verses I am writing have no vitality; they are unattractive and stale.

An image that contains the thought:

They are not pigs, they are not even fish, /Though they have a piggy and a fishy air—(Sylvia Plath, "Stillborn")

Notice that every case of flat writing above is full of abstractions (*actually, affection, power, vitality, before*), generalizations (*everything, all, consequences, verses*), and judgments (*valuable, important, best, unjust, no vitality, unattractive, stale*). When these are replaced with nouns that call up a sense image (*gold, child, dog, ocean, court, pigs, fish*) and with verbs that represent actions we can visualize (*glisten, look, leap, hug, wag, fall*), the writing comes alive. At the same time, the ideas, generalizations, and judgments are *also* present in the images.

Notice too that Miller's image "fall like an ocean" has weight and texture; Plath's image of poems that have a "fishy air" suggests not just the sight of a fish but its smell. All of the five senses go into the making of imagery, and a writer working at full stretch will make use of them all.

It's not that abstractions, generalizations, and judgments are useless or bad writing in themselves; on the contrary, they are important to all human communication.

- *Abstractions* are the names of ideas or concepts, which cannot in themselves be experienced directly through one or more of our senses, such as *intelligence, criticism, love, anger.*

- *Generalizations* can only be vaguely visualized because they include too many of a given group: *something, creatures, kitchen equipment.*

- *Judgments* tell us what to think about something instead of showing it: *beautiful, insidious, suspiciously.*

Human beings are able to communicate largely because they are capable of these kinds of conceptual thinking.

But it is sense impressions that make writing vivid, and there is a physiological reason for this. Information taken in through the five senses is processed in the *limbic system* of the brain, which generates sensuous responses in the body: heart rate, blood/oxygen flow, muscle reaction, and so forth. Emotional response consists of these physiological reactions, and so in order to have an effect on your reader's emotions, you must literally get into the limbic system, which you can only do through the senses. Now, the images of a film strike the eye directly, as *images*, just as the sounds of music strike the ear directly as sound, the smells of perfume or food strike the nose directly, and so forth. But the images of written literature (including sound, smell, taste, feel) strike the eye as little symbols on the page, which must be translated by the brain into the sound that these symbols represent, which must then be translated into the sense that our language signifies by that particular sound. It's a complicated process that demands a lot of a reader, who will thank you for making it worthwhile.

And it is a dynamic process, to which readers actively bring their own memories and experience. Words not only *denote*, or literally refer to their meaning, but *connote*, suggest or imply through layers of connection in our experience and culture. Often using the imagery of one sense will suggest the other senses as well, and will resonate with ideas, qualities, and emotions that are not stated. Strong images tend to demand active verbs that make for energy in the prose or the poetic line.

Here is a single sentence from Margaret Atwood's *Cat's Eye*, in which the heroine describes the zoology building where her father worked when she was a child.

> The cellar smells strongly of mouse droppings, a smell which wafts upward through the whole building, getting fainter as you go up, mingling with the smell of green Dustbane used to clean the floors, and with the other smells, the floor polish and furniture wax and formaldehyde and snakes.

We are ostensibly given only a series of smells from a child's point of view, but as those smells rise we experience traveling upward through the building, also seeing the floors, the furniture, the snakes. The "rising" smells also help build the suggestion of the sinister, from *mouse* to *Dustbane* to *formaldehyde* to *snakes*. There is an echo of fear implied in "getting fainter as you go up," which seems to apply to courage as well as smells.

Notice also how the passage bristles with active verbs. These smells don't just lie there, they *waft, get fainter, mingle;* you *go;* the Dustbane is *used to clean*. This is important. Active verbs are images too. "Look before you leap" contains no visible objects, but we can see the actions. Passive verbs, linking verbs, all forms of the verb *to be*, invite flat, generalized writing, whereas active verbs jump-start the mind.

TRY THIS 1.1

Open a textbook, a how-to book, a form letter, something not intended to be a work of the imagination. Identify words that represent abstractions, generalizations, and/or judgments. Make a list of at least ten of these. Pick two or three of them and invent an image that suggests each word. Let your imagination loose—this is a sense impression, not a definition! Examples:

Capitalism
Dotted line across Nevada
Rollerblade straight:
Sign here.

Shame
Okra in the gumbo.
One cross-section surfaces:
Perfect flower,
Pool of slime.

Or this succinct example from Barbara Drake:

Hunger
How terrible—this little blob of jelly has a mouth.

> The greatest writers are effective largely because they deal
> in particulars and report the details that matter.
>
> *William H. Strunk*

Concrete, Significant Details

Writers are frequently advised: *show, don't tell.* What this means is that it is crucial to address the senses. Vivid writing contains **concrete, significant details.**

- *Concrete* means that there is an image, something that can be seen, heard, smelled, tasted, or touched.
- *Detail* means that there is a degree of focus and specificity.
- *Significant* means that the specific image also suggests an abstraction, generalization, or judgment.

The notion of *detail* is important to the image because it moves away from the generalized and toward the particular. For example, *creature* is a generalized notion, hard to see except in the vaguest way. *Animal* is still vague; *four-legged animal* is a little more specific; *domestic animal* a little more; *dog* narrows the field; *mixed-breed Shepherd* we can see; *old Sammy asleep on the red rug, his haunches twitching in his dream* brings the dog into sharp focus in our minds. At the same time this last sentence resonates with the ideas of age and uneasy sleep. If it said *his teeth bared and gnashing in his dream,* we'd also guess that old Sam has a capacity for meanness. Notice how the narrowing specificity of the noun invites active verbs.

TRY THIS 1.2

Begin with the largest general category you can think of—minerals, food, structures— think big. Then narrow the category step by step, becoming more specific until you have a single detailed image. Try it again with the same large category but narrow in another direction. Can you, *without naming a quality,* make your image suggest an idea or direct our attitude toward the thing you describe?

If specificity as well as concreteness is crucial to vivid writing, so too is the significance carried in those concrete details; the ideas or qualities that they suggest; the way they reveal character, attract or warn us; the way they lead us to think and feel. A list of physical details without such hints will not move us: *The lawn is green; there are four trees; there is a white picket fence about three feet high and a flagstone walk leading up to the white door.* We want to have our intellects and emotions also directed toward the *meaning* of the details.

A survey of any bookshelf will turn up dozens of examples of this principle. Here, for instance, is a scene from Anne Tyler's *Accidental Tourist.* The protagonist's wife has left him and he is having trouble sleeping.

> The dog, sighing, roused himself and dropped off the bed to pad downstairs behind him. The floorboards were cool underfoot, the kitchen linoleum cooler still; there was a glow from the refrigerator as Macon poured himself a glass of milk. He went to the living room and turned on the TV. Generally some black-and-white movie was running—men in suits and felt hats, women with padded shoulders. He didn't try to follow the plot. He took small, steady sips of milk, feeling the calcium traveling to his bones. Hadn't he read that calcium cures insomnia? He absently stroked the cat, who had somehow crept into his lap. It was much too hot to have a cat in his lap, especially this one—a loose-strung, gray tweed female who seemed made of some unusually dense substance. And the dog, most often, would be lying on top of his feet. "It's just you and me, old buddies," Macon would tell them. The cat made a comma of sweat across his bare thighs.

In this passage, Tyler makes continual reference to the senses, letting us feel the floor, the cat, and the heat; see the glow of the refrigerator and the TV; taste the milk and the "calcium traveling to his bones"; hear the dog sigh and the man talking to the animals. The writing is alive because we do in fact live through our sense perceptions, and Tyler takes us past words and through thought to let us perceive the scene in this way.

At the same time, a number of ideas not stated reverberate off the images. We are aware of generalizations the author does not need to make because we will make them ourselves. Tyler could have had her character "tell" us: *The house felt eerie. I was desperately lonely and neither the television nor the animals were really company. I thought if I did something sensible and steady it would help, but I just felt trapped. When I tried to be cheerful it got worse.* This version would be very flat, and none of it is necessary. The eeriness is inherent in the light of the refrigerator and TV; the loneliness in the sigh, the sips, and the absent stroking of the cat. The sense of entrapment is in the cat on his thighs and the dog on his feet. The emotion of the paragraph begins with a sigh and ends in sweat. Notice how deftly Tyler tells us—"men in suits and felt hats, women with padded shoulders"—that at this late hour, all there is on TV is film noir, which adds a connotation of further eeriness, seediness, and despair.

John Gardner in *The Art of Fiction* speaks of concrete details as "proofs," which establish in the reader such firm confidence that the author is an authority, that we will believe whatever she or he tells us. An author who is vague and opinionated, on the other hand, makes us uneasy and suspicious. And this applies to characters as well—a fact you can exploit. Any character—whether in a memoir, a fiction, poetry, or drama—who speaks in generalizations and judgments will undermine our trust.

> It is odd but I must tell you that I have never felt so self-assured, so splendid, so brilliant . . . Apparently, it is necessary to find someone completely inferior to appreciate one's own excellence. To be a prince in name is nothing. To be a prince in essence—it's heaven, it's pure joy.
>
> "*Ivona, Princess of Burgundia,*" *Witold Gombrowicz*

We don't have to know anything about this character or the play he comes from to know that we mistrust his judgment.

This book has begun by insisting on imagery because it is so central to literature and also because many beginning writers try to make their, or their characters', emotions felt by merely naming them, and so fail to let us experience those emotions. Here is a passage from a young writer, which fails through lack of appeal to the senses.

> Debbie was a very stubborn and completely independent person and was always doing things her way despite her parents' efforts to get her to conform. Her father was an executive in a dress manufacturing company and was able to afford his family all the luxuries and comforts of life. But Debbie was completely indifferent to her family's affluence.

This passage contains a number of judgments we might or might not share with the author, and she has not convinced us that we do. What constitutes stubbornness? Independence? Indifference? Affluence? Further, since the judgments are supported by generalizations, we have no sense of the individuality of the characters, which alone would bring them to life on the page. What things was she always doing? What efforts did her parents make to get her to conform? What sort of executive is the father? What dress manufacturing company? What luxuries and comforts?

> Debbie would wear a tank top to a tea party if she pleased, with fluorescent earrings and ankle-strap sandals.
> "Oh, sweetheart," Mrs. Chiddister would stand in the doorway wringing her hands. "It's not *nice*."
> "Not who?" Debbie would say, and add a fringed belt.
> Mr. Chiddister was Artistic Director of the Boston branch of Cardin, and had a high respect for what he called "elegant textures," which ranged from handwoven tweed to gold filigree, and which he willingly offered his daughter. Debbie preferred her laminated wrist bangles.

We have not passed a final judgment on the merits of these characters, but we know a good deal more about them, and we have drawn certain interim conclusions that are our own and have not been forced on us by the author. Debbie is independent of her parents' values, rather careless of their feelings, energetic, a little trashy. Mrs. Chiddister is quite ineffectual. Mr. Chiddister is a snob, though maybe Debbie's taste is so bad we'll end up on his side.

But maybe that isn't at all what the author had in mind. The point is that we weren't allowed to know what the author did have in mind. Perhaps it was more like this version.

> One day Debbie brought home a copy of *Ulysses*. Mrs. Strum called it "filth" and threw it across the sunporch. Debbie knelt on the parquet and retrieved her bookmark, which she replaced. "No, it's not," she said.
> "You're not so old I can't take a strap to you!" Mr. Strum reminded her.
> Mr. Strum was controlling stockholder of Readywear Conglomerates, and was proud of treating his family, not only on his salary, but also on his expense account. The summer before he had taken them to Belgium, where they toured the American Cemetery and the torture chambers of Ghent Castle. Entirely ungrateful, Debbie had spent the rest of the trip curled up in the hotel with a shabby copy of some poems.

Now we have a much clearer understanding of *stubbornness, independence, indifference*, and *affluence*, both their natures and the value we are to place on them. This time our judgment is heavily weighted in Debbie's favor—partly because people who read books have a sentimental sympathy with people who read books—but also because we hear hysteria in "filth" and "take a strap to you," whereas Debbie's resistance is quiet and strong. Mr. Strum's attitude toward his expense account suggests that he's corrupt, and his choice of "luxuries" is morbid. The passage does contain two overt judgments, the first being that Debbie was "entirely ungrateful." Notice that by the time we get to this, we're aware that the judgment is Mr. Strum's and that Debbie has little enough to be grateful for. We understand not only what the author says but also that she means the opposite of what she says, and we feel doubly clever to get it; that is the pleasure of irony. Likewise, the judgment that the book of poems is "shabby" shows Mr. Strum's crass materialism toward what we know to be the finer things.

TRY THIS 1.3

Pick a vivid passage of fiction or creative nonfiction and *spoil it* by replacing specific details with generalizations and judgments. Exchange with a person who has similarly spoiled a favorite passage. Create a new and different passage by replacing the generalizations and judgments with your own choice of sensory details. Compare the results.

> A metaphor goes out and comes back; it is a fetching motion of the imagination.
>
> *Tony Hoagland*

Figures of Speech

English is a language unusually rich in *tropes* or **figures of speech**—that is, expressions not meant to be taken literally, but as standing for something related in some way (the word *trope* comes from a Greek word meaning *to twist* or *turn*). Tropes almost invariably involve an image. The number and variety of common figures of speech make English difficult to learn as a foreign language, but also makes it fertile ground for creative writing. (Notice that *fertile ground* here is a trope, specifically a metaphor in which the language is compared to soil.)

There are many different kinds of figures of speech, but the five major tropes are usually considered to be:

- **Metonymy,** in which one thing is represented by another thing associated with it, as in *all the crowns of Europe* (where *crowns* stands for *kings*)

- **Synecdoche,** in which a part stands for the whole, as in *all hands on deck* (where *hands* stands for *men*)

- **Personification,** in which human characteristics are bestowed on anything nonhuman, as in *the breathing city* or *the gentle breeze*

- **Metaphor,** a comparison as in *the woman is a rose*

- **Simile,** a comparison as in *the woman is like a rose*

Both metaphor and simile bring special intensity to imagery by asking the mind to equate or find similar two unlike things.

Though these are five of the most frequently used figures of speech in English, you may be familiar with others, such as **hyperbole,** which is extreme exaggeration, **oxymoron,** which links two contradictory words, and everybody has enjoyed groaning at **a pun.** In medieval and Renaissance rhetoric, dozens of such tropes were identified, classified, and debated, and skill in using these "ornaments" much admired.

The rhetorical debate has lost its urgency, but the use of figurative language in literature retains its force, slightly turning or twisting the reader's perspective to offer a new or unusual view of the familiar. When Todd McEwen in the memoir of his sister, "A Very Young Dancer," says that her suitor, "Jay, suddenly tired of Moira's perpetual mystery, announced, *The wallet is closed*"—he (and Jay) are using a metonymy in which the wallet stands for love and indulgence. If a fictional narrator observes, "Rub two guilts together and they burst into blame," she is personifying the abstractions *guilt* and *blame* with ironic reference to the notion of rubbing sticks together. If a poems begins:

I keep stepping on the ugly nap
Of all our local comings and disappearings . . .

The "nap" is a synecdoche for the more obvious word "carpet," and moves our focus inward, toward a detail or closeup. It is said of film making that "every closeup is synecdoche," meaning that when, for example, we see a closeup of a hand, we assume that it stands for the whole person. If we see that hand go limp, it may be metonymy suggesting that person's death.

Of all the possible figures of speech to be used by the poet, the playwright, the essayist, and the story writer, metaphor and simile are the most common and the most crucial. A *metaphor* assumes or states a comparison, without acknowledging that it is a comparison: *my electric muscles shock the crowd; her hair is seaweed and she is the sea.* The metaphor may come in the form of an adjective: *they have a piggy and a fishy air.* Or it may come as a verb: *the bees shouldering the grass.*

A simile makes a comparison between two things using the words *like* or *as: his teeth rattled like dice in a box; my head is light as a balloon; I will fall like an ocean on that court!*

Both metaphor and simile compare things that are both alike and different, and it is in the tension between this likeness and difference that their literary power lies.

From earliest infancy, our brains are busy registering likeness and difference. This is a major way we learn, about both behavior and what things mean. A smile on mother's face expresses and promises pleasure, so a smile on a different face also reassures us. If we fall and are told to "be careful," then "be careful" will suggest alarm when we reach for the glass of milk. We compare an experience in the past to a current problem in order to predict the future. The habit of comparison is so natural that our language is full of metaphor and simile we use without knowing we are doing so. *Don't split a gut. Let's go for all the marbles. It doesn't compute. That went belly up. He lays it on with a trowel. I'm fed to the teeth. Read my lips.* Many popular metaphors, like these, are reused until they become *clichés*, comparisons that have lost their freshness.

Metaphor is central to imaginative writing because it offers a particularly exact and resonant kind of concrete detail. When we speak of "the eyes of a potato," or "the eye of the needle," we mean simply that the leaf bud and the thread hole *look like eyes*. We don't mean to suggest that the potato or the needle can see. The comparisons do not suggest any essential or abstract quality to do with sight.

But in literature both metaphor and simile have developed so that the resonance of comparison is precisely in the essential or abstract quality that the two objects share. When a writer speaks of "the eyes of the houses" or "the windows of the soul," the comparison of eyes to windows does contain the idea of transmitting vision between the inner and the outer. When Shakespeare's Jacques claims that "All the world's a stage," the significance lies not in the physical similarity of the world to a stage (he isn't backtracking in history to claim the world is flat), but in the essential qualities that such similarity implies: the pretense of the actors, the briefness of the play, the parts that men and women must inevitably play from babyhood to old age.

A metaphor presents us with a comparison that also conveys an abstraction or a judgment. A good metaphor resonates with the essential, and this is the writer's principle of choice. So Peter Hoeg, in *Smilla's Sense of Snow*, speaks of rain showers that "slap me in the face with a wet towel." Well, rain showers can patter gently on your face, or dribble down your neck, or bring May flowers. But the rain showers that Hoeg is talking about have a vicious nature that lies in the metaphor: they hit hard, they sting, and they seem to hurt on purpose.

Hoeg's metaphor contains a complex of meanings; yet it is *brief*. Because a metaphor condenses so many connotations into the tension between the images, it tends to be not only concrete but concise. So although you might in one context choose to say, "He was so angry that I thought he was going to hit me," if you sense that the moment wants the special intensity of metaphor, you could also pack that meaning into: "His face was a fist."

A metaphor is a particular and particularly imaginative kind of significant detail, comparing two sensible images and letting the abstraction remain unvoiced between them. But even if part of the comparison is an abstraction, that part will be made vivid by the "thingness" of the comparison. Robert Frost's famous "Fire and Ice" develops a simple but striking metaphor in which the objects are compared to the qualities themselves:

> Some say the world will end in fire,
> Some say in ice.
> From what I've tasted of desire
> I hold with those who favor fire.
> But if it had to perish twice,

I think I know enough of hate
To say that for destruction ice
Is also great
And would suffice.

TRY THIS 1.4
Write this poem: The first line consists of an abstraction, plus a verb, plus a place. The second line describes attire. The third line summarizes an action. Let it flow; don't worry too much about making sense.

Examples (by Carissa Neff):

Beauty creeps out the window
Wearing nothing but taut bare skin.
Leaving a trail of wrinkles behind her.

Hunger yells in the hallway,
Draped in cymbals;
He stomps and shouts, "Hear me now!"

The major danger of metaphor is **cliché.** Those "windows of the soul," those "eyes like pools" are so familiar that they no longer hold any interest, whereas a fresh metaphor surprises us with the unlikeness of the two things compared while at the same time convincing us of the aptness or truth of the likeness. A cliché metaphor fails to surprise us and so fails to illuminate. Sometimes as a writer you will find yourself with a gift of fresh comparison, and sometimes the first image that comes to mind will be tired and stale. All writers experience this, and the goods ones learn to overcome it. The first thing to do is to make yourself alert to clichés in your own writing and the world around you, and then to labor (which may mean dream) your way toward those images that illuminate the everyday and make the familiar strange.

TRY THIS 1.5
Quickly list as many cliché metaphors as you can think of: *the path of life, eyes like pools, crazy as a bedbug, nose to the grindstone*, and so forth. Then switch half a dozen of the comparisons: *eyes like bedbugs, nose to the path, the grindstone of life*. Some of these might be fresh and apt! In any case, the exercise will help you become aware of clichés and so help you avoid them.

My own long relationship with cliché is a paradox, for I find that my language is least fresh when I am most determined to write well. If I sit rigid with good intentions, my inner critic takes up residence on my shoulder, sneering *that's silly, that's far-fetched, what a crock, nobody'll believe that!*—with the result that I fall back on usual phrases. But if I knock her off her perch and let myself try anything that comes to mind, *some* of it will be silly, some far-fetched, and among the verbal rubble there is almost bound to be a salvageable building block, a serviceable cooking pot, a precious stone.

More to Read

Burke, Carol, and Molly Best Tinsley. *The Creative Process*. New York: St. Martin's Press, 1993.

Rico, Gabriele Lusser. *Writing the Natural Way*. Los Angeles: J. P. Tarcher, Inc., 1983.

Readings

The readings that follow employ imagery and metaphor in a wide variety of ways. For example, Annie Dillard's "The Giant Water Bug," a short essay from her book *Pilgrim at Tinker Creek*, represents a single sharp observation of nature, dense with metaphor. E.B. White's "The Ring of Time" uses sense details to create a circus scene, and then expands it into a complex metaphor for time.

Read each selection once, fast, for content and pleasure; then a second time consciously aware of images and metaphors. What affect do they have on you? How? What technique might you imitate, absorb, try, steal?

Among the readings you'll find some triggers for play in your journal. These are not connected to the readings in any direct or literal way, but may suggest peripheral ways to practice some shape, subject, or skill the writers display. At the end of this and further chapters you will find suggestions for developing your ideas toward a draft of a finished piece.

CREATIVE NONFICTION

Annie Dillard
The Giant Water Bug

A couple of summers ago I was walking along the edge of the island to see what I could see in the water, and mainly to scare frogs. Frogs have an inelegant way of taking off from invisible positions on the bank just ahead of your feet, in dire panic, emitting a froggy "Yike!" and splashing into the water.

Incredibly, this amused me, and, incredibly, it amuses me still. As I walked along the grassy edge of the island, I got better and better at seeing frogs both in and out of the water. I learned to recognize, slowing down, the difference in texture of the light reflected from mudbank, water, grass, or frog. Frogs were flying all around me. At the end of the island I noticed a small green frog. He was exactly half in and half out of the water, looking like a schematic diagram of an amphibian, and he didn't jump.

He didn't jump; I crept closer. At last I knelt on the island's winter-killed grass, lost, dumb-struck, staring at the frog in the creek just four feet away. He was a very small frog with wide, dull eyes. And just as I looked at him, he slowly crumpled and began to sag. The spirit vanished from his eyes as if snuffed. His skin emptied and drooped; his very skull seemed to collapse and settle like a kicked tent. He was shrinking before my eyes like a deflating football. I watched the taut, glistening skin on his shoulders ruck and rumple and fall. Soon, part of his skin, formless as a pricked balloon, lay in floating folds like bright scum on top of the water: it was a monstrous and terrifying thing. I gaped bewildered, appalled. An oval shadow hung in the water behind the drained frog; then the shadow glided away. The frog skin bag started to sink.

I had read about the giant water bug, but never seen one. "Giant water bug" is really the name of the creature, which is an enormous, heavy-bodied brown beetle. It eats insects, tadpoles, fish, and frogs. Its grasping forelegs are mighty and hooked inward. It seizes a victim with these legs, hugs it tight, and paralyzes it with enzymes injected during a vicious bite. That one bite is the only bite it ever takes. Through the puncture shoot the poisons that dissolve the victim's muscles and bones and organs—all but the skin—and through it the giant water bug sucks out the victim's body, reduced to a juice. This event is quite common in warm fresh water. The frog I saw was being sucked by a giant water bug. I had been kneeling on the island grass; when the unrecognizable flap of frog skin settled on the creek bottom, swaying, I stood up and brushed the knees of my pants. I couldn't catch my breath.

E. B. White

The Ring of Time

Fiddler Bayou, March 22, 1956

After the lions had returned to their cages, creeping angrily through the chutes, a little bunch of us drifted away and into an open doorway nearby, where we stood for a while in semidarkness, watching a big brown circus horse go harumphing around the practice ring. His trainer was a woman of about forty, and the two of them, horse and woman, seemed caught up in one of those desultory treadmills of afternoon from which there is no apparent escape. The day was hot, and we kibitzers were grateful to be briefly out of the sun's glare. The long rein, or tape, by which the woman guided her charge counterclockwise in his dull career formed the radius of their private circle, of which she was the revolving center; and she, too, stepped a tiny circumference of her own, in order to accommodate the horse and allow him his maximum scope. She had on a short-skirted costume and a conical straw hat. Her legs were bare and she wore high heels, which probed deep into the loose tanbark and kept her ankles in a state of constant turmoil. The great size and meekness of the horse, the repetitious exercise, the heat of the afternoon, all exerted a hypnotic charm that invited boredom; we spectators were experiencing a languor—we neither expected relief nor felt entitled to any. We had paid a dollar to get into the grounds, to be sure, but we had got our dollar's worth a few minutes before, when the lion trainer's whiplash had got caught around a toe of one of the lions. What more did we want for a dollar?

Behind me I heard someone say, "Excuse me, please," in a low voice. She was halfway into the building when I turned and saw her—a girl of sixteen or seventeen, politely threading her way through us onlookers who blocked the entrance. As she emerged in front of us, I saw that she was barefoot, her dirty little feet fighting the uneven ground. In most respects she was like any of two or three dozen showgirls you encounter if you wander about the winter quarters of Mr. John Ringling North's circus, in Sarasota—cleverly proportioned, deeply browned by the sun, dusty, eager, and almost naked. But her grave face and the naturalness of her manner gave her a sort of quick distinction and brought a new note into the gloomy octagonal building where we had all cast our lot for a few moments. As soon as she had squeezed through the crowd, she spoke a word or two to the older woman, whom I took to be her mother, stepped to the ring, and waited while the horse coasted to a stop in front of her. She gave the animal a couple of affectionate swipes on his enormous neck and then swung herself aboard. The horse immediately resumed his rocking canter, the woman goading him on, chanting something that sounded like "Hop! Hop!"

In attempting to recapture this mild spectacle, I am merely acting as recording secretary for one of the oldest of societies—the society of those who, at one time or another, have surrendered, without even a show of resistance, to the bedazzlement of a circus rider. As a writing man, or secretary, I have always felt charged with the safekeeping of all unexpected items of worldly or unworldly enchantment, as though I might be held personally responsible if even a small one were to be lost. But it is not easy to communicate anything of this nature. The circus comes as close to being the world in microcosm as anything I know; in a way, it puts all the rest of show business in the shade. Its magic is universal and complex. Out of its wild disorder comes order; from its rank smell rises the good aroma of courage and daring; out of its preliminary shabbiness comes the final splendor. And buried in the familiar boasts of its advance agents lies the modesty of most of its people. For me the circus is at its best before it has been put together. It is at its best at certain moments when it comes to a point, as through a burning glass, in the activity and destiny of a single performer out of so many. One ring is always bigger than three. One rider, one aerialist, is always greater than six. In short, a man has to catch the circus unawares to experience its full impact and share its gaudy dream.

The ten-minute ride the girl took achieved—as far as I was concerned, who wasn't looking for it, and quite unbeknownst to her, who wasn't even striving for it—the thing that is sought by performers everywhere, on whatever stage, whether struggling in the tidal currents of Shakespeare or bucking the difficult motion of a horse. I somehow got the idea she was just cadging a ride, improving a shining ten minutes in the diligent way all serious artists seize free moments to hone the blade of their talent and keep themselves in trim. Her brief tour included only elementary postures and tricks, perhaps because they were all she was capable of, perhaps because her warmup at this hour was unscheduled and the ring was not rigged for a real practice session. She swung herself off and on the horse several times, gripping his mane. She did a few knee-stands—or whatever they are called—dropping to her knees and quickly bouncing back up on her feet again. Most of the time she simply rode in a standing position, well aft on the beast, her hands hanging easily at her sides, her head erect, her straw-colored ponytail lightly brushing her shoulders, the blood of exertion showing faintly through the tan of her skin. Twice she managed a one-foot stance—a sort of ballet pose, with arms outstretched. At one point the neck strap of her bathing suit broke and she went twice around the ring in the classic attitude of a woman making minor repairs to a garment. The fact that she was standing on the back of a moving horse while doing this invested the matter with a clownish significance that perfectly fitted the spirit of the circus—jocund, yet charming. She just rolled the strap into a neat ball and stowed it inside her bodice while the horse rocked and rolled beneath her in dutiful innocence. The bathing suit proved as self-reliant as its owner and stood up well enough without benefit of strap.

The richness of the scene was in its plainness, its natural condition—of horse, of ring, of girl, even to the girl's bare feet that gripped the bare back of her proud and ridiculous mount. The enchantment grew not out of anything that happened or was performed but out of something that seemed to go round and around and around with the girl, attending her, a steady gleam in the shape of a circle—a ring of ambition, of happiness, of youth.

(And the positive pleasures of equilibrium under difficulties.) In a week or two, all would be changed, all (or almost all) lost: the girl would wear makeup, the horse would wear gold, the ring would be painted, the bark would be clean for the feet of the horse, the girl's feet would be clean for the slippers that she'd wear. All, all would be lost.

As I watched with the others, our jaws adroop, our eyes alight, I became painfully conscious of the element of time. Everything in the hideous old building seemed to take the shape of a circle, conforming to the course of the horse. The rider's gaze, as she peered straight ahead, seemed to be circular, as though bent by force of circumstance; then time itself began running in circles, and so the beginning was where the end was, and the two were the same, and one thing ran into the next and time went round and around and got nowhere. The girl wasn't so young that she did not know the delicious satisfaction of having a perfectly behaved body and the fun of using it to do a trick most people can't do, but she was too young to know that time does not really move in a circle at all. I thought: "She will never be as beautiful as this again"—a thought that made me acutely unhappy—and in a flash my mind (which is too much of a busybody to suit me) had projected her twenty-five years ahead, and she was now in the center of the ring, on foot, wearing a conical hat and high-heeled shoes, the image of the older woman, holding the long rein, caught in the treadmill of an afternoon long in the future. "She is at that enviable moment in life [I thought] when she believes she can go once around the ring, make one complete circuit, and at the end be exactly the same age as at the start." Everything in her movements, her expression, told you that for her the ring of time was perfectly formed, changeless, predictable, without beginning or end, like the ring in which she was traveling at this moment with the horse that wallowed under her. And then I slipped back into my trance, and time was circular again—time pausing quietly with the rest of us, so as not to disturb the balance of a performer.

Her ride ended as casually as it had begun. The older woman stopped the horse, and the girl slid to the ground. As she walked toward us to leave, there was a quick, small burst of applause. She smiled broadly, in surprise and pleasure; then her face suddenly regained its gravity and she disappeared through the door.

It has been ambitious and plucky of me to attempt to describe what is indescribable, and I have failed, as I knew I would. But I have discharged my duty to my society; and besides, a writer, like an acrobat, must occasionally try a stunt that is too much for him. At any rate, it is worth reporting that long before the circus comes to town, its most notable performances have already been given. Under the bright lights of the finished show, a performer need only reflect the electric candle power that is directed upon him; but in the dark and dirty old training rings and in the makeshift cages, whatever light is generated, whatever excitement, whatever beauty, must come from original sources—from internal fires of professional hunger and delight, from the exuberance and gravity of youth. It is the difference between planetary light and the combustion of stars.

TRY THIS 1.6

Write down a bumper sticker you like. (It's a good idea to exchange with someone else so you are working with one you don't actually remember.) Describe the car (van, truck, SUV) this bumper sticker is stuck on—make, model, year, color, condition. Open the door. Describe the smells and textures. Name three objects you find. Name a fourth object you're surprised to find there. Look up. Here comes the owner. Who, walking how, wearing what, carrying what, with what facial expression? The owner says something. What?

FICTION

Nadine Gordimer
The Diamond Mine

Love during wartime

I'll call her Tilla. You may call her by another name. You might think you knew her. You might have been the one. It's not by some simple colloquial habit that we "call" someone instead of naming: call him up.

It is during the war, your war, the forties, that has sunk as far away into the century as the grandfathers' 1914. He is blond, stocky in khaki, attractively nearsighted, so that the eyes, which are actually having difficulty with focus, seem to be concentrating attentively on her. This impression is emphasized by his lashes, blond and curly as his hair. He is completely different from the men she knows in the life of films—the only men she knows, apart from her father—and whom she expected to come along one day not too far off, Robert Taylor or even the foreigner, Charles Boyer. He is different because—at last—he is real. She is sixteen. He is no foreigner, no materialization of projection from Hollywood. He's the son of friends of her maternal grandmother, detailed to a military training camp in the province where the girl and her parents live. Some people even take in strangers from the camp for the respite of weekend leave; with a young daughter in the house, this family would not go so far as to risk that, but when the man of the family is beyond call-up age an easy way to fulfill patriotic duty is to offer hospitality to a man vouched for by connections. He's almost to be thought of as an elective grandson of the old lady. In war these strangers, remember, are Our Boys.

When he comes on Friday night and stays until Sunday his presence makes a nice change for the three, mother, father, and daughter, who live a quiet life, not given to socializing. That presence is a pleasant element in the closeness between parents and daughter: he is old enough to be an adult like them and, only eight years ahead of her, young enough to be her contemporary. The mother cooks a substantial lunch on the Sundays he's there; you can imagine what the food must be like in a military camp. The father suggests a game of golf—welcome to borrow clubs—but it turns out the soldier doesn't play. What's his game, then? He likes to fish. But his hospitality is four hundred miles from the sea; the soldier laughs along in manly recognition that there must be a game. The daughter: for her, she could never tell anyone, his weekend presence is a pervasion that fills the house, displaces all its familiar odors of home, is fresh and pungent—he's here. It's the emanation of khaki washed with strong soap and fixed—as in perfume the essence of flowers is fixed by alcohol—by the pressure of a hot iron.

The parents are reluctant cinema-goers, so it is thoughtful of this visiting friend of the family to invite the daughter of the house to choose a film she'd like to see on a Saturday night. She has no driving license yet (seventeen was the qualifying age in those days) and the father does not offer his car to the soldier. So the pair walk down the road from streetlight to streetlight, under the trees, all that autumn, to the small town's center, where only the cinema and the pub in the hotel are awake. She is aware of window dummies, in the closed shops that her mother's friends patronize, observing her as she walks past with a man. If she is invited to a party given by a school friend, she must be home strictly by eleven, usually fetched by her father. But now she is with a responsible friend, a family connection, not among unknown youths on the loose; if the film is a nine-o'clock showing, the pair are not home before midnight, and the lights are already extinguished in the parents' bedroom. It is then that, schoolgirlish, knowing nothing else to offer, she makes cocoa in the kitchen, and it is then that he tells her about fishing. The kitchen is locked up for the night, the windows are closed, and it is amazing how strong that presence of a man can be, that stiff-clean clothing warmed—not a scent, not a breath but, as he moves his arms graphically in description of playing a catch, it comes from the inner crease of his bare elbows, where the sun on Maneuvers hasn't got at the secret fold, from that center of being, the pliant hollow that vibrates between his collarbones as he speaks, the breastplate rosy down to where a few brownish-blond hairs disappear into the open neck of the khaki shirt. He will never turn dark, his skin retains the sun, glows. Him.

Tilla has never gone fishing. Her father doesn't fish. Four hundred miles from the sea, the boys at school kick and throw balls around—they know about, talk about football and cricket. The father knows about, talks about golf. Fishing. It opens the sea before her, the salt wind gets in her narrowed eyes, conveying to her whole nights passed alone on the rocks. He walks from headland to headland on down-wet sand, the tide is out—sometimes in midsentence there's a check, half smile, half breath, because he's thinking of something this child couldn't know. This is his incantation; it shuts out the parade-ground march toward killing and blinds the sights that the gun trains on sawdust-stuffed figures on which he is being drilled to see the face of the enemy, to whom he himself is the enemy, with guts (he pulls the intricately perfect innards out of the fish he's caught, a fisherman's simple skill) in place of sawdust. The sleeping parents are right: he will not touch her innocence of what this century claims, commands from him.

As they walk home where she used to race her bicycle up and down under the trees, the clothing on their arms—the khaki sleeve, the sweater her mother has handed her as a condition of permission to be out in the chill night air—brushes by proximity, not intention. The strap of her sandal slips, and as she pauses to right it, hopping on one leg, he steadies her by the forearm and then they walk on hand in hand. He's taking care of her. The next weekend, they kiss in one of the tree-dark intervals between streetlights. Boys have kissed her; it happened only to her mouth. The next Saturday, her arms went around him, his around her, her face approached, was pressed, breathed in, and breathed against the hollow of neck where the pendulum of heartbeat can be felt, the living place above the breastplate from which the incense of his presence had come. She was there.

In the kitchen there was no talk. The cocoa rose to the top of the pot, made ready. All the sources of warmth that her palms had extended to, everywhere in the house, as a domestic animal senses the warmth of a fire to approach, were in this body against hers, in the current of arms, the contact of chest, belly muscles, the deep strange heat from between his thighs. But he took care of her. Gently loosened her while she was discovering that a man has breasts, too, even if made of muscle, and that to press her own against them was an urgent exchange, walking on the wet sands with the fisherman.

The next weekend leave—but the next weekend leave is cancelled. Instead there's a call from the public phone at the canteen bar. The mother happened to answer and there were expressions of bright and encouraging regret that the daughter tried to piece into what they were responding to. The family was at supper. The father's mouth bunched stoically: Marching orders. Embarkation. The mother nodded round the table, confirming. She—the one

I call Tilla—stood up, appalled at the strength to strike the receiver from her mother and the inability of a good girl to do so. Then her mother was saying, but of course we'll take a drive out on Sunday, say goodbye and Godspeed. Grandma'd never forgive me if she thought . . . Now, can you tell me how to get there, beyond Pretoria, I know . . . I didn't catch it, what mine? And after the turnoff at the main road? Oh, don't bother, I suppose we can ask at a petrol station if we get lost, everyone must know where that camp is. Is there something we can bring you, anything you'll need . . .

It seems they're to make an outing of it. Out of her stun: that essence, ironed khaki and soap, has been swept from the house, from the kitchen, by something that's got nothing to do with a fisherman, except that he is a man and, as her father has stated—embarkation—men go to war. Her mother makes picnic preparations: Do you think a chicken or pickled ox tongue, hard-boiled eggs . . . Don't know where one can sit to eat in a military camp, there must be somewhere for visitors. Her father selects from his stack of travel brochures a map of the local area to place on the shelf below the windshield. Petrol is rationed, but he has been frugal with coupons; there are enough to provide a full tank. Because of this, plans for the picnic are abandoned—no picnic—her mother thinks, Wouldn't it be a nice gesture to take the soldier out for a restaurant lunch in the nearest city? There won't be many such luxuries for the young man on his way to war in the North African desert.

They have never shown her the mine, the diamond mine, although ever since she was a small child they have taken her to places of interest as part of her education. They must have talked about it—her father is a mining-company official himself, but his exploitation is gold, not precious stones—or more likely it has been cited in a general-knowledge text at school: some famous diamond was dug up there.

The camp is on part of the vast mine property, commandeered by the Defense Force. Over the veld there are tents to the horizon, roped and staked, dun as the scuffed and dried grass and the earth scoured by boots—boots tramping everywhere, khaki everywhere, the wearers replicating one another, him. Where will they find him? He did give a tent number. The numbers don't seem to be consecutive. Her father is called to a halt by a replica with a gun, slow-spoken and polite. The car follows given directions retained differently by the mother and the father; the car turns, backs up, take it slowly for heaven's sake.

She is the one: There. There he is.

Of course, when you find him you see that there is no one like him, no bewilderment. They are all laughing in the conventions of greeting, but his eyes have their concentrated attention for her. It is his greeting of the intervals between streetlights, and of the kitchen. This weekend that ends weekends seems also to be the first of winter; it's suddenly cold, wind bellies and whips at that tent where he must have slept, remote, between weekends. It's the weather for hot food, shelter. At the restaurant, he chooses curry and rice for this last meal. He sprinkles grated coconut and she catches his eye and he smiles for her as he adds dollops of chutney. The smile is that of a greedy boy caught out and is also as if it were a hand squeezed under the table. No wine—the father has to drive, and young men oughtn't to be encouraged to drink, enough of that in the Army—but there is ice cream with canned peaches, coffee served, and peppermints with the compliments of the management.

It was too warm in the restaurant. Outside, high-altitude winds carry the breath of what must be early snow on the mountains, far away, unseen, as this drive back to the camp carries the breath of war, far away, unseen, where all the replicas in khaki are going to be shipped. No heating in the family car of those days, the soldier has only his thin, well-pressed khaki and the daughter, of course, like all young girls, has taken no precaution against a change in the weather—she is wearing a skimpy flounced cotton dress (secretly chosen, although he, being older, and a disciple of the sea's mysteries, probably won't even notice) that she was wearing the first time they walked to the cinema. The mother, concealing, she believes, irritation at the fecklessness of the young—next thing she'll have bronchitis and miss school—fortunately keeps a rug handy and insists that the passengers in the back seat put it over their knees.

It was easy to chat in the preoccupations of food along with the budgerigar chitter of other patrons in the restaurant. In the car, headed back for that final place, the camp, the outing is over. The father feels an obligation: at least, he can tell something about the diamond mine that's of interest, and soon they'll actually be passing the site of operations again, though you can't see much from the road.

The rug is like the pelt of some dusty pet animal settled over them. The warmth of the meal inside them is bringing it to life, a life they share, one body. It's pleasant to put their hands beneath it; the hands, his right, her left, find one another.

. . . You know what a diamond is, of course, although you look at it as something pretty a woman wears on her finger, hmm? Well, actually it consists of pure carbon crystallized . . .

He doesn't like to be interrupted, so there's no need to make any response, even if you still hear him. The right hand and the left hand become so tightly clasped that the pad of muscle at the base of each thumb is flattened against the bone and interlaced fingers are jammed down between the joints. It isn't a clasp against imminent parting, it's got nothing to do with any future, it belongs in the urgent purity of this present.

. . . The crystallization in regular octahedrons, that's to say eight-sided, and in allied forms and the cut and polished ones you see in jewelry more or less follow . . .

The hands lay together, simply happened, on the skirt over her left thigh, because that is where she had slipped her hand beneath the woolly comfort of the rug. Now he slowly released, first fingers, then palms—at once awareness signalled between them, that the rug was their tender accomplice, it must not be seen to be stirred by something—he released himself from her and for one bereft moment she thought he had left her behind, his eight-year advantage prevailed against such fusion of palms as it had done, so gently (oh, but why), when they were in the dark between trees, when they were in the kitchen.

. . . colorless or they may be tinted occasionally yellow, pink, even black . . .

The hand had not emerged from the rug. She followed as if her eyes were closed or she were in the dark; it went as if it were playing—looking for a place to tickle, as children do to make one another wriggle and laugh—where her skirt ended at her knee, going under her knee without displacing the skirt and touching the tendons and the hollow there. She didn't want to laugh (what would her father make of such a response to his knowledgeable commentary), so she glided her hand to his and put it back with hers where it had been before.

. . . one of the biggest diamonds in the world after the Koh-i-noor's hundred and nine carats, but that was found in India . . .

The hand, his hand, pressed fingers into her thigh through the cotton flounce, as if testing to see what was real about her, and stopped, and then out of the hesitation went down and, under the rug, up under the gauze of skirt, moved over her flesh. She did not look at him and he did not look at her.

. . . and there are industrial gems you can cut glass with, make bits for certain drills, the hardest substance known . . .

At the taut lip of her panties he hesitated again, no hurry, all something she was learning, he was teaching, the anticipation in his fingertips, he stroked along one of the veins in there in the delicate membranelike skin that is at the crevice between leg and body (like the skin that the sun on Maneuvers couldn't reach in the crook of his elbow), just before the hair begins. And then he went in under the elastic edge and his hand was soft on soft hair, his fingers like eyes attentive to her.

. . . Look at this veld—nothing suggests one of the greatest ever, anywhere, down there, down in what we call Blue Earth, the diamondiferous core . . .

She has no clear idea of where his hand is now, what she feels is that they are kissing, they are in each other's mouths although they cannot look at one another.

Are you asleep back there? The mother is remarking her own boredom with the mine. He is eight years older, able to speak: Just listening.

His finger explores deep down in the dark, the hidden entrance to some sort of cave with its slippery walls and smooth stalagmite. She's found, he's found her.

The car is passing the mine processing plant.

. . . product of the death and decay of forests millennia ago, just as coal is, but down there the ultimate alchemy, you might say . . .

Those others, the parents, they have no way of knowing. It has happened, it is happening under the old woolly rug that was all they could provide for her. She is free of them. Found, and they don't know where she is.

At the camp, the father shakes the soldier's hand longer than in the usual grip. The mother for a moment looks as if she might give him a peck on the cheek, Godspeed, but it is not her way to be familiar.

Aren't you going to say goodbye? She's not a child, good heavens, a mother shouldn't have to remind of manners.

He's standing outside one of the tents with his hands hanging open at his sides as the car is driven away, and his attention is upon her until, with his furry narrowed sight, he'll cease to be able to make her out, while she can still see him, see him until he is made one with all the others in khaki, replicated, crossing and crowding, in preparation to embark.

If he had been killed in that war they would have heard through the grandmother's connections.

Is it still you, somewhere, old.

TRY THIS 1.7

Write a paragraph about a thrilling or anguishing incident from your childhood or adolescence. Evoke the emotion you felt in images of all five senses how the scene (perhaps including your own body) looked to you, sounded, felt, smelled, tasted. Allow yourself whatever personification, metaphor, or simile occurs to you, no matter how extreme.

POEMS

Ted Hughes
The Hawk in the Rain

I drown in the drumming ploughland, I drag up
Heel after heel from the swallowing of the earth's mouth,
From clay that clutches my each step to the ankle
With the habit of the dogged grave, but the hawk

Effortlessly at height hangs his still eye.
His wings hold all creation in a weightless quiet,
Steady as a hallucination in the streaming air.
While banging wind kills these stubborn hedges,

Thumbs my eyes, throws my breath, tackles my heart,
And rain hacks my head to the bone, the hawk hangs
The diamond point of will that polestars
The sea drowner's endurance: and I,

Bloodily grabbed dazed last-moment-counting
Morsel in the earth's mouth, strain towards the master-
Fulcrum of violence where the hawk hangs still.
That maybe in his own time meets the weather

Coming the wrong way, suffers the air, hurled upside down,
Fall from his eye, the ponderous shires crash on him,
The horizon trap him; the round angelic eye
Smashed, mix his heart's blood with the mire of the land.

Billy Collins

Snow Day

Today we woke up to a revolution of snow,
its white flag waving over everything,
the landscape vanished,
not a single mouse to punctuate the blankness,
and beyond these windows

the government buildings smothered,
schools and libraries buried, the post office lost
under the noiseless drift,
the paths of trains softly blocked,
the world fallen under this falling.

In a while, I will put on some boots
and step out like someone walking in water,
and the dog will porpoise through the drifts,
and I will shake a laden branch
sending a cold shower down on us both.

But for now I am a willing prisoner in this house,
a sympathizer with the anarchic cause of snow.

I will make a pot of tea
and listen to the plastic radio on the counter,
as glad as anyone to hear the news

that the Kiddie Corner School is closed,
the Ding-Dong School, closed,
the All Aboard Children's School, closed,
the Hi-Ho Nursery School, closed,
along with—some will be delighted to hear—

the Toadstool School, the Little School,
Little Sparrows Nursery School,
Little Stars Pre-School, Peas-and-Carrots Day School
the Tom Thumb Child Center, all closed,
and—clap your hands—the Peanuts Play School.

So this is where the children hide all day,
these are the nests where they letter and draw,
where they put on their bright miniature jackets,
all darting and climbing and sliding,
all but the few girls whispering by the fence.

And now I am listening hard
in the grandiose silence of the snow,
trying to hear what those three girls are plotting,
what riot is afoot,
which small queen is about to be brought down.

Yusef Komunyakaa

Facing It

My black face fades,
hiding inside the black granite.
I said I wouldn't,
dammit: No tears.
I'm stone. I'm flesh.
My clouded reflection eyes me
like a bird of prey, the profile of night
slanted against morning. I turn
this way—the stone lets me go.
I turn that way—I'm inside
the Vietnam Veterans Memorial
again, depending on the light

to make a difference.
I go down the 58,022 names,
half-expecting to find
my own in letters like smoke.
I touch the name Andrew Johnson;
I see the booby trap's white flash.
Names shimmer on a woman's blouse
but when she walks away
the names stay on the wall.
Brushstrokes flash, a red bird's
wings cutting across my stare.
The sky. A plane in the sky.
A white vet's image floats
closer to me, then his pale eyes
look through mine. I'm a window.
He's lost his right arm
inside the stone. In the black mirror
a woman's trying to erase names:
No, she's brushing a boy's hair.

TRY THIS 1.8

Write a paragraph or a poem exploring your relationship with an animal or a machine. Describe the animal or machine using at least three of the senses.

Or

Write a poem or paragraph about a relationship between surface and depth—in an eye, a mirror, water, metal . . .

Henry Reed

Naming of Parts

To-day we have naming of parts. Yesterday,
We had daily cleaning. And to-morrow morning,
We shall have what to do after firing. But to-day,
To-day we have naming of parts. *Japonica*
Glistens like coral in all of the neighboring gardens,
      And to-day we have naming of parts.

This is the lower sling swivel. And this
Is the upper sling swivel, whose use you will see,
When you are given your slings. And this is the piling swivel,

Which in your case you have not got. *The branches*
Hold in the gardens their silent, eloquent gestures,
  Which in our case we have not got.

This is the safety-catch, which is always released
With an easy flick of the thumb. And please do not let me
See anyone using his finger. You can do it quite easy
If you have any strength in your thumb. *The blossoms*
Are fragile and motionless, never letting anyone see
  Any of them using their finger.

And this you can see is the bolt. The purpose of this
Is to open the breech, as you see. We can slide it
Rapidly backwards and forwards: we call this
Easing the spring. *And rapidly backwards and forwards*
The early bees are assaulting and fumbling the flowers:
  They call it easing the Spring.

They call it easing the Spring: it is perfectly easy
If you have any strength in your thumb: like the bolt,
And the breech, and the cocking-piece, and the point of balance,
Which in our case we have not got; *and the almond-blossom*
Silent in all of the gardens and the bees going backwards and forwards,
  For to-day we have naming of parts.

TRY THIS 1.9

Pick any two strikingly contrasting images. (Can you find two as strikingly contrasted as guns and flowers?) Develop each image with specific details, arranging the two images in alternating lines or paragraphs. What effects do you achieve?

DRAMA

Jim Quinn

Her Deer Story

(This reads more difficultly than it plays. It is not necessary that the characters repeat the tag ends/beginnings absolutely in unison. The point is only to get the man constantly interrupting and being

*interrupted by the woman, whose story it is. We've played this at
headlong speed. And in a quiet, slow, ruminative way, like a couple at
the end of a small party where people have had enough to drink to
tell stories and to squabble in public. But there must be other ways
that work too. The Man part can be divided between two or three or
four men, or one man, who simply adds, Toyota says, Fat says, the
boy says, the tough says, to appropriate lines.)*

WOMAN: I'm driving, we're fighting, I forget about what, his drinking, his druggy son, my possessiveness, my envy, my tone of voice with his wife, I never or is it he never bothers to fill, bothers to fill the tank, check the oil, clean the, the deer must've

MAN ONE: the deer must've tried to leap the car, it slams us sidewise, blocks the light out of the whole windshield,

WOMAN: the whole windshield (*To him.*) Let me tell this! I'm braking through dark, we don't know it's a deer, it stinks like come and piss, it throws itself on the road, rocks us backwards, the hood's all dents, throws itself into a cornfield, one leg's all that can stand. There's no blood.

MAN ONE: It uses its good leg like a hook, the other ones drag and tremble, it's digging through the dirt, won't stop, we get out of the car, we're alone on the road.

WOMAN: "Are you alright?" I blurt or he does, but we don't care about us, we stand there watching it die. But it won't die. (*To him.*) Your shirt sleeve. He looks at it and wipes his nose again. Blood.

MAN ONE: (*To her.*) "It's alright,"

WOMAN: He blows a blood bubble out of one side of his nose, wipes, bleeds. It reaches its good leg out, wobbles half up like a big worm, falls forward, reaches out again. It rattles the cornstalks, keeps going. A rust-colored pickup drives up, it has big wheels it seems to float on top of, it's brown with dirt.

MAN ONE: The driver's young, fat, excited, he wants to know if we have a gun, he says the first one to find an injured deer can kill it, even out of season, his son's eight years old, it'll be the first deer of his life, it's important to a boy, can we watch till he gets back with him? It's only ten minutes? Another car drives up, a guy gets out with a gun in his hands, he's laughing.

MAN THREE: I can see it by the shaking corn!

WOMAN: The fat one gets his gun out of the pickup,

MAN ONE: They both have telescopic sights, remember?

WOMAN: (*To Man One.*) Okay, telescopic sights. Let me tell it. The new car's a Toyota, I remember, white and clean.

MAN TWO: It's mine, I saw it first.

MAN THREE: Okay, line'r up and shoot the fucker if it's yours.

MAN ONE: But the fat one's talking about his son

WOMAN: talking about his son, only ten minutes away

MAN TWO: ten minutes away, a boy of eight? Who never yet got a deer? So close too? This is his chance in a million. It's fate!

MAN THREE: Well, fuck fate. A deer's nobody's fate unless they got a gun. You pop it or I will.

MAN TWO: Isn't this a son of a bitch? (*Appealing to Woman and Man One.*) Ask these people, they could've shot the thing themselves, they see what this'd mean to a kid. And you can't?

WOMAN: We watch the rustling field. Sometimes the head comes up.

MAN TWO: I got a right to first shot. It's like a dream giving it to my son.

MAN ONE: The antlers show, just small yearling spikes. They argue. It heaves and heaves silently, dragging itself away slow. Finally the one in the Toyota shrugs. The fat one gets in the truck, speeds off.

WOMAN: Wait. Toyota watches the field with us, remember? He points to a crow in the white sky. Let me tell it right.

MAN THREE: That crow smells his feed. If it dies before he gets back, the deer's yours. I'll help load it in your car. Run-down deer's good eating same as shot, don't let anybody tell you different.

MAN ONE: We don't think to tell him shoot the damn thing and stop the horrible crawling.

WOMAN: Stupidly, I vomit in the muddy irrigation ditch.

MAN THREE: I'm trying like hell not to laugh. But wow, lady.

WOMAN: The fat one gets back with his kid, who's small but not fat. He hands the kid a gun climbing down from the high truck seat. The gun's littler, no telescope. The kid's clothes are pressed and clean, I wonder if he changed into them special. He holds the gun high, checks it.

MAN ONE: "Safety's on," the boy says in his serious girl-voice. He knows guns.

WOMAN: His eyes see me, go by me, beautiful eyes.

MAN ONE: His father's whispering, pulling him by the elbow.

MAN TWO: Watch your chance. Don't waste your shells, son!

WOMAN: The boy shakes loose from his father, gets ahead of him walking fast. Bugs dance up in the air, we follow in the corn's dragged path, watching. The kid shoots, aims, shoots, walks fast, stops, aims, shoots. "I can see him!" he whispers it, girl-voice calm, shooting, shooting.

MAN TWO: Take your aim!

MAN ONE: Toyota slams back in his car, lays rubber driving off, shouting out the window, not at us, might as well have been at the crow.

MAN THREE: Fuck! Shit!

WOMAN: Trembling head, ear torn bloody with bullets, stink of blood, the kid shooting, kicking dirt bits up all around in tramped corn. I'm not sick. I want this. It's like finally eating when you're dying hungry. I want it dead. He hits the head, doesn't kill it, it hunches itself, it lolls sideways, breathing, deep breaths, tries to kick something away, like you might brush your hand at a fly, and dies that way. It makes me sweat and laugh. They drag it to the truck laughing.

MAN ONE: They open the stomach, insides spill out, they seem to . . . smoke?

WOMAN: No. Driving sometimes, you watch the road ahead, you can almost smell them when you see it, heat waves rising off it? Something like that, but smellier, comes off the body. They leave. "What about us?" I say, to nobody at all. Wind rustles the corn sheaves.

MAN ONE: We get in the car, it starts and dies, it starts and whines, it smokes.

WOMAN: "It won't run," I say, but it does. It leaks water, coughs, overheats, gets us to a gas station where the kid's twenty, no more.

MAN ONE: A country tough, hard rubbery white arms in his t-shirt, blond hair, amazed to see we got this far, wipes dirty hands on a dirty rag and sniffs, knows the story from Chuck and his son.

MAN FOUR: A boy's first deer! He's this week's grade school hero.

MAN ONE: The car's totaled of course, he enjoys telling us. He's got a tow truck that will get us to town, and the wrecker will lend us a loaner. It's nowhere near bad as it could've been.

WOMAN: I walk off, mad, crying, he's after me. I say, "Don't touch! Leave, leave, leave me alone!" He takes my hand. It makes me shake. "You never change the oil," I say, shaking my head, my arms, my whole body. "We're always fighting."

MAN ONE: (*To her.*) Grouch. We're not fighting.

WOMAN: Dried blood around his one nostril.

MAN ONE: (*To her.*) It's nothing. A dead animal. Stand still, calm down.

WOMAN: I close my eyes, I see the boy's wild eyes, beautiful as the deer we
killed. And he's right. He's always right. The whole story's nothing.
Just death. On the way home he's driving, we're fighting, I forget
about what, his son, his wife who's never going to be his ex-wife,
which one of us wants or doesn't need a drink. How could a deer
change us? Everything goes on the same.

MAN ONE: goes on the same.

TRY THIS 1.10

Write a dialogue between two people, in which one tells the other about something that
happened. Have the storyteller use sensory images, so that both the listener and an
audience would be able to see, touch, hear, taste, and smell the experience. Does the
story begin to suggest a metaphor for the relationship between teller and listener?

WORKING TOWARD A DRAFT

Look over the exercises you have done and the passages in your journal, and pick one
that interests you. Brainstorm it (see p. xxv) for how it might be expanded or developed. Ask: *What if . . .* ? and free-associate further images, lines, actions, characters,
incidents. What if this incident led to . . . ? What if so-and-so walked in? What if I
looked at it this way? What if this character said . . . ? What if it took place in . . . ?
And so forth.

Or

Take any passage you have written and underline the abstractions, especially the names
of qualities and judgments. Replace each of these with its opposite. In some instances
this will make nonsense. In some it may provide an insight. Do any of the changes suggest a way of enriching your idea? Pursue the possibility in a few paragraphs of focused
freewrite (see page xxv).

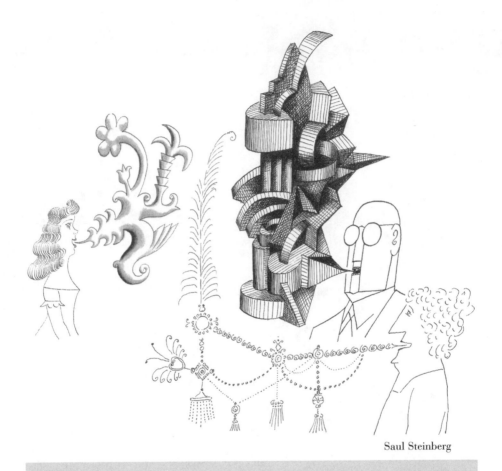

Saul Steinberg

CHAPTER TWO

VOICE

Your Voice
Persona
Character Voice
Point of View

Finding your own voice as a writer is in some ways like
the tricky business of becoming an adult . . . you try on
other people's personalities for size and you fall in love.

A. Alvarez

You pick up the phone and someone says, "Hello. You're home, are you?" and with just these five words you know, although you haven't heard from him for ten years, that Uncle Ed is calling. You turn on the radio and hear ". . . because the American people . . ." and before the familiar phrase is out you know exactly which politician is giving a speech. How do you recognize these voices? How is it possible to be so certain with so little information?

Of course, when you literally *hear* a voice, you have many subtle aural clues—accent, volume, tone, timbre, pitch, rhythm—to help you identify it. As a writer you have only the words, their choice and arrangement, with which to create a unique voice. Yet writers' voices are recognizable, too. They too create patterns that approximate all the qualities named above. As a reader you fall in love with particular poetic or narrative voices and as a writer you may "try on" or imitate those voices as part of the process of finding your own.

Diction (which is a combination of **vocabulary,** the words chosen, and **syntax,** the order in which they are used) can impart particularity to a poem or prose just as tone and pitch and timbre make up a particular voice. Diction will convey not only the facts but what we are to make of them, not only the situation but its emotional coloration, not only the identity but also the attitude of the person who speaks to us from the page. Joan Didion expresses this phenomenon in terms of "grammar," in the essay "Why I Write":

37

All I know about grammar . . . is its infinite power. To shift the structure of a sentence alters the meaning of that sentence, as definitely and inflexibly as the position of a camera alters the meaning of the object photographed. Many people know about camera angles now, but not so many people know about sentences. The arrangement of the words matters, and the arrangement you want can be found in the picture in your mind.

Beyond imitation, if as a writer you pay attention to the image in your mind, and if you develop the flexibility of vocabulary and syntax that allows you to be true to that image, you will be on your way to a voice that is recognizably your own.

> We can only talk about ourselves in the language we have available. If that language is rich, it illuminates us. But if it is narrow or restricted, it represses and conceals us.
>
> *Jaan Whitehead*

Your Voice

An author's voice has a quality developed over time, involving recurrent word choice, syntax, imagery, idiom, rhythm, and range. It comes about by a mostly automatic process, the result of practice and the growing confidence that practice brings. Don't worry about "finding your voice." Worry about saying things as clearly, precisely, and vividly as you can. Make your language as rich, flexible, and varied as you can make it. In other words: seek *to voice*, and *your voice* will follow.

   The language that comes naturally to you is the fine and proper foundation of your voice. Nothing rings more false than a writer who puts on the airs of critical jargon, or medieval fantasy, or high culture, without having a convincing command of that language. On the other hand, training your awareness of language, stretching both the quantity and the flexibility of your vocabulary, playing at different human voices, can all expand your range.

   It can't hurt to go about adding to your vocabulary in even a self-improvement sort of way—buy a word-a-day calendar, subscribe to "Wordsmith" or "Merriam Webster's Word of the Day" online, read "On Language" in the Sunday magazine of the *New York Times*. Buy a really good dictionary. Dissect the diction of the authors you read, and if you don't know a word, look it up. Every writer I know owns a *Roget's Thesaurus*, a blessed aid to locating—not a fancier word to say what you mean! (that *chicken* is not, really, a *chanticleer*)—but the word with that exact shade of meaning you almost have in mind (it might well be a *broiler* or a *bantam* or a *Rhode Island Red*).

   Alert yourself to language as it is used around you. Listen to people talking, note the flavor of different idioms, record bits of conversation, wander around in the dictionary, push the words around on the page. When you get to the point of revising your manuscript, pay attention to the small unease this or that word occasions in you and focus on how it might please you better.

Begin by knowing, and exploring, the fact that you already have a number of different voices. You speak differently in class from the way you speak (even to the same people) at a party or a bar. You have one diction for your diary and another for your history paper. You use one style of vocabulary and syntax to console a friend and another to ditch a date.

You also have a different vocabulary for shades of meaning, so that according to the circumstances you might describe someone as *stuck-up, snobbish, arrogant, haughty,* or *imperious.* There is no such thing as an exact synonym. Each word would be appropriate to a description of a different person, a different mood or tone, a different medium, even a different speaker.

TRY THIS 2.1

Stuck-up, snobbish, arrogant, haughty, imperious. Pick three of these words and produce an image in words of a person who fits each of them. To what extent does "the picture dictate the arrangement" of the words?

Then:

Pick one of the following words and list as many synonyms for it as you can. Pick three of the synonyms and produce an image in words that expresses each. How do the images differ?

    expensive
    shabby
    intelligent
    far
    rapid
    red

And so there exists a definite sense of a *person*, a perfectly *knowable* person, behind the poem.

Mary Oliver

Persona

A **persona** is a mask adopted by the author, which may be a public manifestation of the author's self, or a distorted or partial version of that self, or a fictional, historical, or mythological character. The concept of a persona allows us to acknowledge that, just as no written account can tell the whole truth about an event, so no "I" of a poem, essay, or story is exactly the same as the person who writes. When you write "as yourself" in your own voice—in a personal essay or a lyric poem, for example—there is nevertheless a certain distance between the person you are as you go about living your daily life and the *persona* in which you write. The version of yourself that you choose to reveal is part of your meaning. No matter how earnest your attempt to tell "exactly what happened," "the author" is always a partial or slightly idealized you, writing from a frame of mind more focused and consistent—and probably more virtuous—than any person ever possessed. Even if you are confessing terrible sins, you write as one-who-confesses, which is a particular, and admirable, version of your composite total self.

When you speak in your "own" voice, that voice may be relatively intimate and confiding, one that, though artful, we trust to be as honest with us as possible, as in this memoir-poem of Anne Sexton's, "Young."

> A thousand doors ago
> when I was a lonely kid
> in a big house with four
> garages and it was summer
> as long as I could remember
> I lay on the lawn at night,
> clover wrinkling under me,
> the wise stars bedding over me,
> my mother's window a funnel
> of yellow heat running out,
> my father's window, half shut,
> an eye where sleepers pass
> and the boards of the house
> were smooth and white as wax
> and probably a million leaves
> sailed on their strange stalks
> as the crickets ticked together
> and I, in my brand new body,
> which was not a woman's yet,
> told the stars my questions
> and thought God could really see
> the heat and the painted light,
> elbows, knees, dreams, goodnight.

Here one may feel how the words are "found in the picture" in the poet's mind, how for example the "thousand doors ago" or the "window a funnel of yellow heat running out" reach for an exactness of image, mood, and memory. But the diction might instead signal a more fanciful mask, like this one in which Anne Sexton plays on a conventional image of power and malevolence for her persona:

Her Kind
I have gone out, a possessed witch,
haunting the black air, braver at night;
dreaming evil, I have done my hitch
over the plain houses, light by light:
lonely thing, twelve-fingered, out of mind.
A woman like that is not a woman, quite.
I have been her kind . . .

Prose writers can exercise a similar range of personae. One way of looking at the author of a memoir or personal essay is that that writer is the main character or protagonist of a true story. Again, the persona may be confessional and direct:

When my family packed up and moved from the backwoods of Tennessee to the backwoods of Ohio I was not quite six years old. Like most children at that age I was still a two-legged smudge. Hardly a thing about me was definite except my way of talking, and that soon landed me in trouble. The kids in Ohio took one listen to my Tennessee accent and decided I was a hick. They let me know their opinion by calling me not only hick but hillbilly, ridge runner, clodhopper, and hayseed.
"Coming from the Country," Scott Russell Sanders

But this is far from the only way you might choose to present your "self" as author. Any number of masks may be donned. Here is Dave Barry writing from the persona of Ignorant Literal-Minded Guy, a mask that has been enormously popular among American essayists since Mark Twain:

. . . obviously the real cause of the California electricity shortage is: college students. I base this statement on widespread observation of my son, who is a college student, and who personally consumes more electricity than Belgium. If my son is in a room, then every electrical device within 200 yards of that room—every light, computer, television, stereo, video game, microwave oven, etc.—will be running. My son doesn't even have to turn the devices on; they activate themselves spontaneously in response to his presence.

This comic persona depends partly on exaggeration and an inflated vocabulary, out of tone in relation to the content: *widespread observation, personally consumes, electrical device, spontaneously in response*. It also mocks scientific logic, "basing the statement" on a single case.

TRY THIS 2.2
Imagine (remember?) that you have borrowed ("borrowed"?) a car and been involved in a fender bender. Write an explanation for the police report. Write a **monologue** (a speech for one voice) explaining the accident to the friend whose car you borrowed. Write a letter telling about it to a friend who thinks you are truly cool.

> "I'll tell my state as though 'twere none of mine."
>
> *Robert Browning*

Character Voice

You may also choose to speak in the persona of a character who is largely or totally unlike you. This **character**'s voice is a chosen mimicry and is one of the most rewarding devices of imaginative writing, a skill to pursue in order to develop rich characters both in their narratives and in their dialogue. Your voice will never be entirely absent from the voice of the characters you create, but the characters too can be distinct and recognizable.

The voice of a character requires, beyond invention, an imaginative leap into the mind and diction of another person. The best way to develop this capability is, first, to listen to other people speaking and to become aware of their speech patterns, vocabulary choice, habits of diction; and then to practice launching yourself into the voices you have heard. You already have a foundation for this skill through your knowledge of other writers' efforts. Here, for example, are some very brief examples, most of them familiar to you, of characters announcing their own identities. Notice how much they tell you about themselves, the worlds they inhabit, and their attitudes, in a very few words:

Call me Ishmael. (*Moby Dick*, Herman Melville)

My name is Bond—James Bond. (The series of Bond novels by Ian Fleming)

My name is Ozymandias, King of Kings.
Look on my works, ye mighty, and despair. (*Ozymandias*, Percy Bysshe Shelly)

Out of the ash
I rise with my red hair.
And I eat men like air. (*Lady Lazarus*, Sylvia Plath)

I am but mad north-northwest: when the wind is southerly, I know a hawk from a handsaw. (*Hamlet*, Shakespeare)

I am the Way and the Light. Whosoever believeth in Me shall not perish, but have everlasting life. (John 11:25)

I am a man more sinn'd against than sinning. (*King Lear*, Shakespeare)

If you really want to hear about it, the first thing you'll probably want to know is where I was born, and what my lousy childhood was like, and how my parents were occupied and all before they had me, and all that David Copperfield kind of crap . . . (*The Catcher in the Rye*, J. D. Salinger)

When I look back on my childhood, I wonder how I survived at all. It was, of course, a miserable childhood: the happy childhood is hardly worth your while.

Worse than the ordinary miserable childhood is the miserable Irish childhood, and worse yet is the miserable Irish Catholic childhood. (*Angela's Ashes*, Frank McCourt)

TRY THIS 2.3
Write a short character sketch of someone in your family. Write a monologue in which that person tells you an anecdote from his or her childhood.

You could say, and be roughly accurate, that there is a hierarchy of distance between the author and the voice. The memoirist or personal essayist is most likely to be closest to the person writing; the lyric poet is somewhat more distanced by the artifice of the language; the fiction writer has a range of masks from "author" to characters; and the dramatist speaks only through the characters, theoretically never speaking in his/her own voice except in stage directions.

The voices that you as author create involve not just word choice but the fundamental human capacity for mimicry—which, however, can be deliberately cultivated by careful listening, trial and error. A character's voice comes out of, and can convey, a historical period, a class, a set of circumstances, emotions, and the myriad quirks of typicality and eccentricity. Think of the differences in speech between a televangelist and a hip hop groupie, or even a "master stylist" and the neighborhood barber. Voice, said Philip Roth, is "something that begins at around the back of the knees and reaches well above the head."

Great potential for contrast, irony, and conflict enters the writing when one voice is set off against another. Characters reveal themselves in conversation and confrontation not only in the ideas they consciously express but in the diction they use, the things that "just slip out," and the things they refuse or fail to say. The next chapter will look at dialogue, which can lead not only to character revelation but to the heart of story, which is discovery and decision. In the meanwhile:

TRY THIS 2.4
Go back to the character in your "bumper sticker" exercise on page 20. Find a few more details to describe that character. Then pick a trigger line from those below and use it to start a monologue in that character's voice. If you feel you are not catching the voice, never mind; keep going.
- I don't normally dress this way, but
- I had a dream last night
- I'll tell you what doesn't make any sense
- I'm sorry, I didn't see you
- What I need is some kind of work that
- I remember when you could

> I am the narrator. I am just up in the sky telling the story.
> I just know everything. So pay no attention to me.
>
> *Josiah Sable, ten years old*

Point of View

Closely allied to the concept of voice is **point of view.** We're used to using the phrase "point of view" as a synonym for "opinion," as in, "It's my point of view that young people watch too much television." But point of view as a literary technique is a complex and specific concept, dealing with vantage point and addressing the question: *Who* is standing *where* to watch the scene? The answer will involve the voice of the teller, the intended listener, and the distance or closeness of both the action and the diction. An author's view of the world, as it is and as it ought to be, will ultimately be revealed by manipulation of the point of view, but not vice versa—identifying the author's beliefs will not describe the point of view of the work.

Point of view is a slippery concept, but one over which you gradually gain control as you write. Apart from significant detail, there is no more important skill for a writer to grasp, for, as Carol Bly says in *The Passionate, Accurate Story*, these are the two skills that "divide master from apprentice." Once you have chosen a point of view, you have in effect made a "contract" with the reader, and it will be difficult to break the contract gracefully. If you have restricted yourself to the mind of Sally Anne for five pages, as she longingly watches Chuck and his R&B band, you will violate the contract by suddenly dipping into Chuck's mind to let us know what he thinks of groupies. We are likely to feel misused—and likely to cancel the contract altogether if you suddenly give us an omniscient lecture on the failings of the young.

The first point of view decision that you as a writer must make is the **person** in which you speak: *first person* (I walked out into the rain), *second person* (You walked out into the rain), or *third person* (She walked out into the rain).

All of the examples of persona in this chapter so far are in the **first person:** *I was a lonely kid . . . I have gone out, a possessed witch . . . I was not quite six years old . . . I base this statement . . . Call me Ishmael,* and so forth. The first person is the point of view most frequent in memoir, personal essay, and lyric poetry. Characters in a play speak, of course, in the first person. It is also the voice of much fiction, in which case it will be the voice of the **central narrator,** the *I* writing *my* story as if it were memoir; or else of a **peripheral narrator,** someone on the edge of the action, but nevertheless our eyes and ears in the story and therefore the person with whom we identify and with whom we must be moved or changed if the story is to succeed.

Notice that when you are writing in the first person voice of a fictional or dramatic character, the whole range of intimacy and distance is also possible in the diction. Bohumil Hrabel's young railway employee in the novel *Closely Observed Trains* tells his own story and takes us into his confidence as if he were writing a confessional memoir, in spite of the fact that he never existed:

> I always had the impression—and I still have and always shall have—that behind every window there was at the very least one pair of eyes watching me. If anyone spoke to me I blushed, because I felt uncomfortably aware that there was something about me that disturbed and upset everybody. Three months ago I slashed my wrists, and on the face of it I had no reason to do such a thing, but I did have a reason, and I knew what it was, and I was only afraid that everyone who looked at me was guessing at what that reason could be.

By contrast, in the play *Our Country's Good*, Timberlake Wertenberger's Judge Collins of eighteenth-century Australia uses the distanced diction of profound and self-satisfied authority:

> This land is under English law. The court found them guilty and sentenced them accordingly . . . I commend your endeavor to oppose the baneful influence of vice with the harmonizing acts of civilization, Governor, but I suspect your edifice will collapse without the mortar of fear.

The **second person** is being used whenever the pronoun "you" occurs, but this may simply mean, in dialogue, that one character is addressing another. Sometimes it indicates not the point of view of the story but a general truth, possibly one in a character's mind:

> Maureen was trying to write her weekly letter to Len. It was heavy going; you can't say much in a letter.
>
> *The Ice Age, Margaret Drabble*

Or the pronoun "you" may represent the convention of the author addressing the reader:

> You might think it's a bit rare, having long-distance cross-country runners in Borstal . . . but you're wrong, and I'll tell you why.
>
> *The Loneliness of the Long Distance Runner, Alan Sillitoe*

Often, as in this case, the "you" refers to the person who is assumed to read or receive the piece. The basic point of view is still first person, as it is in Sharon Olds's poem "Feared Drowned," of which these are the first two stanzas:

> Suddenly nobody knows where you are,
> your suit black as seaweed, your bearded
> head slick as a seal's.
>
> Somebody watches the kids. I walk down the
> edge of the water, clutching the towel
> like a widow's shawl around me . . .

This use of the second person, as someone to whom speech, a poem, or story is addressed, can enhance a sense of intimacy, even make us feel as readers/viewers that we are overhearing something private.

The **second person** is the basic point of view of a piece only when the "you" is a character—usually in fact the reader, whom the author *turns into* a character by assuming she knows just how "you" behave in the situation she invents. Here is an example from Lorrie Moore's story "How to Be a Writer":

> First, try to be something, anything, else. A movie star/astronaut. A movie star/ missionary. The movie star/kindergarten teacher. President of the World. Fail miserably. It is best if you fail at an early age—say, fourteen. Early, critical disil- lusionment is necessary so that at fifteen you can write long haiku sequences about thwarted desire. It is a pond, a cherry blossom, a wind brushing against sparrow wing leaving for mountain. Count the syllables. Show it to your mom.

The second person as a basic point of view, in which "you" become the char- acter, tends to be experimental and self-conscious, and may be set aside or saved for special effects.

TRY THIS 2.5

Write about something that happened to you. But write about it in the first person *from the point of view of someone else* who was present.

Or:

Write about it in the second person, keeping in mind that you're trying to make your reader identify and "become you."

The **third person** is frequently used in poetry and fiction, as well as being the basic voice of the nonfiction writer. This is the voice with the greatest range of effects, from total objectivity to great intimacy.

The third person voice in imaginative writing can be roughly divided into three techniques:

- The **omniscient** or godlike narrator, who may know anything past, present, or future and is free to tell us readers what to think or feel
- The **limited omniscient,** who may go into the mind of one or perhaps two characters and also observe from the outside
- The **objective,** who may know no more than a person observing the scene— the facts and whatever is present to the senses

The omniscient author was a frequent stance of nineteenth-century fiction, where the persona of "author" took on an all-knowing quality:

Caroline Helstone was just eighteen years old; and at eighteen the true narrative of life has yet to be commenced. Before that time, we sit listening to a tale, a marvelous fiction; delightful sometimes, and sad sometimes; almost always unreal . . . Hope, when she smiles on us, and promises happiness tomorrow, is implicitly believed;— Love, when he comes wandering like a lost angel to our door, is at once admitted, welcomed, embraced . . . Alas, Experience! No other mentor has so wasted and frozen a face . . .

Shirley, Charlotte Brontë

This voice obviously involves a lot of "telling," and in order to avoid that outdated tone, in the twentieth century it became usual for "the author" to assume the more modest capability of the limited omniscient, able to go into one character's mind and to tell us objectively what, if we were present, we would be able to perceive for ourselves, but not to leap from the mind of one character to another.

Years later, Orno Tarcher would think of his days in New York as a seduction. A seduction and a near miss, a time when his memory of the world around him— the shining stone stairwells, the taxicabs, the sea of nighttime lights—was glinting and of heroic proportion. Like a dream. He had almost been taken away from himself. That was the feeling he had looking back. Smells and sounds: the roll and thunder of the number 1 train; the wind like a flute through the deck rafters of the Empire State Building; the waft of dope in the halls.

For Kings and Planets, Ethan Canin

The perception in these two passages is very much alike, of the vulnerability and ignorance of youth, but in the first the convention of "the author" holds all the answers, whereas in the second "the author" is an unvoiced presence, seeing and remembering through the character's eyes. It is the character himself looking back who "realizes," "feels," and "smells."

In the objective viewpoint, the author may choose a strictly journalistic stance, reporting only what may be seen, heard, smelled, tasted, touched, and objectively known. This is a favorite stance of Ernest Hemingway. In the story, "Hills Like White Elephants," Hemingway reports what is said and done by a quarreling couple, both without any direct revelation of the characters' thoughts and without comment.

The American and the girl with him sat at a table in the shade, outside the building. It was very hot and the express from Barcelona would come in forty minutes. It stopped at this junction for two minutes and went on to Madrid.

"What should we drink?" the girl asked. She had taken off her hat and put it on the table.

"It's pretty hot," the man said.

"Let's drink beer."

"Dos cervezas," the man said into the curtain.

"Big ones?" a woman asked from the doorway.

"Yes. Two big ones."

The woman brought two glasses of beer and two felt pads. She put the felt pads and the beer glasses on the table and looked at the man and the girl. The girl was looking off at the line of hills. They were white in the sun and the country was brown and dry.

The narrative remains clipped, austere, and external. What Hemingway gains by this pretense of objective reporting is that the reader is allowed to discover what is really happening through gestures, repetitions, and slips of the tongue, as in life.

TRY THIS 2.6

Take any passage you have written in the first person and recast it in the objective voice. Try to reveal the thoughts and feelings of the original through speech, gesture, action, and image.

Beyond the choice of person, point of view importantly involves the question of the **distance** between the author/reader and the characters. John Gardner in *The Art of Fiction* succinctly illustrates some of the possibilities of distance in the third person:

1. It was winter of the year 1853. A large man stepped out of a doorway.

2. Henry J. Warburton had never cared much for snowstorms.

3. Henry hated snowstorms.

4. God how he hated these damn snowstorms.

5. Snow. Under your collar, down inside our shoes, freezing and plugging up your miserable soul.

From the impersonality of *large man* through increasingly familiar designations (full name, first name, pronoun), to the identification implied in the second person (*your collar, your shoes, your soul*), these examples reduce the formality of the diction and therefore the psychic and psychological distance between the author-and-reader and the character.

The degree of distance will involve a series of questions, of which "who speaks?" is only the first. It will also involve *to whom?* (the reader? another character? the self?), *in what form?* (a story? a journal? a report? a daydream?), *at what distance?* (an old man telling the story of his youth? a prisoner recounting his crime?), and *with what limitations?* (is the narrator a liar, a child, crazy?). The voice of the speaker, whether autobiographical, poetic persona, narrator, or character, always involves these issues. Because the author *inevitably wants to convince us to share the same perspective*, the answers will also help reveal her or his final opinion, judgment, attitude, or message.

In many ways, our language has been impoverished—by politics, ads, ignorance, and suspicion of eloquence. In the Renaissance it was socially valuable to be able to speak well; you could talk yourself into court or into bed. Whereas in America, and especially from the latter half of the twentieth century, we have tended to equate eloquence with arrogance at best and dishonesty at worst, preferring people who, like, you know, well, kinda couldn't exactly, like, say what they mean. Sort of. Whole concepts have disappeared via advertising from our fund of expression. We no longer have meaningful ways to say *the real thing*, or *the right choice*, or *new and improved*, or *makes you feel young again*, or *just do it*. The words *wonderful, great, grand, distinctive, elegant, exclusive, purity, pleasure, passion, mastery, mystery*, and *natural*, have been co-opted and corrupted. If I say so much as, "Ask your doctor . . . " it's clear that I've got something to sell.

Paradoxically, this impoverishment allows the writer myriad ways to characterize. Though it may be difficult to write convincingly from the lofty perspective of all-knowing author-ity, a rich awareness of voice and voices, their particular idioms and diction, can give you a range of perspectives from which to write. You can make legitimate and revealing use of jargon, cliché, malapropisms (misused words), overstatement, and so forth, in the mouth of a character. Such language is a way of signaling distance between author and character, a distance that the reader understands and shares. A famous example is Amanda Wingfield of Tennessee Williams's *Glass Menagerie*, who here berates her son:

> Oh, I can see the handwriting on the wall as plain as I see the nose in front of my face! It's terrifying! More and more you remind me of your father! He was out all hours without explanation—then *left!* And me with the bag to hold.

TRY THIS 2.7
Write a speech in which a character strings together a bunch of clichés or jargon phrases. Let the clichés characterize. However, be sure you have some sympathy for the character.

If you persevere in writing, "your voice" will inevitably take on a coloration that is entirely your own. At the same time, voice is a powerful force for exploring the inner lives of others. Story writer Grace Paley describes the process: ". . . what we write about is *what we don't know about what we know* . . . when you take this other voice—you're making a 'pull.' You're pulling towards another head. And that pull toward what you *don't* know . . . well, that's the story itself. The story is that stretching . . . that *act* of stretching."

More to Read

Oliver, Mary. *A Poetry Handbook.* New York: Harcourt Brace, 1994.

Alvarez, A. *The Writer's Voice.* New York: W. W. Norton, 2005.

Readings

Of the three prose pieces that begin these readings, two are written in the first person and one in the third person, mostly through the eyes of the central character, but they present three very different voices. Explore what choices of diction and imagery create the childhood pain of Walker, the reflective reminiscence of Cherry, the stark awkwardness of Trevor.

CREATIVE NONFICTION

Alice Walker

Beauty: When the Other Dancer is the Self

It is a bright summer day in 1947. My father, a fat, funny man with beautiful eyes and a subversive wit, is trying to decide which of his eight children he will take with him to the county fair. My mother, of course, will not go. She is knocked out from getting most of us ready: I hold my neck stiff against the pressure of her knuckles as she hastily completes the braiding and then beribboning of my hair.

My father is the driver for the rich old white lady up the road. Her name is Miss Mey. She owns all the land for miles around, as well as the house in which we live. All I remember about her is that she once offered to pay my mother thirty-five cents for cleaning her house, raking up piles of her magnolia leaves, and washing her family's clothes, and that my mother— she of no money, eight children, and a chronic earache—refused it. But I do not think of this in 1947. I am two and a half years old. I want to go everywhere my daddy goes. I am excited at the prospect of riding in a car. Someone has told me fairs are fun. That there is room in the car for only three of us doesn't faze me at all. Whirling happily in my starchy frock, showing off my biscuit-polished patent-leather shoes and lavender socks, tossing my head in a way that makes my ribbons bounce, I stand, hands on hips, before my father. "Take me, Daddy," I say with assurance; "I'm the prettiest!"

Later, it does not surprise me to find myself in Miss Mey's shiny black car, sharing the back seat with the other lucky ones. Does not surprise me that I thoroughly enjoy the fair. At home that night I tell the unlucky ones all I can remember about the merry-go-round, the man who eats live chickens, and the teddy bears, until they say: that's enough, baby Alice. Shut up now, and go to sleep.

It is Easter Sunday, 1950. I am dressed in a green, flocked, scalloped-hem dress (handmade by my adoring sister, Ruth) that has its own smooth satin petticoat and tiny hot-pink roses tucked into each scallop. My shoes, new T-strap patent leather, again highly biscuit-polished. I am six years old and have learned one of the longest Easter speeches to be heard that day, totally unlike the speech I said when I was two: "Easter lilies/pure and white/blossom in/the morning light." When I rise to give my speech I do so on a great wave of love and pride and expectation. People in the church stop rustling their new crinolines. They seem to hold their breath. I can tell they admire my dress, but it is my spirit, bordering on sassiness (womanishness), they secretly applaud.

"That girl's a little *mess*," they whisper to each other, pleased.

Naturally I say my speech without stammer or pause, unlike those who stutter, stammer, or, worst of all, forget. This is before the word "beautiful" exists in people's vocabulary, but "Oh, isn't she the *cutest* thing!" frequently floats my way. "And got so much sense!" they gratefully add . . . for which thoughtful addition I thank them to this day.

It was great fun being cute. But then, one day, it ended.

I am eight years old and a tomboy. I have a cowboy hat, cowboy boots, checkered shirt and pants, all red. My playmates are my brothers, two and four years older than I. Their colors are black and green, the only difference in the way we are dressed. On Saturday nights we all go to the picture show, even my mother; Westerns are her favorite kind of movie. Back home, "on the ranch," we pretend we are Tom Mix, Hopalong Cassidy, Lash LaRue (we've even named one of our dogs Lash LaRue); we chase each other for hours rustling cattle, being outlaws, delivering damsels from distress. Then my parents decide to buy my brothers guns. These are not "real" guns. They shoot "BBs," copper pellets my brothers say will kill birds. Because I am a girl, I do not get a gun. Instantly I am relegated to the position of Indian. Now there appears a great distance between us. They shoot and shoot at everything with their new guns. I try to keep up with my bow and arrows.

One day while I am standing on top of our makeshift garage—pieces of tin nailed across some poles—holding my bow and arrow and looking out toward the fields, I feel an incredible blow in my right eye. I look down just in time to see my brother lower his gun.

Both brothers rush to my side. My eye stings, and I cover it with my hand. "If you tell," they say, "we will get a whipping. You don't want that to happen, do you?" I do not. "Here is a piece of wire," says the older brother, picking it up from the roof; "say you stepped on one end of it and the other flew up and hit you." The pain is beginning to start. "Yes," I say. "Yes, I will say that is what happened." If I do not say this is what happened, I know my brothers will find ways to make me wish I had. But now I will say anything that gets me to my mother.

Confronted by our parents we stick to the lie agreed upon. They place me on a bench on the porch and I close my left eye while they examine the right. There is a tree growing from underneath the porch that climbs past the railing to the roof. It is the last thing my right eye sees. I watch as its trunk, its branches, and then its leaves are blotted out by the rising blood.

I am in shock. First there is intense fever, which my father tries to break using lily leaves bound around my head. Then there are chills: my mother tries to get me to eat soup. Eventually, I do not know how, my parents learn what has happened. A week after the "accident" they take me to see a doctor. "Why did you wait so long to come?" he asks, looking into my eye and shaking his head. "Eyes are sympathetic," he says. "If one is blind, the other will likely become blind too."

This comment of the doctor's terrifies me. But it is really how I look that bothers me most. Where the BB pellet struck there is a glob of whitish scar tissue, a hideous cataract, on my eye. Now when I stare at people—a favorite pastime, up to now—they will stare back. Not at the "cute" little girl, but at her scar. For six years I do not stare at anyone, because I do not raise my head.

Years later, in the throes of a mid-life crisis, I ask my mother and sister whether I changed after the "accident." "No," they say, puzzled. "What do you mean?"

What do I mean?

I am eight, and, for the first time, doing poorly in school, where I have been something of a whiz since I was four. We have just moved to the place where the "accident" occurred. We do not know any of the people around us because this is a different county. The only time I see the friends I knew is when we go back to our old church. The new school is the former state penitentiary. It is a large stone building, cold and drafty, crammed to overflowing with boisterous, ill-disciplined children. On the third floor there is a huge circular imprint of some partition that has been torn out.

"What used to be here?" I ask a sullen girl next to me on our way past it to lunch.

"The electric chair," says she.

At night I have nightmares about the electric chair, and about all the people reputedly "fried" in it. I am afraid of the school, where all the students seem to be budding criminals.

"What's the matter with your eye?" they ask, critically.

When I don't answer (I cannot decide whether it was an "accident" or not), they shove me, insist on a fight.

My brother, the one who created the story about the wire, comes to my rescue. But then brags so much about "protecting" me, I become sick.

After months of torture at the school, my parents decide to send me back to our old community, to my old school. I live with my grandparents and the teacher they board. But there is no room for Phoebe, my cat. By the time my grandparents decide there *is* room, and I ask for my cat, she cannot be found. Miss Yarborough, the boarding teacher, takes me under her wing, and begins to teach me to play the piano. But soon she marries an African— a "prince," she says—and is whisked away to his continent.

At my old school there is at least one teacher who loves me. She is the teacher who "knew me before I was born" and bought my first baby clothes. It is she who makes life bearable. It is her presence that finally helps me turn on the one child at the school who continually calls me "one-eyed bitch." One day I simply grab him by his coat and beat him until I am satisfied. It is my teacher who tells me my mother is ill.

My mother is lying in bed in the middle of the day, something I have never seen. She is in too much pain to speak. She has an abscess in her ear. I stand looking down on her, knowing that if she dies, I cannot live. She is being treated with warm oils and hot bricks held against her cheek. Finally a doctor comes. But I must go back to my grandparents' house. The weeks pass but I am hardly aware of it. All I know is that my mother might die, my father is not so jolly, my brothers still have their guns, and I am the one sent away from home.

"You did not change," they say.

Did I imagine the anguish of never looking up?

I am twelve. When relatives come to visit I hide in my room. My cousin Brenda, just my age, whose father works in the post office and whose mother is a nurse, comes to find me. "Hello," she says. And then she asks, looking at my recent school picture, which I did not want taken, and on which the "glob," as I think of it, is clearly visible, "You still can't see out of that eye?"

"No," I say, and flop back on the bed over my book.

That night, as I do almost every night, I abuse my eye. I rant and rave at it, in front of the mirror. I plead with it to clear up before morning. I tell it I hate and despise it. I do not pray for sight. I pray for beauty.

"You did not change," they say.

I am fourteen and baby-sitting for my brother Bill, who lives in Boston. He is my favorite brother and there is a strong bond between us. Understanding my feelings of shame and ugliness he and his wife take me to a local hospital, where the "glob" is removed by a doctor named O. Henry. There is still a small bluish crater where the scar tissue was, but the ugly white stuff is gone. Almost immediately I become a different person from the girl who does not raise her head. Or so I think. Now that I've raised my head I win the boyfriend of my dreams. Now that I've raised my head I have plenty of friends. Now that I've raised my head classwork comes from my lips as faultlessly as Easter speeches did, and I leave high school as valedictorian, most popular student, and *queen*, hardly believing my luck. Ironically, the girl who was voted most beautiful in our class (and was) was later shot twice through the chest by a male companion, using a "real" gun, while she was pregnant. But that's another story in itself. Or is it?

"You did not change," they say.

It is now thirty years since the "accident." A beautiful journalist comes to visit and to interview me. She is going to write a cover story for her magazine that focuses on my latest book. "Decide how you want to look on the cover," she says. "Glamorous, or whatever."

Never mind "glamorous," it is the "whatever" that I hear. Suddenly all I can think of is whether I will get enough sleep the night before the photography session: if I don't, my eye will be tired and wander, as blind eyes will.

At night in bed with my lover I think up reasons why I should not appear on the cover of a magazine. "My meanest critics will say I've sold out," I say. "My family will now realize I write scandalous books."

"But what's the real reason you don't want to do this?" he asks.

"Because in all probability," I say in a rush, "my eye won't be straight."

"It will be straight enough," he says. Then, "Besides, I thought you'd made your peace with that."

And I suddenly remember that I have.

I remember:

I am talking to my brother Jimmy, asking if he remembers anything unusual about the day I was shot. He does not know I consider that day the last time my father, with his sweet home remedy of cool lily leaves, chose me, and that I suffered and raged inside because of this. "Well," he says, "all I remember is standing by the side of the highway with Daddy, trying to flag down a car. A white man stopped, but when Daddy said he needed somebody to take his little girl to the doctor, he drove off."

I remember:

I am in the desert for the first time. I fall totally in love with it. I am so overwhelmed by its beauty, I confront for the first time, consciously, the meaning of the doctor's words years ago: "Eyes are sympathetic. If one is blind, the other will likely become blind too." I realize I have dashed about the world madly, looking at this, looking at that, storing up images against the fading of the light. *But I might have missed seeing the desert!* The shock of that possibility—and gratitude for over twenty-five years of sight—sends me literally to my knees. Poem after poem comes—which is perhaps how poets pray.

> On Sight
>
> I am so thankful I have seen
> The Desert
> And the creatures in the desert
> And the desert Itself.
>
> The desert has its own moon
> Which I have seen
> With my own eye.
>
> There is no flag on it.
> Trees of the desert have arms
> All of which are always up
> That is because the moon is up
> The sun is up
> Also the sky
> The stars
> Clouds
> None with flags.
>
> If there *were* flags, I doubt
> the trees would point.
> Would you?

But mostly, I remember this:

I am twenty-seven, and my baby daughter is almost three. Since her birth I have worried about her discovery that her mother's eyes are different from other people's. Will she be embarrassed? I think. What will she say? Every day she watches a television program called "Big Blue Marble." It begins with a picture of the earth as it appears from the moon. It is bluish, a little battered-looking, but full of light, with whitish clouds swirling around it. Every time I see it I weep with love, as if it is a picture of Grandma's house. One day when I am putting Rebecca down for her nap, she suddenly focuses on my eye. Something inside me cringes, gets ready to try to protect myself. All children are cruel about physical differences, I know from experience, and that they don't always mean to be is another matter. I assume Rebecca will be the same.

But no-o-o-o. She studies my face intently as we stand, her inside and me outside her crib. She even holds my face maternally between her dimpled little hands. Then, looking every bit as serious and lawyerlike as her father, she says, as if it may just possibly have slipped my attention: "Mommy, there's a *world* in your eye." (As in, "Don't be alarmed, or do anything crazy.") And then, gently, but with great interest: "Mommy, where did you *get* that world in your eye?"

For the most part, the pain left then. (So what, if my brothers grew up to buy even more powerful pellet guns for their sons and to carry real guns themselves. So what, if a young "Morehouse man" once nearly fell off the steps of Trevor Arnett Library because he thought my eyes were blue.) Crying and laughing I ran to the bathroom, while Rebecca mumbled and sang herself off to sleep. Yes indeed, I realized, looking into the mirror. There *was* a world in my eye. And I saw that it was possible to love it: that in fact, for all it had taught me of shame and anger and inner vision, I *did* love it. Even to see it drifting out of orbit in boredom, or rolling up out of fatigue, not to mention floating back at attention in excitement (bearing witness, a friend has called it), deeply suitable to my personality, and even characteristic of me.

That night I dream I am dancing to Stevie Wonder's song "Always" (the name of the song is really "As," but I hear it as "Always"). As I dance, whirling and joyous, happier than I've ever been in my life, another bright-faced dancer joins me. We dance and kiss each other and hold each other through the night. The other dancer has obviously come through all right, as I have done. She is beautiful, whole and free. And she is also me.

TRY THIS 2.8

Everyone hates something about his or her body. Write a poem or a few paragraphs in the first person about what you hate about yours. What tone will you choose? Are you laughing at yourself, genuinely grieving, wry, angry, over it?

Kelly Cherry
A Note About Allen Tate

I took Literary Criticism with Allen Tate. My mind was not on the subject, because—I liked to think—I preferred the abstractions of philosophy and the music of poetry to the explication of the obvious. Literary criticism seemed to me to be mostly paraphrase. But I have since learned to love writing about writing, and perhaps the real reason I was distracted, that bright autumn semester so long ago, was that I had fallen in love. I was going to be married over the Christmas break.

Mr. Tate—we called him "Mr." Tate, not "Dr." or "Professor," and never in our wildest dreams "Allen"—began each class by reading the roll. *Present,* I would say, staring out the window and thinking about licenses, announcements, what dress to wear. *Here.* I wasn't, really.

While he went down the list of last names, Mr. Tate played with his cigarette lighter. It was, I'm sure, a gold lighter. It *looked* gold, and I doubt that Mr. Tate would ever have been happy with something that looked gold but was not gold. He flipped the lid open. Twirled, with his thumb, the little wheel that ignited the wick. The lighter flared. He snapped the lid shut. Sometimes he snapped the lid shut with the thumb of the same hand with which he was holding the lighter; sometimes he gently palmed the lid shut with his other hand.

Oddly, I can't remember whether he smoked in class. It's likely that he did; I think that teachers probably were allowed to smoke in class in those days. But in those days everyone I knew smoked. But not everyone I knew—in fact, no one else I knew—had a gold cigarette lighter. It was the lighter, not the smoking, that was interesting. The lighter, and that Mr. Tate played with it nervously all through class.

He was slender, shortish, with a formal bearing. His manners were of a kind seldom encountered today: the enactment of established rituals of courtesy and consideration. To shake his hand was to participate in a small ceremony. To pass him in the hallway and say hi was to play a minor but, one understood, important part in a well-known drama. (And never a melodrama.)

Maybe there were melodramas in his life. I wouldn't know, because I didn't know him outside of class. He was not the kind of teacher a shy student got to know outside the classroom. Maybe *he* was shy. He certainly did fiddle nervously with that cigarette lighter.

He addressed us with a title, too. We were "Mr." or "Miss." (I have to interrupt myself here to say that although "Ms." had, according to the Oxford English Dictionary, been invented, it had not yet arrived in North Carolina, so he can hardly be faulted for not using it.)

Jonathan Silver and I were married at my parents' house in front of a picture window while the worst blizzard in Richmond's history whited out the view. Guests gazed forlornly at their cars being buried under drifts of snow. Jonathan's mother and father had refused to attend; the mood was solemn, more suited to political and religious history than to romance. There was a sense that we were all engaged in a subversive activity, but against our will, as if we were also surprised, and unsettled, to discover ourselves engaging in anything subversive. People wanted to be in their own homes, not facing the prospect of digging out, putting on snow chains, driving down unplowed roads. As soon as the minister pronounced us husband and wife, coats were grabbed, and people stood in the foyer, sweating in swathes of scarves, waiting only for Jonathan and me to leave first. We had borrowed my father's car. As we turned the corner, I looked back to see the party, which had never quite begun, breaking up. The picture window framed the scene, and it was like something by Hopper, beautiful and sad.

There were two weeks remaining in the semester after the holidays. The first day I returned to Literary Criticism, Mr. Tate, as usual, called the roll, but he did not read my name among the C's. He read most of the roll without stopping. When he reached the S's, he stopped to flick his gold lighter open. Then he called, "Mrs. Silver."

Here, I answered. *Present.*

He flicked his lighter shut and finished the roll call.

That was all. But I knew that this man—this deeply quiet man—had paid more attention to me than I ever had paid to Literary Criticism. Perhaps contemporary women, who prefer "Ms." to "Mrs." and who keep their own names instead of changing them, won't like this story. But I am a contemporary woman, who has reclaimed her own name, and yet I remember the day Mr. Tate called me by my married name as the day I learned what literary criticism is all about. Literary criticism is about the interlineation of text and interpretation. It is about locating new meaning in the words we have been given. It is about knowing how to call the roll—with respect, that is, and observantly, in a way that recognizes change in the world.

FICTION

William Trevor
Sitting With the Dead

His eyes had been closed and he opened them, saying he wanted to see the stable-yard.

Emily's expression was empty of response. Her face, younger than his and yet not seeming so, was empty of everything except the tiredness she felt. 'From the window?' she said.

No, he'd go down, he said. 'Will you get me the coat? And have the boots by the door.'

She turned away from the bed. He would manage on his own if she didn't help him: she'd known him for twenty-eight years, been married to him for twenty-three. Whether or not she brought the coat up to him would make no difference, any more than it would if she protested.

'It could kill you,' she said.

'The fresh air'd strengthen a man.'

Downstairs, she placed the boots ready for him at the back door. She brought his cap and muffler to him with his overcoat. A stitch was needed where the left sleeve met the shoulder, she noticed. She hadn't before and knew he wouldn't wait while she repaired it now.

'What're you going to do there?' she asked, and he said nothing much. Tidy up a bit, he said.

He died eight days later, and Dr Ann explained that tidying the stable-yard with only a coat over his pyjamas wouldn't have hastened anything. An hour after she left, the Geraghtys came to the house, not knowing that he was dead.

It was half past seven in the evening then. At the same time the next morning, Keane the undertaker was due. She said that to the Geraghtys, making sure they understood, not wanting them to think she was turning them away for some other reason. Although she knew that if her husband had been alive he wouldn't have agreed to have the Geraghtys at his bedside. It was a relief that they had come too late.

The Geraghtys were two middle-aged women, sisters, the Misses Geraghty, who sat with the dying. Emily had heard of them, but did not know them, not even to see: they'd had to give their name when she opened the door to them. It had never occurred to her that the Geraghtys would attempt to bring their good works to the sick-room she had lived with herself for the last seven months. They were Legion of Mary women, famed for their charity, tireless in their support of the Society of St Vincent de Paul and their promulgation of the writings of Father Xavier O'Shea, a local priest who, at a young age in the 1880s, had contracted malaria in the mission fields of the East.

'We only heard of your trouble Tuesday,' the thinner and smaller of the two apologized. 'It does happen the occasional time we wouldn't hear.'

The other woman, more robust and older, allowed herself jewellery and make-up and took more care with her clothes. But it was her quiet, sharp-featured sister who took the lead.

'We heard in MacClincy's,' she said.

'I'm sorry you've had a wasted journey.'

'It's never wasted.' There was a pause, as if a pause was necessary here. 'You have our sympathy,' was added to that, the explanation of why the journey had not been in vain.

The conversation took place entirely at the hall door. Dusk was becoming dark, but over the white-washed wall of the small front garden Emily still could see a car drawn up in the road. It was cold, the wind gone round to the east. They meant well, these women, even if they'd got everything wrong, driving out from Carra to visit a man who wouldn't have welcomed them and then arriving too late, a man whose death had spared them an embarrassment.

'Would you like a cup of tea?' Emily offered.

She imagined they'd refuse and then begin to go, saying they couldn't disturb her at a time like this. But the big, wide-shouldered one glanced at her sister, hesitating.

'If you're alone,' the smaller one said, 'you'd be welcome to our company. If it would be of help to you.'

The dead man had been without religion. Anyone could have told them that, Emily reflected, making tea. He would have said that there was more to their sitting at the bedsides of the ill than met the eye, and she wondered if that could possibly be so. Did they in their compassionate travels hope for the first signs of the belief that often came out of nowhere when death declared its intention? Did they drive away from the houses they visited, straight to a presbytery, their duty done? She had never heard that said about the Geraghtys and she didn't want to believe it. They meant well, she said to herself again.

When they left, she wouldn't go back upstairs to look at the dead features. She'd leave him now to Keane in the morning. In the brief time that had elapsed a day had been settled for the funeral, Thursday of next week; in the morning she would let a few people know; she'd put a notice in the *Advertiser*. No children had been born: when Thursday had passed everything would be over except for the unpaid debts. She buttered slices of brack and stirred the tea in the pot. She carried in the tray.

They hadn't taken their coats off, but sat as still as statues, a little apart from one another.

'It's cold,' she said, 'I'll light the fire.'

'Ah no. Ah no, don't bother.' They both protested, but she did anyway, and the kindling that had been in the grate all summer flared up at once. She poured their tea, asking if they took sugar, and then offering the brack. They began to call her Emily, as if they knew her well. They gave their own names: Kathleen the older sister, and Norah.

'I didn't think,' Kathleen began to say, and Norah interrupted her.

'Oh, we know all right,' she said. 'You're Protestant here, but that never made a difference yet.'

They had sat with the Methodist minister, the Reverend Wolfe, Kathleen said. They'd read to him, they'd brought in whatever he wanted. They were there when he went.

'Never a difference,' Norah repeated, and in turn they took a slice of brack. They commented on it, saying it was excellent.

'It isn't easy,' Kathleen said when the conversation lapsed. 'The first few hours. We often stay.'

'It was good of you to think of him.'

'It's cheerful with that fire, Emily,' Kathleen said.

They asked her about the horses because the horses were what they'd heard about, and she explained that they'd become a thing of the past. She'd sell the place now, she said.

'You'd find it remote, Emily,' Kathleen said. Her lipstick had left a trace on the rim of the teacup and Norah drew her attention to it with a gesture. Kathleen wiped it off. 'We're town people ourselves,' she said.

Emily didn't consider the house she'd lived in for nearly thirty years remote. Five minutes in the car and you were in the middle of Carra. Mangan's Bridge, in the other direction, was no more than a minute.

'You get used to a place,' Emily said.

They identified for her the house where they lived themselves, on the outskirts of Carra, on the Athy road. Emily knew it, a pleasant creeper-covered house with silver railings in front of it, not big but prosperous-looking. She'd thought it was Corrigan's, the surveyor's.

'I don't know why I thought that.'

'We bought it from Mr Corrigan,' Norah said, 'when we came to Carra three years ago.' And her sister said they'd been living in Athy before that.

'Carra was what we were looking for,' Norah said.

They were endeavouring to lift her spirits, Emily realized, by keeping things light. Carra had improved in their time, they said, and it would again. You could tell with a town; some of them wouldn't rise out of the doldrums while a century'd go by.

'You'd maybe come in to Carra now?' Kathleen said.

'I don't know what I'll do.'

She poured more tea. She handed round the brack again. Dr Ann had given her pills to take, but she didn't intend to take them. Exhausted as she was, she didn't want to sleep.

'He went out a week ago,' she said. 'He got up and went out to the yard with only a coat over his pyjamas. I thought it was that that hurried it on, but seemingly it wasn't.'

They didn't say anything, just nodded, both of them. She said he had been seven months dying. He hadn't read a newspaper all that time, she said. In the end all the food he could manage was cornflour.

'We never knew your husband,' Norah said, 'any more than yourself. Although I think we maybe met him on the road one day.'

A feeling of apprehension began in Emily, a familiar dread that compulsively caused one hand to clench the other, fingers tightly locking. People often met him, exercising one of the horses. A car would slow down for him but he never acknowledged it, never so much as raised the crop. For a moment she forget that he was dead.

'He was often out,' she said.

'Oh, this was long ago.'

'He sold the last of the horses twelve months ago. He didn't want them left.'

'He raced his horses, we're to understand?' Kathleen said.

'Point-to-points. Punchestown the odd time.'

'Well, that's great.'

'There wasn't much success.'

'It's an up and down business, of course.'

Disappointment had filled the house when yet again a horse trailed in, when months of preparation went for nothing. There had never been much reason for optimism, but even so expectation had been high, as if anything less would have brought bad luck. When Emily married, her husband had been training a string of yearlings on the Curragh. Doing well, he'd said himself, although in fact he wasn't.

'You never had children, Emily?' Kathleen asked.

'No, we never did.'

'I think we heard that said.'

The house had been left to her by an aunt on her mother's side. Forty-three acres, sheep kept; and the furniture had been left to her too. 'I used come here as a child. A Miss Edgill my aunt was. Did you hear of her?'

They shook their heads. Way before their time, Kathleen said, looking around her. A good house, she said.

'She'd no one else to leave it to.' And Emily didn't add that neither the property nor the land would ever have become hers if her aunt had suspected she'd marry the man she had.

'You'll let it go though?' Kathleen pursued her enquiries, doing her best to knit together a conversation. 'The way things are now, you were saying you'd let it go?'

'I don't know.'

'Anyone would require a bit of time.'

'We see a lot of widowing,' Norah murmured.

'Nearly to the day, we were married twenty-three years.'

'God took him because He wanted him, Emily.'

The Geraghtys continued to offer sympathy, one following the other in what was said, the difference in tone and manner continuing also. And again—and more often as more solace was pressed upon her—Emily reflected how fortunate it was that they had escaped the awkwardness of attempting to keep company with her husband. He would have called her back as soon as she'd left them with him. He would have asked her who they were, although he knew; he would have told her to take them away. He'd never minded what he said—the flow of coarse language when someone crossed one of the fields, every word shouted out, frighteningly sometimes. It was always that: raising his voice, the expressions he used; not once, not ever, had there been violence. Yet often she had wished that there had been, believing that violence would have been easier to bear than the power of his articulated anger. It was power she had always felt coming from him, festering and then released, his denial of his failure.

'The horses. Punchestown. The world of the racecourse,' Kathleen said. 'You've had an interesting life, Emily.'

It seemed to Emily that Norah was about to shake her head, that for the first time the sisters were on the verge of a disagreement. It didn't surprise her: the observation that had been made astonished her.

'Unusual is what my sister means.' Norah nodded her correction into place, her tone softening the contradiction.

'There's many a woman doesn't get out and about,' Kathleen said.

Emily poured more tea and added turf to the fire. She had forgotten to draw the curtains over and she did so now. The light in the room was dim; he'd been particular about low-wattage electric bulbs. But the dimness made the room cosy and it seemed wrong that anywhere should be so while he lay only a few hours dead. She wondered what she'd do when another bulb went, either here or somewhere else, if she would replace it with a stronger one or if low-wattage light was part of her now. She wondered if her nervousness was part of her too. It didn't seem that it had always been, but she knew she could be wrong about that.

'I didn't go out and about much,' she said because a silence in the conversation had come. Both visitors were stirring sugar into their tea. When their teaspoons were laid down, Norah said:

'There's some wouldn't bother with that.'

'He was a difficult man. People would have told you.'

They did not contradict that. They did not say anything. She said:

'He put his trust in the horses. Since childhood what he wanted was to win races, to be known for it. But he never managed much.'

'Poor man,' Kathleen murmured. 'Poor man.'

'Yes.'

She shouldn't have complained, she hadn't meant to: Emily tried to say that, but the words wouldn't come. She looked away from the women who had visited her, gazing about her at the furniture of a room she knew too well. He had been angry when she'd taken the curtains down to wash them; everyone staring in, he'd said, and she hadn't known what he'd meant. Hardly anyone passed by on the road.

'He married me for the house,' she said, unable to prevent herself from saying that too. The women were strangers, she was speaking ill of the dead. She shook her head in an effort to deny what she'd said, but that seemed to be a dishonesty, worse than speaking ill.

The women sipped their tea, both lifting the cups to their lips in the same moment.

'He married me for the forty acres,' Emily said, compelled again to say what she didn't want to. 'I was a Protestant girl that got passed by until he made a bid for me and I thought it was romantic, like he did himself—the race cards, the race ribbons, the jockeys' colours, the big crowd there'd be. That's how it happened.'

'Ah now, now,' Kathleen said. 'Ah now, dear.'

'I was a fool and you pay for foolishness. I was greedy for what marriage might be, and you pay for greed. We'd a half acre left after what was paid back a year ago. There's a mortgage he took out on the house. I could have said to him all the time he was dying, "What'll I do?" But I didn't, and he didn't say anything either. God knows what his last thoughts were.'

They told her she was upset. One after the other they told her any widow would be, that it was what you had to expect. Norah said it twice. Kathleen said she could call on them in her grief.

'There's no grief in the house you've come to.'

'Ah now, now,' Kathleen said, her big face puckered in distress. 'Ah, now.'

'He never minded how the truth came out, whether he'd say it or not. He didn't say I was a worthless woman, but you'd see it in his eyes. Another time, I'd sweep the stable-yard and he'd say what use was that. He'd push a plate of food away untouched. We had two collies once and they were company. When they died he said he'd never have another dog. The vet wouldn't come near us. The man who came to read the meter turned surly under the abuse he got for driving his van into the yard.'

'There's good and bad in everyone, Emily.' Norah whispered that opinion and, still whispering, repeated it.

'Stay where you are, Emily,' Kathleen said, 'and I'll make another pot of tea.'

She stood up, the teapot already in her hand. She was used to making tea in other people's kitchens. She'd find her way about, she said.

Emily protested, but even while she did she didn't care. In all the years of her marriage another woman hadn't made tea in that kitchen, and she imagined him walking in from the yard and finding someone other than herself there. The time she began to paint the scullery, it frightened her when he stood in the doorway, before he even said a thing. The time she dropped the sugar bag and the sugar spilt out all over the floor he watched her sweeping it on to the dustpan, turf dust going with it. He said what was she doing, throwing it away when it was still fit to stir into your tea? The scullery had stayed half-painted to this day.

'He lived in a strangeness of his own,' Emily said to the sister who was left in the room with her. 'Even when he was old, he believed a horse could still reclaim him. Even when the only one left was diseased and fit for nothing. When there was none there at all he scoured the empty stables and got fresh straw in. He had it in mind to begin all over again, to find some animal going cheap. He never said it, but it was what he had in mind.'

The house wasn't clean. It hadn't been clean for years. She'd lost heart in the house, and in herself, in the radio that didn't work, her bicycle with the tyres punctured. These visitors would have noticed that the summer flies weren't swept up, that nowhere was dusted.

'Three spoons and one for the pot,' Kathleen said, setting the teapot down in the hearth. 'Is that about right, Emily? Will we let it draw a minute?'

She had cut more brack, finding it on the breadboard, the bread saw beside it, the butter there too. She hoped it wasn't a presumption, she hoped it wasn't interference, she said, but all that remained unanswered.

'He'd sit there looking at me,' Emily said. 'His eyes would follow me about the kitchen. There was a beetle got on the table once and he didn't move. It got into the flour and he didn't reach out for it.'

'Isn't it a wonder,' Norah said, 'you wouldn't have gone off, the way things were, Emily? Not that I'm saying you should have.'

Emily was aware that that question was asked. She didn't answer it; she didn't know why she hadn't gone off. Looking back on it, she didn't. But she remembered how when she had thought of going away what her arguments to herself had been, how she had wondered where she could go to, and had told herself it would be wrong to leave a house that had been left to her in good faith and with affection. And then, of course, there was the worry about how he'd manage.

'Will you take another cup, Emily?'

She shook her head. The wind had become stronger. She could hear it rattling the doors upstairs. She'd left a light burning in the room.

'I'm wrong to delay you,' she said.

But the Geraghtys had settled down again, with the fresh tea to sustain them. She wasn't delaying them in any way whatsoever, Kathleen said. In the shadowy illumination of the single forty-watt bulb the alarm clock on the mantelpiece gave the time as twenty past eleven, although in fact it was half an hour later.

'It's just I'm tired,' Emily said. 'A time like this, I didn't mean to go on about what's done with.'

Kathleen said it was the shock. The shock of death changed everything, she said; no matter now certainly death was expected, it was always a shock.

'I wouldn't want you to think I didn't love my husband.'

The sisters were taken aback, Kathleen on her knees adding turf to the fire, Norah pouring milk into her tea. How could these two unmarried women understand? Emily thought. How could they understand that even if there was neither grief nor mourning there had been some love left for the man who'd died? Her fault, her foolishness from the first it had been; no one had made her do anything.

The talk went on, back and forth between the widow and the sisters, words and commiseration, solace and reassurance. The past came into it when more was said: the wedding, his polished shoes and shiny hair, the party afterwards over on the Curragh, at Jockey Hall because he knew the man there. People were spoken of, names known to the Geraghtys, or people before their time; occasions were spoken of—the year he went to Cheltenham, the shooting of the old grey when her leg went at Glanbyre point-to-point. The Geraghtys spoke of their growing up in Galway, how you wouldn't recognize the City of the Tribes these days so fashionable and lively it had become; how later they had lived near Enniscorthy; how Kathleen had felt the draw of the religious life at that time but then had felt the receding of it, how she had known ever since that she'd been tested with her own mistake. In this way the Geraghtys spread themselves into the conversation. As the night went on, Emily was aware that they were doing so because it was necessary, on a bleak occasion, to influence the bleakness in other ways. She apologized for speaking ill of the dead, and blamed herself again. It was half past three before the Geraghtys left.

'Thank you,' she said, holding open the hall door. The wind that had been slight and then had got up wasn't there any more. The air was fresh and clean. She said she'd be all right.

Light flickered in the car when the women opened the doors. There was the red glow of the tail-light before the engine started up, a whiff of exhaust before the car moved slowly forward and gathered speed.

In the room upstairs, the sheet drawn up over the raddled, stiffening features, Emily prayed. She knelt by the bedside and pleaded for the deliverance of the husband who had wronged her for so long. Fear had drained to a husk the love she had spoken of, but she did not deny that remnant's existence, as she had not in the company of her visitors. She could not grieve, she could not mourn; too little was left, too much destroyed. Would they know that as they drove away? Would they explain it to people when people asked?

Downstairs, she washed up the cups and saucers. She would not sleep. She would not go to bed. The hours would pass and then the undertaker's man would come.

The headlights illuminated low stone walls, ragwort thriving on the verges, gorse among the motionless sheep in gated fields. Kathleen drove, as she always did, Norah never having learnt how to. A visit had not before turned out so strangely, so different from what had been the sisters' familiar expectation. They said all that, and then were silent for a while before Kathleen made her final comment: that what they had heard had been all the more terrible to listen to with a man dead in an upstairs room.

Hunched in the dark of the car, Norah frowned over that. She did not speak immediately, but when they'd gone another mile she said:

'I'd say, myself, it was the dead we were sitting with.'

In the house the silence there had been before the visitors disturbed it was there again. No spectre rose from the carnal remains of the man who was at last at peace. But the woman sitting by the turf fire she kept going was aware, as dawn lightened the edges of the curtains, of a stirring in her senses. Her tiredness afflicted her less, a calm possessed her. In the neglected room she regretted nothing now of what she had said to the women who had meant well; nor did it matter if, here and there, they had not quite understood. She sat for a while longer, then pulled the curtains back and the day came in. Hers was the ghost the night had brought, in her own image as she once had been.

TRY THIS 2.9

Every culture contains the phenomenon of mourners who call on the family of the recently deceased. Unless you come from rural Ireland, these people are likely to look and sound different than those in Trevor's story. Drawing on a culture you know well, write a scene in the third person in which two sympathetic characters call on a widow who does not particularly want to see them.

Then:

Write a speech in which the widow describes her mean husband. What does this woman consider mean? How would she express it?

POEMS

The three poems that follow are written in the first person. What differences of diction distinguish these voices? How intimate or distanced is each? To whom is each poem addressed? Can you copy any of these tricks for your own purposes?

Gary Soto
Black Hair

At eight I was brilliant with my body.
In July, that ring of heat
We all jump through, I sat in the bleachers
Of Romain Playground, in the lengthening
Shade that rose from our dirty feet.
The game before us was more than baseball.
It was a figure—Hector Moreno
Quick and hard with turned muscles,
His crouch the one I assumed before an altar
Of worn baseball cards, in my room.

I came here because I was Mexican, a stick
Of brown light in love with those
Who could do it—the triple and hard slide,
The gloves eating balls into double plays.
What could I do with 50 pounds, my shyness,
My black torch of hair, about to go out?
Father was dead, his face no longer
Hanging over the table or our sleep,
And mother was the terror of mouths
Twisting hurt by butter knives.

In the bleachers I was brilliant with my body,
Waving players in and stomping my feet,
Growing sweaty in the presence of white shirts.
I chewed sunflower seeds. I drank water
And bit my arm through the late innings.
When Hector lined balls into deep
Center, in my mind I rounded the bases

With him, my face flared, my hair lifting
Beautifully, because we were coming home
To the arms of brown people.

Tom Crawford

Ginkgo Tree

The knee-high juvenile smile
in the slender trunk of the little ginkgo tree
planted between the curb and the sidewalk
won't tell you anything
about what happened here
in Kwangju at this intersection a year ago
when our bus smashed into the blue pickup.
It raised up on its right side
the little truck did
almost turning over
then settled back down
in an animal gentleness
in a shower of tempered glass
driverless, the door flung open
going now in a whole new direction
coasting, as it were, toward the little ginkgo tree
rolling ever so slowly
dragging its chrome trim along the street
while one of its silver hubcaps rolled
in the opposite direction,
toward us, pointing an accusing finger, I thought.
But if one discounts the dead driver
lying next to the curb
then the little truck, its black tires
carrying it away down the block
took on a certain charm,
the blue door waving back as it rolled
ever so slowly toward the curb
where it bounced softly like a beach ball
then struck the young tree, not such a hard blow,
but enough to ring all of its bell-shaped, green leaves
causing two or three to fall,
one landing on the hood
the other two on the blue cab.

William Trowbridge

Kong Looks Back on His Tryout With the Bears

If it had worked out, I'd be on a train to Green Bay,
not crawling up this building with the air corps
on my ass. And if it weren't for love, I'd drop
this shrieking little bimbo sixty stories
and let them take me back to the exhibit,
let them teach me to rumba and do imitations.
They tried me on the offensive line, told me
to take out the right cornerback for Nagurski.
Eager to please, I wadded up the whole secondary,
then stomped the line, then the bench and locker room,
then the east end of town, to the river.
But they were not pleased: they said
I had to learn my position, become a team player.
The great father Bear himself said that,
so I tried hard to know the right numbers
and how the arrows slanted toward the little o's.
But the o's and the wet grass and the grunts
drowned out the count, and the tight little cheers
drew my arrow straight into the stands,
and the wives tasted like flowers and raw fish.
So I was put on waivers right after camp,
and here I am, panty sniffer, about to die a clown,
who once opened a hole you could drive Nebraska through.

TRY THIS 2.10

Write from the point of view of anything not human—an insect, an android, a potato, a belly button. Try to invent and develop a diction that represents the frame of reference of this thing. For instance, if you are writing from the point of view of a shoe, it is likely to have extensive knowledge of and opinions about flooring, but a limited concept of the sky or human heads.

Hilða Raz

Father

is never home but she loves him—
adores him, really, and so does Mom:
his big, burly body, his flannel shirts,
woolens over interesting scars
with stories to tell. Oh, he is a raconteur
with racks of bottles in the fragrant breakfront.

He tells her not to talk so much.
His talk holds the world intact;
when it stops, the key piece
drops out the bottom and the whole
plastic globe fragments. Nothing's
the same ever again.

The size of him! The size of them all,
uncles, cousins, the brothers:
wide shoulders jutting through cigar smoke
in the breakfast nook. The deep black marks
of their synthetic heels never quite scrub out.

Under the huge dining table,
under the carpet where his big feet wait,
is the bell. When he pushes it with his shoe
an aunt, or mother, or a maid
brings out another dish
from the steaming kitchen.

But he paid for it, paid for it all,
sweaters, teak tables with brass inlay,
steaks, furs, wicks for the memorial
candles, silk stockings, full tin box
the color of sky, plants
and their white rings on the mahogany,
and the cars, deep greens, metallic,
and the cashmere lap-robes,
and the aunts and out-of-work uncles.

He was best loved, best beloved in the family,
   whose very shadow, even absent,

absorbed all color, sucked short
the seasons, colored grey
even the lavish lilacs of that northern city

she never visits. She sends money
to an old woman who tends the graves,
sends money when the pencilled bills come in.

TRY THIS 2.11

Unlike the preceding three poems, "Father" is written in the third person, as if from the point of view of an outsider, aimed at no one in particular but the convention of "the reader" or "the listener." Try recasting a few lines from one of the earlier poems ("Black Hair," "Ginkgo Tree," or "Kong Looks Back . . .") into prose in the third person. Then try writing a monologue about "Father" in the voice of Mom, a cousin, an uncle, or a maid.

Barbara Hamby

The Language of Bees

The language of bees contains 76 distinct words for stinging,
    distinguishes between a prick, puncture, and mortal wound,
    elaborates on cause and effect as in a sting made to retaliate,
    irritate, insinuate, infuriate, incite, rebuke, annoy,
    nudge, anger, poison, harangue.
The language of the bees has 39 words for queen—regina apiana,
    empress of the hive, czarina of nectar, maharani of the ovum,
    sultana of stupor, *principessa* of dark desire.
The language of bees contains 22 words for sunshine,
Two for rain—big water and small water, so that a man urinating
    on an azalea bush in the full fuchsia of April
    has the linguistic effect of a light shower in September.
For man, two words—roughly translated—"hands" and "feet,"
    the first with the imperialistic connotation of beekeeper,
    the second with the delicious resonance of bareness.
All colors are variations on yellow, from the exquisite
    sixteen-syllable word meaning "diaphanous golden fall,"

to the dirty ochre of the bitter pollen
stored in the honeycomb and used by bees for food.

The language of bees is the language of war. For what is peace
without strife but the boredom of enervating day-after-day,
obese with sweetness, truculent with ennui?
Attack is delightful to bees, who have hundreds of verbs
embracing strategy, aim, location, velocity:
swift, downward swoop to stun an antagonist,
brazen, kamikaze strike for no gain but momentum.
Yet stealth is essential to bees, for they live to consternate
their enemies, flying up pantslegs, hovering in grass.
No insect is more secretive than the bee, for they have two
thousand words describing the penetralia of the hive
—octagonal golden chamber of unbearable moistness,
opaque tabernacle of nectar,
sugarplum of polygonal waxy walls.

The language of bees is the language of aeronautics,
for they have wings—transparent, insubstantial,
black-veined like the fall of an exotic iris.
For they are tiny dirigibles, aviators of orchard and field.
For they have ambition, cunning, and are able to take direct aim.
For they know how to leave the ground, to drift, hover, swarm,
sail over the tops of trees.
The language of bees is a musical dialect, a full, humming
congregation of hallelujahs and amens,
at night blue and disconsolate,
in the morning bright and bedewed.
The language of bees contains lavish adjectives
praising the lilting fertility of their queen
—fat, red-bottomed progenitor of millions,
luscious organizer of coitus,
gelatinous distributor of love.
The language of bees is in the jumble of leaves before rain,
in the quiet night rustle of small animals,
for it is eloquent and vulgar in the same mouth,
and though its wound is sweet it can be distressing,
as if words could not hurt or be meant to sting.

TRY THIS 2.12
Invent a language for something nonhuman. Describe it in poetry or prose.

DRAMA

Jane Martin
French Fries

An old woman in a straight-back chair holding a McDonald's cup. She is surrounded by several bundles of newspapers. She wears thick glasses that distort her eyes to the viewer.

ANNA MAE: If I had one wish in my life, why I'd like to live in McDonald's. Right there in the restaurant. 'Stead of in this old place. I'll come up to the brow of the hill, bowed down with my troubles, hurtin' under my load and I'll see that yellow horseshoe, sort of like part of a rainbow, and it gives my old spirit a lift. Lord, I can sit in a McDonald's all day. I've done it too. Walked the seven miles with the sun just on its way, and then sat on the curb till five minutes of seven. First one there and the last one to leave. Just like some ol' french fry they forgot.

I like the young people workin' there. Like a team of fine young horses when I was growin' up. All smilin'. Tell you what I really like though is the plastic. God gave us plastic so there wouldn't be no stains on his world. See, in the human world of the earth it all gets scratched, stained, tore up, faded down. Loses its shine. All of it does. In time. Well, God he gave us the idea of plastic so we'd know what the everlasting really was. See if there's plastic then there's surely eternity. It's God's hint.

You ever watch folks when they come on in the McDonald's? They always speed up, almost run the last few steps. You see if they don't. Old Dobbin with the barn in sight. They know it's safe in there and it ain't safe outside. Now it ain't safe outside and you know it.

I've see a man healed by a Big Mac. I have. I was just sittin' there. Last summer it was. Oh, they don't never move you on. It's a sacred law in McDonald's, you can sit for a hundred years. Only place in this world. Anyway, a fella, maybe thirty-five, maybe forty, come on in there dressed real nice, real bright tie, bran' new baseball cap, nice white socks and he had him that disease. You know the one I mean, Cerebral Walrus they call it. Anyway, he had him a cock leg. His poor old body had it two speeds at the same time. Now he got him some coffee, with a lid on, and sat him down and Jimmy the tow-head cook knew him, see, and he brought over a Big Mac. Well, the sick fella ate maybe half of it and then he was just sittin', you know, suffering those tremors, when a couple of *ants* come right out of the burger. Now there ain't no ants in McDonald's no way. Lord sent those ants, and the sick fella he looked real sharp at the burger and a bunch *more* ants marched on out nice as you please and his head lolled right over and he pitched himself out of that chair and banged his head on the floor, loud. Thwack! Like a bowling ball dropping. Made you half sick to hear it. We jump up and run over but he was cold out. Well those servin' kids, so cute, they watered him, stuck a touch pepper up his nostril, slapped him right smart, and bang, up he got. Standin' an' blinkin'. 'Well, how are you?,' we say. An he looks us over, looks right in our eyes, and he say, 'I'm fine.' And he was. He was fine! Tipped his Cincinnati Reds baseball cap, big 'jus'-swallowed-the-canary' grin, paraded out of there clean, straight like a pole-bean poplar, walked him a plumb line without no trace of the 'walrus.' Got outside, jumped up, whooped, hollered, sang him the National Anthem, flagged down a Circle Line bus, an' rode off up Muhammad Ali Boulevard wavin' an' smilin' like the King of the Pharoahs. Healed by a Big Mac. I saw it.

McDonald's. You ever seen anybody die in a McDonald's? No sir. No way. Nobody ever has died in one. Shoot, they die in Burger Kings all the time. Kentucky Fried Chicken's got their own damn ambulances. Noooooooooo, you can't die in a McDonald's no matter how hard you try. It's the spices. Seals you safe in this life like it seals in the flavor. Yesssssss, yes!

I asked Jarrell could I live there. See they close up around ten, and there ain't a thing goin' on in 'em till seven a.m. I'd just sit in those nice swingy chairs and lean forward. Rest my head on those cool, cool, smooth tables, sing me a hymn and sleep like a baby. Jarrell, he said he'd write him a letter up the chain of command and see would they let me. Oh, I got my bid in. Peaceful and clean.

Sometimes I see it like the last of a movie. You know how they start the picture up real close and then back it off steady and far? Well, that's how I dream it. I'm living in McDonald's and it's real late at night and you see me up close, smiling, and then you see the whole McDonald's from the outside, lit up and friendly. And I get smaller and smaller, like they do, and then it's just a light in the darkness, like a star, and I'm in it. I'm part of that light, part of the whole sky, and it's all McDonald's, but part of something even bigger, something fixed and shiny . . . like plastic.

I know. I know. It's just a dream. Just a beacon in the storm. But you got to have a dream. It's our dreams make us what we are.

Blackout

TRY THIS 2.13
A prop is a kind of significant detail for the stage. The props in Jane Martin's *French Fries* are subordinated to the voice of the character, but with a little imagination you can see how the actress might make use of the cup, a hamburger, fries, the newspapers, and her glasses. Write a short monologue in which a character reveals him/herself through voice, and also through relation to an object onstage.

WORKING TOWARD A DRAFT
Look over a passage you have written and give voice to one of the minor characters. Try writing a dialogue between the persona or narrator of the piece and this minor character. Try to differentiate the voices through vocabulary and syntax. Does this suggest a way to develop the piece?

Or:

Take a poem or fragment of a poem you have written and develop it in the second person. Who is the "you" to whom this poem might be addressed? How does using the second person alter the meaning?

John Grant

WARM-UP
What does this woman want? Write about what she misses, covets, regrets, dreams of, longs for, deeply desires. What does she want for her daughter? How much of this will she be willing to tell the daughter? What will she admit to no one? Will the daughter share her desires?

CHAPTER THREE

CHARACTER

As Desire
As Image
As Voice
As Action
As Thought
As Presented by the Author
As Conflict
Stock or Flat Characters

I write because I want to have more than one life.

Anne Tyler

Nadia sits across from me at dinner. She is petite, dark-haired. She gestures delicately with her fork. She makes a political point to the famous, bald man beside me, who is sweating and drinking his fourth glass of wine. Nadia's voice is light, her phrases follow each other steadily. The famous man takes another piece of pie. He wipes his forehead with a knuckle, wipes the knuckle on his napkin, flaps the napkin toward Nadia as he replies to her question with a little explosion of sound. I miss some of what he says because his mouth is full of pie. I think: *She's smarter than he is, but he doesn't realize it because he's so impressed with his own fame; actually, underneath, he is terrified of being found out, and he's going to eat and drink himself to death trying to fill the void of his own ego.*

I hardly know these people! How did I come to such conclusions?!

Everything we know about other people we know through our five senses. The outer expresses the inner. Words, actions, and things, which can be seen and heard, express and reveal character and feeling that can be neither seen nor heard. Literature, of course, allows us a freedom that life does not, to be both inside and outside a character, to know thoughts as we can only know them in ourselves, while at the same time seeing the externals as we can for everyone *except* ourselves. In addition, literature can offer an author-itative voice to help us interpret and draw conclusions about the characters.

In nonfiction, fiction, poetry, and drama, there are essentially five possible methods of presenting a character to the reader:
Directly, through:

1. image (or "appearance")

2. voice (or "speech")

3. action

4. thought

Or **indirectly,** through:

5. "telling" or interpreting as an author

Each of these methods is discussed in this chapter, but I want to start with a necessity of all character—the phenomenon of desire—because in order to engage the attention and emotions of your reader you will need, even before you begin to write, to invent, intuit, or decide what each of your characters *wants*.

> We yearn. We are the yearning creatures of this planet . . .
> Yearning is always part of fictional character.
>
> *Robert Olen Butler*

Character as Desire

The importance of desire in creating character can scarcely be overstated. Novelist Butler calls it *yearning,* to indicate its poignant and obsessive nature. Nor is such desire a small thing. Aristotle declared that the nature of a man's desire determined the nature of his morality: he who wants good is good; he who wants evil is evil. (And it follows pretty well that he who wants the trivial is trivial, she who wants peace is peaceful, and so forth.)

Those of us who write are often excellent observers, and we can fall into the trap of creating fictional people who passively observe. Such passive characters lie flat on the page. The characters who stand up and make us care are so in love that they are willing to risk their reputations and their souls (Anna Karenina, for example); or so committed to a cause that they will devote their lives to it (Robin Hood, among many); or driven by a passion to know (like Faust) or to revenge (as in *Hamlet*), or to solve the mystery, climb the mountain, uncover the past, find out who they really are. Of course, the desire need not be as grand as these examples, and in modern literature the questing, conflicted nature of the desire is often and profoundly the point. But it is nevertheless so, that this quality of yearning or determination is what makes us catch our breath, hope for the best, fear the worst, and in short identify with what is, after all, a series of little squiggly lines on a page. "We know rationally," says William Logan, "that Prospero and Miranda never existed, much less Ariel or Caliban; that the real Caesar was not Shakespeare's Caesar; but we can be moved to tears by Ophelia's death, or Cordelia's. The bundles of words behave as if they had private psychologies."

You will have the makings of a character when you can fill out this sentence:
_____(name)_____ is a _____(adj.)_____ _____-year-old _____(noun)_____ who wants _____.

It isn't so important to trace the motive back to some childhood experience or trauma as it is to explore the nature and reality of the character's desire. What is her deepest need, longing, hope, apart from food and air? What can't he live without?

In thinking about your character's desire, it's a good idea to think both generally and specifically, or about the deep desire and the immediate desire. In filling in the sentence above, you might think: *Jeremy Glazer is a belligerent 17-year-old basketball player who wants respect.* "Respect" in this case, an abstraction, represents what Jeremy deeply desires. As a writer you need to ask what, in the particular situation he finds himself in, would represent respect for Jeremy? Being placed on the starting team? Being included in the locker room banter? Or is it his father's acknowledgment that basketball matters as much as his grades? What a character wants deeply (and which can be expressed in an abstraction) will always have a particular manifestation in a particular situation and can be expressed in a way that leads to image and action.

TRY THIS 3.1
Choose a character you have thought and written about before. Fill out the sentence above. Then quickly jot down what makes your character:

- laugh
- afraid
- angry
- ashamed
- tender

Imagine your character in a situation that produces one of these emotions. What does he or she *want* in that situation? What is the deep, abstract desire? What, in this specific situation, does he or she want that would fulfill, at least temporarily, that desire?

> The first thing is to see the people every minute . . . You have
> got to learn to paint with words.
>
> *Flannery O'Connor*

Character as Image

Sometimes a beginning writer skips the externals in order to try to take us directly to the abstract essence of a character. But if you let your reader get to know your characters through the sense details, as in life, these images will convey the essence in the way discussed in Chapter 1, through concrete significant detail: how does this character laugh, what is he wearing, how does she move, what gesture does he make, what objects does he carry, what does she eat and drink, what is the tone of her voice, his laugh, the texture of his skin, the smell of her hair?

> Swollen feet
> tripping on vines in the heat,
> palms thick and green-knuckled,
> sweat drying on top of old sweat.
> She flicks her tongue over upper lip
> where the salt stings her cracked mouth.
>
> *"sus plumas el viento," Gloria Anzaldua*

The first half dozen lines of this sharply realized miniature portrait convey much more than the images themselves. We already know the basic elements of this woman's life, her gender and status, her suffering. We know how poverty feels and tastes, the toll on the body of long overwork.

Especially in fiction and memoir, when a character is first introduced, it's important to let us experience that person through the senses (including sight), and it's often effective to emphasize a particular physical characteristic that can later remind us of the character as a whole. Here is an example from Ayelet Waldeman's *Daughter's Keeper:*

> As a little girl she had been beautiful, rosy-cheeked and blond-ringleted. Today she wore baggy jeans and a ragged green sweatshirt that had been washed so often that its zipper arced in waves from her neck to her waist. Her best feature remained her hair, which hung, an unwashed mass of blond, brown, and red kinky curls, down to the middle of her back. She'd swept part of it off her face and clipped it back with a chipped tortoise-shell barrette.

Here a series of visible clues (*baggy, ragged, unwashed, chipped*) give us a sense of the young woman's attitudes and lifestyle, while the vivid picture of her hair ensures that the next time this character appears on the scene, the author need only mention the hair to evoke the character. But sometimes the images that evoke character are not direct images of that character at all, but of something in the surroundings.

I often wonder who will be the last person to see me alive. If I had to bet, I'd bet on the delivery boy from the Chinese take-out. I order four nights out of seven. Whenever he comes I make a big production of finding my wallet. He stands in the doorway holding the greasy bag while I wonder if this is the night I'll finish off my spring roll, climb into bed, and have a heart attack in my sleep.

The History of Love, Nicole Krauss

Notice how, in this brief passage, the loneliness and longing of the old man are conveyed in the apparently mundane images of the Chinese take-out delivery, as well as in the clipped, almost throw-away rhythm of his voice.

Traditionally, the characters in a play may be minimally described (*Lisa, in her teens, scruffy; Ludovico, blind, a former spy*), for the very good reason that the people in the audience will have the live actor in front of them to offer a sense impression, heightened by costume, makeup, and lighting. But playwrights can and often do vividly signal in their stage directions the physical attributes, gestures, and clothes of their characters, and actors can and often do gratefully make use of this information to explore the character's inner life.

Leaning on the solitary table, his head cupped in one hand as he pages through one of his comic books, is Sam. A black man in his mid-forties. He wears the white coat of a waiter.

"Master Harold" . . . and the Boys, Athol Fugard

Or:

. . . Lou, the magician, enters. He is dressed in the traditional costume of Mr. Interlocutor: tuxedo, bow tie, top hat festooned with all kinds of whatnots that are obviously meant for good luck, he does a few catchy "soft shoe" steps & begins singing a traditional version of a black play song.

spell #7, Ntozake Shange

TRY THIS 3.2
If people are characterized by the objects they choose, own, wear, and carry with them, they are also revealed in what they throw away. *Garbology* is the study of society or culture by examining and analyzing its refuse. Write a character sketch by describing the contents of your character's waste basket.

Character as Voice

As a writer you need to hear a character's voice in your head in order to bring him or her to life successfully. This involves moving beyond inventing or remembering the character to inhabiting his or her persona, a challenging task if your character is significantly different from the person you are. As a first step, it's always good practice to write a monologue in your character's voice. Thinking *from the point of view of that character* will help you to find the diction and the rhythm of his or her speech and thought. Keep going even if you feel you haven't "caught" the character, because sometimes the very fact of continuing will allow you to slip or sidle into the voice you seek.

TRY THIS 3.3

Write a quick sketch of a character you have already worked with, no more than two or three focused details. Then pick one of the trigger lines below and write a monologue in that character's voice. Keep going a little bit past the place you want to stop.

- It doesn't take much, does it, for
- And what I said was true
- I know right away I'm going to
- I've become a different person since
- I don't like anyone to watch me
- You call that music?

Now look over the monologue and highlight a few phrases that seem to you to catch that character's voice. Pick one of these and use it to begin another short monologue.

One of the ways we understand people is by assessing, partly instinctively and partly through experience, what they express voluntarily and involuntarily. When someone chooses to wear baggy jeans as opposed to slim-fits, or a shaved head, a tuxedo, body piercing, a string of pearls—these are choices, largely conscious, that signal: *I am a member of this group.* Other "body language" will strike the viewer as involuntary (dishevelment, poor taste, blushing, slurring, staring, sweating, clumsiness) and so as a betrayal of feelings that have not been chosen. In the same way speech may be consciously chosen both in its style (the rapper's patter, the lawyer convolutions) and content (she tells him she's angry, but not that she's broke). On the whole, it is human nature to give the involuntary more credibility than the chosen. We say that *what he said was very generous, but he kept checking to see how it was going over.* His glances *belied* his words. In this case, we say that the words represent the *text*, and that what we read by other means is the *subtext*.

Speech belongs largely in the voluntary category, though like appearance it can (and does) betray us. Talking is an intentional attempt to express the inner as the outer. But when people talk in literature they convey much more than the information in their **dialogue.** They are also working for the author—to reveal themselves, advance the plot, fill in the past, control the pace, establish the tone, foreshadow the future, establish the mood. What busy talk!

NELL: So just fill me in a bit more could you about what you've been doing.
SHONA: What I've been doing. It's all down there.
NELL: The bare facts are down here but I've got to present you to an employer.
SHONA: I'm twenty-nine years old.
NELL: So it says here.
SHONA: We look young. Youngness runs in our family.
NELL: So just describe your present job for me.
SHONA: My present job at present. I have a car. I have a Porsche. I go up the
      M1 a lot. Burn up the M1 a lot. Straight up the M1 in the fast lane to
      where the clients are, Staffordshire, Yorkshire, I do a lot in Yorkshire.
      I'm selling electric things. Like dishwashers, washing machines, stain-
      less steel tubs are a feature and the reliability of the program . . .

Top Girls, Caryl Churchill

Notice how the characters produce tension by contradicting each other (*Fill me in; it's all down there; but I've got to present you; I'm twenty-nine; so it says*) This is known as "no dialogue," in which characters are in many and various ways saying "no" to each other. They may be angry or polite, disagreeing, contradicting, qualifying, or frankly quarreling, but whatever the tone, they spark our interest because we want to find out what will happen in this overt or implied conflict.

Notice also how Shona's description of her job reveals the subtext. She falters between concrete imagery and flimsy generalization, contradicting in generalization what she tries to prove by making up convincing details. She is spinning lies without sufficient information or imagination, so it's no great surprise when Nell ends the exchange with, "Christ, what a waste of time . . . Not a word of this is true, is it?"

Dramatic dialogue is always **direct** as in this example, all the words spoken. In fiction, nonfiction, or poems, direct dialogue of this sort is lively and vivid, but sometimes the narrative needs to cover ground faster, and then dialogue may be **indirect** or **summarized.** Summarized dialogue, efficient but textureless, gives us a brief report:

Shona claimed she had sales experience, but Nell questioned both her age and her expertise.

Indirect dialogue gives the flavor of the dialogue without quoting directly:

Nell wanted her to fill in the facts, so Shona repeated that she was twenty-nine, claimed that looking young ran in the family, and that she drove a Porsche up to Staffordshire to sell dishwashers and washing machines. But she couldn't seem to come up with the word "appliances."

There's a strong temptation to make dialogue eloquent (you are a writer, after all), and the result is usually that it becomes stilted. People are often *not* eloquent, precisely about what moves them most. Half the time we aren't really sure what we mean, and if we are, we don't want to say it, and if we do, we can't find the words, and if we do, the others aren't listening, and if they are, they don't understand . . . In fact, the various failures to communicate can make the richest sort of dialogue, just as the most stunted language is sometimes the most revealing of character.

In this example from Mark Winegardner's *Crooked River Burning*, David, who has just begun dating a rich society girl, is fishing with his Uncle Stan.

> David had no idea exactly where Uncle Stan came down on yesterday. Finally, he just broke down and asked. "Uncle Stan? What . . . ?"
> But he could not find the words. His uncle just watched him stammer.
> "The thing I was wondering, is . . . " Couldn't do it.
> "This isn't my strong suit," said Stan. "As you know." He licked his lips. "Cigar?"
> "Um, OK," David said. This was a new one.
> Stan killed the engine. They lit up. "Fella at work," he said. "Twins."
> "Great." They drifted.
> "I know you don't feel like this," said Stan.
> "Like what?"
> "Like what I'm about to say," said his uncle. "Don't take this wrong. But you have no idea how young you are . . ."

Debate and argument can make interesting dialogue if the matter itself is interesting, but in imaginative writing debate and argument are usually too static to be of interest, too simple and too single. Eudora Welty explained in an interview with the *Paris Review*, "Sometimes I needed to make a speech do four or five things at once—reveal what the character said but also what he thought he said, what he hid, what others were going to think he meant, and what they misunderstood—and so forth—all in this single speech . . . I used to laugh out loud sometimes when I wrote it."

If a character expresses in dialogue what he/she means, that character has done only one thing, whereas as a writer you are constantly trying to mean more than you say, to give several clues at once to the inner lives of your characters. If Jeannine says:

> I feel that civilization is encroaching on nature, and that the greed of the developers will diminish the value of all our lives—

—she has expressed an opinion, but little of her inner life is revealed, her emotions, her history, her particularities. This is the dialogue equivalent of the vague category images described in Chapter 1. But if she says:

> They should lock up that builder. He's massacred the neighborhood. I remember how the lilac and wisteria used to bloom, and then the peonies, and the daffodils. What fragrance in this room! But now. Smell the stink of that site next door. It just makes me sick.

—the same opinion is expressed, but her emotions—anger, nostalgia, and defeat—also are vividly revealed, and through particular detail.

TRY THIS 3.4

Write a "dialogue" between two characters, only one of whom can speak. The other is physically, emotionally, or otherwise prevented from saying what he/she wants to say. Write only the words of the one, only the appearance and actions of the other.

> By our actions we discover what we really believe and, simultaneously, reveal ourselves to others.
>
> *John Gardner*

Character as Action

I have said that a character is first of all someone who *wants*. Whatever the nature of that desire, it will lead the character toward action and therefore toward potential change. The action may be as large as a military charge or as small as removing a coffee cup, but it will signal or symbolize for the reader that a significant change has occurred. The characters who interest and move us are those who are capable of such change.

Playwright Sam Smiley observes that, "Any significant discovery forces change in conditions, relationships, activity or all three." And, he says, "The quickest and best way to know someone is to see that person make a significant decision . . . At the instant a character makes a choice, he changes from one state to another; his significant relationships alter; and usually he must follow a new line of action as a consequence."

If we grant that *discovery* and *decision* are the two agents of human change, characters will be *in action* when these are possible. Action as in *action-packed* is a crude but effective way of getting discovery and decision into a work:

> There's the bad guy! (discovery) Quick, I will load my revolver, hide behind this pillar, turn and shoot. (decision) But wait! There's his accomplice on the catwalk above me! (discovery) I will roll under this forklift to avoid his bullet! (decision)

The thriller, the cop show, the alien, and the spy are enormously popular (and money-making) genres because they simplify and exaggerate our experience of what action is. But of course most human discovery, decision, and change take place in the realm of work, love, relationship, and family, and it's important for the literary writer to recognize discovery and decision in these areas, where they are likely to be both complex and difficult.

One reason that debate and argument seem static is that characters holding forth with well thought-out positions seem unlikely to change, whereas dialogue

that represents potential change *becomes* itself dramatic action. In dramatic dialogue, in ways large and small, characters are constantly making discoveries and
decisions. Look again at the exchange above between Nell and Shona. What does
Nell discover about Shona? What does Shona decide to say to prove herself? Look
at the exchange between David and his Uncle Stan. What change occurs between
them when Stan decides to offer his nephew a cigar? How is the relationship further changed, when he decides (with difficulty: "Don't take this wrong.") to speak
his mind?

Change may seem most obvious in literature with a strong story line, and
of course discovery and decision will often involve a physical action: she opens
the letter, he picks up the phone, she slams the door, he steps on the gas. But
change also importantly occurs in the mind, and even in the gentlest piece of
memoir or the slightest nature lyric, the persona is made aware of something that
seems important, something that has not before been present to the mind, and
now is, and so changes the entire mental landscape. Frequently (by no means
always; still, frequently) in the tradition of memoir this mental change has to
do with a new perspective of the complexity of life and human beings; frequently
in lyric poetry it has to do with the ephemeral quality of beauty, and therefore
an awareness of death.

The change from alive-to-dead is a major one, as is the change from in-
danger-to-triumphant-hero. But discovery and decision are no less present in the
subtle and profound exchanges of ordinary life.

> Loveliest of trees, the cherry now
> Is hung with snow along the bough
> And stands about the woodland ride
> Wearing white for Easter tide.
>
> Now of my threescore years and ten
> Twenty will not come again,
> And take from seventy springs a score,
> That only leaves me fifty more.
>
> And since, to look at things in bloom,
> Fifty years is little room,
> About the woodland I will go
> To see the cherry hung with snow.
>
> *"II" from A Shropshire Lad, A. E. Housman*

In this very low-key poem (you can hear the stillness, the deliberate pace,
in the rhythm), the poet makes two discoveries and a decision. The first discovery
is of the snow on the trees; the second is of the brevity of life. The decision is simply to walk in the woods, but in following this "new line of action" he also
"changes from one state to another," and acknowledges his mortality.

TRY THIS 3.5
Take a monologue you have already written and add actions, in the form of either narration or stage directions. Make the action contradict or qualify the speech. ("I'm not worried about it at all. These things don't throw me." [*She twists her hands.*]) and so forth. Remember that a good way to reveal characters' feelings is through their relationships to objects.

Character as Thought

Although discovery and decision necessarily *imply* thought, image, speech, and action are all external manifestations—things that we could observe. Imaginative writing has the power also to take us inside the minds of characters to show us directly what they are thinking. Again, different degrees of the revelation of thought are appropriate to different forms of literature:

- In a memoir or personal essay we can't credibly see into the minds of other characters. (Though even this quasi-rule is sometimes broken; Tom Wolfe in his techniques of "new journalism" frequently turns what his interviewees say into a kind of mental patter or stream of consciousness, as if these quotations were in fact their thoughts.)

- A character in a drama is necessarily speaking and therefore making his thoughts external, but there are a number of theatrical traditions to let us know that we are overhearing his/her thoughts—as in soliloquy, aside, voice-over. Many characters in modern drama speak directly to the audience, and usually do so with an assumed honesty toward what is going on in their minds, whereas in dialogue with other characters they may lie, conceal, stumble, or become confused.

- Fiction usually (except in the case of the objective narrator) gives us the thoughts of at least the central character.

- A persona in poetry is usually sharing thoughts. Poetry also has the same freedom as fiction, to be presented from the point of view of a character—and this character may reveal what's on her mind.

Aristotle suggested a useful way of looking at thought in relation to desire. A persona or character begins with a certain desire, and therefore a certain specific goal in mind. Thought is the process by which she works backward to decide what to do in the immediate situation that presents itself. "Loveliest of Trees" is a condensed poetic demonstration of this process. *The chances are I will die at about seventy. I'm twenty now. That means I have fifty years left. That's not many years to look at these trees. I will look at them now.* My apologies to Housman for this rude paraphrase—but it does show not only Aristotle's understanding of the thought process, but also how crucial to the beauty of the poem is Housman's diction.

Thought, like dialogue, is also action when it presents us with the process of change. Since both discovery and decision take place in the mind, thought is material to every character and is in fact the locus of action and the dwelling place of desire. In the first lines of any poem, the first page of every story, the curtain rise of every drama, you can find a human consciousness yearning for whatever might occur in the last line, on the last page, in the last scene. The action proceeds because that consciousness makes a lightning-fast leap backward to the present moment, to decide what action can be taken now, at this moment, in this situation, to achieve that goal. At every new discovery, the mind repeats the process, ever changing in the service of a fixed desire.

Character as Presented by the Author

Appearance, speech, action, and thought are the direct methods of presenting character. The *indirect method* is **authorial interpretation**—"telling" us the character's background, motives, values, virtues, and the like. The advantages of the indirect method are enormous, for its use leaves you free to move in time and space; to know anything you choose to know whether the character knows it or not; and godlike, to tell us what we are to feel. The indirect method allows you to convey a great deal of information in a short time.

> The port town of Veracruz is a little purgatory between land and sea for the traveler, but the people who live there are very fond of themselves and the town they have helped to make . . . and they carry on their lives of alternate violence and lethargy with a pleasurable contempt for outside opinion . . .
>
> Katherine Anne Porter, *Ship of Fools*

The disadvantage of this indirect method is that it bars us readers from sharing the immediacy and vividness of detail and the pleasure of judging for ourselves. In the summarized judgments of the passage above, for example, we learn more about the attitude of the narrator than about the town. Nevertheless, the indirect method is very efficient when you want to cover the exposition quickly, as A.S. Byatt does in this passage from "Crocodile Tears."

> The Nimmos spent their Sundays in those art galleries that had the common sense to open on that dead day . . . They liked buying things, they liked simply looking, they were happily married and harmonious in their stares, on the whole. They engaged a patch of paint and abandoned it, usually simultaneously, they lingered in the same places, considering the same things. Some they remembered, some they forgot, some they carried away.

Thus in a few sentences of the first paragraph, Byatt tells us everything we need to know about the Nimmos's marriage—especially since Mr. Nimmo is going to die on the next page, and the story will concern itself with Mrs. Nimmo's flight from the scene. Notice that although this passage is full of analysis and interpretation, we are given some images to look at: ". . . harmonious in their stares . . . They engaged a patch of paint and abandoned it . . ." In an instance like this, authorial interpretation functions for pace and structure. But it is not a very useful mode to describe human change, which involves action and therefore calls for the immediacy of scene, and of the direct presentation of character.

TRY THIS 3.6
Write a paragraph of no more than a hundred words presenting a character through authorial interpretation. Cover at least five years in the character's life, four qualities he or she possesses, three important events, and two habitual actions.

> The meaning of life must be conceived in terms of the specific meaning of a personal life in a given situation.
>
> *Victor Frankl*

Character as Conflict

Rich characterization can be effectively (and quite consciously) achieved by producing a conflict between methods of presentation. A character can be directly revealed to us through *image, voice, action*, and *thought*. If you set one of these methods at odds with the others, then dramatic tension will be produced. Imagine, for example, a character who is impeccable and expensively dressed, who speaks eloquently, who acts decisively, and whose mind is revealed to us as full of order and determination. He is inevitably a flat character. But suppose that he is impeccable, eloquent, decisive, and that his mind is a mess of wounds and panic. He is at once interesting.

Here is the opening passage of Saul Bellow's *Seize the Day*, in which appearance and action are blatantly at odds with thought. Notice that it is the tension between suppressed thought and what is expressed through appearance and action that produces the rich character conflict.

> When it came to concealing his troubles, Tommy Wilhelm was not less capable than the next fellow. So at least he thought, and there was a certain amount of evidence to back him up. He had once been an actor—no, not quite, an extra—and he knew what acting should be. Also, he was smoking a cigar, and when a man is smoking a cigar, wearing a hat, he has an advantage: it is harder to find out how he feels. He came from the twenty-third floor down to the lobby on the mezzanine to collect his mail before breakfast, and he believed—he hoped—he looked passably well: doing all right.

Thought is most frequently at odds with one or more of the other three methods of direct presentation—reflecting the difficulty we have expressing ourselves openly or accurately—but this is by no means always the case. The author may be directly telling us what to think and contradicting herself by showing the character to be someone else entirely. A character may be successfully, calmly, even eloquently expressing fine opinions while betraying himself by pulling at his ear, or herself by crushing her skirt. Captain Queeg of Herman Wouk's *The Caine Mutiny* is a memorable example of this, maniacally clicking the steel balls in his hand as he defends his disciplinary code. Often we are not privy to the thoughts of a character at all, so that the conflicts must be expressed in a contradiction between the external methods of direct presentation, appearance, speech, and action. Notice that the notion of "betraying oneself" is again important here. We're more likely to believe the evidence unintentionally given than deliberate expression.

TRY THIS 3.7
Write a short character sketch (it may be from life), focusing on how your character makes a living. Put your character in a working situation and let us know by a combination of direct and indirect methods what that work is, how well he/she does it, what it looks, sounds, smells like, and how the character feels about it. Contrast the methods.

Stock and Flat Characters

I have insisted on the creation of character through an understanding of desire and through many methods of presentation. But it would be impractical and unnecessary to go through this process for every passerby on the fictional street, and boring to present such characters fully.

Flat characters are those defined by a single idea or quality. They may exist only to fulfill function, and we need know little about them. It's true nevertheless that they can be brought to brief life in an image—notice that the take-out delivery boy in the passage above from Nicole Krauss's *History of Love*, "stands in the doorway holding the greasy bag"—but neither the author nor the reader needs to stop to explore their psychology, or to give them the complexity that would make them *round*.

Stock characters or *caricatures* are related to flat characters in that they insistently present a single idea or quality. If you have aimed for a lifelike and complex character, and someone says you've created a stock character, that's not good. But some writers, especially in drama, effectively use stock characters as a way of satirizing human types. Eugene Ionesco takes the technique to its extreme in *The Bald Soprano*:

Mrs. Smith: There, it's nine o'clock. We've drunk the soup, and eaten the fish and chips, and the English salad. The children have drunk English water. We've eaten well this evening. That's because we live in the suburbs of London and because our name is Smith.

TRY THIS 3.8

Go back to something you have written and find a character who appears only briefly or is named or referred to without appearing. Characterize that person with a single vivid image.

Or:

Pick two stock characters from the list below. Decide what one wants from the other. Caricature them by writing a dialogue between them.
   Absent-minded professor
   Drug pusher
   Naïve girl
   Rock or hip hop wannabe
   Rich widow
   Evangelist

More to Read

Chiarella, Tom. *Writing Dialogue*. Cincinnati: Story Press, 1998.

Minot, Stephen. *Three Genres*. Upper Saddle River, N.J.: Prentice Hall, 2002.

Readings

CREATIVE NONFICTION

Scott Russell Sanders
The Inheritance of Tools

At just about the hour when my father died, soon after dawn one February morning when ice coated the windows like cataracts, I banged my thumb with a hammer. Naturally I swore at the hammer, the reckless thing, and in the moment of swearing I thought of what my father would say: "If you'd try hitting the nail it would go in a whole lot faster. Don't you know your thumb's not as hard as that hammer?" We both were doing carpentry that day, but far apart. He was building cupboards at my brother's place in Oklahoma; I was at home in Indiana putting up a wall in the basement to make a bedroom for my daughter. By the time my mother called with news of his death—the long distance wires whittling her voice until it seemed too thin to bear the weight of what she had to say—my thumb was swollen. A week or so later a white scar in the shape of a crescent moon began to show above the cuticle, and month by month it rose across the pink sky of my thumbnail. It took the better part of a year for the scar to disappear, and every time I noticed it I thought of my father.

The hammer had belonged to him, and to his father before him. The three of us have used it to build houses and barns and chicken coops, to upholster chairs and crack walnuts, to make doll furniture and bookshelves and jewelry boxes. The head is scratched and pockmarked, like an old plowshare that has been working rocky fields, and it gives off the sort of dull sheen you see on fast creek water in the shade. It is a finishing hammer, about the weight of a bread loaf, too light really for framing walls, too heavy for cabinetwork, with a curved claw for pulling nails, a rounded head for pounding, a fluted neck for looks, and a hickory handle for strength.

The present handle is my third one, bought from a lumberyard in Tennessee down the road from where my brother and I were helping my father build his retirement house. I broke the previous one by trying to pull sixteen-penny nails out of floor joists—a foolish thing to do with a finishing hammer, as my father pointed out. "You ever heard of a crowbar?" he said. No telling how many handles he and my grandfather had gone through before me. My grandfather used to cut down hickory trees on his farm, saw them into slabs, cure the planks in his hayloft, and carve handles with a drawknife. The grain in hickory is crooked and knotty, and therefore tough, hard to split, like the grain in the two men who owned this hammer before me.

After proposing marriage to a neighbor girl, my grandfather used this hammer to build a house for his bride on a stretch of river bottom in northern Mississippi. The lumber for the place, like the hickory for the handle, was cut on his own land. By the day of the wedding he had not quite finished the house, and so right after the ceremony he took his wife home and put her to work. My grandmother had worn her Sunday dress for the wedding, with a fringe of lace tacked on around the hem in honor of the occasion. She removed this lace and folded it away before going out to help my grandfather nail siding on the house. "There she was in her good dress," he told me some fifty-odd years after that wedding day, "holding up them long pieces of clapboard while I hammered, and together we got the place covered up before dark." As the family grew to four, six, eight, and eventually thirteen, my grandfather used this hammer to enlarge his house room by room, like a chambered nautilus expanding his shell.

By and by the hammer was passed along to my father. One day he was up on the roof of our pony barn nailing shingles with it, when I stepped out the kitchen door to call him for supper. Before I could yell, something about the sight of him straddling the spine of the roof and swinging the hammer caught my eye and made me hold my tongue. I was five or six years old, and the world's commonplaces were still news to me. He would pull a nail from the pouch at his waist, bring the hammer down, and a moment later the *thunk* of the blow would reach my ears. And that is what had stopped me in my tracks and stilled my tongue, that momentary gap between seeing and hearing the blow. Instead of yelling from the kitchen door, I ran to the barn and climbed two rungs up the ladder—as far as I was allowed to go—and spoke quietly to my father. On our walk to the house he explained that sound takes time to make its way through air. Suddenly the world seemed larger, the air more dense, if sound could be held back like any ordinary traveler.

By the time I started using this hammer, at about the age when I discovered the speed of sound, it already contained houses and mysteries for me. The smooth handle was one my grandfather had made. In those days I needed both hands to swing it. My father would start a nail in a scrap of wood, and I would pound away until I bent it over.

"Looks like you got ahold of some of those rubber nails," he would tell me. "Here, let me see if I can find you some stiff ones." And he would rummage in a drawer until he came up with a fistful of more cooperative nails. "Look at the head," he would tell me. "Don't look at your hands, don't look at the hammer. Just look at the head of that nail and pretty soon you'll learn to hit it square."

Pretty soon I did learn. While he worked in the garage cutting dovetail joints for a drawer or skinning a deer or tuning an engine, I would hammer nails. I made innocent blocks of wood look like porcupines. He did not talk much in the midst of his tools, but he kept up a nearly ceaseless humming, slipping in and out of a dozen tunes in an afternoon, often running back over the same stretch of melody again and again, as if searching for a way out. When the humming did cease, I knew he was faced with a task requiring great delicacy or concentration, and I took care not to distract him.

He kept scraps of wood in a cardboard box—the ends of two-by-fours, slabs of shelving and plywood, odd pieces of molding—and everything in it was fair game. I nailed scraps together to fashion what I called boats or houses, but the results usually bore only faint resemblance to the visions I carried in my head. I would hold up these constructions to show my father, and he would turn them over in his hands admiringly, speculating about what they might be. My cobbled-together guitars might have been alien spaceships, my barns might have been models of Aztec temples, each wooden contraption might have been anything but what I had set out to make.

Now and again I would feel the need to have a chunk of wood shaped or shortened before I riddled it with nails, and I would clamp it in a vice and scrape at it with a handsaw. My father would let me lacerate the board until my arm gave out, and then he would wrap his hand around mine and help me finish the cut, showing me how to use my thumb to guide the blade, how to pull back on the saw to keep it from binding, how to let my shoulder do the work.

"Don't force it," he would say, "just drag it easy and give the teeth a chance to bite."

As the saw teeth bit down the wood released its smell, each kind with its own fragrance, oak or walnut or cherry or pine—usually pine, because it was the softest and easiest for a child to work. No matter how weathered and gray the board, no matter how warped and cracked, inside there was this smell waiting, as of something freshly baked. I gathered every smidgen of sawdust and stored it away in coffee cans, which I kept in a drawer of the workbench. When I did not feel like hammering nails I would dump my sawdust on the concrete floor of the garage and landscape it into highways and farms and towns, running miniature cars and trucks along miniature roads. Looming as huge as a colossus, my father worked over and around me, now and again bending down to inspect my work, careful not to trample my creations. It was a landscape that smelled dizzyingly of wood. Even after a bath my skin would carry the smell, and so would my father's hair, when he lifted me for a bedtime hug.

I tell these things not only from memory but also from recent observation, because my own son now turns blocks of wood into nailed porcupines, dumps cans full of sawdust at my feet and sculpts highways on the floor. He learns how to swing a hammer from the elbow instead of the wrist, how to lay his thumb beside the blade to guide a saw, how to tap a chisel with a wooden mallet, how to mark a hole with an awl before starting a drill bit. My daughter did the same before him, and even now, on the brink of teenage aloofness, she will occasionally drag out my box of wood scraps and carpenter something. So I have seen my apprenticeship to wood and tools reenacted in each of my children, as my father saw his own apprenticeship renewed in me.

The saw I use belonged to him, as did my level and both of my squares, and all four tools had belonged to his father. The blade of the saw is the bluish color of gun barrels, and the maple handle, dark from the sweat of hands, is inscribed with curving leaf designs. The level is a shaft of walnut two feet long, edged with brass and pierced by three round windows in which air bubbles float in oil-filled tubes of glass. The middle window serves for testing whether a surface is horizontal, the others for testing whether it is plumb or vertical. My grandfather used to carry this level on the gun rack behind the seat in his pickup, and when I rode with him I would turn around to watch the bubbles dance. The larger of the two squares is called a framing square, a flat steel elbow so beat up and tarnished you can barely make out the rows of numbers that show how to figure the cuts on rafters. The smaller one is called a try square, for marking right angles, with a blued steel blade for the shank and a brass-faced block of cherry for the head.

I was taught early on that a saw is not to be used apart from a square: "If you're going to cut a piece of wood," my father insisted, "you owe it to the tree to cut it straight."

Long before studying geometry, I learned there is a mystical virtue in right angles. There is an unspoken morality in seeking the level and the plumb. A house will stand, a table will bear weight, the sides of a box will hold together only if the joints are square and the members upright. When the bubble is lined up between two marks etched in the glass tube of a level, you have aligned yourself with the forces that hold the universe together. When you miter the corners of a picture frame, each angle must be exactly forty-five degrees, as they are in the perfect triangles of Pythagoras, not a degree more or less. Otherwise the frame will hang crookedly, as if ashamed of itself and of its maker. No matter if the joints you are cutting do not show. Even if you are butting two pieces of wood together inside a cabinet, where no one except a wrecking crew will ever see them, you must take pains to insure that the ends are square and the studs are plumb.

I took pains over the wall I was building on the day my father died. Not long after that wall was finished—paneled with tongue-and-groove boards of yellow pine, the nail holes filled with putty and the wood all stained and sealed—I came close to wrecking it one afternoon when my daughter ran howling up the stairs to announce that her gerbils had escaped from their cage and were hiding in my brand-new wall. She could hear them scratching and squeaking behind her bed. Impossible! I said. How on earth could they get inside my drum-tight wall? Through the heating vent, she answered. I went downstairs, pressed my ear to the honey-colored wood, and heard the scritch scritch of tiny feet.

"What can we do?" my daughter wailed. "They'll starve to death, they'll die of thirst, they'll suffocate."

"Hold on," I soothed. "I'll think of something."

While I thought and she fretted, the radio on her bedside table delivered us the headlines. Several thousand people had died in a city in India from a poisonous cloud that had leaked overnight from a chemical plant. A nuclear-powered submarine had been launched. Rioting continued in South Africa.

An airplane had been hijacked in the Mediterranean. Authorities calculated that several thousand homeless people slept on the streets within sight of the Washington Monument. I felt my usual helplessness in face of all these calamities. But here was my daughter weeping because her gerbils were holed up in a wall. This calamity I could handle.

"Don't worry," I told her. "We'll set food and water by the heating vent and lure them out. And if that doesn't do the trick, I'll tear the wall apart until we find them."

She stopped crying and gazed at me. "You'd really tear it apart? Just for my gerbils? The *wall?*" Astonishment slowed her down only for a second, however, before she ran to the workbench and began tugging at drawers, saying, "Let's see, what'll we need? Crowbar. Hammer. Chisels. I hope we don't have to use them—but just in case."

We didn't need the wrecking tools. I never had to assault my handsome wall, because the gerbils eventually came out to nibble at a dish of popcorn. But for several hours I studied the tongue-and-groove skin I had nailed up on the day of my father's death, considering where to begin prying. There were no gaps in that wall, no crooked joints.

I had botched a great many pieces of wood before I mastered the right angle with a saw, botched even more before I learned to miter a joint. The knowledge of these things resides in my hands and eyes and the webwork of muscles, not in the tools. There are machines for sale—powered miter boxes and radial arm saws, for instance—that will enable any casual soul to cut proper angles in boards. The skill is invested in the gadget instead of the person who uses it, and this is what distinguishes a machine from a tool. If I had to earn my keep by making furniture or building houses, I suppose I would buy powered saws and pneumatic nailers; the need for speed would drive me to it. But since I carpenter only for my own pleasure or to help neighbors or to remake the house around the ears of my family, I stick with hand tools. Most of the ones I own were given to me by my father, who also taught me how to wield them. The tools in my workbench are a double inheritance, for each hammer and level and saw is wrapped in a cloud of knowing.

All of these tools are a pleasure to look at and to hold. Merchants would never paste NEW NEW NEW! signs on them in stores. Their designs are old because they work, because they serve their purpose well. Like folksongs and aphorisms and the grainy bits of language, these tools have been pared down to essentials. I look at my claw hammer, the distillation of a hundred generations of carpenters, and consider that it holds up well beside those other classics—Greek vases, Gregorian chants, *Don Quixote*, barbed fishhooks, candles, spoons. Knowledge of hammering stretches back to the earliest humans who squatted beside fires chipping flints. Anthropologists have a lovely name for those unworked rocks that served as the earliest hammers. "Dawn stones" they are called. Their only qualification for the work, aside from hardness, is that they fit the hand. Our ancestors used them for grinding corn, tapping awls, smashing bones. From dawn stones to this claw hammer is a great leap in time, but no great distance in design or imagination.

On that iced-over February morning when I smashed my thumb with the hammer, I was down in the basement framing the wall that my daughter's gerbils would later hide in. I was thinking of my father, as I always did whenever I built anything, thinking how he would have gone about the work, hearing in memory what he would have said about the wisdom of hitting the nail instead of my thumb. I had the studs and plates nailed together all square and trim, and was lifting the wall into place when the phone rang upstairs. My wife answered, and in a moment she came to the basement door and called down softly to me. The stillness in her voice made me drop the framed wall and hurry upstairs. She told me my father was dead. Then I heard the details over the phone from my mother. Building a set of cupboards for my brother in Oklahoma, he had knocked off work early the previous afternoon because of cramps in his stomach. Early this morning, on his way into the kitchen of my brother's trailer, maybe going for a glass of water, so early that no one else was awake, he slumped down on the linoleum and his heart quit.

For several hours I paced around inside my house, upstairs and down, in and out of every room, looking for the right door to open and knowing there was no such door. My wife and children followed me and wrapped me in arms and backed away again, circling and staring as if I were on fire. Where was the door, the door, the door? I kept wondering. My smashed thumb turned purple and throbbed, making me furious. I wanted to cut it off and rush outside and scrape away the snow and hack a hole in the frozen earth and bury the shameful thing.

I went down into the basement, opened a drawer in my workbench, and stared at the ranks of chisels and knives. Oiled and sharp, as my father would have kept them, they gleamed at me like teeth. I took up a clasp knife, pried out the longest blade, and tested the edge on the hair of my forearm. A tuft came away cleanly, and I saw my father testing the sharpness of tools on his own skin, the blades of axes and knives and gouges and hoes, saw the red hair shaved off in patches from his arms and the backs of his hands. "That will cut bear," he would say. He never cut a bear with his blades, now my blades, but he cut deer, dirt, wood. I closed the knife and put it away. Then I took up the hammer and went back to work on my daughter's wall, snugging the bottom plate against a chalkline on the floor, shimming the top plate against the joists overhead, plumbing the studs with my level, making sure before I drove the first nail that every line was square and true.

FICTION

Jhumpa Lahiri
Interpreter of Maladies

AT THE TEA STALL Mr. and Mrs. Das bickered about who should take Tina to the toilet. Eventually Mrs. Das relented when Mr. Das pointed out that he had given the girl her bath the night before. In the rearview mirror Mr. Kapasi watched as Mrs. Das emerged slowly from his bulky white Ambassador, dragging her shaved, largely bare legs across the back seat. She did not hold the little girl's hand as they walked to the restroom.

They were on their way to see the Sun Temple at Konarak. It was a dry, bright Saturday, the mid-July heat tempered by a steady ocean breeze, ideal weather for sightseeing. Ordinarily Mr. Kapasi would not have stopped so soon along the way, but less than five minutes after he'd picked up the family that morning in front of Hotel Sandy Villa, the little girl had complained. The first thing Mr. Kapasi had noticed when he saw Mr. and Mrs. Das, standing with their children under the portico of the hotel, was that they were very young, perhaps not even thirty. In addition to Tina they had two boys, Ronny and Bobby, who appeared very close in age and had teeth covered in a network of flashing silver wires. The family looked Indian but dressed as foreigners did, the children in stiff, brightly colored clothing and caps with translucent visors. Mr. Kapasi was accustomed to foreign tourists; he was assigned to them regularly because he could speak English. Yesterday he had driven an elderly couple from Scotland, both with spotted faces and fluffy white hair so thin it exposed their sunburnt scalps. In comparison, the tanned, youthful faces of Mr. and Mrs. Das were all the more striking. When he'd introduced himself, Mr. Kapasi had pressed his palms together in greeting, but Mr. Das squeezed hands like an American so that Mr. Kapasi felt it in his elbow. Mrs. Das, for her part, had flexed one side of her mouth, smiling dutifully at Mr. Kapasi without displaying any interest in him.

As they waited at the tea stall, Ronny, who looked like the older of the two boys, clambered suddenly out of the back seat, intrigued by a goat tied to a stake in the ground.

"Don't touch it," Mr. Das said. He glanced up from his paperback tour book, which said "INDIA" in yellow letters and looked as if it had been published abroad. His voice, somehow tentative and a little shrill, sounded as though it had not yet settled into maturity.

"I want to give it a piece of gum," the boy called back as he trotted ahead.

Mr. Das stepped out of the car and stretched his legs by squatting briefly to the ground. A clean-shaven man, he looked exactly like a magnified version of Ronny. He had a sapphire-blue visor and was dressed in shorts, sneakers, and a T-shirt. The camera slung around his neck, with an impressive telephoto lens and numerous buttons and markings, was the only complicated thing he wore. He frowned, watching as Ronny rushed toward the goat, but appeared to have no intention of intervening. "Bobby, make sure that your brother doesn't do anything stupid."

"I don't feel like it," Bobby said, not moving. He was sitting in the front seat beside Mr. Kapasi, studying a picture of the elephant god taped to the glove compartment.

"No need to worry," Mr. Kapasi said. "They are quite tame." Mr. Kapasi was forty-six years old, with receding hair that had gone completely silver, but his butterscotch complexion and his unlined brow, which he treated in spare moments to dabs of lotus-oil balm, made it easy to imagine what he must have looked like at an earlier age. He wore gray trousers and a matching jacket-style shirt, tapered at the waist, with short sleeves and a large pointed collar, made of a thin but durable synthetic material. He had specified both the cut and the fabric to his tailor—it was his preferred uniform for giving tours because it did not get crushed during his long hours behind the wheel. Through the windshield he watched as Ronny circled around the goat, touched it quickly on its side, then trotted back to the car.

"You left India as a child?" Mr. Kapasi asked when Mr. Das had settled once again into the passenger seat.

"Oh, Mina and I were both born in America," Mr. Das announced with an air of sudden confidence. "Born and raised. Our parents live here now, in Assansol. They retired. We visit them every couple years." He turned to watch as the little girl ran toward the car, the wide purple bows of her sundress flopping on her narrow brown shoulders. She was holding to her chest a doll with yellow hair that looked as if it had been chopped, as a punitive measure, with a pair of dull scissors. "This is Tina's first trip to India, isn't it, Tina?"

"I don't have to go to the bathroom anymore," Tina announced.

"Where's Mina?" Mr. Das asked.

Mr. Kapasi found it strange that Mr. Das should refer to his wife by her first name when speaking to the little girl. Tina pointed to where Mrs. Das was purchasing something from one of the shirtless men who worked at the tea stall. Mr. Kapasi heard one of the shirtless men sing a phrase from a popular Hindi love song as Mrs. Das walked back to the car, but she did not appear to understand the words of the song, for she did not express irritation, or embarrassment, or react in any other way to the man's declarations.

He observed her. She wore a red-and-white-checkered skirt that stopped above her knees, slip-on shoes with square wooden heels, and a close-fitting blouse styled like a man's undershirt. The blouse was decorated at chest level with a calico appliqué in the shape of a strawberry. She was a short woman, with small hands like paws, her frosty pink fingernails painted to match her lips, and was slightly plump in her figure. Her hair, shorn only a little longer than her husband's, was parted far to one side. She was wearing large dark brown sunglasses with a pinkish tint to them, and carried a big straw bag, almost as big as her torso, shaped like a bowl, with a water bottle poking out of it. She walked slowly, carrying some puffed rice tossed with peanuts and chili peppers in a large packet made from newspapers. Mr. Kapasi turned to Mr. Das.

"Where in America do you live?"

"New Brunswick, New Jersey."

"Next to New York?"

"Exactly. I teach middle school there."

"What subject?"

"Science. In fact, every year I take my students on a trip to the Museum of Natural History in New York City. In a way we have a lot in common, you could say, you and I. How long have you been a tour guide, Mr. Kapasi?"

"Five years."

Mrs. Das reached the car. "How long's the trip?" she asked, shutting the door.

"About two and a half hours," Mr. Kapasi replied.

At this Mrs. Das gave an impatient sigh, as if she had been traveling her whole life without pause. She fanned herself with a folded Bombay film magazine written in English.

"I thought that the Sun Temple is only eighteen miles north of Puri," Mr. Das said, tapping on the tour book.

"The roads to Konarak are poor. Actually it is a distance of fifty-two miles," Mr. Kapasi explained.

Mr. Das nodded, readjusting the camera strap where it had begun to chafe the back of his neck.

Before starting the ignition, Mr. Kapasi reached back to make sure the cranklike locks on the inside of each of the back doors were secured. As soon as the car began to move the little girl began to play with the lock on her side, clicking it with some effort forward and backward, but Mrs. Das said nothing to stop her. She sat a bit slouched at one end of the back seat, not offering her puffed rice to anyone. Ronny and Tina sat on either side of her, both snapping bright green gum.

"Look," Bobby said as the car began to gather speed. He pointed with his finger to the tall trees that lined the road. "Look."

"Monkeys!" Ronny shrieked. "Wow!"

They were seated in groups along the branches, with shining black faces, silver bodies, horizontal eyebrows, and crested heads. Their long gray tails dangled like a series of ropes among the leaves. A few scratched themselves with black leathery hands, or swung their feet, staring as the car passed.

"We call them the hanuman," Mr. Kapasi said. "They are quite common in the area."

As soon as he spoke, one of the monkeys leaped into the middle of the road, causing Mr. Kapasi to brake suddenly. Another bounced onto the hood of the car, then sprang away. Mr. Kapasi beeped his horn. The children began to get excited, sucking in their breath and covering their faces partly with their hands. They had never seen monkeys outside of a zoo, Mr. Das explained. He asked Mr. Kapasi to stop the car so that he could take a picture.

While Mr. Das adjusted his telephoto lens, Mrs. Das reached into her straw bag and pulled out a bottle of colorless nail polish, which she proceeded to stroke on the tip of her index finger.

The little girl stuck out a hand. "Mine too. Mommy, do mine too."

"Leave me alone," Mrs. Das said, blowing on her nail and turning her body slightly. "You're making me mess up."

The little girl occupied herself by buttoning and unbuttoning a pinafore on the doll's plastic body.

"All set," Mr. Das said, replacing the lens cap.

The car rattled considerably as it raced along the dusty road, causing them all to pop up from their seats every now and then, but Mrs. Das continued to polish her nails. Mr. Kapasi eased up on the accelerator, hoping to produce a smoother ride. When he reached for the gearshift the boy in front accommodated him by swinging his hairless knees out of the way. Mr. Kapasi noted that this boy was slightly paler than the other children. "Daddy, why is the driver sitting on the wrong side in this car too?" the boy asked.

"They all do that here, dummy," Ronny said.

"Don't call your brother a dummy," Mr. Das said. He turned to Mr. Kapasi. "In America, you know . . . it confuses them."

"Oh yes, I am well aware," Mr. Kapasi said. As delicately as he could, he shifted gears again, accelerating as they approached a hill in the road. "I see it on *Dallas*, the steering wheels are on the left-hand side."

"What's *Dallas?*" Tina asked, banging her now naked doll on the seat behind Mr. Kapasi.

"It went off the air," Mr. Das explained. "It's a television show."

They were all like siblings, Mr. Kapasi thought as they passed a row of date trees. Mr. and Mrs. Das behaved like an older brother and sister, not parents. It seemed that they were in charge of the children only for the day; it was hard to believe they were regularly responsible for anything other than themselves. Mr. Das tapped on his lens cap and his tour book, dragging his thumbnail occasionally across the pages so that they made a scraping sound. Mrs. Das continued to polish her nails. She had still not removed her sunglasses. Every now and then Tina renewed her plea that she wanted her nails done too, and so at one point Mrs. Das flicked a drop of polish on the little girl's finger before depositing the bottle back inside her straw bag.

"Isn't this an air-conditioned car?" she asked, still blowing on her hand. The window on Tina's side was broken and could not be rolled down.

"Quit complaining," Mr. Das said. "It isn't so hot."

"I told you to get a car with air conditioning," Mrs. Das continued. "Why do you do this, Raj, just to save a few stupid rupees? What are you saving us, fifty cents?"

Their accents sounded just like the ones Mr. Kapasi heard on American television programs, though not like the ones on *Dallas*.

"Doesn't it get tiresome, Mr. Kapasi, showing people the same thing every day?" Mr. Das asked, rolling down his own window all the way. "Hey, do you mind stopping the car? I just want to get a shot of this guy."

Mr. Kapasi pulled over to the side of the road as Mr. Das took a picture of a barefoot man, his head wrapped in a dirty turban, seated on top of a cart of grain sacks pulled by a pair of bullocks. Both the man and the bullocks were emaciated. In the back seat Mrs. Das gazed out another window at the sky, where nearly transparent clouds passed quickly in front of one another.

"I look forward to it, actually," Mr. Kapasi said as they continued on their way. "The Sun Temple is one of my favorite places. In that way it is a reward for me. I give tours on Fridays and Saturdays only. I have another job during the week."

"Oh? Where?" Mr. Das asked.

"I work in a doctor's office."

"You're a doctor?"

"I am not a doctor. I work with one. As an interpreter."

"What does a doctor need an interpreter for?"

"He has a number of Gujarati patients. My father was Gujarati, but many people do not speak Gujarati in this area, including the doctor. And so the doctor asked me to work in his office, interpreting what the patients say."

"Interesting. I've never heard of anything like that," Mr. Das said.

Mr. Kapasi shrugged. "It is a job like any other."

"But so romantic," Mrs. Das said dreamily, breaking her extended silence. She lifted her pinkish brown sunglasses and arranged them on top of her head like a tiara. For the first time, her eyes met Mr. Kapasi's in the rearview mirror: pale, a bit small, their gaze fixed but drowsy.

Mr. Das craned to look at her. "What's so romantic about it?"

"I don't know. Something." She shrugged, knitting her brows together for an instant. "Would you like a piece of gum, Mr. Kapasi?" she asked brightly. She reached into her straw bag and handed him a small square wrapped in green-and-white-striped paper. As soon as Mr. Kapasi put the gum in his mouth a thick sweet liquid burst onto his tongue.

"Tell us more about your job, Mr. Kapasi," Mrs. Das said.

"What would you like to know, madam?"

"I don't know." She shrugged again, munching on some puffed rice and licking the mustard oil from the corners of her mouth. "Tell us a typical situation." She settled back in her seat, her head tilted in a patch of sun, and closed her eyes. "I want to picture what happens."

"Very well. The other day a man came in with a pain in his throat."

"Did he smoke cigarettes?"

"No. It was very curious. He complained that he felt as if there were long pieces of straw stuck in his throat. When I told the doctor, he was able to prescribe the proper medication."

"That's so neat."

"Yes," Mr. Kapasi agreed, after some hesitation.

"So these patients are totally dependent on you," Mrs. Das said. She spoke slowly, as if she were thinking aloud. "In a way, more dependent on you than the doctor."

"How do you mean? How could it be?"

"Well, for example, you could tell the doctor that the pain felt like a burning, not straw. The patient would never know what you had told the doctor, and the doctor wouldn't know that you had told the wrong thing. It's a big responsibility."

"Yes, a big responsibility you have there, Mr. Kapasi," Mr. Das agreed.

Mr. Kapasi had never thought of his job in such complimentary terms. To him it was a thankless occupation. He found nothing noble in interpreting people's maladies, assiduously translating the symptoms of so many swollen bones, countless cramps of bellies and bowels, spots on people's palms that changed color, shape, or size. The doctor, nearly half his age, had an affinity for bell-bottom trousers and made humorless jokes about the Congress party. Together they worked in a stale little infirmary where Mr. Kapasi's smartly tailored clothes clung to him in the heat, in spite of the blackened blades of a ceiling fan churning over their heads.

The job was a sign of his failings. In his youth he'd been a devoted scholar of foreign languages, the owner of an impressive collection of dictionaries. He had dreamed of being an interpreter for diplomats and dignitaries, resolving conflicts between people and nations, settling disputes of which he alone could understand both sides. He was a self-educated man. In a series of notebooks, in the evenings before his parents settled his marriage, he had listed the common etymologies of words, and at one point in his life he was confident that he could converse, if given the opportunity, in English, French, Russian, Portuguese, and Italian, not to mention Hindi, Bengali, Orissi, and Gujarati. Now only a handful of European phrases remained in his memory, scattered words for things like saucers and chairs. English was the only non-Indian language he spoke fluently anymore. Mr. Kapasi knew it was not a remarkable talent. Sometimes he feared that his children knew better English than he did, just from watching television. Still, it came in handy for the tours.

He had taken the job as an interpreter after his first son, at the age of seven, contracted typhoid—that was how he had first made the acquaintance of the doctor. At the time Mr. Kapasi had been teaching English in a grammar school, and he bartered his skills as an interpreter to pay the increasingly exorbitant medical bills. In the end the boy had died one evening in his mother's arms, his limbs burning with fever, but then there was the funeral to pay for, and the other children who were born soon enough, and the newer, bigger house, and the good schools and tutors, and the fine shoes and the television, and the countless other ways he tried to console his wife and to keep her from crying in her sleep, and so when the doctor offered to pay him twice as much as he earned at the grammar school, he accepted. Mr. Kapasi knew that his wife had little regard for his career as an interpreter. He knew it reminded her of the son she'd lost, and that she resented the other lives he helped, in his own small way, to save. If ever she referred to his position, she used the phrase "doctor's assistant," as if the process of interpretation were equal to taking someone's temperature, or changing a bedpan. She never asked him about the patients who came to the doctor's office, or said that his job was a big responsibility.

For this reason it flattered Mr. Kapasi that Mrs. Das was so intrigued by his job. Unlike his wife, she had reminded him of its intellectual challenges.

She had also used the word *romantic*. She did not behave in a romantic way toward her husband, and yet she had used the word to describe him. He wondered if Mr. and Mrs. Das were a bad match, just as he and his wife were. Perhaps they too had little in common apart from three children and a decade of their lives. The signs he recognized from his own marriage were there—the bickering, the indifference, the protracted silences. Her sudden interest in him, an interest she did not express in either her husband or her children, was mildly intoxicating. When Mr. Kapasi thought once again about how she had said "romantic," the feeling of intoxication grew.

He began to check his reflection in the rearview mirror as he drove, feeling grateful that he had chosen the gray suit that morning and not the brown one, which tended to sag a little in the knees. From time to time he glanced in the mirror at Mrs. Das. In addition to glancing at her face, he glanced at the strawberry between her breasts and the golden brown hollow in her throat. He decided to tell Mrs. Das about another patient, and another: the young woman who had complained of a sensation of raindrops in her spine, the gentleman whose birthmark had begun to sprout hairs. Mrs. Das listened attentively, stroking her hair with a small plastic brush that resembled an oval bed of nails, asking more questions, for yet another example. The children were quiet, intent on spotting more monkeys in the trees, and Mr. Das was absorbed by his tour book, so it seemed like a private conversation between Mr. Kapasi and Mrs. Das. In this manner the next half hour passed, and when they stopped for lunch at a roadside restaurant that sold fritters and omelette sandwiches, usually something Mr. Kapasi looked forward to on his tours so that he could sit in peace and enjoy some hot tea, he was disappointed. As the Das family settled together under a magenta umbrella fringed with white and orange tassels, and placed their orders with one of the waiters who marched about in tricornered caps, Mr. Kapasi reluctantly headed toward a neighboring table.

"Mr. Kapasi, wait. There's room here," Mrs. Das called out. She gathered Tina onto her lap, insisting that he accompany them. And so together they had bottled mango juice and sandwiches and plates of onions and potatoes deep-fried in graham-flour batter. After finishing two omelette sandwiches, Mr. Das took more pictures of the group as they ate.

"How much longer?" he asked Mr. Kapasi as he paused to load a new roll of film in the camera.

"About half an hour more."

By now the children had gotten up from the table to look at more monkeys perched in a nearby tree, so there was a considerable space between Mrs. Das and Mr. Kapasi. Mr. Das placed the camera to his face and squeezed one eye shut, his tongue exposed at one corner of his mouth. "This looks funny. Mina, you need to lean in closer to Mr. Kapasi."

She did. He could smell a scent on her skin, like a mixture of whiskey and rosewater. He worried suddenly that she could smell his perspiration, which he knew had collected beneath the synthetic material of his shirt. He polished off his mango juice in one gulp and smoothed his silver hair with his hands. A bit of the juice dripped onto his chin. He wondered if Mrs. Das had noticed.

She had not. "What's your address, Mr. Kapasi?" she inquired, fishing for something inside her straw bag.

"You would like my address?"

"So we can send you copies," she said. "Of the pictures." She handed him a scrap of paper which she had hastily ripped from a page of her film magazine. The blank portion was limited, for the narrow strip was crowded by lines of text and a tiny picture of a hero and heroine embracing under a eucalyptus tree.

The paper curled as Mr. Kapasi wrote his address in clear, careful letters. She would write to him, asking about his days interpreting at the doctor's office, and he would respond eloquently, choosing only the most entertaining anecdotes, ones that would make her laugh out loud as she read them in her house in New Jersey. In time she would reveal the disappointment of her marriage, and he his. In this way their friendship would grow, and flourish. He would possess a picture of the two of them, eating fried onions under a magenta umbrella, which he would keep, he decided, safely tucked between the pages of his Russian grammar. As his mind raced, Mr. Kapasi experienced a mild and pleasant shock. It was similar to a feeling he used to experience long ago when, after months of translating with the aid of a dictionary, he would finally read a passage from a French novel, or an Italian sonnet, and understand the words, one after another, unencumbered by his own efforts. In those moments Mr. Kapasi used to believe that all was right with the world, that all struggles were rewarded, that all of life's mistakes made sense in the end. The promise that he would hear from Mrs. Das now filled him with the same belief.

When he finished writing his address Mr. Kapasi handed her the paper, but as soon as he did so he worried that he had either misspelled his name or accidentally reversed the numbers of his postal code. He dreaded the possibility of a lost letter, the photograph never reaching him, hovering somewhere in Orissa, close but ultimately unattainable. He thought of asking for the slip of paper again, just to make sure he had written his address accurately, but Mrs. Das had already dropped it into the jumble of her bag.

They reached Konarak at two-thirty. The temple, made of sandstone, was a massive pyramid-like structure in the shape of a chariot. It was dedicated to the great master of life, the sun, which struck three sides of the edifice as it made its journey each day across the sky. Twenty-four giant wheels were carved on the north and south sides of the plinth. The whole thing was drawn by a team of seven horses, speeding as if through the heavens. As they approached, Mr. Kapasi explained that the temple had been built between A.D. 1243 and 1255, with the efforts of twelve hundred artisans, by the great ruler of the Ganga dynasty, King Narasimhadeva the First, to commemorate his victory against the Muslim army.

"It says the temple occupies about a hundred and seventy acres of land," Mr. Das said, reading from his book.

"It's like a desert," Ronny said, his eyes wandering across the sand that stretched on all sides beyond the temple.

"The Chandrabhaga River once flowed one mile north of here. It is dry now," Mr. Kapasi said, turning off the engine.

They got out and walked toward the temple, posing first for pictures by the pair of lions that flanked the steps. Mr. Kapasi led them next to one of the wheels of the chariot, higher than any human being, nine feet in diameter.

"'The wheels are supposed to symbolize the wheel of life,'" Mr. Das read. "'They depict the cycle of creation, preservation, and achievement of realization.' Cool." He turned the page of his book. "'Each wheel is divided into eight thick and thin spokes, dividing the day into eight equal parts. The rims are carved with designs of birds and animals, whereas the medallions in the spokes are carved with women in luxurious poses, largely erotic in nature.'"

What he referred to were the countless friezes of entwined naked bodies making love in various positions, women clinging to the necks of men, their knees wrapped eternally around their lovers' thighs. In addition to these were assorted scenes from daily life, of hunting and trading, of deer being killed with bows and arrows and marching warriors holding swords in their hands.

It was no longer possible to enter the temple, for it had filled with rubble years ago, but they admired the exterior, as did all the tourists Mr. Kapasi took there, slowly strolling along each of its sides. Mr. Das trailed behind, taking pictures. The children ran ahead, pointing to figures of naked people, intrigued in particular by the Nagamithunas, the half-human, half-serpentine couples who were said, Mr. Kapasi told them, to live in the deepest waters of the sea. Mr. Kapasi was pleased that they liked the temple, pleased especially that it appealed to Mrs. Das. She stopped every three or four paces, staring silently at the carved lovers, and the processions of elephants, and the topless female musicians beating on two-sided drums.

Though Mr. Kapasi had been to the temple countless times, it occurred to him, as he too gazed at the topless women, that he had never seen his own wife fully naked. Even when they had made love she kept the panels of her blouse hooked together, the string of her petticoat knotted around her waist. He had never admired the backs of his wife's legs the way he now admired those of Mrs. Das, walking as if for his benefit alone. He had, of course, seen plenty of bare limbs before, belonging to the American and European ladies who took his tours. But Mrs. Das was different. Unlike the other women, who had an interest only in the temple and kept their noses buried in a guidebook or their eyes behind the lens of a camera, Mrs. Das had taken an interest in him.

Mr. Kapasi was anxious to be alone with her, to continue their private conversation, yet he felt nervous to walk at her side. She was lost behind her sunglasses, ignoring her husband's requests that she pose for another picture, walking past her children as if they were strangers. Worried that he might disturb her, Mr. Kapasi walked ahead, to admire, as he always did, the three life-sized bronze avatars of Surya, the sun god, each emerging from its own niche on the temple facade to greet the sun at dawn, noon, and evening. They wore elaborate headdresses, their languid, elongated eyes closed, their bare chests draped with carved chains and amulets. Hibiscus petals, offerings from previous visitors, were strewn at their gray-green feet. The last statue, on the northern wall of the temple, was Mr. Kapasi's favorite. This Surya had a tired expression, weary after a hard day of work, sitting astride a horse with folded legs. Even his horse's eyes were drowsy. Around his body were smaller sculptures of women in pairs, their hips thrust to one side.

"Who's that?" Mrs. Das asked. He was startled to see that she was standing beside him.

"He is the Astachala-Surya," Mr. Kapasi said. "The setting sun."

"So in a couple of hours the sun will set right here?" She slipped a foot out of one of her square-heeled shoes, rubbed her toes on the back of her other leg.

"That is correct."

She raised her sunglasses for a moment, then put them back on again. "Neat."

Mr. Kapasi was not certain exactly what the word suggested, but he had a feeling it was a favorable response. He hoped that Mrs. Das had understood Surya's beauty, his power. Perhaps they would discuss it further in their letters. He would explain things to her, things about India, and she would explain things to him about America. In its own way this correspondence would fulfill his dream of serving as an interpreter between nations. He looked at her straw bag, delighted that his address lay nestled among its contents. When he pictured her so many thousands of miles away he plummeted, so much so that he had an overwhelming urge to wrap his arms around her, to freeze with her, even for an instant, in an embrace witnessed by his favorite Surya. But Mrs. Das had already started walking.

"When do you return to America?" he asked, trying to sound placid.
"In ten days."

He calculated: a week to settle in, a week to develop the pictures, a few days to compose her letter, two weeks to get to India by air. According to his schedule, allowing room for delays, he would hear from Mrs. Das in approximately six weeks' time.

The family was silent as Mr. Kapasi drove them back, a little past four-thirty, to Hotel Sandy Villa. The children had bought miniature granite versions of the chariot's wheels at a souvenir stand, and they turned them round in their hands. Mr. Das continued to read his book. Mrs. Das untangled Tina's hair with her brush and divided it into two little ponytails.

Mr. Kapasi was beginning to dread the thought of dropping them off. He was not prepared to begin his six-week wait to hear from Mrs. Das. As he stole glances at her in the rearview mirror, wrapping elastic bands around Tina's hair, he wondered how he might make the tour last a little longer. Ordinarily he sped back to Puri using a shortcut, eager to return home, scrub his feet and hands with sandalwood soap, and enjoy the evening newspaper and a cup of tea that his wife would serve him in silence. The thought of that silence, something to which he'd long been resigned, now oppressed him. It was then that he suggested visiting the hills at Udayagiri and Khandagiri, where a number of monastic dwellings were hewn out of the ground, facing one another across a defile. It was some miles away, but well worth seeing, Mr. Kapasi told them.

"Oh yeah, there's something mentioned about it in this book," Mr. Das said. "Built by a Jain king or something."

"Shall we go then?" Mr. Kapasi asked. He paused at a turn in the road. "It's to the left."

Mr. Das turned to look at Mrs. Das. Both of them shrugged.

"Left, left," the children chanted.

Mr. Kapasi turned the wheel, almost delirious with relief. He did not know what he would do or say to Mrs. Das once they arrived at the hills. Perhaps he would tell her what a pleasing smile she had. Perhaps he would compliment her strawberry shirt, which he found irresistibly becoming. Perhaps, when Mr. Das was busy taking a picture, he would take her hand.

He did not have to worry. When they got to the hills, divided by a steep path thick with trees, Mrs. Das refused to get out of the car. All along the path, dozens of monkeys were seated on stones, as well as on the branches of the trees. Their hind legs were stretched out in front and raised to shoulder level, their arms resting on their knees.

"My legs are tired," she said, sinking low in her seat. "I'll stay here."

"Why did you have to wear those stupid shoes?" Mr. Das said. "You won't be in the pictures."

"Pretend I'm there."

"But we could use one of these pictures for our Christmas card this year. We didn't get one of all five of us at the Sun Temple. Mr. Kapasi could take it."

"I'm not coming. Anyway, those monkeys give me the creeps."

"But they're harmless," Mr. Das said. He turned to Mr. Kapasi. "Aren't they?"

"They are more hungry than dangerous," Mr. Kapasi said. "Do not provoke them with food, and they will not bother you."

Mr. Das headed up the defile with the children, the boys at his side, the little girl on his shoulders. Mr. Kapasi watched as they crossed paths with a Japanese man and woman, the only other tourists there, who paused for a final photograph, then stepped into a nearby car and drove away. As the car disappeared out of view some of the monkeys called out, emitting soft whooping sounds, and then walked on their flat black hands and feet up the path. At one point a group of them formed a little ring around Mr. Das and the children. Tina screamed in delight. Ronny ran in circles around his father. Bobby bent down and picked up a fat stick on the ground. When he extended it, one of the monkeys approached him and snatched it, then briefly beat the ground.

"I'll join them," Mr. Kapasi said, unlocking the door on his side. "There is much to explain about the caves."

"No. Stay a minute," Mrs. Das said. She got out of the back seat and slipped in beside Mr. Kapasi. "Raj has his dumb book anyway." Together, through the windshield, Mrs. Das and Mr. Kapasi watched as Bobby and the monkey passed the stick back and forth between them.

"A brave little boy," Mr. Kapasi commented.

"It's not so surprising," Mrs. Das said.

"No?"

"He's not his."

"I beg your pardon?"

"Raj's. He's not Raj's son."

Mr. Kapasi felt a prickle on his skin. He reached into his shirt pocket for the small tin of lotus-oil balm he carried with him at all times, and applied it to three spots on his forehead. He knew that Mrs. Das was watching him, but he did not turn to face her. Instead he watched as the figures of Mr. Das and the children grew smaller, climbing up the steep path, pausing every now and then for a picture, surrounded by a growing number of monkeys.

"Are you surprised?" The way she put it made him choose his words with care.

"It's not the type of thing one assumes," Mr. Kapasi replied slowly. He put the tin of lotus-oil balm back in his pocket.

"No, of course not. And no one knows, of course. No one at all. I've kept it a secret for eight whole years." She looked at Mr. Kapasi, tilting her chin as if to gain a fresh perspective. "But now I've told you."

Mr. Kapasi nodded. He felt suddenly parched, and his forehead was warm and slightly numb from the balm. He considered asking Mrs. Das for a sip of water, then decided against it.

"We met when we were very young," she said. She reached into her straw bag in search of something, then pulled out a packet of puffed rice. "Want some?"

"No, thank you."

She put a fistful in her mouth, sank into the seat a little, and looked away from Mr. Kapasi, out the window on her side of the car. "We married when we were still in college. We were in high school when he proposed. We went to the same college, of course. Back then we couldn't stand the thought of being separated, not for a day, not for a minute. Our parents were best friends who lived in the same town. My entire life I saw him every week-end, either at our house or theirs. We were sent upstairs to play together while our parents joked about our marriage. Imagine! They never caught us at anything, though in a way I think it was all more or less a setup. The things we did those Friday and Saturday nights, while our parents sat downstairs drinking tea . . . I could tell you stories, Mr. Kapasi."

As a result of spending all her time in college with Raj, she continued, she did not make many close friends. There was no one to confide in about him at the end of a difficult day, or to share a passing thought or a worry. Her parents now lived on the other side of the world, but she had never been very close to them anyway. After marrying so young she was overwhelmed by it all, having a child so quickly, and nursing, and warming up bottles of milk and testing their temperature against her wrist while Raj was at work, dressed in sweaters and corduroy pants, teaching his students about rocks and dinosaurs. Raj never looked cross or harried, or plump as she had become after the first baby.

Always tired, she declined invitations from her one or two college girl-friends to have lunch or shop in Manhattan. Eventually the friends stopped calling her, so that she was left at home all day with the baby, surrounded by toys that made her trip when she walked or wince when she sat, always cross and tired. Only occasionally did they go out after Ronny was born, and even more rarely did they entertain. Raj didn't mind; he looked forward to coming home from teaching and watching television and bouncing Ronny on his knee. She had been outraged when Raj told her that a Punjabi friend, someone whom she had once met but did not remember, would be staying with them for a week for some job interviews in the New Brunswick area.

Bobby was conceived in the afternoon, on a sofa littered with rubber teething toys, after the friend learned that a London pharmaceutical company had hired him, while Ronny cried to be freed from his playpen. She made no protest when the friend touched the small of her back as she was about to make a pot of coffee, then pulled her against his crisp navy suit. He made love to her swiftly, in silence, with an expertise she had never known, without the meaningful expressions and smiles Raj always insisted on afterward. The next day Raj drove the friend to JFK. He was married now, to a Punjabi girl, and they lived in London still, and every year they exchanged Christmas cards with Raj and Mina, each couple tucking photos of their families into the envelopes. He did not know that he was Bobby's father. He never would.

"I beg your pardon, Mrs. Das, but why have you told me this information?" Mr. Kapasi asked when she had finally finished speaking and had turned to face him once again.

"For God's sake, stop calling me Mrs. Das. I'm twenty-eight. You probably have children my age."

"Not quite." It disturbed Mr. Kapasi to learn that she thought of him as a parent. The feeling he had had toward her, that had made him check his reflection in the rearview mirror as they drove, evaporated a little.

"I told you, because of your talents." She put the packet of puffed rice back into her bag without folding over the top.

"I don't understand," Mr. Kapasi said.

"Don't you see? For eight years I haven't been able to express this to anybody, not to friends, certainly not to Raj. He doesn't even suspect it. He thinks I'm still in love with him. Well, don't you have anything to say?"

"About what?"

"About what I've just told you. About my secret, and about how terrible it makes me feel. I feel terrible looking at my children, and at Raj, always terrible. I have terrible urges, Mr. Kapasi, to throw things away. One day I had the urge to throw everything I own out the window—the television, the children, everything. Don't you think it's unhealthy?"

He was silent.

"Mr. Kapasi, don't you have anything to say? I thought that was your job."

"My job is to give tours, Mrs. Das."

"Not that. Your other job. As an interpreter."

"But we do not face a language barrier. What need is there for an interpreter?"

"That's not what I mean. I would never have told you otherwise. Don't you realize what it means for me to tell you?"

"What does it mean?"

"It means that I'm tired of feeling so terrible all the time. Eight years, Mr. Kapasi, I've been in pain eight years. I was hoping you could help me feel better, say the right thing. Suggest some kind of remedy."

He looked at her, in her red plaid skirt and strawberry T-shirt, a woman not yet thirty, who loved neither her husband nor her children, who had already fallen out of love with life. Her confession depressed him, depressed him all the more when he thought of Mr. Das at the top of the path, Tina clinging to his shoulders, taking pictures of ancient monastic cells cut into the hills to show his students in America, unsuspecting and unaware that one of his sons was not his own. Mr. Kapasi felt insulted that Mrs. Das should ask him to interpret her common, trivial little secret. She did not resemble the patients in the doctor's office, those who came glassy-eyed and desperate, unable to sleep or breathe or urinate with ease, unable, above all, to give words to their pains. Still, Mr. Kapasi believed it was his duty to assist Mrs. Das. Perhaps he ought to tell her to confess the truth to Mr. Das. He would explain that honesty was the best policy. Honesty, surely, would help her feel better, as she'd put it. Perhaps he would offer to preside over the discussion, as a mediator. He decided to begin with the most obvious question, to get to the heart of the matter, and so he asked, "Is it really pain you feel, Mrs. Das, or is it guilt?"

She turned to him and glared, mustard oil thick on her frosty pink lips. She opened her mouth to say something, but as she glared at Mr. Kapasi some certain knowledge seemed to pass before her eyes, and she stopped. It crushed him; he knew at that moment that he was not even important enough to be properly insulted. She opened the car door and began walking up the path, wobbling a little on her square wooden heels, reaching into her straw bag to eat handfuls of puffed rice. It fell through her fingers, leaving a zigzagging trail, causing a monkey to leap down from a tree and devour the little white grains. In search of more, the monkey began to follow Mrs. Das. Others joined him, so that she was soon being followed by about half a dozen of them, their velvety tails dragging behind.

Mr. Kapasi stepped out of the car. He wanted to holler, to alert her in some way, but he worried that if she knew they were behind her, she would grow nervous. Perhaps she would lose her balance. Perhaps they would pull at her bag or her hair. He began to jog up the path, taking a fallen branch in his hand to scare away the monkeys. Mrs. Das continued walking, oblivious, trailing grains of puffed rice. Near the top of the incline, before a group of cells fronted by a row of squat stone pillars, Mr. Das was kneeling on the ground, focusing the lens of his camera. The children stood under the arcade, now hiding, now emerging from view.

"Wait for me," Mrs. Das called out. "I'm coming."

Tina jumped up and down. "Here comes Mommy!"

"Great," Mr. Das said without looking up. "Just in time. We'll get Mr. Kapasi to make a picture of the five of us."

Mr. Kapasi quickened his pace, waving his branch so that the monkeys scampered away, distracted, in another direction.

"Where's Bobby?" Mrs. Das asked when she stopped.

Mr. Das looked up from the camera. "I don't know. Ronny, where's Bobby?"

Ronny shrugged. "I thought he was right here."

"Where is he?" Mrs. Das repeated sharply. "What's wrong with all of you?"

They began calling his name, wandering up and down the path a bit. Because they were calling, they did not initially hear the boy's screams. When they found him, a little farther down the path under a tree, he was surrounded by a group of monkeys, over a dozen of them, pulling at his T-shirt with their long black fingers. The puffed rice Mrs. Das had spilled was scattered at his feet, raked over by the monkeys' hands. The boy was silent, his body frozen, swift tears running down his startled face. His bare legs were dusty and red with welts from where one of the monkeys struck him repeatedly with the stick he had given to it earlier.

"Daddy, the monkey's hurting Bobby," Tina said.

Mr. Das wiped his palms on the front of his shorts. In his nervousness he accidentally pressed the shutter on his camera; the whirring noise of the advancing film excited the monkeys, and the one with the stick began to beat Bobby more intently. "What are we supposed to do? What if they start attacking?"

"Mr. Kapasi," Mrs. Das shrieked, noticing him standing to one side. "Do something, for God's sake, do something!"

Mr. Kapasi took his branch and shooed them away, hissing at the ones that remained, stomping his feet to scare them. The animals retreated slowly, with a measured gait, obedient but unintimidated. Mr. Kapasi gathered Bobby in his arms and brought him back to where his parents and siblings were standing. As he carried him, he was tempted to whisper a secret into the boy's ear. But Bobby was stunned, and shivering with fright, his legs bleeding slightly where the stick had broken the skin. When Mr. Kapasi delivered him to his parents, Mr. Das brushed some dirt off the boy's T-shirt and put the visor on him the right way. Mrs. Das reached into her straw bag to find a bandage, which she taped over the cut on his knee. Ronny offered his brother a fresh piece of gum. "He's fine. Just a little scared, right, Bobby?" Mr. Das said, patting the top of his head.

"God, let's get out of here," Mrs. Das said. She folded her arms across the strawberry on her chest. "This place gives me the creeps."

"Yeah. Back to the hotel, definitely," Mr. Das agreed.

"Poor Bobby," Mrs. Das said. "Come here a second. Let Mommy fix your hair." Again she reached into her straw bag, this time for her hairbrush, and began to run it around the edges of the translucent visor. When she whipped out the hairbrush, the slip of paper with Mr. Kapasi's address on it fluttered away in the wind. No one but Mr. Kapasi noticed. He watched as it rose, carried higher and higher by the breeze, into the trees where the monkeys now sat, solemnly observing the scene below. Mr. Kapasi observed it too, knowing that this was the picture of the Das family he would preserve forever in his mind.

TRY THIS 3.10

Write about an incident from the point of view of someone hired to serve someone else—a waiter, taxi driver, airline attendant, cleaner, or the like. Let us know the thoughts of the server but see the person who has hired him or her through appearance, speech, and action.

POEMS

Theodore Roethke

I Knew a Woman

I knew a woman, lovely in her bones,
When small birds sighed, she would sigh back at them;
Ah, when she moved, she moved more ways than one:
The shapes a bright container can contain!
Of her choice virtues only gods should speak,
Or English poets who grew up on Greek
(I'd have them sing in chorus, cheek to cheek).

How well her wishes went! She stroked my chin,
She taught me Turn, and Counter-turn, and Stand;
She taught me Touch, that undulant white skin;
I nibbled meekly from her proffered hand;
She was the sickle; I, poor I, the rake,
Coming behind her for her pretty sake
(But what prodigious mowing we did make).

Love likes a gander, and adores a goose:
Her full lips pursed, the errant note to seize;
She played it quick, she played it light and loose;
My eyes, they dazzled at her flowing knees;
Her several parts could keep a pure repose,
Or one hip quiver with a mobile nose
(She moved in circles, and those circles moved).

Let seed be grass, and grass turn into hay:
I'm martyr to a motion not my own;
What's freedom for? To know eternity.
I swear she cast a shadow white as stone.
But who would count eternity in days?
These old bones live to learn her wanton ways:
(I measure time by how a body sways).

Carole Simmons Oles

Stonecarver

for Father

Don't look at his hands now.
Stiff and swollen, small finger
curled in like a hermit:
needing someone to open the ketchup,
an hour to shave.
That hand held the mallet,
made the marble say
Cicero, Juno, and *laurel.*

Don't think of his eyes
behind thick lenses squinting
at headlines, his breath
drowning in stonedust and Camels,
his sparrow legs.

Think of the one who slid
3 floors down scaffolding ropes
every lunchtime,
who stood up to Donnelly the foreman
for more time to take care.

Keep him the man in the photo,
straight-backed on the park bench
in Washington, holding hands
with your mother.
Keep his hands holding
calipers, patterns, and pointer,
bringing the mallet down
fair on the chisel,
your father's hands sweeping off dust.

Allen Ginsberg
To Aunt Rose

Aunt Rose—now—might I see you
with your thin face and buck tooth smile and pain
        of rheumatism—and a long black heavy shoe
           for your bony left leg
    limping down the long hall in Newark on the running carpet
        past the black grand piano
        in the day room
              where the parties were
and I sang Spanish loyalist songs
        in a high squeaky voice
           (hysterical) the committee listening
      while you limped around the room
      collected the money—
Aunt Honey, Uncle Sam, a stranger with a cloth arm
      in his pocket
        and huge young bald head
          of Abraham Lincoln Brigade

—your long sad face
    your tears of sexual frustration
        (what smothered sobs and bony hips
           under the pillows of Osborne Terrace)
    —the time I stood on the toilet seat naked
        and you powdered my thighs with Calomine
        against the poison ivy—my tender
          and shamed first black curled hairs
what were you thinking in secret heart then
    knowing me a man already—
and I an ignorant girl of family silence on the thin pedestal
    of my legs in the bathroom—Museum of Newark.

           Aunt Rose
   Hitler is dead, Hitler is in Eternity; Hitler is with
        Tamburlane and Emily Brontë

Though I see you walking still, a ghost on Osborne Terrace
        down the long dark hall to the front door
    limping a little with a pinched smile
        in what must have been a silken
          flower dress
welcoming my father, the Poet, on his visit to Newark

—see you arriving in the living room
     dancing on your crippled leg
and clapping hands his book
     had been accepted by Liveright

Hitler is dead and Liveright's gone out of business
The Attic of the Past and *Everlasting Minute* are out of print
     Uncle Harry sold his last silk stocking
     Claire quit interpretive dancing school
     Buba sits a wrinkled monument in Old
       Ladies Home blinking at new babies

last time I saw you was the hospital
     pale skull protruding under ashen skin
      blue veined unconscious girl
       in an oxygen tent
     the war in Spain has ended long ago
      Aunt Rose

Elizabeth Jennings
One Flesh

Lying apart now, each in a separate bed,
He with a book, keeping the light on late,
She like a girl dreaming of childhood,
All men elsewhere—it is as if they wait
Some new event: the book he holds unread,
Her eyes fixed on the shadows overhead,

Tossed up like flotsam from a former passion,
How cool they lie. They hardly ever touch,
Or if they do it is like a confession
Of having little feeling—or too much.
Chastity faces them, a destination
For which their whole lives were a preparation.

Strangely apart, yet strangely close together,
Silence between them like a thread to hold
And not wind in. And time itself's a feather
Touching them gently. Do they know they're old,
These two who are my father and my mother
Whose fire from which I came, has now grown cold?

Howard Nemerov
Life Cycle of Common Man

Roughly figured, this man of moderate habits,
This average consumer of the middle class,
Consumed in the course of his average life span
Just under half a million cigarettes,
Four thousand fifths of gin and about
A quarter as much vermouth; he drank
Maybe a hundred thousand cups of coffee,
And counting his parents' share it cost
Something like half a million dollars
To put him through life. How many beasts
Died to provide him with meat, belt and shoes
Cannot be certainly said.
                        But anyhow,
It is in this way that a man travels through time,
Leaving behind him a lengthening trail
Of empty bottles and bones, of broken shoes,
Frayed collars and worn out or outgrown
Diapers and dinnerjackets, silk ties and slickers.

Given the energy and security thus achieved,
He did . . .? What? The usual things, of course,
The eating, dreaming, drinking and begetting,
And he worked for the money which was to pay
For the eating, et cetera, which were necessary
If he were to go on working for the money, et cetera,
But chiefly he talked. As the bottles and bones
Accumulated behind him, the words proceeded
Steadily from the front of his face as he
Advanced into the silence and made it verbal.
Who can tally the tale of his words? A lifetime
Would barely suffice for their repetition;
If you merely printed all his commas the result
Would be a very large volume, and the number of times
He said "thank you" or "very little sugar, please,"
Would stagger the imagination. There were also
Witticisms, platitudes, and statements beginning
"It seems to me" or "As I always say."

Consider the courage in all that, and behold the man
Walking into deep silence, with the ectoplastic
Cartoon's balloon of speech proceeding

Steadily out of the front of his face, the words
Borne along on the breath which is his spirit
Telling the numberless tale of his untold Word
Which makes the world his apple, and forces him to eat.

TRY THIS 3.11
Write a poem about an ordinary person or ordinary people doing something ordinary.
Focus on and list the details of appearance, speech, and/or action that are involved in
this ordinary scene, so that we recognize it. Can you by doing this at the same time tell
us something amazing, or moving, or new?

DRAMA

Mary Gallagher

Brother

Inquiries concerning all rights (including Live Stage Performances, TV, and
Film Rights) should be addressed to Harden-Curtis Associates, 850 Seventh
Avenue, Suite 903, New York, NY 10019 ATTN: Mary Harden.

CHARACTERS
Kitty
Charlie

*It's five o'clock in the morning. Kitty's entering in her bathrobe and heading
for the refrigerator as Charlie enters from outside, wearing a worn-looking
winter jacket.*

KITTY: Oh God,   **CHARLIE:** Oh great—
    you scared me—   I was afraid Mom was
    Hi! How *are* you . . . ?   up—How the hell are ya?

(They kiss and hug awkwardly, he whirls her around as:)

CHARLIE: Jeez, whenja get so skinny?
KITTY: God, I don't know . . . has it been that long since we—?

CHARLIE: Yeah, gotta be a couple years or something . . .

KITTY: Well, yeah, I guess we didn't make it last Christmas, so—

KITTY: You look big! I always forget, I expect you to look weedy, like when you were sixteen or something . . .

CHARLIE: That was many moons ago.

KITTY: I know, but I forget. Listen, I still picture you in that dalmatian outfit you had to wear in the kindergarten play.

CHARLIE: Oh, yeah? You wanta wrestle? Now that you're a fly-weight. Give you two falls out of three. How was the trip down?

KITTY: Average. There was a wreck on 90 so everything was backed up— and poor Matt got carsick, twice—your average turnpike nightmare . . . Are you just getting home?

CHARLIE: Yup. Had too good a time tonight, couldn't tear myself away. What is it, five o'clock or something? What're you doing up?

KITTY: I just *got* up, I've gotta make this damn potato salad for the reception and I want to get it done before the kids get up. I must've been crazy to say I'd do this . . .

(She takes a bowl of hard-boiled eggs from the fridge and starts peeling them.)

KITTY: So what's the story, you seeing somebody?

CHARLIE: Nah. I was just up at Dink's.

KITTY: That biker bar? I mean, it *was* . . . now is it . . . like, fun, or—?

CHARLIE: That's my club. There're some good guys hang out there. They call me the King. I walk in, they say, "The King is here." Plus they got a pool table—

KITTY: You didn't walk home, did you? God. I mean, it's none of my business, but you don't want to get mugged again—

CHARLIE: I was a kid when I got mugged, I don't even remember it. *You* remember—

KITTY: Well, but it's cold out, too—

CHARLIE: Haddaya *think* I get around? It's not like I can use Mom's car. Hey, I'm the champeen walker.

KITTY: Right . . . don't you have gloves, at least?

CHARLIE: I had some great gloves. Did you give me those? Blue wool with leather pads?

KITTY: Yeah, probably . . .

CHARLIE: They were great. But I lost 'em. That red shirt you gave me was great too, I lost that too. They're great while they last, though. Man, I am starving. Mom made that chicken stuff for dinner, right?

KITTY: We killed it.

CHARLIE: Thanks, guys.

KITTY: There's salad left, though.

CHARLIE: Salad! Hey, this is me you're talking to—Oh shit, I better close this door or Mom'll be out here bitching, make me do the Breathalyzer . . .

(He closes the door to the hall, goes to cupboards, takes out a can of Chef Boy-ar-Dee Ravioli and a loaf of Wonder Bread, opens the can and makes cold ravioli sandwiches.)

CHARLIE: Couple months ago I was a bad boy, really let myself go . . . she tell you about this?

KITTY: *(nods yes, but blankly)* What.

CHARLIE: It was pretty funny, or it woulda been if somebody'd been there to see it besides us . . . I came in real late, and I mean I was loaded, and coming through the living room, I tripped over her fucking sewing box and I fell flat, like, with this huge crash! And I couldn't get back up. It was wild, the whole room was going nuts around me . . . and then, Jesus, here comes Mom, with the electric carving knife!— she thought someone was breaking in—

KITTY: *(appalled but has to laugh)* What was she gonna do with the electric knife, she would've had to go get the extension cord so she could plug it in—

CHARLIE: *(laughs)* Yeah, right . . . yeah . . . but she doesn't sleep through stuff like she used to. That was great, how when she was sleeping, we'd go in and ask her stuff, like if we could do stuff or buy stuff, like donuts or something, and she'd always say—

BOTH: "Sure, honey . . . "

KITTY: She'd still be asleep . . .

CHARLIE: We got away with fucking everything. Forget it, *now*. The slightest thing, she wakes up screaming . . .

KITTY: Listen though, Mom says you're doing great at your new job, she says they really like you.

CHARLIE: Well, my boss keeps telling me I'm the best worker they got . . .

KITTY: Well, good for you . . . just keep it up. I mean I always knew if you got on a good roll . . .

CHARLIE: I figure she'd be telling you to shape me up—

KITTY: No, listen . . . I mean sure, she . . . she *cares*, that's all . . . but I don't want to . . . be telling you . . . we oughta be past that . . .

CHARLIE: Jesus, *I* think so, but Mom . . . she's really getting crotchety. Like ever since that night, she won't give me a ride anywhere except to work, and that's just if I oversleep. It's like, in her mind, the only life I should have is work. You know? I go, "Hey, Ma, I'm not gonna just work and come straight home and sit around watching the boob tube all night long, like the living dead . . . "

(*starts eating ravioli sandwiches, sees her watching*)

    What.

KITTY: You really do still eat like that.

CHARLIE: Hey, the Chef's my man. Mom, once in a while she'll try to palm off some gourmet brand, what they call "pasta" now. I tell her, "Ma, I got my loyalties."

KITTY: So you psyched for the wedding?

CHARLIE: . . . Oh, right! Right . . . great!

KITTY: All the cousins are coming in—

CHARLIE: Oh yeah? Old Eddie's coming, too?

KITTY: Yeah, didn't Mom tell you?

CHARLIE: Hey. You're the one she talks to.

KITTY: Well . . . that's because I'm gone. But listen, Jen has hot plans to dance with you. Uncle Charlie. Like, rad.

CHARLIE: Oh, yeah?

KITTY: Oh, please. Don't tell her I said so, but she never stops playing that Jackson Browne tape you gave her.

CHARLIE: She's a babe, that kid, she's gonna break some hearts. Yeah, I wanted to make it home to see her tonight, but . . .

KITTY: And Matt's dying to see you too. You'll have to show him your MAD collection one more time.

CHARLIE: He remembers that?

KITTY: Are you serious? That's on the list now, that's required.

CHARLIE: Oh, shit.

KITTY: What.

CHARLIE: I think I have to work today.

KITTY: Oh, no, Charlie, you can't miss this—

CHARLIE: Shit. Get me up at eight, I'll call in sick.

KITTY: Well . . . wait . . .

CHARLIE: Nah, fuck it. If he doesn't like it, he can fire me.

KITTY: No, wait, Charlie, I shouldn't've . . . that wouldn't be too cool with Mom, or . . . you know, just . . . for *you*, I mean . . . this is a decent job . . .

CHARLIE: Pearl-diving, it's a privilege—

KITTY: Well, but if you stick it out there, maybe you can move up—

CHARLIE: Move up, how? To waiter? I'd rather wash dishes my whole life than be a fucking waiter. You know how much shit they have to take from these assholes? Come in ordering "Chivas and Coke," like that's a sign of class!

KITTY: Well, but you'd make a lot more money—

CHARLIE: Hey, I go in, I do my job, and I don't have to take any shit from anybody—including my "superior." The crew chief? What a dickhead! Keeps telling me about "technique"—which he doesn't know zilch what he's talking about—and when I tell him "Back off," he goes, "I am your superior!" Dickhead's never read a book, can't even speak English hardly, here he is telling me . . .

KITTY: Well, sure, but on any job—

CHARLIE: Then yesterday, I had a couple beers in the bar on my lunch hour—then my boss comes in and tells me the staff isn't *allowed* to drink on the "premises"—how's that for life in a democracy?

KITTY: That stinks. But, you know, why give them your money anyway—

CHARLIE: Man, I was seeing red, I went back in the kitchen, my "superior" starts in on me about "technique," I told him, "Yeah, you spent your whole life washing other people's dirty dishes, and you think that make you my *superior?* I find that sad."

KITTY: Well, but Charlie, don't . . . this looks like a job you can keep for a while, right?

CHARLIE: Listen, there are a million—a zillion jobs like this. Pearl-diving, busing tables, washing floors—nobody wants these fucking jobs. Every kitchen is a zoo, they got no-shows, they got walkouts, guys right off the boat who can't even speak English, you gotta do a pan-tomime to show 'em what they're sposeta do. . . . This is one thing I know more about than you, okay? With my experience, I can walk into any restaurant and any bar in this city, and I can get hired, and I am not exaggerating, any day I ask—

KITTY: Okay, but asking is the hard part, and—Jésus, I swore I wasn't get-ting into this—Mom wants you to be working—

CHARLIE: No matter what scutwork it is—

KITTY: Now that's not fair—or true—God, Charlie—you're so bright—

CHARLIE: Oh shit, what, did you guys spend the whole night talking about getting me motivated—?

KITTY: (*overlapping*) No, I told her, I told everyone, I don't want to get into this! But when I hear you talking about—

CHARLIE: (*overlapping*) You come home every two years—

KITTY: (*overlapping*) It's not just me who's saying it—

CHARLIE: You wouldn't last one day washing dishes in a restaurant.

KITTY: Okay, fine . . . let's not do this, huh? I'm really . . . want to see you, I want to spend some time with you—

CHARLIE: You know, she keeps ragging me about "if you'd just get your equivalency"—like a high school diploma's gonna open the golden doors—McDonald's, that's the golden doors it'll open—and I'd rather haul shit! Listen, I couldn't make Mom happy unless I wore a suit to work—Shit.

KITTY: What.

CHARLIE: I forgot to get my good pants cleaned.

KITTY: I'll just iron 'em, they'll be fine—

CHARLIE: No, they're gross, got puke on 'em or something . . .

KITTY: Well, maybe Joe brought extra pants—

CHARLIE: Well, I was gonna ask him if he brought extra shoes. All I've got is tennis shoes.

KITTY: God, I sort of doubt it. Joe's not exactly Mr. Style, you know. I mean you don't have to worry about the family standards here. Last week his boss took us out to dinner, and they wouldn't even let Joe in the restaurant because no tie, right?

CHARLIE: (*half-listening*) Assholes . . .

KITTY: So Joey takes off down the street and zips into some discount store and zips out with this plastic tie—God, did it feel sleazy, like it was made out of a shower curtain, or—well, most likely he'll wear it tomorrow at the wedding—

CHARLIE: I've got ties to lend him, God, they're still in the boxes—but I better find that white shirt, throw it in the washer. Can you wake me? Like at nine. And I'll call in. What time's the wedding?

KITTY: Noon. I'll prob'ly still be making this goddamn potato salad as they're marching down the aisle . . .

CHARLIE: Joe's gonna wear a suit, right?

KITTY: No, just a sportscoat, you don't have to—

CHARLIE: Would he have an extra one?

KITTY: . . . I don't think . . . but you don't have to . . . or we can go buy one, in a couple hours here. We can put it on the card and you can pay us back.

CHARLIE: Yeah? When?

KITTY: Oh, who cares? Shoes, too. Charlie. You should have a decent pair of shoes, you know? A decent jacket . . . for your life. Okay?

CHARLIE: (*beat; then:*) I can get away with a shirt and tie, huh?

KITTY: . . . Sure, this is very casual . . . home-catering, the whole trip . . .

CHARLIE: Okay, I'm gonna hit the rack. Wake me up, okay? Wake me at ten, ten's good enough.

KITTY: I'll send the kids in—
CHARLIE: Better not, you ain't seen my room.

(*as he exits*)

> And listen, at the wedding? Just keep Uncle Bill away from me. I
> can get through anything if he just doesn't ask me what I'm "up to
> these days."

(*He exits, with remains of sandwiches. She keeps peeling eggs.*)

Blackout

TRY THIS 3.12
Write a short dialogue in which one person explains or defends him/herself to another.
The listener is sympathetic, and believes the explanation. We aren't and don't. How
can you make the talker unreliable in both image/action and speech? Why does the
listener believe what we do not?

WORKING TOWARD A DRAFT
Look back over your exercises and your journal. Pick two characters who interest you
and brainstorm how they might meet. Under what circumstances? How would they
feel about each other? What might one want from the other? Is there a story in this
confrontation?

Or:

Pick an autobiographical passage you have written. Develop and extend it by describing the people more fully, in appearance, action, and speech. Explore and record more
fully your own thoughts in that situation. What did you learn from the experience
recounted in the passage?

John Coffer, "Coney Island, 2002"

WARM-UP

Drawing on your own experience, describe a carnival or fair. Include the weather and time of day, the smells, the sounds, tastes. How do these concrete details also establish the mood or atmosphere? Place two people on the midway. One wants to go home, the other wants to stay. Which? Why?

CHAPTER FOUR

SETTING

As the World
As a Camera
As Mood and Symbol
As Action

"... place is a definer and a confiner of what I'm doing ...
It saves me. Why, you couldn't write a story that happened
nowhere."

Eudora Welty

A love of home. A passion for travel. The grief of exile. The fragility of nature.
The excitement of the metropolis. A fascination with the past. An obsession
with the future. The search to belong. The need to flee. A sense of alienation. The
thrill of outer space. The romance of real estate. Fear of the dark. The arctic
waste. The swamp. The summit. The sea. The slums. The catacombs. The palace.
The rocking chair. The road.

Writer after writer will tell you that **setting** fuels the drive to write. Virtually any writer you ask will profess a profound relation to place and time, whether
as patriot, refugee, homebody, adventurer, flaneur, or time traveler; and each will
tell you that creating the sensuous particularity of a place and period is crucial
to writing. Setting is not merely scenery against which the significant takes place;
it is part and parcel of the significant; it is heritage and culture; it is identity or
exile, and the writer's choice of detail directs our understanding and our experience of it.

Like so many Americans raised in suburbia [Deborah Tall writes], I have never
really belonged to an American landscape . . . The land's dull tidiness was hard
to escape, except in the brief adventures of childhood when I could crawl beneath
a bush or clothe myself in a willow tree. Before long, tall enough to look out the
kitchen window, I saw the tree tamed by perspective, the bush that could be

hurdled, my yard effectively mimicked all up and down the block: one house, two trees, one house, two trees, all the way to the vanishing point.

"Here"

In rejecting the suburban landscape as her rightful home, Tall creates its oppressive tidiness for us, its suggestive or even symbolic importance to her sense of the "vanishing point." Though the description is of a deliberately static scene, the forceful verbs—*escape, crawl, clothe, tame, hurdle, mimic*—carry the energy of her desire to be gone from it. And readers can connect with the pictures and emotions she evokes in many ways: the image of suburbia itself, the childhood desire to hide, the changing perspective as she grows, the need for independence. For myself, though I grew up in the desert and would have been grateful for two trees, I powerfully identify with the sense of knowing even as a child that the place I lived was not the place I belonged, and the implication that this sense of exile is common among writers.

If a piece of literature does not create the setting for us, if it seems to occur in no-place no-time or in vague-place fuzzy-time, we cannot experience it, or else we must experience that vagueness itself as crucial to the action. Samuel Butler's Utopia is set in *Erewhon* (*nowhere* spelled backward) because the point of such a place, where philosophers reign and children select their parents, is that it cannot exist. Tom Stoppard's heroes in *Rosencrantz and Guildenstern Are Dead* do not know where they are, or where they came from, or where the sun comes up, or what time it is, and therefore *do not know who they are.*

Yet there's a resistance and even a measure of boredom that greets the subject of setting, and I can think of at least two reasons for this. The first is that tedious and sentimental descriptions of nature tend to be part of our early schooling, operating as a sort of admonishment that we should pay less attention to Mickey Mouse and Beyoncé, and more to the (ho-hum) wonders of nature. The other is that in daily life we take our surroundings ninety percent for granted. The world you know is what you're told to write about. What's the big deal? Isn't it everybody's world? Well, no.

Don't think that any place is "typical."

Steven Schoen

Setting as the World

Your routine, your neighborhood, your take on home, history, climate, and the cosmos is unique, like your voice, and inseparable from your voice. As a writer you need to be alert to your own vision and to create for us, even make strange to us, the world you think most familiar. Richard Ford demonstrates the technique in his description of "Seminary Street" in the novel *Independence Day:*

> The 4th is still three days off, but traffic is jamming into Frenchy's Gulf and through the parking lot at Pelcher's Market, citizens shouting out greetings from the dry cleaners and Town Liquors, as the morning heat is drumming up . . . all merchants are staging sidewalk "firecracker sales," setting out derelict merchandise they haven't moved since Christmas and draping sun racks with patriotic bunting and gimmicky signs that say wasting hard-earned money is the American way.

Ford's portrait here of a typical American town is given immediacy and life with names, quotations, and just slightly unexpected diction like *jamming, drumming, staging, "firecracker sales," derelict, sun racks, bunting, gimmicky*. These words and images are deliberate choices on Ford's part to particularize not only the town but our response to it. We may know this street well, but we would not see it well nor would we experience it in any particular way if we were told it was "a typical small town on 4th of July weekend."

If, on the other hand, the world you are writing about is itself in some way exotic, you may want to work in the opposite direction, to make it seem as familiar to us as the nearest mall.

> A server is woken at hour four-thirty by stimulin in the airflow, then yellow-up in our dormroom. After a minute in the hygiener and streamer, we put on fresh uniforms before filing into the restaurant. Our seer and aides gather us around Papa's Plinth for Matins, we recite the Six Catechisms, then our beloved Logoman appears and delivers his Sermon.
>
> *Cloud Atlas, David Mitchell*

Here, the familiar tone and casual delivery help readers accept the futuristic setting as the norm, at least for the duration of this fiction, in spite of the unusual words.

TRY THIS 4.1
Draw the floor plan of the first house you remember living in. Take a mental tour through this house, pausing (and marking on the floor plan) where significant events occurred. Walk through again, making a list of these events. Pick one of them and write about it. Pay attention to the setting and the atmosphere of the event. How does your relation to the space, light, weather, walls, furniture, and objects affect what you are doing and feeling? Does the place represent safety or confinement?

Description has earned a bad rap with overlong, self-indulgent eulogies to wildflowers, furniture, or alien planets. But setting involves everything that supports and impinges on your characters. The props of the world—artifacts and architecture, infrastructure, books, food, fabrics, tools and technology—create and sustain identity. People behaving in relation to their surroundings define both space and time, and reveal much more.

Take the example of a simple stage setting. The stage is bare; it could be any-where at any time. Now place on it an ordinary straight-backed chair. What portion of history is now eliminated? How much of the contemporary world can the setting now *not* represent—in what portion of the planet do people not sit on chairs? You don't know the answer. Neither do I. That neither of us knows the answer proves how particular and limited is our vision of the world.

A male actor enters the space. He sits in the chair. He holds his arms and head rigid, as if strapped. Where is he now? What will happen? Or he sweeps in and sits, miming the flinging aside of his robe. Where is he now? To what tradition does the scene belong? He drops a briefcase, slumps in the chair, and slips off his shoes with a toe on the heel of each. Where? What is he feeling? Or he sets the briefcase down, opens it, removes something, clears a space before him and begins to study, frowning. Where? Who is he? He tips back, one fist over the other in front of him, fighting the pull of the thing in his hands. Where? How much do you know about him? He kneels in front of the chair, one hand on his heart. What is he up to? He stands on the chair, fingering his neck, eyeing the ceiling. What is he thinking?

The male actor exits. A female actor enters. What does *she* do in relation to the chair? Which of the above actions would she not be likely to perform? What would she do that he would not?

Each of these actions, in relation to the absolute rock-bottom-simplest setting, represents a narrowing of possibility, an intensifying of situation, a range of emo-tions, and a shape of story. Each depends on the historical, geographical, psy-chological, and narrative potential that we have learned throughout a lifetime. Dancers have been so enamored of these possibilities that the use of chairs in dance has become a cliché. When a playwright wishes to indicate the most minimal set imaginable, she will usually indicate something like: *bare stage, three chairs.*

TRY THIS 4.2

Write about a landscape with a single tree. Describe the tree in as exact detail as you would a human being. Add a human being to the scene. What is the relationship of the human to the tree?

In choosing the most minimal stage set, the playwright is relying on the body and mobility of the actor to create the world around the chair, and those rep-resent a powerful collaborative presence. If your medium is poetry, essay, or fiction, you need to supply the whole of that vitality in words. Think of your char-acters as the point and center of what you write. Setting is everything else. It is the world. You need to make that world for us even as you present your char-acters, in order to let us care about them. Novelist and short-story writer Ron Carlson nicely catches the necessity and the priority:

> . . . if the story is about a man and a woman changing a tire on a remote highway . . .
> you've nonetheless got to convince me of the highway, the tire, the night, the
> margin, the shoulder, the gravel under their knees, the lug nuts, the difficulty
> getting the whole thing apart and back together, and the smells. You must do that.
> But that's not what you're there to deliver. That's the way you're going to seduce
> me . . . after you've got my shirt caught in the machine of the story and you've
> drawn me in, what you're really going to crush me with are these hearts and these
> people. Who are they?
>
> *interview with Ron Carlson by Susan McInnis*

The techniques of setting—"the machine of the story"—are those you have
already encountered as image and voice. Create a place by the selection of concrete detail in your particular diction or that of your narrating character. When
you focus on offering us the particularity of place, time, and weather, you will also
be able to manipulate the mood, reveal the character, and advance the action.

The details you choose to evoke place will also, if you choose them well, signal the period. Albert Einstein invented the word *chronotope* to indicate the
"space-time-continuum," or the fact that space and time are different manifestations of the same thing. Metaphorically this is true of imagery, and of the
imagery of space and time. You will indicate something about period as well as
architecture if your characters live in a *hogan, bungalow, cottage, sod house,*
split-level, or *high-rise*. Likewise you will tell us something about where and when
we are likely to be if your heroine is carrying a *reticule, porte monnaie, poke,*
duffle, or *fanny pack*.

> My father walked beside me to give me courage, his palm touching gently the back
> laces of my bodice. In the low-angled glare already baking the paving stones of
> the piazza and the top of my head, the still shadow of the Inquisitor's noose
> hanging above the Tor di Nona, the papal court, stretched grotesquely down the
> wall, its shape the outline of a tear.
>
> "A brief unpleasantness, Artemesia," my father said, looking straight ahead.
> "Just a little squeezing."
>
> *The Passion of Artemesia, Susan Vreeland*

This is a voice of relative calm in a situation of high drama. Can you identify the images and the diction that indicate period and locale?

If you have, as a reader, been impatient with description, it is probably either
because the author relied on a cliché picture-postcard image to evoke the scene,
or else because the description existed as a pedestal for the author's piety or clev-
erness. The techniques that convincingly create the world are the same as those
that create image and character: be alert to the sense impressions of your inner
eye (remembering that place and time can be created by smells and sounds, by
textures and even tastes as well as the visible). As with character, a single vivid
detail may accomplish more than a catalogue. Originality often means a genuine

connection with some particularity that you have noticed, and the ability to dream that particularity into your scene, however fictional.

An example from my own ignorance: in a novel set in Mexico in 1914, I needed to establish the threatening atmosphere of a small town. I decided I had better endow the town with a cockfight—everybody knows a cockfight is scary— and went looking for fictional and nonfiction accounts as models. I made notes about factual details, tried several pale drafts, and despaired at the brilliance of Nathaniel West and Ernest Hemingway. I'd never seen a cockfight, but I thought my imagination ought to be up to the task. It was not. Then it occurred to me that what frightened *me* in the desert was Gila monsters. I wrote a scene in which an old man with a Gila monster on a leash taunts the town by tossing frogs and snakes that his lizard paralyzes with its venomous tongue. There was more invention required by this scene than the cockfight I'd been trying to write (so far as I know nobody puts a leash on a Gila monster), but because it came out of my own emotion, feeling, and observation, it moved my character and his story in the direction needed.

TRY THIS 4.3
A memory, a poem, or a short-short story: Two characters sit down to eat. Don't tell us where or when, but let us know through the architecture, décor, implements, and food when and where the scene takes place.

". . . my favorite sentence may be, 'Last Wednesday at the Black Cat Night Club.' I mean, I just love knowing where I am."

Ron Carlson

Setting as a Camera

Setting often begins a piece, for the very good reason that this is the first thing we register in life. Entering a place, we take it in as a panorama (sit in a restaurant and watch people enter; their eyes go left and right, even up and down before they fix on the approaching hostess). Waking with the sense "where am I?" is notoriously disconcerting. It is no less so in literature. This does not mean setting has to be the very first thing writers address, but it does mean that their audience can't go far without some sort of orientation.

As a model, consider the western, which typically begins with a *long shot* (the camera at distance) of the horsemen coming over the rise. We get a sense of the landscape, then we see the far-off arrival of the riders. Then there might be a *middle shot*, say four riders in the frame, to give us a sense of the group. Then a *close-up:* this is our hero, his head and shoulders. Screenwriters and directors are taught that they need such an "establishing shot" at the beginning of *each* scene. This parallels the action that often takes place on stage: the curtain opens on an empty room; we register it, read its clues. Someone enters. What is the relationship of this person to this space? Someone else comes in; they begin to talk and the situation is revealed.

Carl Sandburg, in "Good Morning, America," demonstrates the long shot opening:

In the evening there is a sunset sonata to the cities.
There is a march of little armies to the dwindling of drums.
The skyscrapers throw their tall lengths of walls into black bastions on the red west.

Only once this cityscape, its sound, sight, and time of day, is established, does he introduce the puny maker of these great structures, man.

The process of orientation somehow takes place in every piece that tells a story. Consider again the beginning of the Housman poem in the last chapter:

Loveliest of trees, the cherry now
Is hung with snow along the bough
And stands about the woodland ride
Wearing white for Easter tide

Now of my threescore years and ten
Twenty will not come again . . .

Notice how this poem follows both the pattern of a film opening (and also, incidentally, the "seduction" process that Ron Carlson describes above). Actually, we begin with a middle shot (cherry tree, bough with the snow that tells us the season), pull back to a long shot (woodland ride), and then zoom in on the persona in relation to the scene (my whole life, and where I am in it now).

The practice of beginning with a wide angle and moving to closer focus is important for introducing us to an exotic locale:

The thin light of the approaching daybreak always seemed to emphasize the strangeness and foreignness of our battalion's bivouac area on a country road outside Casablanca. Every morning a heavy mist covered the land just before the sun rose. Then, as the light grew, odd-looking shapes and things came slowly into view . . . . Dim, moving figures behind the mist, dressed in ghostly white, materialized as Arabs perched on the hindquarters of spindly donkeys or walking along the road.

"On the Fedala Road," John McNeel

But this technique is no less useful to present a domestic scene:

Throughout my childhood our family's evening meals were expeditious and purposeful, more reliable than imaginative. We were French Canadians, which meant we knew pork and maple syrup. My grandfather liked to eat salt pork, sautéed in a frying pan, or cold, right out of the fridge, with a schmear of horseradish, a side of string beans, and a bottle of Tadcaster ale.

"Nothing to Eat but Food: Menu as Memoir," John Dufresne

Part of the long shot is temporal here, involving the whole sweep of *throughout my childhood*. Then it places us at table (*evening meals*). The diction also begins on a wide scale, with the generalizations (*expeditious, purposeful*) narrowing to an ethnicity and a region (*French Canadians*) and then comically to an image (*pork and maple syrup*). The character of grandfather is introduced and the close-up begins, narrowing toward his plate while the details and diction also give us the ethnic oddities of voice and flavor: *sautéed* and *schmear* and *Tadcaster ale*.

Of course, it is equally possible, and potentially interesting, to begin with the close-up and then move to middle and long shots—an opening image, say, of a fly crawling up three-days' worth of stubble to disappear in a nostril—only then you had better pull back to show us the bad guy's whole face, and the way he is wedged in the rock, and the wide-sky emptiness of the desert he has to cross. Sandra Cisneros demonstrates the technique in the short story "Salvador Late or Early":

> Salvador with eyes the color of a caterpillar, Salvador of the crooked hair and crooked teeth, Salvador whose name the teacher cannot remember, is a boy who is no one's friend, runs along somewhere in that direction where homes are the color of bad weather, lives behind a raw wood doorway, shakes the sleepy brothers awake, ties their shoes, combs their hair with water, feeds them milk and corn flakes from a tin cup in the dim dark of morning.

In this dense miniature portrait, notice how the focus begins on Salvador, then places him in a classroom, then chases him *somewhere in that direction*, so that we know the very vivid images of his poverty are the narrator's invention, impressions of the *dim dark* setting in which he lives.

Or observe, in this excerpt from Michael Ignatieff's memoir, *August in My Father's House*, how a storm is evoked in three sentences, first in middle shot, then close-up, and then sweeping away to a long shot:

> . . . A shutter bangs against the kitchen wall and a rivulet of sand trickles from the adobe wall in the long room where I sit. The lamp above my head twirls in the draught. Through the poplars, the forks of light plunge into the flanks of the mountains and for an instant the ribbed gullies stand out like skeletons under a sheet.

Notice also how the energy of the verbs (some of them personifications) mimic the energy of the storm: *bangs, trickles, twirls, plunge, stand out,* and how the scene is capped with a simile that suggests its malevolence: *ribbed gullies . . . like skeletons.* So active is this storm and the "camera" swinging to capture it, so forcefully does it suggest the emotion of the narrator, that it's unlikely anyone would refer to it as a "description of nature," though it is also that.

As this example shows, the "camera" may record the scene, but it is a subjective, not an impartial observer. The angle and distance are, like the details themselves, a choice made by the author that conveys a sense of viewpoint, of *someone* standing *somewhere* to watch the scene.

> If the atmosphere is to be foreboding, you must forebode
> on every page. If it is to be cold, you must chill, not once
> or twice, but until your readers are shivering.
>
> *Jerome Stern*

Setting as Mood and Symbol

Each of the scenes above creates a **mood** or **atmosphere** for the events that will unfold there—fearful in the Vreeland, majestic in the Sandburg, elegiac in the Housman, mysterious in the McNeel, comic in the Dufresne, poignant in the Cisneros, malevolent in the Ignatieff. (Do you agree with these characterizations? Which words and images are responsible for the mood created?)

Setting in the sense of atmosphere is one of the writer's most adaptable tools. Mood will inevitably contain some element of time and weather—wet or dry, dark or light, winter or summer, calm or storm, and so forth. These, together with the textures and colors of objects, the smells of vegetation, the shapes of buildings, are all rich with the mood from which the unique action and its meaning emerge.

> When we came back to Paris it was clear and cold and lovely. The city had accommodated itself to winter, there was good wood for sale at the wood and coal place across our street, and there were braziers outside of many of the good cafés so that you could keep warm on the terraces.
>
> *A Moveable Feast, Ernest Hemingway*

Mood is a state of mind or emotion, and when we speak of setting as mood, we are speaking of an external manifestation of the inner, the concrete expressing the abstract, the contingent standing for the essential. In this sense, setting is often to some degree **symbolic**. It may be deliberately and specifically so, like the deranged planets that stand for the disordered society in *King Lear*, or the subway that is "the flying underbelly of the city . . . heaped in modern myth" in Imamu Amiri Baraka's play *Dutchman*.

More often, the setting is suggestive of a larger meaning, reaching out from a particular place and time toward a cosmic or universal reading. In this opening passage from Don DeLillo's *Underworld*, a boy is playing hookey to be at a New York baseball stadium that becomes the symbolic locus of American longing. (Notice the close-up/long-shot/close-up/long-shot structure.)

It's a school day, sure, but he's nowhere near the classroom. He wants to be here instead, standing in the shadow of this old rust-hulk of a structure, and it's hard to blame him . . .

Longing on a large scale is what makes history. This is just a kid with a local yearning but he is part of an assembling crowd, anonymous thousands off the buses and trains, people in narrow columns tramping over the swing bridge above the river, and even if they are not a migration or a revolution, some vast shaking of the soul, they bring with them the body heat of a great city and their own small reveries and desperations, the unseen something that haunts the day . . .

Our relation to place, time, and weather, like our relation to clothes and other objects, is charged with emotion more or less subtle, more or less profound. It is filled with judgment mellow or harsh. And it alters according to what happens to us. In some rooms you are always trapped; you enter them with grim purpose and escape them as soon as you can. Others invite you to settle in, to nestle or carouse. Some landscapes lift your spirits; others depress you. Cold weather gives you energy and bounce, or else it clogs your head and makes you huddle, struggling. You describe yourself as a night person or a morning person. The house you loved as a child now makes you, precisely because you were once happy there, think of loss and death.

TRY THIS 4.5
As a prompt for a memoir, poem, or fiction, choose one of the clichés below. Using concrete details rather than the words of the cliché, create the setting suggested by it. You might begin with a single sharply focused image, then pull back to reveal the larger landscape. Use a persona or introduce a character if you choose.
- a dark and stormy night
- raining cats and dogs
- freeze you to death
- scorching hot
- foggy as pea soup
- balmy weather
- fragrant as new-mown hay

The potential for emotion inherent in place, time, and weather can be used or heightened (or invented) to dramatic effect in your writing. Nothing happens nowhere. Just as significant detail calls up a sense impression and also an abstraction, so setting and atmosphere impart both information and emotion. Just as dialogue must do more than one thing at a time, so can setting characterize, reveal mood, and signal change. Here from Saul Bellow's "Memoir of a Bootlegger's Son" is a picture of the place his father worked after he lost the fortune he brought from Russia:

The bakery was a shanty. The rats took refuge from the winter there, and drowned in the oil and fished out suffocated from the jelly. The dogs and cats could not police them, they were so numerous. The thick ice did not float leisurely, it ran the swift current. In March and even April the snow still lay heavy. When it melted, the drains couldn't carry off the water. There were gray lagoons in the hollows of old ice; they were sullen or flashing according to the color of the sky.

Bellow's choices of imagery here are so rich with mood that they amount to a prophecy: *refuge, drowned, suffocated, heavy, gray, hollows, old ice.* The impotence of dogs and cats, ice, snow and drains, the lagoons "sullen or flashing according to the color of the sky" convey not only the scene but also the man's loss of self-determination.

TRY THIS 4.6

On the left is a list of times, places, and/or weather. On the right are words that represent a mood or quality of atmosphere. Pick one item from the left and one from the right. Write a poem or paragraph in which you make the setting suggest the atmosphere. If the connection is not obvious, your piece will be more interesting. Introduce a character if you please.

the city in the rain	sinister
midnight on the farm	sick with love
1890, in the parlor	full of promise
high noon on the river	suicidal
a spring morning	dangerous
in the bar, after hours	suspense
the dusty road	happy-go-lucky
dawn in a foreign place	lonely

Setting as Action

If character is the foreground and setting the background, then there may be harmony or conflict between character and background. The persons of your poem, play, memoir, or fiction may be comfortably at ease in the world around them, or they may be uneasy, uncomfortable, full of foreboding.

I will wait for her in the yard that Maggie and I made so clean and wavy yesterday afternoon. A yard like this is more comfortable than most people know. It is not just a yard. It is like an extended living room. When the hard clay is swept clean as a floor and the fine sand around the edges lined with tiny, irregular grooves, anyone can come and sit and look up into the elm tree and wait for the breezes that never come inside the house.

"Everyday Use," Alice Walker

Here the setting is a place full of comfort and community, and any conflict comes from an outside threat to that balance—perhaps, we suspect, the "her" being waited for. But where there is menace in the setting, or conflict between the character and the setting, there is already an element of "story."

> There is a city surrounded by water with watery alleys that do for streets and roads and silted up back ways that only the rats can cross. Miss your way, which is easy to do, and you may find yourself staring at a hundred eyes guarding a filthy palace of sacks and bones. Find your way, which is easy to do, and you may meet an old woman in a doorway. She will tell your fortune, depending on your face.
>
> *The Passion, Jeanette Winterson*

When a character is in harmony with his/her surroundings, the atmosphere suggested is static, and it will take a disruption of some kind to introduce the possibility of change. But when setting and character, background and foreground, are set in opposition to each other, the process of discovery and decision is already in motion, and we know we are in for a seismic or a psychic shift.

One great advantage of being a writer is that you may create the world. Places and the elements have the significance and the emotional effect you give them in language. As a person you may be depressed by rain, but as an author you are free to make rain mean freshness, growth, bounty, and God. You may love winter, but you are free to make the blank white field symbolize oblivion.

As with character, the first requisite of effective setting is to know it fully, to experience it mentally, and the second is to create it through significant detail. What sort of place is this, and what are its peculiarities? What is the weather like, the light, the season, the time of day? What are the contours of the land and architecture? What are the social assumptions of the inhabitants, and how familiar and comfortable are the characters with this place and its lifestyle? These things are not less important in literature than in life, but more, since their selection inevitably takes on significance.

TRY THIS 4.7

Take a road map, close your eyes, and point to it at random. Have a character drive or walk through the nearest town and stop in at a bank, shop, or restaurant. Study the surrounding area on the map if you like. Invent the details.

Or:

Write about a place you can't return to.

More to Read

Baxter, Charles. *Burning Down the House: Essays on Fiction*. St. Paul: Graywolf Press, 1997.

Bickham, Jack M. *Setting*. Cincinnati: Writer's Digest Books, 1994.

Readings

CREATIVE NONFICTION

Joan Didion

At the Dam

Since the afternoon in 1967 when I first saw Hoover Dam, its image has never been entirely absent from my inner eye. I will be talking to someone in Los Angeles, say, or New York, and suddenly the dam will materialize, its pristine concave face gleaming white against the harsh rusts and taupes and mauves of that rock canyon hundreds or thousands of miles from where I am. I will be driving down Sunset Boulevard, or about to enter a freeway, and abruptly those power transmission towers will appear before me, canted vertiginously over the tailrace. Sometimes I am confronted by the intakes and sometimes by the shadow of the heavy cable that spans the canyon and sometimes by the ominous outlets to unused spillways, black in the lunar clarity of the desert light. Quite often I hear the turbines. Frequently I wonder what is happening at the dam this instant, at this precise intersection of time and space, how much water is being released to fill downstream orders and what lights are flashing and which generators are in full use and which just spinning free.

I used to wonder what it was about the dam that made me think of it at times and in places where I once thought of the Mindanao Trench, or of the stars wheeling in their courses, or of the words *As it was in the beginning, is now and ever shall be, world without end, amen.* Dams, after all, are commonplace: we have all seen one. This particular dam had existed as an idea in the world's mind for almost forty years before I saw it. Hoover Dam, showpiece of the Boulder Canyon project, the several million tons of concrete that made the Southwest plausible, the *fait accompli* that was to convey, in the innocent time of its construction, the notion that mankind's brightest promise lay in American engineering.

Of course the dam derives some of its emotional effect from precisely that aspect, that sense of being a monument to a faith since misplaced. "They died to make the desert bloom," reads a plaque dedicated to the 96 men who died building this first of the great high dams, and in context the worn phrase touches, suggests all of that trust in harnessing resources, in the meliorative power of the dynamo, so central to the early Thirties. Boulder City, built in 1931 as the construction town for the dam, retains the ambience of a model city, a new town, a toy triangular grid of green lawns and trim bungalows, all fanning out from the Reclamation building. The bronze sculptures at the dam itself evoke muscular citizens of a tomorrow that never came, sheaves of wheat clutched heavenward, thunderbolts defied. Winged Victories guard the flagpole. The flag whips in the canyon wind. An empty Pepsi-Cola can clatters across the terrazzo. The place is perfectly frozen in time.

But history does not explain it all, does not entirely suggest what makes the dam so affecting. Nor, even, does energy, the massive involvement with power and pressure and the transparent sexual overtones to that involvement. Once when I revisited the dam I walked through it with a man from the Bureau of Reclamation. For a while we trailed behind a guided tour, and then we went on, went into parts of the dam where visitors do not generally go. Once in a while he would explain something, usually in that recondite language having to do with "peaking power," with "outages" and "dewatering," but on the whole we spent the afternoon in a world so alien, so complete and so beautiful unto itself that it was scarcely necessary to speak at all. We saw almost no one. Cranes moved above us as if under their own volition. Generators roared. Transformers hummed. The gratings on which we stood vibrated. We watched a hundred-ton steel shaft plunging down to that place where the water was. And finally we got down to that place where the water was, where the water sucked out of Lake Mead roared through thirty-foot penstocks and then into thirteen-foot penstocks and finally into the turbines themselves. "Touch it," the Reclamation man said, and I did, and for a long time I just stood there with my hands on the turbine. It was a peculiar moment, but so explicit as to suggest nothing beyond itself.

There was something beyond all that, something beyond energy, beyond history, something I could not fix in my mind. When I came up from the dam that day the wind was blowing harder, through the canyon and all across the Mojave. Later, toward Henderson and Las Vegas, there would be dust blowing, blowing past the Country-Western Casino FRI & SAT NITES and blowing past the Shrine of Our Lady of Safe Journey STOP & PRAY, but out at the dam there was no dust, only the rock and the dam and a little greasewood and a few garbage cans, their tops chained, banging against a fence. I walked across the marble star map that traces a sidereal revolution of the equinox and fixes forever, the Reclamation man had told me, for all time and for all people who can read the stars, the date the dam was dedicated. The star map was, he had said, for when we were all gone and the dam was left. I had not thought much of it when he said it, but I thought of it then, with the wind whining and the sun dropping behind a mesa with the finality of a sunset in space. Of course that was the image I had seen always, seen it without quite realizing what I saw, a dynamo finally free of man, splendid at last in its absolute isolation, transmitting power and releasing water to a world where no one is.

Bill Capoſſere
A Wind from the North

When three days had passed and the snow still lay in smooth unbrushed drifts across the cold glass and silvery metal of the car, the neighbors, curious or concerned, began a trail of telephone calls that led, eventually, to my own heated home. Later that night, inside a sky of utter clarity and simplicity, it began once more to snow.

The coroner said my uncle had been dead five or six days, dead of a heart attack sometime earlier in the week, dead perhaps in his sleep, or perhaps not, but dead at least quickly, and certainly quietly. It is the quiet part I often wonder about. Five or six days of lying there in his chair while outside the snow piled softly atop his car like all the pale moments of his life gathered together in a cold and singular space. Five or six days gone by, the snow filling in the gaps between the stiff branches of the pine bushes outside the apartment, filling in the hollow between the wheel and the chassis, filling in, even, at last, the cavity formed by his own absence, an absence gone unmarked under the glare of a stark midwinter sun.

What sort of life creates this sort of death? Where after six days, a week, no one turns and says, "Hey, have you seen Louie lately?" Where no one pours an eight a.m. coffee-to-go, then watches it sit atop the counter growing colder by the minute, wondering at least a little before pouring it out into the stainless steel sink. Where no one rings once, twice, many times, before knocking then pounding against an unyielding door. How do sixty years of a man's tracks disappear so completely under a blanket of snow that the world seems a cold and pathless place?

My own memories of him are dim. I seldom saw him off the couch at home, and remember few conversations. Usually the ones we had were brief and one-sided and came about because I had wandered between him and the golf game on television or had strayed too close to his new car—always the same: sleek and sporty and untouchable. I never rode in one.

When he and my aunt divorced, I remember little feeling of loss, inured, perhaps, to such annual occurrence in our lives, or simple acknowledgment maybe of a presence never felt, a connection never made. When he moved back in with my aunt for a while due to finances, I recall only a sense of awkwardness. The two of them did not speak to one another; he moved through the house like the family madman, let out this time from the attic, but still unseen, not to be spoken to. He would come down the stairs when I visited and grasp my hand firmly as if to hold me there until, forced by the pressure of our palms, I would at last acknowledge his existence.

That was perhaps as far as I could go. His hands were thin and dry and bloodless; cool to the touch, they held no history for me. We would stand that way for a moment as he asked a question or two, the right questions, I suppose, the ones he had finally learned one cannot get along without, but we were two strangers by then, and it was all the conversation one might expect to have while waiting in line someplace wide and empty.

I think he began to realize even then the fort he had built round himself, began then to notice the metallic taste of loneliness, like an old coin held too long in the mouth. As he sat in that chair and the snow began to pile up outside, I wonder if he saw in its slow accumulation the heavy weight of a lifetime's chances gone by and felt in its cool accusation the smothering force that pressed him back into his seat and finally crowded out the untethered motions of his heart.

The Eskimo, it is said, have many words for snow, different words for snow falling and snow already fallen. They use *muruaneq* for soft deep snow, *natquik* for the snow which covers the ground and clings to the feet, *kanevvluk* for fine snow, and *quaniisqineq* for snow floating on water. But, as far as I can find, they have no word for the snow that covers a man's death so that even the wake of his passage is obliterated. Unless it be *natquigte*, snow that drifts perpetually along the ground, resting nowhere, holding to nothing, ever-moving particles aloft on the wind.

TRY THIS 4.8
Remember or invent a person in a particular landscape or kind of weather. Make the setting characterize the person.

FICTION

Donald Barthelme
The School

Well, we had all these children out planting trees, see, because we figured that . . . that was part of their education, to see how, you know, the root systems . . . and also the sense of responsibility, taking care of things, being individually responsible. You know what I mean. And the trees all died. They were orange trees. I don't know why they died, they just died. Something wrong with the soil possibly or maybe the stuff we got from the nursery wasn't the best. We complained about it. So we've got thirty kids there, each kid had his or her own little tree to plant, and we've got these thirty dead trees. All these kids looking at these little brown sticks, it was depressing.

It wouldn't have been so bad except that just a couple of weeks before the thing with the trees, the snakes all died. But I think that the snakes—well, the reason that the snakes kicked off was that . . . you remember, the boiler was shut off for four days because of the strike, and that was explicable. It was something you could explain to the kids because of the strike. I mean, none of their parents would let them cross the picket line and they knew there was a strike going on and what it meant. So when things got started up again and we found the snakes they weren't too disturbed.

With the herb gardens it was probably a case of overwatering, and at least now they know not to overwater. The children were very conscientious with the herb gardens and some of them probably . . . you know, slipped them a little extra water when we weren't looking. Or maybe . . . well, I don't like to think about sabotage, although it did occur to us. I mean, it was something that crossed our minds. We were thinking that way probably because before that the gerbils had died, and the white mice had died, and the salamander . . . well, now they know not to carry them around in plastic bags.

Of course we *expected* the tropical fish to die, that was no surprise. Those numbers, you look at them crooked and they're belly-up on the surface. But the lesson plan called for tropical-fish input at that point, there was nothing we could do, it happens every year, you just have to hurry past it.

We weren't even supposed to have a puppy.

We weren't even supposed to have one, it was just a puppy the Murdoch girl found under a Gristede's truck one day and she was afraid the truck would run over it when the driver had finished making his delivery, so she stuck it in her knapsack and brought it to school with her. So we had this puppy. As soon as I saw the puppy I thought, Oh Christ, I bet it will live for about two weeks and then . . . And that's what it did. It wasn't supposed to be in the classroom at all, there's some kind of regulation about it, but you can't tell them they can't have a puppy when the puppy is already there, right in front of them, running around on the floor and yap yap yapping. They named it Edgar—that is, they named it after me. They had a lot of fun running after it and yelling, "Here, Edgar! Nice Edgar!" Then they'd laugh like hell. They enjoyed the ambiguity. I enjoyed it myself. I don't mind being kidded. They made a little house for it in the supply closet and all that. I don't know what it died of. Distemper, I guess. It probably hadn't had any shots. I got it out of there before the kids got to school. I checked the supply closet each morning, routinely, because I knew what was going to happen. I gave it to the custodian.

And then there was this Korean orphan that the class adopted through the Help the Children program, all the kids brought in a quarter a month, that was the idea. It was an unfortunate thing, the kid's name was Kim and maybe we adopted him too late or something. The cause of death was not stated in the letter we got, they suggested we adopt another child instead and sent us some interesting case histories, but we didn't have the heart. The class took it pretty hard, they began (I think, nobody ever said anything to me directly) to feel that maybe there was something wrong with the school. But I don't think there's anything wrong with the school, particularly, I've seen better and I've seen worse. It was just a run a bad luck. We had an extraordinary number of parents passing away, for instance. There were I think two heart attacks and two suicides, one drowning, and four killed together in a car accident. One stroke. And we had the usual heavy mortality rate among the grandparents, or maybe it was heavier this year, it seemed so. And finally the tragedy.

The tragedy occurred when Matthew Wein and Tony Mavrogordo were playing over where they're excavating for the new federal office building. There were all these big wooden beams stacked, you know, at the edge of the excavation. There's a court case coming out of that, the parents are claiming that the beams were poorly stacked. I don't know what's true and what's not. It's been a strange year.

I forgot to mention Billy Brandt's father, who was knifed fatally when he grappled with a masked intruder in his home.

One day, we had a discussion in class. They asked me, where did they go? The trees, the salamander, the tropical fish, Edgar, the poppas and mommas, Matthew and Tony, where did they go? And I said, I don't know, I don't know. And they said, who knows? and I said, nobody knows. And they said, is death that which gives meaning to life? and I said, no, life is that which gives meaning to life. Then they said, but isn't death, considered as a fundamental datum, the means by which the taken-for-granted mundanity of the everyday may be transcended in the direction of—

I said, yes, maybe.

They said, we don't like it.

I said, that's sound.

They said, it's a bloody shame!

I said, it is.

They said, will you make love now with Helen (our teaching assistant) so that we can see how it is done? We know you like Helen.

I do like Helen but I said that I would not.

We've heard so much about it, they said, but we've never seen it.

I said I would be fired and that it was never, or almost never, done as a demonstration. Helen looked out of the window.

They said, please, please make love with Helen, we require an assertion of value, we are frightened.

I said that they shouldn't be frightened (although I am often frightened) and that there was value everywhere. Helen came and embraced me. I kissed her a few times on the brow. We held each other. The children were excited. Then there was a knock on the door, I opened the door, and the new gerbil walked in. The children cheered wildly.

TRY THIS 4.9
Using what you have learned about voice, pick a character who belongs to a certain place—preacher, prisoner, coach, nurse, Little Leaguer or the like—and write a monologue in which that place is evoked through the voice.

POEMS

Sherman Alexie

At Navajo Monument Valley Tribal School

from the photograph by Skeet McAuley

the football field rises
to meet the mesa. Indian boys
gallop across the grass, against

the beginning of their body.
On those Saturday afternoons,
unbroken horses gather to watch

their sons growing larger
in the small parts of the world.
Everyone is the quarterback.

There is no thin man in a big hat
writing down all the names
in two columns: winners and losers.

This is the eternal football game,
Indians versus Indians. All the Skins
in the wooden bleachers, fancydancing,

stomping red dust straight down
into nothing. Before the game is over,
the eighth-grade girls' track team

comes running, circling the field,
their thin and brown legs echoing
wild horses, wild horses, wild horses.

Heather McHugh

Earthmoving Malediction

Bulldoze the bed where we made love,
bulldoze the goddamn room.
Let rubble be our evidence
and wreck our home.

I can't give touching up
by inches, can't give beating up
by heart. So set the comforter
on fire, and turn the dirt

to some advantage—palaces of pigweed,
treasuries of turd. The fist
will vindicate the hand,
and tooth and nail

refuse to burn, and I
must not look back, as Mrs. Lot
was named for such a little—
something in a cemetery,

or a man. Bulldoze the coupled
ploys away, the cute exclusives
in the social mall. We dwell

on earth, where beds
are brown, where swoops
are fell. Bulldoze

the pearly gates:
if paradise comes down
there is no hell.

Annie Tibble
Trials of a Tourist

It is three o'clock in the morning.
I am in a hurry.
I will have some fried fish.
It does not smell nice.
Bring some coffee now—and some wine.
Where is the toilet? There is a mistake in the bill.
You have charged me too much.
I have left my glasses, my watch and my ring, in the toilet.
Bring them.

Porter, here is my luggage.
I have only a suitcase and a bag.
I shall take this myself.
Be very careful with that.
Look out! The lock is broken.
Don't forget that.
I have lost my keys.
Help me to close this.
How much do I owe you? I did not know I had to pay.
Find me a non-smoking compartment, a corner seat, facing the engine.
Put the case on the rack.
Someone has taken my seat.
Can you help me to open the window.

Where is the toilet?
I have left my ticket, my gloves and my glasses in the toilet.
Can they be sent on?
Stop! I want to get off again. I have got into the wrong train.

Who is speaking?
Wrong number!
I don't understand you.
Do you speak English?
I am an Englishwoman. Does no-one here speak English?
Wait. I am looking for a phrase in my book.

My bag has been stolen.
That man is following me everywhere.
Go away. Leave me alone.
I shall call a policeman.

You are mistaken. I didn't do it.
It has nothing to do with me. I have done nothing.
Let me pass. I have paid you enough.
Where is the British Consulate?
Beware!

Bring me some cottonwool.
I think there is a mistake in your calculations.
I do not feel well.
Ring a doctor.

Can you give me something for diarrhoea?
I have a pain. Here.
I have pains all over.
I can't eat.
I do not sleep.
I think I have a temperature.
I have caught a cold.
I have been burnt by the sun.
My skin is smarting. Have you nothing to soothe it?
My nose is bleeding.
I feel giddy.
I keep vomiting.
I have been stung by sea-urchins.
I have been bitten by a dog.
I think I have food-poisoning.
You are hurting me.
I shall stay in bed.
Bring me some brandy—please.
Help!
Fire!
Thief!

TRY THIS 4.10
"Trials of a Tourist" is a "found poem," all of its lines being taken from phrases found
in a mini-dictionary for tourists. Choose another text about a place—a guidebook,
travel article, brochure, government pamphlet, field guide, Internet site, even a map—
and arrange phrases from it to form a poem. Comedy allowed.

Yusef Komunyakaa
Nude Interrogation

Did you kill anyone over there? Angela shifts her gaze from the Janis Joplin poster
to the Jimi Hendrix, lifting the pale muslin blouse over her head. The blacklight

deepens the blues when the needle drops into the first groove of "All Along the Watchtower." I don't want to look at the floor. *Did you kill anyone? Did you dig a hole, crawl inside, and wait for your target?* Her miniskirt drops into a rainbow at her feet. Sandalwood incense hangs a slow comet of perfume over the room. I shake my head. She unhooks her bra and flings it against a bookcase made of plywood and cinderblocks. *Did you use an M-16, a handgrenade, a bayonet, or your own two strong hands, both thumbs pressed against that little bird in the throat?* She stands with her left thumb hooked into the elastic of her sky-blue panties. When she flicks off the blacklight, snowy hills rush up to the windows. *Did you kill anyone over there? Are you right-handed or left-handed? Did you drop your gun afterwards? Did you kneel beside the corpse and turn it over?* She's nude against the falling snow. *Yes.* The record spins like a bull's-eye on the far wall of Xanadu. *Yes,* I say. *I was scared of the silence. The night was too big. And afterwards, I couldn't stop looking up at the sky.*

TRY THIS 4.11
Below are some themes associated with setting, suggested by the preceding poems. Pick one, remember or imagine the place it refers to, and brainstorm a list of images. Arrange them into lines. Use the name of the place as your title, perhaps?
- ghosts of the past live here
- I will destroy this place
- I want to go home
- history happened there

DRAMA

David Ives
The Philadelphia

This play is for Greg Pliska, who knows what a Philadelphia can be.

CHARACTERS
AL: California cool; 20s or 30s
MARK: frazzled; 20s or 30s
WAITRESS: weary; as you will

SETTING
A bar/restaurant. A table, red-checkered cloth, two chairs, and a specials board.

AL is at the restaurant, with the WAITRESS.

WAITRESS: Can I help you?

AL: Do you know you would look fantastic on a wide screen?

WAITRESS: Uh-huh.

AL: Seventy millimeters.

WAITRESS: Look. Do you want to see a menu, or what?

AL: Let's negotiate, here. What's the soup du jour today?

WAITRESS: Soup of the day you got a choice of Polish duck blood or cream of kidney.

AL: Beautiful. Beautiful! Kick me in a kidney.

WAITRESS: *(Writes it down.)* You got it.

AL: Any oyster crackers on your seabed?

WAITRESS: Nope. All out.

AL: How about the specials today, spread out your options.

WAITRESS: You got your deep fried gizzards.

AL: Fabulous.

WAITRESS: Calves' brains with okra.

AL: You are a *temptress.*

WAITRESS: And pickled pigs' feet.

AL: Pigs' feet, *I love it.* Put me down for a quadruped.

WAITRESS: If you say so.

AL: Any sprouts to go on those feet?

WAITRESS: Iceberg.

AL: So be it. *(Waitress exits, as MARK enters, looking shaken and bedraggled.)*

MARK: Al!

AL: Hey there, Marcus. What's up?

MARK: Jesus!

AL: What's going on, buddy?

MARK: Oh man . . .!

AL: What's the matter? Sit down.

MARK: I don't get it, Al. I don't understand it.

AL: You want something? Want a drink? I'll call the waitress—

MARK: *(Desperate.) No!* No! Don't even try. *(Gets a breath.)* I don't know what's going on today, Al. It's really weird.

AL: What, like . . . ?

MARK: Right from the time I got up.

AL: What is it? What's the story?

MARK: Well—just for an example. This morning I stopped off at a drug-store to buy some aspirin. This is at a big drugstore, right?

AL: Yeah . . .

MARK: I go up to the counter, the guy says what can I do for you, I say, Give me a bottle of aspirin. The guy gives me this funny look and he says, "Oh we don't have *that*, sir." I said to him, You're a drugstore and you don't have any aspirin?

AL: Did they have Bufferin?

MARK: Yeah!

AL: Advil?

MARK: Yeah!

AL: Extra-strength Tylenol?

MARK: Yeah!

AL: But no aspirin.

MARK: No!

AL: Wow . . .

MARK: And that's the kind of weird thing that's been happening all day. It's like, I go to a newsstand to buy the *Daily News*, the guy never even *heard* of it.

AL: Could've been a misunderstanding.

MARK: I asked everyplace—*nobody* had the *News!* I had to read the *Toronto Hairdresser*. Or this. I go into a deli at lunch time to buy a sandwich, the guys tells me they don't have any *pastrami*. How can they be a deli if they don't have pastrami?

AL: Was this a Korean deli?

MARK: This was a kosher from *Jerusalem* deli. "Oh we don't carry *that*, sir," he says to me. "Have some tongue."

AL: Mmm.

MARK: I just got into a cab, the guy says he doesn't go to 56th Street! He offers to take me to Newark instead!

AL: Mm-hm.

MARK: Looking at me like I'm an alien or something!

AL: Mark. Settle down.

MARK: "Oh I don't go *there*, sir."

AL: Settle down. Take a breath.

MARK: Do you know what this is?

AL: Sure.

MARK: What is it? What's happening to me?

AL: Don't panic. You're in a Philadelphia.

MARK: I'm in a what?

AL: You're in a Philadelphia. That's all.

MARK: But I'm in—

AL: Yes, physically you are in New York. But *meta*physically you are in a Philadelphia.

MARK: I've never heard of this!

AL: You see, inside of what we know as reality there are these pockets, these black holes called Philadelphias. If you fall into one, you run up against exactly the kinda shit that's been happening to you all day.

MARK: Why?

AL: Because in a Philadelphia, no matter what you ask for, you can't get it. You ask for something, they're not gonna have it. You want to do something, it ain't gonna get done. You want to go somewhere, you can't get there from here.

MARK: Good God. So this is very serious.

AL: Just remember, Marcus. This is a condition named for the town that invented the *cheese steak*. Something that nobody in his right mind would willingly ask for.

MARK: And I thought I was just having a very bad day . . .

AL: Sure. Millions of people have spent entire lifetimes inside a Philadelphia and never even knew it. Look at the city of Philadelphia itself. Hopelessly trapped forever inside a Philadelphia. And do they know it?

MARK: Well what can I do? Should I just kill myself now and get it over with?

AL: You try to kill yourself in a Philadelphia, you're only gonna get hurt, babe.

MARK: So what do I do?

AL: Best thing you can do is wait it out. Someday the great cosmic train will whisk you outa the City of Brotherly Love and off to someplace happier.

MARK: *You're* pretty goddamn mellow today.

AL: Yeah well. Everybody has to be someplace. (*WAITRESS enters.*)

WAITRESS: Is your name Allen Chase?

AL: It is indeed.

WAITRESS: There was a phone call for you. Your boss?

AL: Okay.

WAITRESS: He says you're fired.

AL: Cool! Thanks. (*WAITRESS exits.*) So anyway, you have this problem . . .

MARK: Did she just say you got *fired?*

AL: Yeah. I wonder what happened to my pigs' feet . . .

MARK: Al—!? You *loved* your job!

AL: Hey. No sweat.

MARK: How can you be so calm?

AL: Easy. You're in a Philadelphia? *I* woke up in a Los Angeles. And life is beautiful! You know Susie packed up and left me this morning.

MARK: Susie left you?

AL: And frankly, Scarlett, I don't give a shit. I say, go and God bless and may your dating pool be Olympic-sized.

MARK: But your job? The garment district is your life!

AL: So I'll turn it into a movie script and sell it to Paramount. Toss in some sex, add a little emotional blah-blah-*blah*, pitch it to Jack and Dusty, you got a buddy movie with a garment background. Not relevant enough? We'll throw in the hole in the ozone, make it E.C.

MARK: E.C.?

AL: Environmentally correct. Have you heard about this hole in the ozone?

MARK: Sure.

AL: Marcus, I *love* this concept. I *embrace* this ozone. Sure, some people are gonna get hurt in the process, meantime everybody else'll tan a little faster.

MARK: (*Quiet horror.*) So this is a Los Angeles . . .

AL: Well. Everybody has to be someplace.

MARK: Wow.

AL: You want my advice? *Enjoy your Philadelphia.* Sit back and order yourself a beer and a burger and chill out for a while.

MARK: But I can't order anything. Life is great for you out there on your cosmic beach, but whatever *I* ask for, I'll get a cheese steak or something.

AL: No. There's a very simple rule of thumb in a Philadelphia. *Ask for the opposite.*

MARK: What?

AL: If you can't get what you ask for, ask for the opposite and you'll get what you want. You want the *Daily News,* ask for the *Times.* You want pastrami, ask for tongue.

MARK: Oh.

AL: Works great with women. What is more opposite than the opposite sex?

MARK: Uh-huh.

AL: So. Would you like a Bud?

MARK: I sure could use a—

AL: No. Stop. (*Very deliberately.*) Do you want . . . a Bud?

MARK: (*Also deliberately.*) No. I *don't* want a Bud. (*WAITRESS enters and goes to the specials board.*)

AL: Good. Now there's the waitress. Order Yourself a Bud and a burger. But do not *ask* for a Bud and a burger.

MARK: Waitress!

AL: Don't call her. She won't come.

MARK: Oh.

AL: You're in a Philadelphia, so just figure, fuck her.

MARK: Fuck *her*.

AL: You don't need that waitress.

MARK: *Fuck* that waitress.

AL: And everything to do with her.

MARK: *Hey waitress! FUCK YOU!* (*WAITRESS turns to him.*)

WAITRESS: Can I help you, sir?

AL: *That's* how you get service in a Philadelphia.

WAITRESS: Can I help you?

MARK: Uh—no thanks.

WAITRESS: Okay, what'll you have? (*Takes out her pad.*)

AL: Excellent.

MARK: Well—how about some O.J.

WAITRESS: Sorry. Squeezer's broken.

MARK: A glass of milk?

WAITRESS: Cow's dry.

MARK: Egg nog?

WAITRESS: Just ran out.

MARK: Cuppa coffee?

WAITRESS: Oh we don't have *that*, sir. (*MARK and AL exchange a look, and nod. The WAITRESS has spoken the magic words.*)

MARK: Got any ale?

WAITRESS: Nope.

MARK: Stout?

WAITRESS: Nope.

MARK: Porter?

WAITRESS: Just beer.

MARK: That's too bad. How about a Heineken?

WAITRESS: Heineken? Try again.

MARK: Rolling Rock?

WAITRESS: 'Outa stock.

MARK: Schlitz?

WAITRESS: Nix.

MARK: Beck's?

WAITRESS: Next.

MARK: Sapporo?

WAITRESS: Tomorrow.

MARK: Lone Star?

WAITRESS: Hardy-har.

MARK: Bud Lite?

WAITRESS: Just plain Bud is all we got.

MARK: No thanks.

WAITRESS: (*Calls.*) *Gimme a Bud!* (*To MARK.*) Anything to eat?

MARK: Nope.

WAITRESS: Name it.

MARK: Pork chops.

WAITRESS: (*Writes down.*) Hamburger . . .

MARK: Medium.

WAITRESS: Well done . . .

MARK: Baked potato.

WAITRESS: Fries . . .

MARK: And some zucchini.

WAITRESS: Slice of raw. (*Exits, calling.*) Burn one!

AL: Marcus, that was excellent.

MARK: Thank you.

AL: *Excellent.* You sure you've never done this before?

MARK: I've spent so much of my life asking for the wrong thing without
      knowing it, doing it on purpose comes easy.

AL: I hear you.

MARK: I could've saved myself a lot of trouble if I'd screwed up on purpose
      all those years. Maybe I was in a Philadelphia all along and never
      knew it!

AL: You might've been in a Baltimore. They're practically the same.
      (*WAITRESS enters, with a glass of beer and a plate.*)

WAITRESS: Okay. Here's your Bud. (*Sets that in front of MARK.*) And one
      cheese steak. (*She sets that in front of AL, and starts to go.*)

AL: Excuse me. Hey. Wait a minute. What is that?

WAITRESS: It's cheese steak.

AL: No. I ordered cream of kidney and two pairs of feet.

WAITRESS: Oh we don't have *that*, sir.

AL: I beg your pardon?

WAITRESS: We don't have that, sir. (*Small pause.*)

AL: (*To MARK.*) You son of a bitch! *I'm in your Philadelphia!*

MARK: I'm sorry, Al.

AL: You brought me into your fucking Philadelphia!

MARK: I didn't know it was contagious.

AL: Oh God, please don't let me be in a Philadelphia! Don't let me in a—

MARK: Shouldn't you ask for the opposite? I mean, since you're in a
      Philad—

AL: Don't you tell *me* about life in a Philadelphia.

MARK: Maybe you're not really—

AL: I taught you everything you know about Philly, asshole. Don't tell *me* how to act in a Philadelphia!

MARK: But maybe you're not really in a Philadelphia!

AL: Do you see the cheese on that steak? What do I need for proof? The fucking *Liberty Bell?* Waitress, bring me a glass of water.

WAITRESS: Water? Don't have that, sir.

Al: (*To MARK.*) "We don't have *water*"—? What, you think we're in a sudden drought or something? (*Suddenly realizes.*) Holy shit, I just lost my job . . . ! Susie left me! I gotta make some phone calls! (*To WAITRESS.*) 'Scuse me, where's the pay phone?

WAITRESS: Sorry, we don't have a pay ph—

AL: Of *course* you don't have a pay phone, of *course* you don't! Oh shit, let me outa here! (*Exits.*)

MARK: I don't know. It's not that bad in a Philadelphia.

WAITRESS: Could be worse. I've been in a Cleveland all week.

MARK: A Cleveland. What's that like?

WAITRESS: It's like death, without the advantages.

MARK: Really. Care to stand?

WAITRESS: Don't mind if I do. (*She sits.*)

MARK: I hope you won't reveal your name.

WAITRESS: Sharon.

MARK: (*Holds out his hand.*) Good-bye.

WAITRESS: Hello. (*They shake.*)

MARK: (*Indicating the cheese steak.*) Want to starve?

WAITRESS: Thanks! (*She picks up the cheese steak and starts eating.*)

MARK: Yeah, everybody has to be someplace . . . (*Leans across the table with a smile.*) So.

Blackout

TRY THIS 4.12
The Greek and Roman method of comedy was to take an absurd idea and follow it very logically, very precisely, and straight-faced to its conclusion. If you have a good, really absurd idea, write a ten-minute comedy. (This is a good place to brainstorm *what if. . .?*)

TRY THIS 4.13
Write a stage direction, using no more than five elements—backdrop, structure, pieces of furniture, objects?—to set the scene onstage. See how much you can tell us with these five things about the place and time and the characters who are likely to enter here.

Or:

Set a short scene in a place as banal or characterless as you can think of. Make the dialogue bizarre.

WORKING TOWARD A DRAFT
From among the things you have written, find a piece in which you feel you have inadequately set the scene. Rewrite it incorporating elements of place, time, and weather. How can you use these elements to make the piece not merely longer and not merely clearer, but more intense and meaningful?

Or:

Take something you have written and rewrite it, setting it in some altogether different space. If it took place in private, set it in public; if in the past, set it in the future; if on a playground, set it in a cemetery, and so forth. Does this displacement offer possibilities for enriching the piece?

Helen Levitt, "From Crosstown"

CHAPTER FIVE

STORY

As a Journey
As a Power Struggle
As Connection and Disconnection

Act I, get your guy up a tree. Act II, throw rocks at him.
Act III, get your guy outta the tree.

Julius Epstein

Story as a Journey

The late great novelist and teacher John Gardner used to say that there are only two stories: *someone went on a journey* and *a stranger came to town.*

I once ran into a poet at the Yaddo writers' colony who reduced the formula still further: "You fiction writers," he said. "Everything you write is the same: two worlds collide; a love story."

The novelist Chaim Potok used to say that the only a subject he wanted to write about was a clash between cultures, the Insider encountering The Other.

These are all ways of expressing the fundamental form of a story. When worlds (cultures, generations, genders, 'hoods) encounter each other, conflict will inevitably occur (in a thousand different guises). When conflict occurs, human beings will band together in some form of love. Sometimes allies, families, races, gangs, nations, will draw closer together to repel a common antagonist. Sometimes connection will be made across the divide of *self* and *other.*

In Chapter 3, I said that a dynamic character is someone capable of change. The encounter or collision of one character with others will force such change, and the story is the process of that change. The altered state may be from alive to dead, from ugly to beautiful, from ignorant to wise, callous to compassionate, from certain to uncertain or vice versa. But the change occurs because the character confronts a situation that will challenge her/his assumptions and somehow shake up the easy beliefs—hence the prevalence, in such a formulation, of strangers, journeys, and worlds. I like the metaphor of the two worlds, too, because it suggests both the importance of setting and the necessity of discovery and decision. The new world that the character discovers may be the house next door, it may be a different set of assumptions or the next stage of life (puberty is a foreign country, marriage is an undiscovered planet)—but the story will always end in an altered state in at least the character whose point of view we share. Usually the character will have his or her scope enlarged—but not always. Usually the story will result in greater wisdom, compassion, or understanding—though it can end in diminishment or narrowing. As *readers*, however, we will *always*, if the story succeeds, have our capacity for empathy enlarged by having lived in the character's skin for the duration. Every story is in this important human sense a "love story."

A story is a journey is only one of many useful metaphors for the shape of a story, but it is the one almost always used by actors and directors when they set out to produce a play. Where does the protagonist want to go (what does she/he desire)? What are the obstacles encountered (what discoveries are made, what conflicts arise)? What does she/he do to overcome these obstacles (what decisions are made)? Is the goal reached? Is it as expected? Sometimes the journey of the story ends in fulfillment, sometimes not; sometimes the goal is reached and proves not worth the trip; sometimes a detour leads to paradise.

Here is a **short-short story** (only 101 words) about a long journey. Written in the diction of a five-year-old, it manages to give a panorama in space and time, as well as details that particularize both the setting and the characters. What change takes place in the character? How does the single line of dialogue at the end show this change?

I've never been this far from home. I've never stayed up this late. I'm out west.

We rode the train. I slept upstairs. You put your clothes in a hammock. They have Dixie cups.

The world has mountains on the edge, where the sun sets, big black things, and that's where we're going.

I'm in the front seat with my mother. I'm five. We're going to a dude ranch. There will be cowboys.

There's a soft green glow on the dash board. My mother wears perfume.

I'm traveling. I've never been this old.

"The stars are ablaze," I tell my mother.

"Frontiers," John M. Daniel

TRY THIS 5.1
Write a brief memoir or short-short story about a journey. Give us the setting and
at least two characters. They discover something that causes trouble. Let the main
character make a decision and take an action.

Or:

Write about a time that you started out on a trip but failed to arrive at your destination. What was the obstacle—weather, accident, mechanical failure, human failure,
human conflict? Characterize both the people involved and the setting through significant detail; give us a sense of the trip itself. What changed from the beginning
expectations? How did you change?

Story as a Power Struggle

Another, perhaps the most common, way of looking at story structure is in terms
of **conflict, crisis,** and **resolution,** a shape that comes from Aristotle's insistence
on *a beginning, a middle,* and *an end.*

This model acknowledges that, in literature, only trouble is interesting. *Only*
trouble is interesting. This is not so in life. Life offers periods of comfortable communication, peaceful pleasure, and productive work, all of which are extremely
interesting to those involved. But passages about such times make for dull reading;
they cannot be used as a plot.

Suppose, for example, you go on a picnic. You find a beautiful deserted
meadow with a lake nearby. The weather is splendid and so is the company.
The food's delicious, the water's fine, and the insects have taken the day off.
Afterward, someone asks you how your picnic was. "Terrific," you reply, "really
perfect." No story.

But suppose the next week you go back for a rerun. You set your picnic
blanket on an anthill. You all race for the lake to get cold water on the bites,
and one of your friends goes too far out on the plastic raft, which deflates. He
can't swim and you have to save him. On the way in you gash your foot on a broken bottle. When you get back to the picnic, the ants have taken over the cake
and a possum has demolished the chicken. Just then the sky opens up. When you
gather your things to race for the car, you notice a bull has broken through the
fence. The others run for it, but because of your bleeding heel the best you can
do is hobble. You have two choices: try to outrun him or stand perfectly still
and hope he's interested only in a moving target. At this point, you don't know
if your friends can be counted on for help, even the nerd whose life you saved.
You don't know if it's true that a bull is attracted by the smell of blood.

A year later, assuming you're around to tell about it, you are still saying, "Let me *tell* you what happened last year." And your listeners are saying, "What a story!"

This pattern of trouble and the effort to overcome it is repeated in every story on a larger or smaller scale. It may seem, for example, that the five-year-old in the short-short above is not in much trouble. But look at the huge dangers he faces: *never been this far from home, never up this late; mountains on the edge, big black things where we're going.* The clear and intense desire to get to the dude ranch is countered by the awesome strangeness of the adventure. Two worlds collide, in fact.

In the conflict-crisis-resolution model, story is seen as a power struggle between two nearly equal forces, a **protagonist** or central character and an **antagonist,** who represents the obstacles to the protagonist's desires and may be another human being or some other force—God, nature, the self, and so forth. If the antagonist is some abstract force, then, like the character's desire, it will also have a very specific manifestation: not "nature" but "seven miles of white water rapids on the lower Colorado"; not "the supernatural" but "a mutant reptile embryo capable of hatching in a human middle ear."

It is crucial that the opposing forces have approximately equal force, so that our uncertainty about the outcome keeps us reading. We begin with a situation in which the power is with the protagonist or the antagonist. Something happens, and the power shifts to the other. Something else, and it shifts back again. Each time the power shifts, the stakes are raised, each battle is bigger, more intense than the last, until (at the crisis moment), one of the two opposing forces manifests its power in a way that the other cannot match.

Here is another short-short story (a lavish 232 words this time), also in a child's voice, in which the conflict-crisis-resolution pattern is intense.

Watching Joey pop the red berries into his mouth like Ju-Ju Bees and Mags only licking them at first, then chewing, so both of their smiles look bloody and I laugh though I don't eat even one . . . then suddenly our moms are all around us (although mine doesn't panic till she looks at the others, then screams along with them things like *God dammit did you eat these?* and shakes me so my "No" sounds like "oh-oh-oh") and then we're being yanked toward the house, me for once not resisting as my mother scoops me into her arms, and inside the moms shove medicine, thick and purple, down our throats in the bathroom; Joey in the toilet, Mags in the sink, me staring at the hair in the tub drain as my mom pushes my head down, and there is red vomit everywhere, splashing on the mirror and powder-blue rugs, everywhere except the tub where mine is coming out yellow, the color of corn muffins from lunch, not a speck of red, *I told you,* I want to scream, and then it is over and I turn to my mother for a touch or a stroke on the head like the other moms (but she has moved to the doorway and lights a cigarette, pushes hair out of her eyes) and there is only her smeared lips saying, *This will teach you anyway.*

"*This Is How I Remember It,*" Betsy Kemper

In this classical pattern, the story begins with an **exposition,** or statement of the situation at the beginning of the action, which is typically, as here, a state of unstable equilibrium (*I laugh, though I don't eat even one . . .*). **Conflict** arrives with the mothers, and that conflict undergoes a series of **complications** involving force, blame, mistake, submission, anger, and so forth. The power struggle between mother and daughter escalates through a change of setting. Details build the contrast between the kinds of *mom* and the kinds of vomit. The **crisis action** occurs as a moment of martyred triumph for the narrator (*I told you*) and then there is a **falling action** or **denouement** in which the mother and daughter retreat to their respective corners and settle back into what (we know by now) is their habit of being. This is the **resolution.** Some questions to consider: Why did the author choose to tell this story in a single sentence? What does the narrator want? Who wins? Is it worth it?

This very short story is very much of the twentieth century, in that the crisis occurs in the mind of the narrator and the "resolution" does not offer a "solution." The completion of the action has changed the characters not by a dramatic reversal, but by moving them deeper into their *impasse.*

Order is a major value that literature offers us, and order implies that the subject has been brought to closure. In life this never quite happens. Even the natural "happy endings," marriage and birth, leave domesticity and child-rearing to be dealt with; the natural "tragic endings," separation and death, leave trauma and bereavement in their wake. Literature absolves us of these nuisances. Whether or not the lives of the characters end, the story does, and we are left with a satisfying sense of completion. This is one reason we enjoy crying or feeling terrified or even nauseated by fiction; we know in advance that it's going to be over, and by contrast with the continual struggle of living, all that ends, ends well.

TRY THIS 5.2

Write a short story on a postcard. (Write small.) Make sure it has a conflict, a crisis, and a resolution. Send it to a friend in another place (meaning you have published it), or to yourself (when it arrives you will be able to see it fresh).

Or:

A story, a memoir, or a play: Place two characters in a dangerous setting. Each has half of something that is no good without the other half. Neither wants to give up his/her half. What happens?

Connection is human substance, the substance of story. Its
gain and loss provides the emotional power.

Claudia Johnson

Story as Connection and Disconnection

Every story presents some sort of journey, literal or psychological or both, that results in a change in the central character. Every story shows a pattern of conflict between approximately equal forces, which leads to a crisis and a resolution. Every story also offers a pattern of connection and disconnection between human beings, which is the source of meaning and significance in the story. Conflict is exciting; it keeps the reader wondering what will happen next. But conflict itself is sterile unless it is given human dimension through the connections and disconnections of the characters.

Therefore, boy meets girl, boy loses girl, boy gets girl (connection, disconnection, connection). Therefore Hamlet's father dies (disconnects), but comes back (connects) as a ghost, Hamlet rages against his mother (disconnects), welcomes his school friends (connects), breaks off with Ophelia (disconnects), kills her father (disconnects), betrays his school friends (disconnects), kills his stepfather (disconnects) and, in the arms (connects) of his best friend, dies (disconnects). It will be evident that a story that ends in disconnection, especially death, tends toward tragedy, and one that ends in connection, traditionally marriage, is a comedy. Examine any story that makes you care, and you will see that people *who matter to each other* perform, as in life, patterns of love and hate, alienation and community, anger and forgiveness, connection and disconnection. As Claudia Johnson puts it, "The conflict and surface events are like waves, but underneath is an emotional tide—the ebb and flow of human connection."

Even in the very short compass of the two short-short stories above, these patterns occur. In "Frontiers," the boy is frighteningly separated from home, but his mother is there with him, to take him to the glamorous and grown-up connection with *cowboys*. In "This Is How I Remember It," the girl is connected to her friends, but not so close that she will dare the bloodred berries; the moms arrive to connect, each with her own child; but the heroine deeply disconnects from her punitive and unjust mother.

TRY THIS 5.3

Write down a memory of a time you seriously disconnected from someone close to you. Know that the person will never read it.

Or:

Write a poem about a death, a breakup, a divorce, a house moving, a quarrel. Find some small positive aspect of the disconnection.

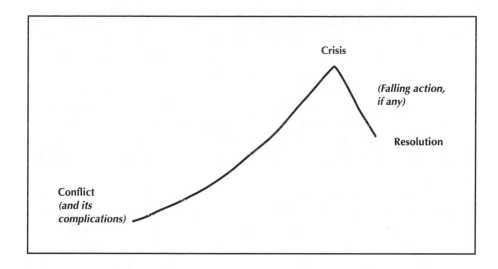

It is useful to think of story shape as an inverted check mark, rising from left to right and ending in a short downswing. The story begins with an *exposition* of the opening situation, develops a conflict through a series of complications in which the power changes back and forth, and culminates in a crisis. Then there is a brief walking-away (falling action or denouement), leading to resolution.

If we take the familiar tale of Cinderella, we can see how even this simple children's story relates to each of the models—as journey, as power struggle, and as pattern of connection/disconnection.

At the opening of the tale we're given the basic conflict: Cinderella's mother has died, and her father has married a brutal woman with two waspish daughters. Cinderella is made to do all the dirtiest and most menial work, and she weeps among the cinders. Cinderella's desire is to be treated equally, or treated well. Her journey is on the literal level from the hearth to the palace, and on the mythic level from slave to Princess. Along the way she encounters the obstacles of powerlessness, evil, short-lived magic, and chance. With the aid of goodness, beauty, magic, and chance, she also reaches her goal.

Next consider the story in relation to the "check mark" diagram in terms of the power struggle. The Stepmother has on her side the strength of ugliness and evil (two very powerful qualities in literature as in life). With her daughters she also has the strength of numbers, and she has parental authority. Cinderella has only beauty and goodness, but (in literature and life) these are also very powerful.

At the beginning of the struggle in "Cinderella," the power is very clearly on the Stepmother's side. But the first event of the story is that an invitation arrives from the Prince, which explicitly states that *all* the ladies of the land are invited to a ball. Notice that Cinderella's desire is not to triumph over her Stepmother (though she eventually will, much to our satisfaction); such a desire would diminish her goodness. She simply wants to be relieved of her mistreatment. She wants equality, so that the Prince's invitation, which specifically gives her a right equal to the Stepmother's and Stepsisters' rights, shifts the power to her.

The Stepmother takes the power back by blunt force: You may not go; you must get us ready to go. Cinderella does so, and the three leave for the ball.

Then what happens? The Fairy Godmother appears. It is very powerful to have magic on your side. The Fairy Godmother offers Cinderella a gown, glass slippers, and a coach with horses and footmen, giving her more force than she has yet had.

But the magic is not all-potent. It has a qualification that portends bad luck. It will last only until midnight (unlike the Stepmother's authority), and Cinderella must leave the ball before the clock strikes twelve or risk exposure and defeat.

What happens next? She goes to the ball and the Prince falls in love with her—and love is an even more powerful weapon than magic in a literary war. In some versions of the tale, the Stepmother and Stepsisters are made to marvel at the beauty of the princess they don't recognize, pointing to the irony of Cinderella's new power.

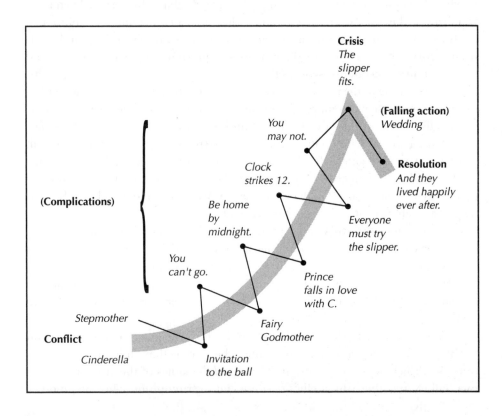

And then? The magic quits. The clock strikes twelve, and Cinderella runs down the steps in her rags to her rats and pumpkin, losing a slipper, bereft of her power in every way.

But after that, the Prince sends out a messenger with the glass slipper and a dictum (a dramatic repetition of the original invitation in which all ladies were invited to the ball) that every female in the land is to try on the slipper. Cinderella is given her rights again by royal decree.

What happens then? In most good retellings of the tale, the Stepmother also repeats her assumption of brute authority by hiding Cinderella away, while our expectation of triumph is tantalizingly delayed with grotesque comedy: one sister cuts off a toe, the other a heel, trying to fit into the heroine's rightful slipper.

After that, Cinderella tries on the slipper and it fits. *This is the crisis action.* Magic, love, and royalty join to recognize the heroine's true self; evil, numbers, and authority are powerless against them. At this point, the power struggle has been decided; the outcome is inevitable. When the slipper fits, no further action can occur that will deprive Cinderella of her desire. The change in the lives of all concerned is significant and permanent.

In many of the finest modern short stories and novels, the true territory of struggle is the main character's mind, and so the real crisis action must occur there. Yet it is important to grasp that any mental reversal that takes place in the crisis of a story must be triggered or shown by an action. The slipper must fit. It would not do if the Stepmother just happened to change her mind and give up the struggle; it would not do if the Prince just happened to notice that Cinderella looked like his love. The moment of recognition must be manifested in an action.

The *crisis*, also referred to as the *turning point* or *climax* of a story, is often the most difficult for beginning writers to identify and to produce. It is likely to be the moment of greatest emotional intensity in the story, and it is by definition the point at which the change in the protagonist is decisive and inevitable. In Charles Baxter's "Snow" in the readings of Chapter 8, for example, the crisis occurs when Stephanie—alarmingly—turns to the narrator for advice and takes off her shoes in a failed attempt to "interest" his brother. (This story can in fact be read as an anti-Cinderella story, in which the shoes come off instead of on and the romantic connection fails to occur.) In "Red Sky in the Morning," a memoir that tells a story in the Readings section of this chapter, the crisis moment occurs quite early, as an "indelible bittersweetness," on which the rest of the essay reflects. In the story "Missing," also in this chapter, the narrator explains his past to the villagers in their own terms, and a potential disconnection is averted.

In "Cinderella," after the crisis of the fitting slipper, the tale has a brief falling action: the Prince sweeps Cinderella up on his white horse and gallops away to their wedding. The story comes to closure with the classic resolution of all comedy: They lived happily ever after. (In "Snow," on the other hand, the resolution occurs in our point-of-view character, who comes to know "what it feels like . . . in a few years.")

If we look at "Cinderella" in terms of connection/disconnection we see a pattern as clear as that represented by the power struggle. The first painful disconnection is that Cinderella's mother has died; her father has married (connected with) a woman who spurns (disconnects from) her; the Prince's invitation offers connection, the Stepmother's cruelty alienates again. The Fairy Godmother connects as a magical friend, but the disappearance of the coach and gown disconnect Cinderella temporarily from that grand and glorious fairy tale union, marriage to the Prince. If we consult the emotions that this tale engenders—pity, anger, hope, fear, romance, anticipation, disappointment, triumph—we see that both the struggle between antagonist/protagonist and the pattern of alienation/connectedness is necessary to ensure, not only that there is an action, but also that we care about its outcome.

Forms of imaginative writing are not mutually exclusive. Often a memoir is dramatic, dialogue can be lyrical, narrative turns to poetry. Above all, many essays, poems, and plays have the fundamental form of story. This form—in its incarnations as journey, conflict-crisis-resolution, and connection/disconnection—is so prevalent in human culture that scarcely any communication is free of it. The most casual conversation includes anecdotes of destination and detour. The company report boasts of obstacles overcome. The trip to school shapes up as power struggle between protagonist child and antagonist mom, resolved with a connecting hug or a parting blast. Awareness of these shapes can inform any genre of writing and help to bridge the gap between mind and mind, helping to achieve the first desire of any writer: connection with that intimate stranger, the reader.

TRY THIS 5.4

Write a memory that tells a story.

Or:

Write a dialogue that is a poem.

More to Read

Burroway, Janet. *Writing Fiction: A Guide to Narrative Craft.* New York: Longman, 2006.

Forster, E. M. *Aspects of the Novel.* New York: Harcourt Brace Jovanovich, 1972.

Readings

Patricia Hampl
Red Sky in the Morning

Years ago, in another life, I woke to look out the smeared window of a Grey-hound bus I had been riding all night, and in the still-dark morning of a small Missouri river town where the driver had made a scheduled stop at a grimy diner, I saw below me a stout middle-aged woman in a flowered housedress turn and kiss full on the mouth a godlike young man with golden curls. But I've got that wrong: *he* was kissing *her*. Passionately, without regard for the world and its incomprehension. He had abandoned himself to his love, and she, stolid, matronly, received this adoration with simple grandeur, like a socialist-realist statue of a woman taking up sheaves of wheat.

Their ages dictated that he must be her son, but I had just come out of the cramped, ruinous half sleep of a night on a Greyhound and I was clairvoyant: This was that thing called love. The morning light cracked bloodred along the river.

Of course, when she lumbered onto the bus a moment later, lurching forward with her two bulging bags, she chose the empty aisle seat next to me as her own. She pitched one bag onto the overhead rack, and then heaved herself into the seat as if she were used to hoisting sacks of potatoes onto the flatbed of a pickup. She held the other bag on her lap, and leaned toward the window. The beautiful boy was blowing kisses. He couldn't see where she was in the dark interior, so he blew kisses up and down the side of the bus, gazing ardently at the blank windows. "Pardon me," the woman said without looking at me, and leaned over, bag and all, to rap the glass. Her beautiful boy ran back to our window and kissed and kissed, and finally hugged himself, shutting his eyes in an ecstatic pantomime of love-sweet-love. She smiled and waved back.

Then the bus was moving. She slumped back in her seat, and I turned to her. I suppose I looked transfixed. As our eyes met she said, "Everybody thinks he's my son. But he's not. He's my husband." She let that sink in. She was a farm woman with hands that could have been a man's; I was a uni-versity student, hair down to my waist. It was long ago, as I said, in another life. It was even another life for the country. The Vietnam War was the time we were living through, and I was traveling, as I did every three weeks, to visit my boyfriend who was in a federal prison. "Draft dodger," my brother said. "Draft resister," I piously retorted. I had never been kissed the way this woman had been kissed. I was living in a tattered corner of a romantic idyll, the one where the hero is willing to suffer for his beliefs. I was the girlfriend. I lived on pride, not love.

My neighbor patted her short cap of hair, and settled in for the long haul as we pulled onto the highway along the river, heading south. "We been married five years and we're happy," she said with a penetrating satisfaction, the satisfaction that passeth understanding. "Oh," she let out a profound sigh as if she mined her truths from the bountiful, bulky earth, "Oh, I could tell you stories." She put her arms snugly around her bag, gazed for a moment, apparently made pensive by her remark. Then she closed her eyes and fell asleep.

I looked out the window smudged by my nose which had been pressed against it at the bus stop to see the face of true love reveal itself. Beyond the bus the sky, instead of becoming paler with the dawn, drew itself out of a black line along the Mississippi into an alarming red flare. It was very beautiful. The old caution—*Red sky in the morning, sailor take warning*—darted through my mind and fell away. Remember this, I remember telling myself, hang on to this. I could feel it all skittering away, whatever conjunction of beauty and improbability I had stumbled upon.

It is hard to describe the indelible bittersweetness of that moment. Which is why, no doubt, it had to be remembered. The very word—*Remember!*—spiraled up like a snake out of a basket, a magic catch in its sound, the doubling of the m—*re memmemem*—setting up a low murmur full of inchoate associations as if a loved voice were speaking into my ear alone, occultly.

Whether it was the unguarded face of love, or the red gash down the middle of the warring country I was traveling through, or this exhausted farm woman's promise of untold tales that bewitched me, I couldn't say. Over it all rose and remains only the injunction to remember. This, the most impossible command we lay upon ourselves, claimed me and then perversely disappeared, trailing an illusive silken tissue of meaning, without giving a story, refusing to leave me in peace.

Because everyone "has" a memoir, we all have a stake in how such stories are told. For we do not, after all, simply *have* experience; we are entrusted with it. We must do something—make something—with it. A story, we sense, is the only possible habitation for the burden of our witnessing.

The tantalizing formula of my companion on the Greyhound—*oh, I could tell you stories*—is the memoirist's opening line, but it has none of the delicious promise of the storyteller's "Once upon a time . . ." In fact, it is a perverse statement. The woman on the bus told me nothing—she fell asleep and escaped to her dreams. For the little sentence inaugurates nothing, and leads nowhere after its *dot dot dot* of expectation. Whatever experience lies tangled within its seductive promise remains forever balled up in the woolly impossibility of telling the-truth-the-whole-truth of life, any life.

Memoirists, unlike fiction writers, do not really want to "tell a story." They want to tell it *all*—the all of personal experience, of consciousness itself. That includes a story, but also the whole expanding universe of sensation and thought that flows beyond the confines of narrative and proves every life to be not only an isolated story line but a bit of the cosmos, spinning and streaming into the great, ungraspable pattern of existence. Memoirists wish to tell their mind, not their story.

The wistfulness implicit in that conditional verb—*I could tell*—conveys an urge more primitive than a storyteller's search for an audience. It betrays not a loneliness for someone who will listen but a hopelessness about language itself and a sad recognition of its limitations. How much reality can subject-verb-object bear on the frail shoulders of the sentence? The sigh within the statement is more like this: I could tell you stories—if only stories could tell what I have in me to tell.

For this reason, autobiographical writing is bedeviled. It is caught in a self which must become a world—and not, please, a narcissistic world. The memoir, once considered a marginal literary form, has emerged in the past decade as the signature genre of the age. "The triumph of memoir is now established fact," James Atlas trumpeted in a cover story on "The Age of the Literary Memoir" in the *New York Times Magazine*. "Fiction," he claimed, "isn't delivering the news. Memoir is."

With its "triumph," the memoir has, of course, not denied the truth and necessity of fiction. In fact, it leans heavily on novelistic assumptions. But the contemporary memoir has reaffirmed the primacy of the first person voice in American imaginative writing established by Whitman's "Song of Myself." Maybe a reader's love of memoir is less an intrusive lust for confession than a hankering for the intimacy of this first-person voice, the deeply satisfying sense of being spoken to privately. More than a story, we want a voice speaking softly, urgently, in our ear. Which is to say, to our heart. The voice carries its implacable command, the ancient murmur that called out to me in the middle of the country in the middle of a war—remember, remember (*I dare you, I tempt you*).

Looking out the Greyhound window that red morning all those years ago, I saw the improbable face of love. But even more puzzling was the cryptic remark of the beloved as she sat next to me. I think of her more often than makes sense. Though he was the beauty, she was the one who comes back. How faint his golden curls have become (he also had a smile, crooked and charming, but I can only remember the idea of it—the image is gone). It is she, stout and unbeautiful, wearing her flowery cotton housedress with a zipper down the middle, who has taken up residence with her canny eye and her acceptance of adoration. To be loved like that, loved improbably: of course, she had stories to tell. She took it for granted in some unapologetic way, like being born to wealth. Take the money and run.

But that moment before she fell asleep, when she looked pensive, the red morning rising over the Mississippi, was a wistful moment. *I could tell you stories*—but she could not. What she had to tell was too big, too much, too *something*, for her to place in the small shrine that a story is.

When we met—if what happened between us was a meeting—I felt nothing had ever happened to me and nothing ever would. I didn't understand that riding this filthy Greyhound down the middle of bloodied America in the middle of a mutinous war was itself a story and that something *was* happening to me. I thought if something was happening to anybody around me it was happening to people like my boyfriend: They were the heroes, according to the lights that shined for me then. I was just riding shotgun in my own life. I could not have imagined containing, as the farm woman slumped next to me did, the sheer narrative bulk to say, "I could tell you stories," and then drifting off with the secret heaviness of experience into the silence where stories live their real lives, crumbling into the loss we call remembrance.

The boastful little declaration, pathetically conditional (not "I'll tell you a story" but "I could") wavered wistfully for an instant between us. The stranger's remark, launched in the dark of the Greyhound, floated across the human landscape like the lingering tone of a struck bell from a village church, and joined all the silence that ever was, as I turned my face to the window where the world was rushing by along the slow river.

FICTION

Robert Olen Butler
Missing

It was me you saw in that photo across a sugarcane field. I was smoking by the edge of the jungle and some French journalist, I think it was, took that photo with a long lens, and you couldn't even see the cigarette in my hand but you could see my blond hair, even blonder now than when I leaned my rifle against a star apple tree with my unit on up the road in a terrible fight and I put my pack and steel pot beside it and I walked into the trees. My hair got blonder from the sun that even up here in the highlands crouches on us like a mama-san with her feet flat and going nowhere. Though my hair should've gone black, by rights. It should have gone as black as the hair of my wife.

Somebody from the village went into Da Lat and came back with an American newspaper that found its way there from Saigon, probably, brought by some Aussie businessman or maybe even an American GI come back to figure out what it was he left over here in Vietnam. There are lots of them come these days, I'm told, the GIs, and it makes things hard for me, worrying about keeping out of their sight. I've got nothing to do with them, and that's why the photo pissed me off. As soon as I saw it, I knew it was me. I knew the field. I knew my own head of hair. And because you can't see the cigarette; my hand coming down from my face looks like some puny little wave, like I'm saying come help me. And that's the last goddamn thing I want.

I grew the tobacco myself. That's what we do in my village. And up here we grow coffee, too. The first time I saw the girl who would be my wife she was by the side of a road spreading the coffee beans out to dry. Spreading them with her bare feet. And when her family finally let me marry her and we lay down at last in our little house—with wood walls and a wood ceiling in this place in Vietnam where there are hardwood trees and cool nights—she rubbed her hands through my hair, calling it sunlight, and I held her feet in my hands and kissed them and they tasted of coffee.

I'm not missing, I'm here. I know the smell of the wood fires and the incense my wife burns for the dead father and mother who gave her to me and the smell of my daughter's hair washed from the big pot in our backyard to catch the rainwater, and instead, the "USA Today" has got me on the run, waving pitifully across a field at a photographer to put the word out to the world, but they don't wonder why I'm apparently not smart enough to walk on across that field and say, Take me back to my mama and papa and my brothers and my sisters who are living ruined lives in America because I'm missing in action. I don't even have the sense to get close enough to the road so I can be identified, so I'm the lost child of every family in the country with someone whose body was never found.

But I walked away. I just walked away. And there were a thousand of them like me. Two thousand. More, I heard, a lot more. In the back alleys of Saigon, the little villages in the highlands and along the sea, trying to keep out of the way of the killing just like these people who took us in and didn't ask any questions.

Though I could see the questions all come back in the faces of my people when the newspaper showed up. We all went out to see it. It's the way here. The village is small and our elder is Binh and he knew me from the first, he was the first man I saw when I walked in here in 1970 unarmed and bareheaded and I said in the little bit of Vietnamese I had that I was a friend, I wanted to lie down and sleep. He knew what I was doing.

It was yesterday that we sat on mats in front of Tiên's house and she brought us tea and we looked at the paper.

"It's you, I think," Binh said, and he curved his lower lip upward, lifting the little wisp of a Hô' Chí Minh beard, a beard that he wore not from approval of the man but with a kind of irony.

Tri, who had brought the paper, put it before me again now, and the dozen faces around watched me for the final word. I nodded. Thào, my wife, touched my shoulder. She could see it, too. "Yes," I said.

"What does it say about you?" Binh asked.

"Nothing," I said. "They don't know who I am."

Binh nodded and he did it slow enough that I knew he wanted me to say more. I waited, though, looking away beyond the circle, across the dirt street to the tobacco-drying racks, and some kids were there, two of Tiên's boys squatting and looking back at me and Tri's little girl, who stood staring at a dragon head set on a table in the sun. Tiên had been working on the head, repainting the green and red ridges in its face, getting it ready for T'êt, the new year. When I looked away from Binh, I thought my daughter, Hoa, might be there, but she wasn't. And I didn't want to cast my gaze farther with Binh waiting for me to say more.

But I'd waited a little too long already. Binh asked, "Does it speak of some other man?"

"Not one particular man. No. It says some people in America have seen the photo and think it's proof that Americans are still alive over here, men being held by the communists."

"MIA," Binh said, pronouncing each letter with a flat American inflection that he'd picked up from me long ago.

"Yes," I said.

At this, Binh turned his face, in respect, away from Quang who sat next to him. Quang was almost as old as Binh, clean-shaven, with skin the color of this dirt street moments after a rain. But I glanced at him briefly, and there were others from our little circle who did, too. He was holding the newspaper spread tight in his two hands as if trying to stretch any wrinkles out of it. He was looking at my image there, and I think his mind now was on his own lost son. Most of the people of a certain age in my village have dead children from the war. But Quang's boy is missing, still, after more than twenty years, and he worries about where the body might be, the spirit lost and hovering around it waiting for rites that would never come.

My village believes in spirits. Last night we all burned incense in our kitchens for the god of the hearth. Such a god lives in each of our houses, and seven days before T'êt he goes up to heaven to report on the family. A family is very important in Vietnam. We work and we care for each other and we live under one roof and there is no ending for such a thing. My wife's mother and father slept on straw mats in our house until the day that each of them died. I will sleep on a straw mat in the house of my daughter until I die. That is my wish.

Perhaps that's why I'm so frightened now to see this image of myself in an American newspaper. Why I looked again across to where the children were, more of them now, gathering to watch us and wonder, and I looked for my daughter and I wanted to see her in that moment, a brief glance even. We are meant to protect our families in all their linked parts like we protect our bodies. And the god of the hearth takes special note in his report of how careful we are about that. And how we respect the spirits, the spirits of our family gone to the afterlife before us and the spirits of all the others in the air around us. And we must respect the gods, as well. The minds and wills that animate the universe. Look where they have brought me.

And Hoa appeared. My daughter is tall now, her body changing from a girl to a woman, and her hair is the brown of the dried tobacco, not black but the color of what we grow and prepare here, and I don't know why I was caught by her hair at that moment but it is long and it has this color that belongs to no one else here, not my wife, not me. And she stepped behind Tri's daughter and she looked to me, briefly, and then at the little girl staring at the dragon.

Binh still had something on his mind. "Do you think some people in America will look at this picture and remember?"

"There will be many who do that," I said, and my eyes moved to Quang, and I was thinking of the grief he was drawing from the paper in his hands even then, and Binh knew what I was saying. But I also understood him. He meant: Do you have other people in that past life of yours who will recognize this son or husband or brother of theirs and suffer from this?

I felt my wife stir beside me. She heard this beneath Binh's words as well, and grew angry at him, I think. It made her fear another woman. I should speak, I knew. But I looked again at Hoa and she was bending to the table and she picked up the dragon head and turned to face Tri's daughter and I could see Hoa's face for a moment there, caught full in the sunlight, and in this light the parts of her body that she had because of me seemed very clear, the highness of her brow, the half-expressed roundness of the lids of her eyes, the length of her nose, the wideness of her mouth, her hair neither dark nor light. And I had a twist of sadness for her, as if she had gotten from me imperfect cells that had made a club foot or an open spine or a weak heart.

She lifted the dragon high with both hands and raised it over her, and she slowly brought it down; her hair, her brow disappeared into the dragon, her eyes and her nose and her mouth, my daughter's face disappeared into great bright eyes, flared nostrils, cheeks of blood red and a brow of green. And Tri's daughter clapped her hands and laughed and the dragon head angled and opened its mouth to her as if to cry out.

I looked at Binh and he was waiting for me to speak and I looked at the others and then at Thào. Her face was slightly turned to me but her eyes were lowered. I thought, It's been nearly twenty years since I first lay down with you and touched those places on your body that were smooth and soft and that are coarser now, and I love them still, I love them more for their very coarseness. I do not wish to open the past either, my wife. But this is my village and I was seen across a field by millions and the eyes of that other country turn this way.

I let a little of the past back into me then, and I did not know what to say. A house with a wraparound porch and maple trees and a grass yard cut close and edged each week in a perfect line along a sidewalk; things unknown in this place. Things that I could see without pain only when they sat unpeopled in my head. Things of a family that were worth keeping only from a summer day when the maple leaves did not stir and when no one from inside this house was visible, no sounds could be heard from inside. How to say that for these Vietnamese who sensed—always—even the dead spirits of a family? Who in this circle could imagine that only this was good in that past life of mine: a maple tree and the smell of fresh paint on the porch, just dried into a Victorian green and smelling like something new, and the creak of a chain on a swing there, my feet touching and pushing, lifting me as if I was flying away.

And these thoughts frightened me. I was thinking about these Vietnamese now from a distance, how they could not know me, and I wanted to blame this distance on that other self that was creeping back in, but it was hard now entirely to do that. After all, this was my past and the haunches it crept on could find strength only from me. And Tri's daughter shrieked and laughed across the way and there was a faint, muffled roaring that I recognized as my daughter's voice and I knew not to look. I could not look at that.

And I rose up from where I crouched and I said, "I'm sorry," and I stepped out of the circle and I did not look at my wife and I did not look at my daughter and I hesitated only for a moment and I knew that no one here would ask me again to speak of this and that was their way and I looked along our village street, down a little slope to a closing of the trees, the road I had followed when Binh first saw me weary and ready to sleep. And I took one step now in that direction, toward the trees, and another step, and I walked away.

I walked for a long time and went up, into a piney wood, and this was an American smell, as American as it was Vietnamese. There were two tall pine trees in the yard behind the house with the wraparound porch and it smelled just like this and there was a chill that made me tremble briefly, tremble in the chest, in the heart, right then, passing through the shadow of a great isolated pine in a little clearing and open to the wind, and the nights in the highlands could be American, too, it could be cold at times here in Vietnam, even in this country of rice paddies and water buffalo.

And I stopped and I sat on a knoll and I looked at my hands darkened by the sun, not as dark as my wife's skin or Binh's or any of the others in the circle I'd broken but as dark as the skin of a Vietnamese child, that dark. This could be the skin of a Vietnamese child. Except for the blond hairs on my knuckles, and I looked at my arms and there was a forest of blond hair on this dark arm, and I was on the porch swing, in the very center, and my arms were taut, my legs were just long enough now to touch and push and lift and my arms were rigid grasping the lip of the seat, and for a moment there was only the cry of the chain above me: I pushed and the chain cried out, over and over, and it seemed painful to this thing for it to carry me, and I rose but always came down again and I never did move from the porch, and I stopped and I sat and still there was silence from the house but I knew I would go in. Against all that I desperately desired, I would go in.

Binh was asking me to go in. They all asked me that now. Just to have me speak. I was to walk into the great bland jaws of that house and what I feared was this: perhaps a family scattered even to the other side of the earth did not truly cease. Once I went in again, perhaps I could never return to Vietnam. I sat now and waited and trembled and nothing came to me to do.

But I could not sit in the woods and I rose and I went back down to the path and I walked again into the village and I went past the vegetable garden and there were three women there in conical straw hats and I knew their names and I knew their children and I passed the house of Tri and the house of Quang and the houses of others whose names I knew, whose children I knew, and I stopped in front of Tiên's house and there was the smell of wood fire from her kitchen and the smell of incense and the dragon's head was sitting in her doorway now and smelling of paint. There was the smell of fresh paint in her doorway and they all came, gradually. Tiên first and then Binh and then the others, all of them came, and my wife came and Hoa was with her and about to go away and I shook my head no and then nodded her to the circle that was forming.

Hoa crouched beside me and Thào next to her, anxious still, I knew, and my daughter turned her face up to me and then away and I leaned near and her hair smelled of the rain, smelled of the water that we gathered in a

great stone pot, as is our way here, and we believe that the spirits of our ancestors come close to us and need our prayers, the prayers in our houses with the
smoke of incense rising, and I understood how odd and wonderful the air
of this village was now because I came here and married and made this child.
The air here was filled with the spirits of Thào's coffee farmers and tobacco
farmers and woodcutters but also filled with the spirits of my clothiers and
newspapermen and bankers, all drawn into this place, into my house, by
our incense and our prayers, all brought together by my child, the confluence
of families who were, in that invisible realm, astonished to find themselves
together.

And I said, "Each new year when I was a child, the god of the hearth
went to heaven from my house in America. He came to the council of the gods
and he said, There are children in this house and they sleep each night in great
fear and they have places on their bodies that are the color of the sky in the
highlands of Vietnam just after the sun has disappeared. And they pray,
even the youngest of them, a boy, for escape and when they love each other,
these children, it is to pray that each of the others escapes. And they know
that this will happen for them, if at all, one at a time. And this house is empty
of incense. And this house sees no spirits in the world."

And I stopped speaking and the faces in the circle lowered their eyes in
deference to me and they understood and they said no more and we all rose
and we went away and that night I lay in the dark on a straw mat and my
wife lay awake next to me. I could hear her faintly jagged breath and I said,
"There was no woman in that life." And my wife sighed softly and her breathing grew as smooth as her body when I first touched her and I closed my eyes.

And I thought of this place in Vietnam where I lay and how it grows
coffee and it grows tobacco, and in that other life there was time in the morning when I could slip out of the house and there was no one around but me
and I knew that one day I would escape, and inside they drank coffee and
smoked cigarettes and read the newspaper.

TRY THIS 5.5

Recall an experience that changed you. Write about it with one of the traditional
openings of story:
- Once upon a time
- Long ago and far away
- In the beginning
- Let me tell you a story
- Listen!
- It all began

Amy Bloom
The Story

You wouldn't have known me a year ago.

A year ago I had a husband, and my best friend was Margeann at the post office. In no time at all my husband got cancer, house prices tumbled in our part of Connecticut, and I got a new best friend. Realtors' signs came and went in front of the house down the road: from the elegant forest green-and-white FOR SALE BY OWNER, nicely handmade to show that they were in no hurry and in no need, to MARTHA BRAE LEWIS AND COMPANY, Realtors who sold only very expensive houses and rode horses in the middle of the day when there was nothing worthwhile on the market and then down, down to the big national relocator company's fiberboard sign practically shouting, "Fire Sale, You Can Have This House for Less Than They Paid for It." My place was nothing special compared to my neighbor's, but it did have the big stained-glass windows Ethan had made, so beautiful, sightseers drove right up our private road, parked by the birches, and begged to come in, just to stand there in the rays of purple and green light, to be charmed by twin redheaded mermaids flanking the front door, to run their fingers over the cobalt blue drops sprayed across the hall, bezel set into the plaster. They stood between the cantering cinnabar legs of the centaur in the middle of the kitchen wall and sighed. After coffee and cookies they would order two windows or six or, one time, wild with real estate money, people from Gramercy Park ordered a dozen botanical panels for their new house in Madison, and Ethan always said, "Why do you do that?" I did it for company and for money, since I needed both and Ethan didn't care. When he asked for the mail, without looking up, or even when he made the effort to ask about my bad knee, not noticing that we'd last spoken two full days ago, it was worse than the quiet. If I didn't ask the New Yorkers for money, he'd shuffle around in his moccasins, picking at his nails until they made an insulting offer or got back in their cars, baffled and rich.

Six months after Ethan caught cancer like a terrible cold and died; I went just once to the Unitarian widows group in which all the late husbands were much nicer than mine had been and even the angriest woman only said, "Goddamn his smoking," and I thought, His smoking? Almost all that I liked about Ethan was his stained glass, his small, wide hands, and the fact that he was willing to marry Plain Jane me when I thought no one would, and willing to stay by me when I lost the baby. That was such a bad time I didn't leave the house for two months and Ethan invited the New Yorkers in just to get me out of bed. Other than that, I only thought that if you didn't hate your silent, moody husband after twenty years, and he didn't seem to hate you and your big blob of despair, you could call it a good thing, no worse than other marriages. That last month was like the honeymoon we never took, and when strangers talk to me now, I sound like a woman who lost her beloved and grieves still.

I have dead parents—the best kind, I think, at this stage of life—two sisters, whom I do love at a little distance, a garden that is as close to God as I need it to be, and a book group I've been in for fourteen years, which also serves as mastectomy hot line, menopause watch, and PFLAG. I don't mind being alone, having been raised by hard-drinking, elderly parents, a German and a Swede, with whom I never had a fight or a moment's pleasure, and I took off for college at sixteen, with no idea of what to say to these girls with outerwear for every season (fall coats and spring jackets and pale blue anoraks) and underwear that was nicer than my church clothes. Having made my own plain, dark way, and having been with plain, dark but talented Ethan such a long time, I've been pleasantly surprised in middle age, to have yoga and gardening for my soul, and bookkeeping to pay the bills. Clearly, my whole life was excellent training for money managing of all kinds, and now I do the books for twenty people like Ethan, gifted and without a clear thought in their heads about organizing their finances or feeding their families, if they're lucky enough to have more than a tiny profit to show for what they do.

I didn't call my new neighbors the Golddust Twins. Margeann, our postmaster, called them that. She nicknamed all the New Yorkers, and pre-read their magazines and kept the catalogues that most appealed to her. Tall-blondgorgeous, she said. And gobs of money, she said. Just gobs of money, and Mr. Golddust had a little sense but she had none and they had a pretty little blond baby who would grow up to be hell on wheels if the mother didn't stop giving her Coca-Cola at nine in the morning and everything else she asked for. And they surely needed a bookkeeper, Margeann said, because Doctor Mrs. Golddust was a psychiatrist and he did something mysterious in the import and export of art. I could tell, just from that, that they would need me, the kind of bookkeeper and accountant and paid liar who could call black white and look you straight in the eye. I put my business card in their mailbox, which they (I assumed she) had covered in bits of fluorescent tile, making a rowdy little work of art, and they called me that night. She invited themselves over for coffee on Sunday morning.

"Oh my God, this house is gorgeous. Completely charming. And that stained glass. You are a genius, Mrs. Baker. Mrs.? Not Ms.? Is Janet all right?

This is unbelievable. Oh my God. And your garden. Unbelievable. Miranda, don't touch the art. Let Mommy hold you up to the light. Like a fairy story."

Sam smiled and put out his hand, my favorite kind of male hand, what I would call shapely peasant, auburn hairs on the first joint of each finger and just a little ginger patch on the back. His hands must have been left over from early Irish farmers; the rest of him looked right out of a magazine.

"I know I'm carrying on, but I can't help it. Sam, darlingdarling, please take Miranda so Janet and I can just explore for two minutes."

We walked out to the centauries, and she brushed her long fingers against their drooping blue fringe.

"Can I touch? I'm not much of a gardener. That card of yours was just a gift from God. Not just because of the bookkeeping, but because I wanted to meet you after I saw you in town. I don't think you saw me. At the Dairy Mart."

I had seen her, of course.

"Sam, Janet has forgiven me for being such a loony. Maybe she'll help us out of our financial morass."

Sam smiled and scooped Miranda up just before she smacked into the coffee table corner. He said he would leave the two of us to it and any help at all would be better than what he had currently. He pressed my hands together in his and put two files between them, hard clear plastic with "MoBay Exports, Incorporated" embossed across the front and a manila folder with stationery from Dr. Sandra Saunders sticking out of it. I sent them away with blueberry jam and a few begonia cuttings. Coming from New York, she thought any simple thing you could do in a garden was wonderful.

Sandra called, "I can tell Miranda's fallen in love with you. Could you possibly watch her tomorrow? Around five? Just for a half hour? Sam has to go to the city."

After two tantrums, juice instead of Coke, stories instead of videos, and no to her organdy dress for playing in the sandbox, it was seven o'clock, then eight. I gave Miranda dinner and a bath. She was, in fact, a very sweet child, and I thought that her mother, like mine, meant well but seemed not to have what was called for. When Sandra came home, Miranda ran to her but looked out between her legs and blew me a kiss.

"Say 'We love you, Janet,'" Sandra said.

"We love you, Jah-net."

"Say 'Please come tomorrow for drinks, Janet.'"

Miranda sighed. "Drinks, Jah-net," she said, indulgently.

I kissed them both good-bye. I had never had such fresh, sweet skin under my lips, Miranda's peach and Sandra's apricots-and-cream moisturizer, and although I wasn't attracted to women or girls, I could see why a person would be.

I planted a small square garden near Sam's studio, sweet William and campanula and Violet Queen asters with a little rosemary bonsai that Miranda could put her pinkie-sized plastic babies around. Sandra was gone more than Sam was. He worked in the converted barn with computers and screens and two faxes and four phone lines, and every time I visited, he brought me a cup of tea and admired our latest accomplishments.

He said, "It's very good of you to do this."

"I don't mind," I said.

"We could always get a sitter," he said, but he knew I knew that wasn't true, because I had done their books.

Can I say that the husband was not any kind of importer? Can I say that he was what he really was, a successful cartoonist? That they lived right behind me, in a house I still find too big and too showy, even now that I am in it?

I haven't even described the boyfriend, the one Sandra went off to canoodle with while I baby-sat. Should I write him as tall and blond when in fact he was dark and muscular, like the husband? It will be too confusing for readers if both men are dark and fit, with long ponytails, but they both were. And they drove the same kind of truck, making for more confusion.

I've given them blandly wholesome, modern names, wishing for the days of Aunt Ada Starkadder and Martin Chuzzlewit and Pompeo Lagunima. Sam's real name conveys more of his rather charming shy stiffness and rectitude, but I keep "Sam," which has the advantage of suggesting an unlikely, misleading blend of Jewish and New England, and I'll call the boyfriend "Joe," suggesting a general good-natured lunkishness. Sandra, as I've named her, actually was a therapist, just as I've written her, but not a psychiatrist, and I disliked her so much, I can't bear to make you think, even in this story, that she had the discipline and drive and intellectual persistence to become a physician. She had nothing but appetite and brass balls, and she was the worst mother I ever saw. Even now, I regard her destruction as a very good thing, which may undermine the necessary fictive texture of deep ambiguity, the roiling ambivalence that gives tension to the narrator's affection.

Sandy pinched her child for not falling asleep quickly enough; she gave her potato chips for breakfast and Slurpees for lunch; she cut her daughter's hair with pinking shears and spent two hundred dollars she didn't have on her own monthly Madison Avenue haircuts. She left that child in more stores than I can remember, cut cocaine on her changing table, and blamed the poor little thing for every disappointment and heartache in her own life, until Miranda's eyes welled up at the sound of her mother calling her name. And if Sandy was not evil, she was worse than foolish, and sick, and, more to the point, incurable. If Sandra were smooshed inside a wrecked car splattered against the inside of a tunnel, I wouldn't feel even so sad for her as I did for Princess Diana, for whom I felt very little indeed.

I think the opening works, and the part about the widows group is true, although I've left out the phone call I got a week after the group met, when the nicest widow, an oversized Stockard Channing, invited me to a dinner with unmistakable overtones and I didn't go. I wish I had gone; that dinner and its aftermath might make a better story than this one I've been fooling with.

I don't want to leave out the time Sandra got into a fistfight with Joe's previous girlfriend, who knocked Sandra down into the middle of her own potato salad at the Democrats annual picnic, or the time Joe broke into the former marital home after Sandra moved out and threw Sam's library into the fire, not realizing that he was also destroying Sandra's collection of first editions. And when he was done, drunk and sweating, I sat on my porch, watching through my late husband's binoculars ("Ethan" is very much my late husband, a sculptor, not a glassmaker, but correct in the essentials of character; my husband wasn't dead before I met them; he died a year later, and Sam was very kind and Sandra was her usual charming, useless self). I saw Joe trip on little Miranda's Fisher-Price roller skate and slide down the ravine. I went to sleep, and when Sam called me the next day, laughing and angry, watching an ambulance finally come up his long gravel drive and the EMTs put splints all over Joe the Boyfriend, I laughed too and brought over corn chowder and my own rye bread for Sam and Miranda.

I don't have any salt-of-the-earth-type friends like Margeann. Margeanns are almost always crusty and often black and frequently given to pungent phrases and earth wisdom. Sometimes, they're someone's grandmother. In men's stories they're either old and disreputable drinking buddies, someone's tobacco-chewing, trout-fishing grandpaw, or the inexplicably devoted sidekick of color, caustic and true.

My friends in real life are two other writers—the movie critic for our nearest daily newspaper and a retired home-and-garden freelancer I've been playing tennis with for twenty years. Estelle, my tennis buddy, has more the character of the narrator than I do, and I thought I could use her experience with Sandra to make a story line. Sandra had sprinkled her psychobabble all over poor Estelle, got her coming three times a week, cash on the table, and had almost persuaded her to leave Dev, her very nice husband, in order to "explore her full potential." Estelle's entire full potential is to be the superb and good-natured tennis partner she is, a gifted gardener (which is where I got all that horticultural detail), and a poor cook and worse housekeeper for an equally easygoing, rosy-cheeked man who inherited two million dollars when he was fifty and about whom I can say nothing worse than at eighty-three Dev's not quite as sharp as he was—although he's nicer. I could not imagine how else Estelle's full potential, at seventy-seven, with cataracts in her left eye, bad hearing, and not the least interest in art, theater, movies, or politics, would express itself. I persuaded Dev to take her on a fancy cruise, two weeks through the canals of France, and when they came back, beaming pinkly, a little chubby, and filled with lively remarks about French bread and French cheese, Estelle said nothing more about her underdeveloped potential and nothing more about meeting with Sandra.

I see that I've made Sam sound more affably dodgy than he really is. He wouldn't have caught my eye in the first place if he was no more than the cardboard charmer I describe, and he was tougher than Joe, in the end. Even if Sandra hadn't been a bad mother, I might have imagined a complex but rosy future with Sam and Miranda, if I was capable of imagining my future.

I don't know what made Sandra think I would be her accomplice. If you are thin and blondly pretty and used to admirers, maybe you see them wherever there are no rivals. But, hell, I read the ladies' magazines and drove all the way to Westport for a new haircut and spent money on clothes, and although she didn't notice that I was coming over in silk knit T-shirts and black jeans, Sam did. When Sandra called me, whispering from Joe's bed, "Ohmigod, make something up, I lost track of time," I didn't. I walked over with dinner for Sam and Miranda, and while Miranda sat in front of her computer, I said, "I'm a bad liar. Sandra called from Joe's. She asked me to make something up, but I can't."

There is no such thing as a good writer and a bad liar.

After she moved out, she called me most mornings, just to report on the night before. She was in heaven. Joe was wonderful in every way but terribly jealous of Sam. Very silly, of course. Very flattering.

I called Joe in the late afternoons. I said, "Oh, Sandy's not there? Oh, of course." Joe was possibly the most easily led person God ever made. I didn't even have to drop a line, I just dangled it loosely and flicked. I said, "She's not at the office. She must be at home. I mean, at Sam's. It's great that they're getting along, for Miranda's sake. Honestly, I think they're better friends now that they're separated."

I did that twice a week, making up different reasons for calling. Joe hit her, once. She told me and I touched the round bruise on her jaw, begging her to press charges, but she didn't.

The part where Joe drove his truck into the back of Sam's house is too good to leave out, and tells funnier than it really was, although the rear end of his pickup sticking out through acres of grape arbor was pretty funny, as was the squish-squish of the grapes as Joe tried to extricate himself, and the smell of something like wine sweeping over us as he drove off, vines twirling around his tires.

I reported Sandy to the ethics committee of the Connecticut Association of Family Counselors. All the things she shouldn't have told me—how she did things in her office, and her financial arrangements with her patients, and the stock tips they gave her, and her insistence on being paid in cash in advance— and the fact that I, who was no kind of therapist at all, knew all these things and all their names, was enough to make them suspend her license for six months.

Sophisticated readers understand that writers work out their anger, their conflicts, their endless grief and rolling list of loss, through their stories. That however mean-spirited or diabolical, it's only a story. That the darkness in the soul is shaped into type and lies there, brooding and inert, black on the page but active, dangerous, only in the reader's mind. Actually, harmless. I am not harmless.

The story I had hoped to write would have skewered her, of course. Anyone who knew her would have read it, known it was her, and thought badly of her while reading. She would have been embarrassed and angry. That really was not what I had in mind. I wanted her skin like a rug on my floor, her slim throat slit, heart still beating behind the newly bricked-up wall. In stories, when someone behaves uncharacteristically, we know a meaningful, even pivotal, moment has come. If we are surprised too often, we either vacillate or just give up and close the book. In real life, when people think they know you, know you well enough not only to say, "It's Tuesday, she must be helping out at the library today," but well enough to have said to the librarian, after you've left the building, "You know, she just loves reading to the four-year-olds. I think it's been such a comfort to her since her little boy died"—when they know you like that, you can do almost any bad, secretive thing and if they hear about it, they will, as readers do, simply disbelieve the narrator.

I find that I have no sympathy with the women who have nannies, on top of baby sitters on top of beepers and pagers and party coordinators, or with the older ones who want to give back their damaged, distressing adopted children, or with the losers who sue to get their children back when they had given them to adequate and loving parents three years before. In my world, none of them would be allowed to be mothers, and if they had slipped through my licensing bureau, their children would be promptly removed and all traces of their maternal claims erased.

As Sandra's dear friend and reliable baby sitter, it was easy to hire Joe to do a little work on my front porch, easy to have him bump into my research assistant, the two of them as much alike as a pair of pretty quarter horses, easy to fuel Sandra's sudden wish to move farther out of town. Easy to send the ethics committee the information they needed to remove her license permanently, easy to suggest she manage Joe's business, easy to suggest that children need quality time not quantity, and that young, handsome lovers need both, easy to wave Sandra and Joe off in their new truck (easy to arrange a ten-thousand-dollar loan when you are such a steady customer of the local bank and own your home outright).

I can't say I didn't intend harm. I did and would not have minded even death, and if death is beyond my psychological reach, then disappearance, which is worse because it's not permanent but better, because there is no body.

And I am like a wife now to this lovely, appreciative man who thinks me devoted and kind, who teases me for trembling at dead robins on the patio, for crying openly at AT&T commercials. And I am like a mother to this girl as rapacious and charming and roughly loving as a lion cub. The whole house creaks with their love, and I walk the floors at night, up and down the handsome distressed pine stairs, in and out of the library and the handmade-in-England kitchen through a family room big enough for anything but contact sports. In the daylight, I make myself garden—fruit trees, flowers, and herbs—and it's no worse than doing the crossword puzzle, as I used to. I have taken a bookkeeping class; we don't need an accountant anymore. I don't write so much as an essay for the library newsletter, although I still volunteer there and at Miranda's school, of course, and I keep our nice house nice. I go to parties where people know not to ask writers how it's going and I still play tennis. Although I feel like a fool and worry that the Tai Chi teacher will sense that I am not like the others, I go twice a week, for whatever balance it will give me.

I slip into the last row and I do not look at the pleasant, dully focused faces of the women on either side of me. *Bear Catching Fish*, she says, and moves her long arms overhead and down, trailing through the imaginary river. *Crane*, and we rise up on one single, shaky leg. At the end of class, we are all sweating lightly, lying in the dusty near-dark of the Lyman School gym. The floor smells of boys and rubber and rosin, and I leave before they rise and bow to each other, hands in front of sternum, ostentatiously relaxed and transcendent.

In the farthest northwest corner of our property, on the far side of the last stand of skinny maples, I put up an arbor and covered it with Markham's Pink clematis and Perle d'Azur. The giant heart-shaped leaves of Dutchman's pipe turn my corner into a secret place. I carried the pieces of a large cedar bench down there one night last fall and assembled it by flashlight.

There is no one in this world now who knew my baby or me, when I was twenty-eight, married four years and living in the graduate student apartments of the University of California at Berkeley. Our apartment was next to a pale, hunched engineer from New Jersey, who lived next to an anguished physicist from Chad and his good-natured Texan wife, baking Derby pie and corn bread for the whole floor, and we were all across from the brilliant Indian brothers, both mathematicians, both with gold-earringed little girls and wives so quick with numbers that when Berkeley's power went out, as it often did during bad weather, the cash registers were replaced by two thin, dark women in fuchsia and turquoise saris rustling over their raw silk *cholis*, adding up the figures without even a pencil. Our babies and toddlers played in the courtyard and the fathers watched and played chess and drank beer and we watched and brushed sand out of the children's hair and smoked Marlboros and were friends in a very particular, young, and hopeful way.

When Eddie died, they all came to the little funeral at the university chapel and filled our apartment with biscuits and samosas and brisket and with their kindness and their own sickening relief. We left the next day, like thieves. I did not finish my Ph.D. in English literature. My husband did not secure a teaching position at the University of San Francisco, and when I meet people who remember Mario Savio's speeches on the steps of Sproul Hall and their cinder-block apartments on Dwight Way, I leave the room. My own self is buried in Altabates Hospital, still between the sheet and the mattress of his peach plastic Isolette, twisted around the tubes that wove in and out of him like translucent vines, trapped inside that giant ventilator, four times Eddie's size without being of any use to him or his little lungs.

I have made the best and happiest ending that I can, in this world, made it out of the flax and netting and leftover trim of someone else's life, I know, but I made it to keep the innocent safe and the guilty punished, and I made it as the world should be and not as I have found it.

TRY THIS 5.6
Write about a memory in which you responded with revenge, and are glad you did so. What did this experience change in you?

POEMS

Robert Hass
A Story About the Body

The young composer, working that summer at an artist's colony, had watched her for a week. She was Japanese, a painter, almost sixty, and he thought he was in love with her. He loved her work, and her work was like the way she moved her body, used her hands, looked at him directly when she made amused and considered answers to his questions. One night, walking back from a concert, they came to her door and she turned to him and said, "I think you would like to have me. I would like that too, but I must tell you that I have had a double mastectomy," and when he didn't understand, "I've lost both my breasts." The radiance that he had carried around in his belly and chest cavity—like music—withered very quickly, and he made himself look at her when he said, "I'm sorry. I don't think I could." He walked back to his own cabin through the pines, and in the morning he found a small blue bowl on the porch outside his door. It looked to be full of rose petals, but he found when he picked it up that the rose petals were on top; the rest of the bowl—she must have swept them from the corners of her studio—was full of dead bees.

TRY THIS 5.7

"Nude Interrogation" on page 152 and "A Story About the Body" above are **prose poems,** poems that are not written in lines but continue to the margins of the page like prose. Earlier in this chapter you read two short-short stories within the text—"Frontier" and "This Is How I Remember It." The borderline between a prose poem and a short-short story is very fine, and you could (probably not very fruitfully) argue about whether any given piece is one or the other. In a general way, you could say that a prose poem will pay central attention to the language and its pattern of sound, whereas a short-short story will be first of all structured on the narrative arc conflict-crisis-resolution. You will, however, find many exceptions to this general—not even rule, but—observation. If you contrast "Nude Interrogation" and "Frontiers," you will see the difference relatively clearly.

Write either a prose poem or a short-short story such that no one would claim it was the other. If a poem, dwell on the language but tell *no story*. If a story, plain-speak a plot.

Albert Goldbarth
Columbine High School/ Littleton, CO

Here, thirteen high school students died,
murdered by two other high school students
—the memorial consists
of fifteen crosses. In this photograph, a woman
rests her head against one upright beam
as if decanting
(*trying* to) everything that's in her brain
—only the wood, only something
inhuman now, could hold what flows from her.
This grief's too vast for us, a color of its own,
not from our limited strip of the spectrum.

Really all that makes this picture comprehensible
to us—to we who view, but haven't
lived, this news—is the take-out cup
for her cola. You know, with the plastic lid
and the straw. A summer movie
advertised around it. Droplets
on the side, from where its ice and the heat
of the afternoon commune.
It's a large. You've had it
on maybe a thousand occasions. Any of us
might hold this drink,
might take it into our systems.

TRY THIS 5.8

Write a poem or a few paragraphs about a photograph of a horrific event. Focus as
Goldbarth does on a mundane detail. What point can you make, what effect can you
achieve, what story can you tell, with this contrast between horrific and mundane?

Ellen Bryant Voigt

Short Story

My grandfather killed a mule with a hammer,
or maybe with a plank, or a stick, maybe
it was a horse—the story varied
in the telling. If he was planting corn
when it happened, it was a mule, and he was plowing
the upper slope, west of the house, his overalls
stiff to the knees with red dirt, the lines
draped behind his neck.
He must have been glad to rest
when the mule first stopped mid-furrow;
looked back at where he'd come, then down
to the brush along the creek he meant to clear.
No doubt he noticed the hawk's great leisure
over the field, the crows lumped
in the biggest elm on the opposite hill.
After he'd wiped his hatbrim with his sleeve,
he called to the mule as he slapped the line
along its rump, clicked and whistled.

My grandfather was a slight, quiet man,
smaller than most women, smaller
than his wife. Had she been in the yard,
seen him heading toward the pump now,
she'd pump for him a dipper of cold water.
Walking back to the field, past the corncrib,
he took an ear of corn to start the mule,
but the mule was planted. He never cursed
or shouted, only whipped it, the mule
rippling its backside each time
the switch fell, and when that didn't work
whipped it low on its side, where it's tender,
then cross-hatched the welts he'd made already.
The mule went down on one knee,
and that was when he reached for the blown limb,
or walked to the pile of seasoning lumber; or else,
unhooked the plow and took his own time to the shed
to get the hammer.
        By the time I was born,
he couldn't even lift a stick. He lived
another fifteen years in a chair,
but now he's dead, and so is his son,
who never meant to speak a word against him,
and whom I never asked what his father
was planting and in which field,
and whether it happened before he married,
before his children came in quick succession,
before his wife died of the last one.
And only a few of us are left
who ever heard that story.

Maxine Kumin
Woodchucks

Gassing the woodchucks didn't turn out right.
The knockout bomb from the Feed and Grain Exchange
was featured as merciful, quick at the bone
and the case we had against them was airtight,
both exits shoehorned shut with puddingstone,
but they had a sub-sub-basement out of range.

Next morning they turned up again, no worse
for the cyanide than we for our cigarettes
and state-store Scotch, all of us up to scratch.

They brought down the marigolds as a matter of course
and then took over the vegetable patch
nipping the broccoli shoots, beheading the carrots.

The food from our mouths, I said, righteously thrilling
to the feel of the .22, the bullets' neat noses.
I, a lapsed pacifist fallen from grace
puffed with Darwinian pieties for killing,
now drew a bead on the littlest woodchuck's face.
He died down in the everbearing roses.

Ten minutes later I dropped the mother. She
flipflopped in the air and fell, her needle teeth
still hooked in a leaf of early Swiss chard.
Another baby next. O one-two-three
the murderer inside me rose up hard,
the hawkeye killer came on stage forthwith.

There's one chuck left. Old wily fellow, he keeps
me cocked and ready day after day after day.
All night I hunt his humped-up form. I dream
I sight along the barrel in my sleep.
If only they'd all consented to die unseen
gassed underground the quiet Nazi way.

Li-Young Lee
The Hammock

When I lay my head in my mother's lap
I think how day hides the stars,
the way I lay hidden once, waiting
inside my mother's laughter. And I remember
how she carried me on her back
between home and the kindergarten,
once each morning and once each afternoon.
I don't know what my mother's thinking.

When my son lays his head in my lap, I worry
his lips, swollen with his father's kisses,
won't keep his father's worries from becoming
his. I think, *Dear God*, and remember
there are stars we haven't heard from yet
they have so far to arrive: *Amen*,
and I think, and I feel almost comforted.
I've no idea what my child is thinking.

Between two unknowns, I live my life.
And what's it like? Between my mother's hopes,
older than me by coming before me,
and my child's wishes, older than me
by outliving me, what's it like?
Is it a door, and good-bye on either side?
Is it a window, and eternity on either side?
Yes, Yes, and a little singing between two great rests.

TRY THIS 5.9

Several of the preceding poems are also memoirs. All of them tell a story. Write a poem of no more than a dozen lines with the title of one of the traditional tales below. Make it contemporary. Can you base it on your own experience?

- Beauty and the Beast
- Ugly Duckling
- Mulan
- Baba Yaga
- Humpty Dumpty
- Noah's Ark
- Three Little Pigs
- Aladdin's Lamp

DRAMA

Carole Real
The Battle of Bull Run Always Makes Me Cry

CHARACTERS

DONNA: 34, single, successful, lonely, funny.
LINDA: Donna's friend, married, with a toddler.
AMY: Donna's friend, also married, practical.
PATRICK: 35, Irish American, single, well dressed, attractive.

(A coffee shop. Linda and Amy are awaiting Donna, who enters, frazzled.)

DONNA: Hi, I'm sorry, I just, oh God what a thing. I got pulled over! By a cop! And he noticed my emissions sticker was expired and I'm like oh God what's that going to be, like another seventy-five-dollar thing? So I started crying!

LINDA: You did?

AMY: Good move.

DONNA: Yeah, I know. But it wasn't even like I had to try.

LINDA: Was he cute?

DONNA: *(Disappointed.)* No.

LINDA: *(Disappointed.)* Oh, too bad.

DONNA: So I said to him that I was on my way to pick up my little girl, Enid. It just came out of my mouth. So, of course he knows I'm lying. I can tell. Because no one has a little girl named Enid.

AMY: Right.

LINDA: What'd he do?

DONNA: He softened.

AMY: Oh good.

DONNA: Yeah, and told me that I should get the emissions thing done and that he'd let me go this time.

AMY: Great!

DONNA: But it freaked me out, let me tell you. That and . . . you know I keep having dreams about Sai Baba.

LINDA: Who?

DONNA: Sai Baba. He's a guru of some sort. They chant for him in Norwalk and places. The guy, who came to clean my rug, Gary? I assumed he was, you know, a pod, and then he picked up one of my Alan Watts books and started talking about it and kundalini and stuff and then he mentioned Sai Baba. But the weird thing is . . . they think he's God. Really God. "The avatar" is what Gary said, which I guess means God. And every night since then, I've had these dreams where I'm someplace, doing something, then all of a sudden people are chanting or talking about Sai Baba. I tried to get one of his books, but they were out.

LINDA: Oh for God's sake!

DONNA: Well, I'm not saying I'll convert . . .

LINDA: For God's sake, for God's sake, for God's sake! Tell us about your date!

DONNA: Oh . . . my date . . .

LINDA: Yes, your . . .

DONNA: My . . . You want to hear . . . ?

LINDA: My God, yes! I got a babysitter so I could meet you!

AMY: We want to hear . . . we're here to hear.
DONNA: Well, it's a thing, let me tell you.
LINDA: What happened?

(*Patrick crosses to opposite Donna, Amy, and Linda. He is good-looking and well dressed. He stands, waiting to meet someone. During the play, Donna, Amy, and Linda can see Patrick, and he can see them, though he interacts only with Donna.*)

DONNA: Well! We met at the movie theater. And he looked really cute.
AMY: Yeah?
LINDA: No, he's really cute.
DONNA: Right. So, he was there, really cute. And I thought, "Oh God." You
      know?
AMY and **LINDA:** (three syllables) Yeaaaaah.
DONNA: So we saw the movie, and then we went . . .
LINDA: Wait wait wait. I did not get a babysitter to hear a summary. Start
      from the beginning. Did you have popcorn. Did he pay for it.
DONNA: I had popcorn. He did not pay for it.

(*Linda and Amy react visably negatively.*)

      He had bought the tickets.

(*Linda and Amy take this in and give him a few points.*)

      So we saw the movie . . .

LINDA: Which movie.
DONNA: Dark Rain.

(*We see Patrick seated at the movie.*)

AMY: That's supposed to be really sad . . .
DONNA: Oh, it is. It's really really sad.
LINDA: Is it sad?
DONNA: No, it's sad.
LINDA: It has that really cute, that . . .
DONNA: Yes. And he *dies.*
AMY: Oh
DONNA: Alone, in a prison in Istanbul, like a thousand miles from his girl-
      friend, who really loves him. I was like, distraught.

(*Patrick hands a napkin to an invisible person next to him.*)

AMY: Did you cry?
DONNA: Yes! Plus I was so tense, from the date thing.
LINDA: Did he cry?

DONNA: No. Actually. He was sort of smirking.

LINDA: Oh, I don't like that. Did he notice you were crying?

DONNA: Yes, he gave me a napkin.

LINDA: That's good.

DONNA: Then after the movie as we were walking to the restaurant he started talking about politics.

AMY *and* **LINDA:** *(sympathetic, been there.)* Oh . . .

DONNA: And then, over dinner? The Civil War.

(Patrick is now at dinner, holding forth about the Civil War. We see his lips move, but we cannot hear him.)

AMY: The whole war?

DONNA: One battle in particular.

LINDA: Well, he was probably trying to impress you.

DONNA: Don't people understand how totally unimpressed I am with people trying to impress me?

LINDA: He probably wanted you to think he's smart.

DONNA: Would I be eating with him if he weren't smart? Have I eaten with a man who is not smart?

LINDA: Well, he doesn't know that.

AMY: So, what happened?

DONNA: He talked for about forty-five minutes about this one particular battle.

LINDA: Which one?

DONNA: Oh, like it would mean something to you.

LINDA: Well . . .

DONNA: Anyway, I can't really say which battle. I was feigning. I was sittin' there thinkin' "Cat food, kitty litter, broccoli, I'd like to fuck this guy . . . "

(Patrick and Donna lock eyes for a moment.)

DONNA: And he's like blah blah blah Shiloh, blah blah blah Lee.

(During Patrick's speech, Donna crosses to him and joins him at a dinner table.)

PATRICK: . . . then Chamberlain, who was really a remarkable person, a professor of classical language at Bowdoin . . . he had asked for leave to go fight, they said no, so he asked to go to England to study and then joined the army instead . . . he served throughout the war, and at Gettysburg had the job of holding the flank at Little Round Top. This is all in Shelby Foote's book.

DONNA: *(to Amy and Linda)* Like I'm gonna read Shelby Foote's book, you know?

PATRICK: The Union had set up artillery on the ridge. Of course if you can turn the flank and get behind the Yankees . . .

DONNA: (*feigning*) Right . . .

PATRICK: Anyway, Chamberlain had withstood several charges, he was running out of men and ammunition, but at the next charge he made a countercharge with bayonets and the South freaked and didn't try to take Round Hill after that. He got the Congressional Medal of Honor. One person *can* make a difference.

DONNA: (*to Linda and Amy*) Why do they do that? Why do they talk to me about the Civil War?

AMY: Did you see that documentary?

DONNA: Are you talking about the Civil War?

LINDA: (*to Amy*) Yes.

AMY: Did you see that part, that letter . . .

LINDA: Please, I'll go hysterical crying.

AMY: This army officer knows he's going to die in the next battle, and he writes his wife . . .

LINDA: I can't listen to this! I'll start sobbing!

AMY: The most beautiful letter . . . I cried.

LINDA: I sobbed.

AMY: I boo-hooed. I couldn't watch the rest of the show, I had to lie down.

DONNA: Well, why couldn't he talk about something like that about the Civil War? Why did he have to go on and on about a battle?

AMY: Because men think *out* (*makes a gesture with her hands indicating the outside world*) . . . in (*gesture meaning inner life*). Women think *in* (*gesture*) . . . out (*gesture*)

DONNA: Oh . . .

LINDA: No, that's true.

AMY: So the reason they think of you last, after all the stuff that's out there in the world, is because they think of themselves last, and you and your relationship with them is part of them.

DONNA: That's why they like military history.

AMY: Right.

DONNA: Because it's all *out.* (*gestures*)

AMY: Right.

LINDA: What happened next? I have a two-year-old, I need to live vicariously here.

DONNA: So then I said to him . . . (*to Patrick*) Are you nervous because you know I want to sleep with you?

(*Patrick stares at her*)

AMY and **LINDA:** (*They turn towards one another and squeal, at once horrified and thrilled.*) AAAAAAAHHHHHH!

LINDA: You didn't.

AMY: Oh my God.

DONNA: Naah, I didn't have the balls. What I really wanted to say was. (*To Patrick*) Shut up and kiss me! Just please *God* shut the *fuck* up and kiss me! (*To Linda and Amy*) But instead I just said (*to Patrick*) I'm not really a Civil War fan. Per se.

(*Patrick looks hurt, and moves the food around on his plate with his fork. To Linda and Amy.*)

Then he was sort of hurt, I could tell, and he sort of moved the food around on his plate. And I started to think, I'm such an asshole, you know, here's this guy taking me out, trying to talk to me, okay, so it's about the battle of Bull Run, whatever, but I can't even be nice to him. And here I am, I'm thirty-four, I haven't had a boyfriend since . . .

LINDA: Ron . . .

DONNA: Ron, who was . . .

LINDA: Unkind.

DONNA: Unkind . . . I need to be more . . . I need . . . I don't know.

AMY: Now, why do you want to date Patrick?

DONNA: What?

AMY: I mean, aside from that he's cute.

DONNA: Well. He looks like my father. A *lot.*

(*Linda and Amy take this in.*)

And we have a lot in common. Weird things. And, when I look in his eyes I feel like I'm falling down a long tunnel towards ancient Celtic mysteries.

AMY: Wow. Okay. That's a good reason.

LINDA: Did you tell him that thing? That we talked about? About how you've got all this stuff going for you, a career, and a nice place to live, and now you're really ready for a serious relationship, and looking forward to it? You know, really strong and confident and knowing what you want, but letting him know that you want something more than just a fling?

DONNA: Oh, right. The thing. Right. Okay. (*to Patrick*) You know, Patrick, actually, over the past year it's become sort of clear to me that, well, I have this career, that is going well, and I have a nice home and friends, but the truth is that, without, you know, someone to share it with, it can be really . . . really . . .

(*She starts tearing up.*)

. . . lonely and . . . empty.

(She cries outright.)

Really lonely.

(She sobs. Patrick, a little stunned, hands her a napkin.)

I'm sorry.

(She wipes her eyes.)

I have to go to the ladies room.

(She gets up and crosses back to the table with Linda and Amy. She sits between them, resting her elbows on the table, and crying into the napkin. To Linda.)

It didn't really go how we planned.

AMY: **LINDA:**

(Amy and Linda both rub/pat her back.)

Ooooh.   No.

DONNA: It just gets very lonely when they talk about the Civil War.

AMY   **LINDA:**

(Amy and Linda both rub/pat her back.)

Ooooh.   I know.

DONNA: Or politics.

AMY   **LINDA:**

(Amy and Linda both rub/pat her back.)

Ooooh.   I know.

DONNA: Or books.

AMY   **LINDA:**

(Amy and Linda both rub/pat her back.)

Ooooh.   I know.

DONNA: Because they're lecturing! And you don't want a lecture. You want back and forth.

(She makes a back and forth gesture.)

LINDA: I know. That's the thing.
DONNA: That's the thing. You want the back and forth.

AMY: You want back and forth.

DONNA: That's the thing.

LINDA: Then what happened?

DONNA: I stayed in the ladies room a while. There were some other women there and we chatted, you know, about the toilet paper.

AMY: That must have been a nice break.

DONNA: It was.

(*She crosses back to Patrick's table.*)

The Battle of Bull Run always makes me cry.

PATRICK: That's all right. Do you want to go for a walk?

DONNA: (*Noticing that he's paid the check.*) Yes.

(*They leave the restaurant and start to stroll.*)

Do you ever think there's just so much that we don't understand? Like, my cat? Kitty? She's been staring at this cat next door, for like two years. But I never let her out, so all she can do is stare at him from the deck. Sometimes I sing the theme from *Romeo and Juliet* when I see them doing this. Anyway, I had problems with her, pee problems. It's a long story, but I decided it was time for her to be able to go outdoors. So I got her all her shots, which cost like two hundred dollars. And then I had to keep her in till the shots kicked in and then the very day she was finally okay to go outside, I came home from work, thinking, okay this is *the* day Kitty gets to go outside and I see Woody, the cat from next door, on my path. And what's at my door but a tiny little freshly killed bird. Like a present. Which he had never done before, in the whole two years I've been there. But my question is, how did he know? How did he know that this was the day, the first day in the two years I've been there that she could come out? Then I realized this is *much much* bigger than we think.

PATRICK: What is.

DONNA: Courtship. I mean, forget trying to analyze it. Because most of it will always remain completely . . . mysterious. And we should just honor the mystery. (*To Linda and Amy.*) Do you think men do that, and women sort of don't? Honor the mystery?

AMY: (*thinking about it*) Maybe.

DONNA: Why is that?

LINDA: What'd he do then?

DONNA: He . . .

PATRICK: (*Thinks it's funny.*) Where's your coat?

DONNA: (*Knows it was dumb.*) I didn't wear one. I always do that.

PATRICK: (*takes his raincoat off*) Here.

(*puts the raincoat on her, and buttons it*)

DONNA: You'll get wet.
PATRICK: It's okay.
DONNA: Thanks.
PATRICK: My pleasure.
LINDA: What'd he do?
DONNA: He . . .
PATRICK: (*Offers her his arm*)
LINDA: What?
DONNA: It's hard to describe.

(*She takes his arm.*)

> **AMY:**   **LINDA:**
> Tell us!   Tell!

DONNA: He gave me his coat. And he buttoned it up.

> **AMY:**   **LINDA:**
> Oooooo.   Oooooooh.

LINDA: That is so hot.
DONNA: And then he gave me his arm, and he walked me home. And he
was quiet the whole way.
LINDA: Uncomfortable quiet, or nice like you're in a bubble together quiet?
DONNA: Bubble together.
LINDA: Then, when you got to your place, what did he do?
PATRICK: Goodnight.

(*He kisses her.*)

DONNA: He said, "goodnight" and kissed me.
LINDA: How was the kiss?

(*Donna taps Patrick on the shoulder. Patrick kisses her again.*)

DONNA: Very nice. It was a very nice kiss.
LINDA: You had a nice date.
DONNA: Did I?
AMY: Yes.
LINDA: No, you did.
DONNA: I did. I had a nice date.

End

TRY THIS 5.10
Write a dialogue between yourself and two friends in which you tell about something
that happened to you. How do the friends' comments affect the way you tell the tale?
You might think of the telling as a journey and the friends' comments as detours.

WORKING TOWARD A DRAFT

Comb your journal and exercises for the passages that represent a confrontation, or "collision" of "two worlds," whether these worlds represent a power struggle between different ages, backgrounds, assumptions, territories, religions—whatever. Now look at the passages you have flagged and see which present a "journey" in the sense that the central persona or character changes in the course of the piece. Whether these are written in the form of nonfiction, fiction, poetry, or drama, they are likely to provide the richest possibilities for expansion. Pick one and jot down in your journal a plan for how you would turn it into something more substantial. What would you expand, trim, change? What human disconnections and connections would occur? What would you hope to show by the end? What effect would you like it to have on the reader?

Pick another passage and repeat the process.

Photos (clockwise from top left): Pam Valois, Rueters/Corbis, Pam Valois, Dirk Westphal

CHAPTER SIX

DEVELOPMENT AND REVISION

Developing a Draft
Structuring
Research
Revision
Editing
The Workshop

Ultimately my hope is to amaze myself.

Jerry Uelsmann

Imaginative writing has its source in dream, risk, mystery, and play. But if you are to be a good—and perhaps a professional—writer, you will need discipline, care, and ultimately even an obsessive perfectionism. As poet Paul Engle famously said, "Writing is rewriting what you have rewritten."

Just as a good metaphor must be both apt and surprising, so every piece of literary work must have both unity and variety, both craft and risk, both form and invention. Having dreamt and played a possibility into being, you will need to sharpen and refine it in action, character, and language, in a continual process of development and revision. You may need both to research and to re-dream. This will involve both disciplined work and further play, but it won't always be that easy to tell one from the other. Alice Munro describes the duality of a process in which seeking order remains both mysterious and a struggle:

> So when I write a story, I want to make a certain kind of structure, and I know the feeling I want to get from being inside that structure . . . There is no blueprint for this structure . . . It seems to be already there, and some unlikely clue, such as a shop window or a bit of conversation, makes me aware of it. Then I start accumulating the material and putting it together. Some of the material I may have

lying around already, in memories and observations, and some I invent, and some I have to go diligently looking for (factual details), while some is dumped in my lap (anecdotes, bits of speech). I see how this material might go together to make the shape I need, and I try it. I keep trying and seeing where I went wrong and trying again . . . I feel a part that's wrong, like a soggy weight; then I pay attention to the story, as if it were happening somewhere.

The concept of "development" seems to contain the notion of making something longer and fuller, whereas that of "revision" suggests mere changing or polishing. But in fact both terms are part of a continual process toward making the piece the best that it can be, and it isn't always easy to say which comes first or even which is which. Sometimes adding a paragraph to a character description will suggest a whole new theme or structure; sometimes a single word change proves a clue to a core meaning. Once when I had a fictional character describing her sister, she said, "She needs to be important," and for no reason but the rhythm I added, "especially if it means being dangerous." I didn't at once know what I meant, but I'm afraid that small addition led, two hundred pages later, to the sister's death. Much of development and revision, especially in the early stages, relies on your being receptive to the small interior voice that nudges you in this direction or feels vaguely unsatisfied with that paragraph.

Developing a Draft

Your journal is now a warehouse of possibilities, and you probably already have a sense of the direction in which many of its entries might be developed. Consider the following suggestions as you choose the form best suited to bring out the strengths of your journal work.

- If you wrote of a memory or an event that seems to you to contain a point or to lead toward reflection, if you came up with ideas that mattered to you and that you wanted both to illustrate and to state, then you probably have creative nonfiction, perhaps a memoir or personal essay in the works.

- If a journal entry has a strong setting, with characters who engage each other in action and dialogue, whose thoughts and desires may lead them into conflict and toward change, perhaps a short story is brewing.

- If the sound and rhythm of the language seem integral to the thought, if the images seem dense and urgent, if the idea clusters around imagery and sound rather than playing itself out in a sequence of events, then a poem is probably forming.

- If you have characters who confront each other in dialogue, especially if they are concealing things that they sometimes betray in word or action, and if they face discovery and decision that will lead to change in one or more of their lives, then you very likely have a play.

TRY THIS 6.1

Go quickly through your journal and identify the passages that seem to you on first sight to belong to the genres of creative nonfiction, fiction, poetry, and drama. Star those that interest you most. What is it about each of those pieces that seems worth more development? Make notes to yourself in the margin; circle or highlight ideas, images, connections you might want to pursue.

Chapters 7 through 10 of this book will discuss the techniques peculiar to each of the four forms—creative nonfiction, fiction, poetry, and drama—and you'll want to look at those chapters as you work toward a finished draft. In the meantime, there are a number of ways to develop your ideas in order to find your direction. Some of these are repetitions or adaptations of ideas you have already used for play.

TRY THIS 6.2

Take a journal entry you like and highlight any word that seems particularly evocative, that seems to capture the spirit of the whole. Free-associate around that word. Freewrite a paragraph on the subject.

And:

Pick another journal piece. Read it over, set it aside, and begin writing, starting every sentence with the words, "It's like . . . It's like . . . It's like . . . " Sometimes the sentence will evoke colors, sometimes memories, sometimes metaphors, and so forth. Keep writing, fast, until you're moderately tired.

Or:

Pick a journal entry that does not depend on setting, and give it a setting; describe the place and atmosphere in detail. Think of "setting" loosely. Perhaps the setting of a piece is someone's face. Perhaps the weather is internal.

When I was eight or nine, my brother, who was four years older, made up wonderful stories with which he used to pass the hot boring afternoons of Arizona summer. I would whine and beg for another episode. At some point he got tired of it and decided I should make up stories on my own. Then he would drill me by rapping out three nouns. "Oleanders, wastebasket, cocker spaniel!" "Factory, monkey bars, chop suey!" I was supposed to start talking immediately, making up as I went along a story about a dog who used to scrounge around in the garbage until one day he made the mistake of eating a poison flower . . . or a tool and die worker who went to a Chinese restaurant and left his son on the playground . . . My brother was the expert writer (and eventually went on to become an editor at the *Los Angeles Times*). I myself had not considered storytelling—I wrote ill-advised love letters and inspirational verse—and was amazed that I could—almost always—think of some way to include his three arbitrary things in a tale of mystery, disaster, or romance.

Neither of us knew that my brother had stumbled on a principle of literary invention, which is that creativity occurs when things not usually connected are seen as connected. It is the *unexpected* juxtaposition that generates literature. A more sophisticated version of this game is used in film writing. Screenwriter Claudia Johnson tells me that she and collaborator Pam Ball once went to a restaurant to celebrate the finishing of a film script. They had no idea what they were going to write next and decided to test the nimbleness of their plotting by outlining a film based on the next three things they overheard. The three conversations turned out to concern a cigarette, a suicide in Chicago, and origami. By the time they had their coffee they had a treatment for the next film.

Novelist Margaret Drabble describes the same process as organic and largely unconscious. "It's an accumulation of ideas. Things that have been in the back of my mind suddenly start to swim together and to stick together, and I think, 'Ah, that's a novel beginning.'"

TRY THIS 6.3

Pick, without too much thought about it—random would be fine—three entries in your journal. Take one element from each (a character, an image, a theme, a line of dialogue) and write a new passage that combines these three elements. Does it suggest any way that the three entries might in fact be fused into a single piece and be enriched by the fusion?

Or:

Take one of your journal entries and rewrite it in the form of one of the following: an instruction pamphlet, a letter to the complaints department, a newspaper item, a television ad, a love song. Does the new juxtaposition of form and content offer any way you can enrich your idea?

Structuring

Once you've identified a piece you want to develop, there are basically two ways to go about structuring the finished work—though they are always in some way used in combination.

Outlining

At one extreme is the **outline.** You think through the sequence of events of a story or drama, the points of an essay, the verse form of a poem. Then when you have an outline roughly in mind (or written down in detail), you start at the beginning and write through to the end of a draft.

Do not underestimate the power and usefulness of this method. However amorphous the vision of the whole may be, most writers begin with the first sentence and proceed to the last. Though fiction writer/essayist Charles Baxter has mourned the "tyranny of narrative," his stories and novels show the most careful attention to narrative sequence. (That one of them, *First Light*, presents its events in reverse order makes precise sequencing all the more necessary.) E. M. Forster spoke of writing a novel as moving toward some imagined event that loomed as a distant mountain. Eudora Welty advised a story writer to take walks pondering the story until it seemed whole, and then to try to write the first draft at one sitting. Though playwrights may first envision a climactic event and poets may start with the gift of a line that ends up last in the finished poem, still, the pull is strong to write from left to right and top to bottom.

TRY THIS 6.4

Take a pack of 3×5 cards and jot down, only a few words per card, any images, scenes, reflections you have in mind for a particular piece. Arrange them in a possible sequence. What's missing? Dream or freewrite or ponder what might be needed. Put each of these possible additions on a card and place them in sequence. Now you have a rough outline. You may want to write it down in outline or list form or you may not. Perhaps the cards, which can be reshuffled as you and the piece evolve, are what you need.

Quilting

At the opposite end of the spectrum from the outline is *quilting*, or "piece work," in which you carry on writing without attention to shape or structure. To use this method, you decide that this paragraph or verse or incident is the kernel of the thing you're going to write, and you continue to doodle and noodle around it, seeing what will emerge. You freewrite a dialogue passage, sketch in a description of the setting, try it in this character's voice and then as an omniscient narrator, let yourself go with a cascade of images. Two or three time a day, sit down and dash out a potential section of such a piece—a few lines, a paragraph, a monologue, images, a character sketch. Talk to yourself in your journal about what theme or idea matters to you, what you'd like to accomplish, what you fear will go wrong. If you do this for several days, you will have roughed out a sizeable portion of your project.

When you have a small mountain of material (I like to write or copy it into a single computer file I label a "ruff," then identify each paragraph by page number so I can find it easily), you print it, chop it into sections, spread it out on a large surface, and start moving pieces around till you seem to have a composition. Tape the sections together and make notes on them, discarding what seems extraneous, indicating what's missing, what needs rewriting, where a transition is in order, and so forth. Then cut-and-paste on the computer to put them in that order, noting the needed changes. When you print out this version, you have a rough shape of your piece.

TRY THIS 6.5
Doodle a series of lists—of the characteristics of someone you have written about, or of phrases and idioms that character would use; or of objects associated with a person, place, profession, or memory you have written about. Generate, rapidly, a list of metaphors for some central object in a piece you want to develop.

This cut-jot-and-sort system can work for any genre, and it's worth getting used to the process. However, sometimes it works better than others, and sometimes it just isn't the best way. The advantages of the outline method tend to be clarity, unity, and drive; of the cut-and-paste method, richness, originality, and surprise. The problem with writing from an outline is that the piece may seem thin and contrived; the trouble with piece work is that it can end up formless, diffuse, and dull.

You will already have a sense of which method is your natural tendency, and I'd urge you, whichever it is, to work in the opposite direction. The methods are not mutually exclusive, and each can benefit from the particular discipline of the other.

If you start with a clear sense of direction, a determination to follow a plan, then detour from time to time. Too tight a rein on the author's part, too rigid a control of where the imagery is headed, what the protagonist will do next, how the remembered event exactly happened—any of these can squeeze the life out of the work. When you feel the action or the language becoming mechanical, stop and freewrite a monologue, a list of images, an exploration of character, or conflict, or the weather. One freeing trick, if you find your piece flat, is to go through and put some arbitrary line or sentence in each paragraph or verse, something that absolutely does not belong and that you would never put there. Then go away from it for a while, and when you go back, see if there's anything in the nonsense that might in fact improve the sense.

If, on the other hand, you can generate lovely stuff but have trouble finding a through-line for it, if you find yourself in successive drafts generating new possibilities and never settling on a form or sequence, then you probably need to focus on a plan and push yourself through one draft based on it. Set your quilt aside and consider the questions of unity and shape: What is the heart of this piece? What is its emotional core? What, in one word, is it *about?* How can I focus on that, make each part illuminate it, raise the intensity, and get rid of the extraneous?

And don't give up. "The big secret," says fiction writer Ron Carlson, "is the ability to stay in the room. The writer is the person who stays in the room . . . People have accused me . . . 'You're talking Zen here.' And I just say, 'Zen this: The secret is to stay in the room.'"

TRY THIS 6.6

Practice in brief form each of the methods above. Pick an entry in your journal—not one you intend to make into a finished work. Before lunch, write an outline of a piece based on that entry. In late afternoon or evening, take *no more than one hour* to write a draft of the piece that covers the whole outline. Your work will have holes, cracks, and sloppy writing. Never mind; get through to the end. Leave it for a day or two, then make marginal notes on what you would want to do in the next draft.

Pick another entry and over the next two or three days, freewrite something or other about it every four hours. Print, cut, and arrange into a sequence or shape. Print out the result and make marginal notes on what the next draft would need.

Discuss in class what you learned from the two methods. Which would suit you best when you come to write an essay, a story, a poem, a play?

Research

Any piece of writing, to be convincing and rich with detail, needs solid knowledge of its subject matter. Nothing is more irritating to a reader than to be told a character is a doctor when it's clear he doesn't know a stethoscope from a stegosaur. For any genre of writing there will come a time when you need to research through library, interview, Internet, or some other way.

But research for imaginative writing has a rather different nature and purpose than the research you've been taught. Whereas the "research paper" has as its first requirement a rigorous attention to both facts and sources, the watchword of imaginative research is *immersion*. Depending on the kind of piece you're writing, you may need accuracy, and you may need to credit or quote someone, but you certainly need the flavor, the imagery and the atmosphere of whatever you seek to know. If you make yourself wholly available to whatever information you seek, what you need will be there when you come to write about it.

I once had the luck, just as I was starting on a novel set in Mexico and Arizona in 1914, to hear a lecture by the great novelist Mary Lee Settle. She offered three rules for historical fiction research:

- Don't read *about* the period; read *in* the period. Read letters, journals, newspapers, magazines, books written at the time. You will in this way learn the cadences, the turn of mind and phrase, the obsessions and quirks of the period.

- Don't take notes. If you save everything that interests you, you'll be tempted to use it whether it fits or not, and your fiction will smell of research. Immerse yourself and trust that what you need will be there.

- Don't research beyond the period you're writing about. If you know too much about the future, your characters will inevitably know it too.

Now, these rules are particular to historical fiction, but I think the spirit of them is applicable to any sort of imaginative research.

You may need to interview someone in order to write a piece about your family, and you may want to quote exactly. But don't take down everything, and don't think you have to use everything. Much more important than notes is to listen with an absolutely open mind. Hear the rhythms and the images of the particular voice. Sponge up the sounds and the peculiarities.

For any genre of imaginative work, you may need to search the library or the Internet for information on an object, a profession, a region, a building, a kind of clothing, and so forth. Read ravenously. Reread, read a second book or site. Look into a third that suggests something vaguely connected. But understand that you are reshaping the information into something that is not primarily information, and the crucial thing is to absorb it, toss it on the compost of your imagination, let it feed your piece, not devour it.

TRY THIS 6.7

Bring your research skills to your imaginative work. Identify something in a piece that you aren't sure about. You don't know the facts, don't understand the process or the equipment, aren't clear on the history or the statistics, don't know the definition. Find out. Consult books, reference works, newspapers, the Internet; interview someone, email someone, ask the experts.

Interviewer: Was there some technical problem? What was it that had stumped you?
Hemingway: Getting the words right.

Revision

Most people dread revision and put it off; and most find it the most satisfying part of writing once they are engaged in it and engaged by it. The vague feelings of self-dissatisfaction and distress that accompany an imperfect draft are smoothed away as the pleasure of small perfections and improvements come.

To write your first draft, you banished the internal critic. Now make the critic welcome. The first round of rewrites is probably a matter of letting your misgivings surface. Revision is a holistic process, unique to each piece of writing, and though this chapter includes questions you might use as a guide, there is no substitute for your own receptivity and concentration. What do *you* think is needed here? What are you sure of, and where are you dissatisfied?

Focus for a while on what seems awkward, overlong, undeveloped, flat, or flowery. Tinker. Tighten. Sharpen. Let that small unease surface and look at it squarely. More important at this stage than finishing any given page or phrase is that you're getting to know your story in order to open it to new possibilities. Novelist Rosellen Brown says, "What I love about being in the revision stage is that it means you've got it. It's basically there. And so then you've got to chip away at it, you've got to move things around, you've got to smooth it down. But the fact of the matter is, you've got it in hand."

It is when you have a draft "in hand" that you will experience development and revision as a continuum of invention and improvement, re-seeing and chiseling. Sometimes the mere altering of punctuation will flash forth a necessary insight. Sometimes inspiration will necessitate a change of tense or person. To find the best way of proceeding, you may have to "see again" more than once. The process involves external and internal insight; you'll need your conscious critic, your creative instinct, and readers you trust. You may need each of them several times, not necessarily in that order. Writing gets better not just by polishing and refurbishing, not only by improving a word choice here and image there, but by taking risks with the structure, re-envisioning, being open to new meaning itself. Sometimes, Annie Dillard advises in *The Writing Life*, what you must do is knock out "a bearing wall." "The part you jettison," she says, "is not only the best written part; it is also, oddly, that part which was to have been the very point. It is the original key passage, the passage on which the rest was to hang, and from which you yourself drew the courage to begin."

There are many kinds of work and play that go under the name of "revision." It would be useful to go back to the film metaphor—long shot, middle shot, close-up—in order to think of ways of re-visioning your work. You will at some point early or late need to step back and view the project as a whole, its structure and composition, the panorama of its tones: does it need fundamental change, reversal of parts, a different shape or a different sweep? At some point you will be working in obsessive close-up, changing a word to alter the coloration of a mood, finding a fresher metaphor or a more exact verb, even changing a comma to a semicolon and changing it back again. Often you'll be working in middle shot, moving this paragraph from page one to page three, chopping out an unnecessary description, adding a passage of dialogue to intensify the atmosphere. Read each draft of your piece aloud and listen for rhythm, word choice, unintended repetition. You'll move many times back and forth among these methods, also walking away from the piece in order to come back to it with fresh eyes.

> **TRY THIS 6.8**
> Make a list of things a character or persona in your piece might fear. Add a scene, line, or image in which a character or persona is in great fear.
>
> *Or:*
>
> Show the character doing something genuinely dangerous. But the character/persona is not afraid. Why not?

If you feel stuck on a project, put it away. Don't look at it for a matter of days or weeks, until you feel fresh again. In addition to getting some distance on your work, you're mailing it to your unconscious. You may even discover that in the course of developing a piece, you have mistaken its nature. I once spent a year writing a screenplay—which I suppose I thought was the right form because the story was set in an Arizona cow town in 1914—finally to realize that I couldn't even *find out* what the story was until I got inside the characters' heads. Once I understood this, that story became a novel.

As you plan your revisions and as you rewrite, you will know (and your critics will tell you) what problems are unique to your piece. You may also be able to focus your own critique by asking yourself these questions:

What is this piece about? The answer may be different according to the genre, may involve a person, an emotion, an action, or a realization rather than an idea. But centering your consciousness on what the piece is about will help to center the piece itself.

> **TRY THIS 6.9**
> State your central subject or idea in a single sentence. Reduce it to a word. Express it in an image. Express it in a line of dialogue that one of your characters might say. Probably none of these things will appear in your finished piece, but they will help you focus. Are you clear about what you're writing about? Does it need thinking and feeling through again?

Is the language fresh? Have you used concrete imagery, the active voice to make the language vivid? Are these abstractions necessary? Does your opening line or sentence make the reader want to read on?

> **TRY THIS 6.10**
> Go through your work and highlight generalizations in one color, abstractions in another, clichés in a third. Replace each of them with something specific, wild, inappropriate, far-fetched. Go back later to see if any of these work. Replace the others, working toward the specific, the precise, and the concrete.

Is it clear? Do we know who, what, where, when, what's happening? Can we see the characters, keep their names straight, follow the action?

TRY THIS 6.11

Go through your manuscript and highlight the answers to these questions: *Where are we? When are we? Who are they? How do things look? What period, time of year, day or night is it? What's the weather? What's happening?* If you can't find the answers in your text, the reader won't find them either. Not all of this information may be necessary, but you need to be aware of what's left out.

Where is it too long? The teacher William Strunk, long revered for his little book *The Elements of Style,* used to bark at his students, "Omit unnecessary words!" Do so. Are there too many adjectives, adverbs, flowery descriptions, explanations—as perhaps there are in this sentence, since you've already got the point?

TRY THIS 6.12

Carefully save the current draft of your piece. Then copy it into a new document on which you play a cutting game—make your own rules in advance. Cut all the adjectives and adverbs. Or remove one line from every verse of a poem. Delete a minor character. Fuse two scenes into one. Cut half of every line of dialogue. Or simply require yourself to shorten it somehow by a third. You will have some sense of what tightening might improve your work. Compare the two drafts. Does the shortened version have any virtues that the longer one does not?

Where is it underdeveloped? This question may simply involve the clarity of the piece: What necessary information is in your head that has not made it to the page, and so to the mind of the reader? But underdevelopment may also involve depth or significance, what memoirist Patricia Foster calls "the vertical drop . . . when an essay drops deeper—into character, into intimacy, into some sense of the hidden story."

TRY THIS 6.13

In any first, second, or third draft of a manuscript there are likely to be necessary lines, images, or passages that you have skipped or left skeletal. Make notes in your margins wherever you feel your piece is underdeveloped. Then go back and quickly freewrite each missing piece. At this point, just paste the freewrites in. Then read over the manuscript (long shot) to get a feel for how these additions change, add, or distort. Are some unnecessary after all? Do some need still fuller expanding? Should this or that one be reduced to a sentence or image? Do some suggest a new direction?

Does it end? The ending of a piece is its most powerful point in terms of its impact on the reader (the beginning is the second most important). So it matters that it should have the effect you want. Does the character change? Does the essay reveal? Does the poem offer a turn or twist on its image? Does the drama move? (Actually, any of these questions might apply to any genre.) This is not to say that the piece should clunk closed with a moral or a stated idea. Novelist Elizabeth Dewberry puts it this way: "When you get to the end you want to have a sense that you understand for the first time—and by *you* I mean the writer and the reader and even the characters—for the first time, how the whole story fits together."

TRY THIS 6.14

As an experiment only, end your piece with a poetic line, a line of dialogue, or a paragraph that is the direct opposite of the meaning or effect you want. You might try ending by repeating the opening (which can, in fact, turn out to be effective if the line or paragraph takes on a new and changed meaning). Consider the impact of what you have done. Does it help to clarify what the ending should be?

Editing

Just as there is no clear line between development and revision, so revision and editing are part of the same process, helping the piece to be as good as it can possibly be. Editing addresses such areas as clarity, precision, continuity, and flow. One way to see the distinction is that editing can be done by an editor, someone other than the author, whereas revision is usually turned back to the author. (For example, noting a lack of transition from the last section to this one, my editor has just asked, "Can you insert a short paragraph here explaining the relationship between revision and editing, and the difference between editing and line editing?") Line editing is the last in the care-and-feeding process of the manuscript, a line-by-line check that spelling, grammar, and punctuation—including agreement, comma placement, quotation marks, modifiers, and so forth—are accurate (and perhaps in the "style" of the publication or press). Although these jobs can be invaluably done by an editor and copy editor, and many a genius has been saved from embarrassment by their intervention, it's also true that the more carefully you edit and **line edit** your own manuscript the more professional you will appear, and that "clean copy" is most likely to be given serious consideration.

Spelling, grammar, and punctuation are a kind of magic; their purpose is to be invisible. If the sleight of hand works, we will not notice a comma or a quotation mark but will translate each instantly into a pause or an awareness of voice; we will not focus on the individual letters of a word but extract its sense whole. When the mechanics are incorrectly used, the trick is revealed and the magic fails; the reader's focus is shifted from the story to its surface. The reader is irritated at the author, and of all the emotions the reader is willing to experience, irritation at the author is not one.

There is no intrinsic virtue in standardized mechanics, and you can depart from them whenever you produce an effect that adequately compensates for the attention called to the surface. But only then. Unlike the techniques of narrative, the rules of spelling, grammar, and punctuation can be coldly learned anywhere in the English-speaking world—and they should be learned by anyone who aspires to write.

No one really has an eagle eye for his/her own writing. It's harder to keep your attention on the mechanics of your own words than any other—for which reason a friend or a copy editor with the skill is invaluable. In the meantime, however, try to become a good surface editor of your work. Reading aloud always helps.

TRY THIS 6.15

Particularly frequent problems in grammar and punctuation are these: dangling modifiers, unclear antecedents of pronouns, the use of the comma in compound sentences, the use of *lay* and *lie*. If you're unsure of yourself with regard to any of these giveaway errors, look them up in a standard grammar text. Spend the time to learn them—the effort will repay itself a hundredfold throughout your writing life.

Then:

What follows is a passage with at least three punctuation mistakes, three spelling mistakes, one dangling modifier, four typos, two awkward repetitions, one unclear antecedent, two misused words, and a cliché (though some may fit more than one category and a few may cause disagreement—that is the nature of proofreading). Spot and correct them. Make any necessary judgment calls.

> Together, Lisel and Drakov wondered through Spartanvilles noisy, squalid streets. Goats clogged the noisy streets and the venders cursed them. Walking hand in hand, the factory generater seemed to send it's roar overhead at the level of a low plane.
>
> A homeless man leared up at them crazy as a cuckoo. They were astonished to see the the local police had put up a barrier at the end of Main Street, plus the government were making random passport checks at the barrier.
>
> "What could they be looking for on a georgeous day like this"? Lisel wondered. Drakov said, "Us, Maybe."

Then:

Your manuscript as you present it to your workshop, an agent, or an editor, is dressed for interview. If it's sloppy it'll be hard to see how brilliant it really is. Groom it. Consult the end of each genre chapter for the traditional and professional formats.

Line Edit: Check through for faulty grammar, inconsistent tenses, unintended repetitions of words, awkwardness. *Proofread:* Run a spell check (but don't rely on it entirely). Read through for typos, punctuation errors, any of those goblins that slip into a manuscript. If you are in doubt about the spelling or meaning of a word, look it up.

> *Whatever can't be taught, there is a great deal that can,*
> *and must, be learned.*
>
> Mary Oliver

The Workshop

Once you have a draft of a piece and have worked on it to the best of your ability, someone else's eyes can help refresh the vision of your own. That's where the workshop can help. Professionals rely on their editors and agents in this process, and as Kurt Vonnegut has pointed out, "A creative writing course provides experienced editors for inspired amateurs. What could be simpler or more dignified?"

In preparation for the workshop, each class member should read the piece twice, once for its content, a second time with pen in hand to make marginal comments, observations, suggestions. A summarizing end note is usual and helpful. This should be done with the understanding that the work at hand is *by definition* a work in progress. If it were finished then there would be no reason to bring it into the workshop.

Keep in mind that the goal of the workshop is to make the piece under consideration *the best that it can be.* The group should continue to deal, first, in neutral and inquiring ways with each piece before going on to discuss what does and doesn't "work." It's often a good idea to begin with a detailed summary of what the poetry, story, essay, or drama actually says—useful because if class members understand the characters or events differently, find the imagery confusing, or miss an irony, this is important information for the author, a signal that she has not revealed what, or all, she meant. The exploratory questions suggested in the introduction may still be useful. In addition, the class might address such questions as:

- What kind of piece is this?
- What other works does it remind you of?
- How is it structured?
- What is it about?
- What does it say about what it is about?
- What degree of identification does it invite?
- How does its imagery relate to its theme?
- How is persona or point of view employed?
- What effect on the reader does it seem to want to produce?

Only then should the critique begin to deal with whether the work under consideration is successful in its effects: *is the language fresh, the action clear, the point of view consistent, the rhythm interesting, the characters fully drawn, the imagery vivid?* Now and again it is well to pause and return to more substantive matters: *what's the spirit of this piece, what is it trying to say, what does it make me feel?* Take another look also at the suggestions for workshop etiquette on page xxviii of the "Invitation to the Writer." Your workshop leader will also have ground rules for the conducting of the workshop.

If the process is respectfully and attentively addressed, it can be of genuine value not only to the writer but to the writer-critics, who can learn, through the articulation of their own and others' responses, what "works" and what doesn't, and how to face similar authorial problems. In workshop discussion, disagreements are as often as instructive as consensus; lack of clarity often teaches what clarity is.

For the writer, the process is emotionally strenuous, because the piece under discussion is a sort of baby on the block. Its parent may have a strong impulse to explain and plead. Most of us feel not only committed to what we have put on the page, but also defensive on its behalf—wanting, really, only to be told that it is a work of genius or, failing that, to find out that we have gotten away with it. We may even want to blame the reader. If the criticism is: *this isn't clear,* it's hard not to feel: *you didn't read it right*—even if you understand that although the workshop members have an obligation to read with special care, it is not up to them to "get it" but up to the author to be clear. If the complaint is: *this isn't credible,* it's very hard not to respond: *but it really happened!*—even though you know perfectly well that credibility is a different sort of fish than fact. There is also a self-preservative impulse to keep from changing the core of what you've done: *why should I put in all that effort?*

The most important part of being a writer in a workshop is to learn this: be still, be greedy for suggestions, take everything in, and don't defend. The trick to making good use of criticism is to be utterly selfish about it. Ultimately you are the laborer, the arbiter, and the boss in any dispute about your story, so you can afford to consider any problem and any solution. Therefore, the first step toward successful revision is learning to hear, absorb, and accept criticism.

It *is* difficult. But only the effort of complete receptivity will make the workshop work for you. The chances are that your draft really does not say the most meaningful thing inherent in it, and that most meaningful thing may announce itself sideways, in a detail, a parenthesis, an afterthought, a slip. Somebody else may spot it before you do. Sometimes the best advice comes from the most surprising source. The thing you resist the hardest may be exactly what you need.

After the workshop, the writer's obligation alters slightly. It's important to take the written critiques and take them seriously, let them sink in with as good a will as you brought to workshop. But part of the need is also not to let them sink in too far. Reject without regret whatever seems on reflection wrong-headed, dull, destructive, or irrelevant to your vision. Resist the impulse to write "for the workshop" what you think your peers or teacher will praise. It's just as important to be able to discriminate between helpful and unhelpful criticism as it is to be able to write. It is in fact the same thing as being able to write. So listen to everything and receive all criticism as if it is golden. Then listen to yourself and toss the dross.

More to Read

Bunge, Nancy, *Master Class*. Iowa City: University of Iowa Press, 2005.

Kaplan, David Michael. *Revision: A Creative Approach to Writing and Rewriting Fiction*. Cincinnati: Story Press, 1997.

Strunk, William Jr. and E. B. White. *The Elements of Style*, Fourth Edition. New York: Longman, 2000.

And to Watch

Burroway, Janet, *So Is It Done? Navigating the Revision Process*. Chicago: Elephant Rock Productions, 2005.

Examples

What follows in this chapter are three examples of revision, two of them with a narrative by the author explaining what changes were made in the manuscripts and why. Two are poems that change their forms, and one is the opening of a novel.

ELIZABETH BISHOP: FIRST AND FINAL DRAFTS OF "ONE ART"

The first and final drafts of Elizabeth Bishop's poem "One Art" show an evolution from a focused freewrite toward the very intricate poetic form of a **villanelle,** in which the first and third lines are repeated at the end of alternating successive verses and as a couplet at the end. In spite of this very demanding scheme, the finished version is about half the length of the freewrite. Notice how the ideas are increasingly simply stated, the tone of the final version calm and detached until the burst of emotion in the last line. In these two drafts, Bishop plays with various points of view, trying "one" and "I" and "you" before settling on the final combination of instruction and confession. The title too works toward simplicity, from "How to Lose Things," "The Gift of Losing Things," and "The Art of Losing Things" to the most concise and understated "One Art."

The First Draft

HOW TO LOSE THINGS /? / THE GIFT OF LOSING THINGS?

One might begin by losing one's reading glasses
oh 2 or 3 times a day - or one's favorite pen.

THE ART OF LOSING THINGS
The thing to do is to begin by "mislaying".

Mostly, one begins by "mislaying":
keys, reading-glasses, fountain pens
- these are almost too easy to be mentioned,
and "mislaying" means that they usually turn up
in the most obvious place, although when one
is making progress, the places grow more unlikely
- This is by way of introduction. I really
want to introduce myself -   I am such a
fantastic lly good at losing things
I think everyone shd. profit from my experiences.

You may find it hard to believe, but I have actually lost
I mean lost, and forever two whole houses,
one a very big one.   A third house, also big, is
at present, I think, "mislaid" - but
maybe it's lost, too. I won't know for sure for some time.
I have lost one/long peninsula and one island.
I have lost - it can never be has never been found -
a small-sized town on that same island.
I've lost smaller bits of geography, like   and many smaller bits of geography or scenery
a splendid beach , and a good-sized bay.
Two whole cities, two of the
world's biggest cities (two of the most beautiful
although that's beside the point)
A piece of one continent -
and one entire continent.   All gone, gone forever and ever.

One might think this would have prepared me
for losing one average-sized not especially------- exceptionally
beautiful or dazzlingly intelligent person
(except for blue eyes)   (only the eyes were exceptionally beautiful and
But it doesn't seem to have, at all...   the hands looked intelligent)
                                  the fine hands

a good piece of one continent
and another continent - the whole damned thing!
He who loseth his life, etc. - but he who
loses his love - neever, no never never never again -

A
 x
B

The Final Draft

Elizabeth Bishop

One Art

The art of losing isn't hard to master;
so many things seem filled with the intent
to be lost that their loss is no disaster.

Lose something every day. Accept the fluster
of lost door keys, the hour badly spent.
The art of losing isn't hard to master.

Then practice losing farther, losing faster:
places, and names, and where it was you meant
to travel. None of these will bring disaster.

I lost my mother's watch. And look! my last, or
next-to-last, of three loved houses went.
The art of losing isn't hard to master.

I lost two cities, lovely ones. And, vaster,
some realms I owned, two rivers, a continent.
I miss them, but it wasn't a disaster.

—Even losing you (the joking voice, a gesture
I love) I shan't have lied. It's evident
the art of losing's not too hard to master
though it may look like (*Write it!*) like disaster.

> *A detailed comparison of the many drafts of this poem appears in the*
> *fine essay "A Moment's Thought" in Ellen Bryant Voigt's,* The Flexible
> Lyric (*Athens and London, The University of Georgia Press, 1999*).

Notice also that "One Art" is a "list poem" or "catalogue poem," built on a list of things that can be lost. It's almost impossible to overstate the importance of the list in literature. You can use lists of images to build a description or a portrait, extend a metaphor by listing the aspects of a comparison, or structure an essay as a list of ways to look at your subject. (Margaret Atwood's "The Female Body," on page 249, is structured in such a way.) It could even be argued that a story is based on a list of events one after the other.

TRY THIS 6.16
Choose one of the lists in your journal and play around with it, extending each item on the list into a sentence or two, adding an image, an idea, a memory. When you have a page or so, look it over and see what repeated images or ideas emerge. What do the parts have in common? What do you seem to be saying? Can you give it a title? If so, you may have a theme. Try arranging the parts into lines. Now try cutting whatever seems extraneous to your theme. Are you partway to a poem?

JANET BURROWAY: THE OPENING OF *INDIAN DANCER:* A REVISION NARRATIVE

As I write this, I am still in the process of revising a novel, *Indian Dancer.* The novel tells the story of a girl born in Belgium in 1930, who escapes to England during the Second World War and later emigrates to America. Most of the novel deals with her adolescent and adult life, but after I had written many of the later scenes, it seemed to me that the novel should begin with an image of that childhood escape, which affects everything she later does. I felt "inspired" when I woke up one morning and tapped out this:

> Always,
> she retained one image from the boat, too fleeting for a memory but too substan-
> tial for a dream, like a few frames clipped from a kinetoscope. She was standing
> in the stern, embraced from behind by a woman who was wrapping her in rough
> blanket stuff. Her shoes and the hem of her coat above her knees were wet. She
> knew that the woman was kind, but the smell of anxiety and too many nights'
> sweat filled her with dark judgment. There was no moon at all, which was the
> point, but all the same she could watch the wake of the boat widening behind
> them. She also knew, in a cold, numbed way, that her father was bleeding on the
> shore, but what presented itself as monstrous was the wake, dark and glutinous,
> ever spreading toward the land, as if she herself were a speck being washed from
> a wound. *I will never go back. I will never.* This was experienced as grief, not yet
> a vow.

After a day or so I felt this was melodramatic—that "dark judgment," her father "bleeding on the shore," the "monstrous" and "glutinous" sea. I noticed that "kinetoscope" stuck out like a piece of show-off research. I thought there should be more sense of the woman trying to help her, and of the others on the boat. The past tense also troubled me. If she "always retained," then wouldn't the memory be in the present?

Always,

also, she is standing in the stern, embraced from behind by a woman who swaddles her in coarse blanket stuff. Her shoes and the hem of her coat above her knees are wet. There is no moon—which is the point—but all the same she can see the wake widening in the Channel, and close beside her on the deck the boy who broke his shin, the bone stub moving under the flesh like a tongue in a cheek. The man—his father?—still has the boy's mouth stuffed with a forearm of loden coat to keep him from crying out, although they are far enough from shore that the oars have been shipped and the motor roped into life. It sputters like a heart. Behind her the people huddle—you can't tell heroes from refugees—over flasks of tea and Calvados whose fireapple smell flings up on the smell of sea. She will never see any of these people again. The woman's armpit cups her chin, old wet wool and fear. She knows unflinchingly that her father has been left behind. What presents itself as monstrous is the wake—dark, glutinous—which seems to be driving them from the land on its slubbed point as if the boat is a clot being washed from a wound.

I will never go back. I will never. This is experienced as grief, not yet a vow.

I fiddled with this a lot, still dissatisfied with its tone, which seemed to set the book on a loftier course than I intended, but it was several months before it struck me that *the woman should tell this scene.* I think it was the image of the boy's broken bone "like a tongue in a cheek" that gave me the first hint of the woman's voice. She was a British woman; I imagined her as working class, one of the accidental heroes of the Resistance, a practical, solid sort. This revelation must have occurred to me on an airplane (the disembodied feeling of airplanes *always* sets me writing) because I scribbled on a page of a yellow pad:

Mostly they ~~all~~ all run together, ~~but sometimes~~ ~~its the youngsters stick in~~ ~~the ones that~~ mind ~~stick in mind are the youngsters~~. One I recall, ~~and~~ a skinny little thing ~~on her own~~, very grown in her coat and collar. This must have been about 'forty, we ~~was~~ doing the ~~Ostend Dover run~~ run from the Ostend coast ~~to Ostend~~ to Dover in Sart ~~Spoot~~ Dunahy's trawler, once a month maybe. We had ~~half~~ a dozen crannies of that coast marked out and underground runners all through Flanders ~~and beyond~~ to set up the ~~rendezvous~~ times. ~~One reason~~ I ~~remember this~~ ~~one~~ we expected two of them, the girl and her ~~father~~ father, and ~~but we~~ near as spit didn't wait for them. Hell, ~~because the other~~ there was a ~~hanging jumped~~ ~~catchcorner~~ squeejam off the dock and broke a leg in the boat. One of the men ~~Dunahy~~ gave him a monthful of loden coat to keep him quiet, but it saved us, and Dunahy cast off. Then I saw her running down the dune, ~~edging~~ like, where she ~~could have~~ run straight ~~up~~ ~~to~~ ~~us~~ ~~if she chose~~, and I went ~~down~~ ~~to~~ coax her into ~~the water~~ running straight and ~~up~~ ~~us~~ up to her

Now I started over, putting the scene back in chronological order but always chasing the woman's voice, also reading up on the period and the events of the war, checking out British expressions with my son who lives in London:

They came in all sorts, talk about misery and scared, and I never saw a one of them again.

This must have been about 'forty, the Vicar and I were coming down from Teddington maybe once a month to make the crossing from Dover to Ostend and back again. We had the use of Duck Henley's trawler and half a dozen meeting points along the coast, underground runners all through that part of Flanders setting up the times. ~~Usually they came on foot, talk about misery and scared, and~~ They mostly run together, only it's the children that stick out in your mind.

~~Sometimes they were that dumb brave. There were babies never made a peep, and~~ I remember one boy landed squeejaw off the dock and broke his shin so the bone rolled under his skin like a tongue in a cheek. It was maybe the same trip we ~~was~~ were expecting a girl and her father and nearly pushed off without them when we saw her running ~~all by herself~~ down the rocks, straight into the water up to her coat hem. O'Hannaughy swung his arm signalling her to go round the dock and lowered her down with her shoes full of water. I wrapped her up and she says po-faced, "My Father sends me to come ahead." She says, "My fah-zer."

or maybe another

What I remember ~~about her~~ is, we had a little bunsen and usually when you got out far enough to rope the motors alive, they were all glad to hunker down over a cuppa. But this one didn't leave the stern six, maybe eight hours of rough crossing, looking back where we'd come from. ~~It was black dark—we always picked nights with no moon—but all the same you could see the wake~~. Very polite she was in her soggy shoes, but couldn't be budged. ~~I knew not to ask about her father~~. And I remember I tucked the blanket around her, which she let me, and I thought the way we must have looked to God, that greasy little trawler in the black ~~water~~ wake, like a clot being washed ~~out of~~ from a wound.

in the ~~black~~ dark. ~~with no moon~~.

arrives not. He ~~keeps back but~~ ~~is not able to~~

Over the course of several months I kept coming back to this scene, trying to imagine it more fully, to heighten the sense of danger as the little boat flees the mines and U-boats, but to keep it in the chatty, down-to-earth voice of the woman who was—when? I asked myself suddenly; why?—telling this story—to whom? At some point, having spent perhaps a couple of full-time work weeks on this tiny but crucial scene, it came to me that the woman was being interviewed on television, for one of those anniversary documentaries of the war. At once, though I do not describe the scene of the interview, I could see and hear her more clearly.

The book now begins this way:

Transit: Ostend–Dover

All that spring and summer we brought back boatloads of the refugees. The Vicar organized us. They didn't mind I was a woman because I was able-bodied. We traveled down from Teddington once a month to make the crossing, and we had the use of Duck Henley's trawler and half a dozen meeting points along the Flemish coast. Underground runners all through Belgium setting up the rendezvous.

It's a wonder what you remember. Great swollen blanks, and then some daft thing bobs up like flotsam. Such as, I'd never worn a pair of trousers, and what I couldn't get used to was the twill going swish between my thighs. Is that camera running? Don't show me saying *thighs*, will you? Anyway, that and the smells. Tar, old fish in the wet boards. Seasick, of course. And off your own skin a bit of metal smell, with a sourness like fireworks. When they say "sweating bullets" I expect that's what they mean.

The ones we ferried came in every sort—rich man, poor man, tinker, tailor. I never saw a one of them again. Now and then I cross via Newhaven over to Normandy for the shopping, and I look around and think: they're not so different, take away their pocket books and their sunburn. What struck me, in Teddington everybody got raw noses from the cold and spider veins from the fire, but those ones were always drained-looking like they hadn't been out of doors, although most had been living rough or walking nights. You probably think I misremember it from a newsreel—not that we ever made it into the Movietone—but I said it at the time: every one of them gray, and eyes like drain holes that the color washed right down.

It's the children stick in your mind—a wee tiddler with its eyes wide open and its mouth tight shut. I remember one boy landed crooked off the dock and broke his shin, so the bone stub rolled under the skin like a tongue in a cheek. Somebody gave him a mouthful of coat sleeve to keep him quiet.

It was that same trip we were expecting a father and daughter that didn't show up, and we about pushed off without them. We'd heard dogs, and you never knew the meaning of dogs—it could be the patrols, or just somebody's mutt in a furore. One thing I've never understood, you pick a night with no moon and a piece of shore without a light—a disused lighthouse this was, great dark lump in the dark—and you can't see a whit, *can not see*. And then there's a click, like, in the back of your eyes, and you can. Sandiford was pressing off the piling, and the Vicar said, *no, steady on*. Duck was reluctant—you couldn't know when the boy would yell out—and then he felt it too and had them put up the oars. The waves were thick as black custard, and the black shore, and now, click! there's this girl, maybe ten or twelve, gawky little tyke, slogging straight into the water up to her coat hem. Sandiford swung his arm signaling her to go round the dock and fetched her down with her shoes full of water. She's got one hand done up in a fist against her collar bone. I wrapped her up, and she says po-faced, "My father arrives not. I arrive alone." She says, "My fah-zer." I knew better than to ask.

From there across—you understand, nobody said *U-boats*. Nobody said *mines*. Mostly you didn't keep an eye out, except for Duck and Sandiford whose job it was, because you were superstitious you would call them up. All the same that's what was in everybody's mind. You just hoped the kiddies didn't know the odds.

What I remember is, we had a little paraffin stove, and usually when you got out far enough to rope the motors into life, they were all glad to settle down over a cuppa. But this one didn't leave the stern maybe eight hours of rough crossing, looking back where we'd come from in the dark. She held that one hand tight as lockjaw, and I thought she had some money in there, maybe, or a bit of jewelry, something she'd been told to keep from harm. You'd think you wouldn't be curious under the circumstances, but eight hours is a long time to be standing, your mind must be doing something. I remember I tucked the blanket tighter around her and held it there, which she let me, and for most of the way we just stood till it was lightening a little down by the horizon. She dozed, I thought. She sagged against me and bit by bit her hand relaxed over the top of the blanket. There was nothing in it. Not a thing. I cupped it in my own and chafed it back to life a little. And I thought the way we must have looked to God, that greasy little trawler in the black wake, like a clot being washed from a wound.

My folder of drafts of this passage now runs to forty pages, excessive and obsessive perhaps, but it is after all the beginning of the book and must be right. I have noticed over the years that my digging at, fiddling with, scratching away at a scene will often turn up something much more fundamental than a new image or a livelier verb. In this case, I gradually realized that the reason the scene must be in somebody else's voice is that *the heroine does not remember it.* Traumatized by her flight, she cannot recall witnessing her father's death until she is nearly fifty years old. When I realized that, I understood much better what story I was telling and how the plot could be shaped and resolved. I had the delicious chance to let my heroine see the television documentary in the 1980s—in a twenty-year-old rerun—and let that chunk of interview, which contained the reader's first view of her, finally jog her memory.

TRY THIS 6.17
Choose a scene in your journal, either of fiction or memoir, and rewrite it from another point of view, in another voice. Try to choose a character as different from the original voice as possible, so that we get not just a change of "person" (from *he* or *she* to *I*), but a different set of attitudes, a different take on the events. Under what circumstances would this character be telling the story? To whom? Set the scene if you like.

Or:

Interview one of your characters. Write the questions out as if you were in fact conducting a radio, television, or newspaper interview, and then answer them.

Or:

Trade brief character descriptions with another writer. Make up a list of questions for that writer's character, then trade lists and write your own character's answers to the questions.

JAMES KIMBRELL: GROWING "FOUR TANGERINES"

A letter came in the mail that announced the twentieth reunion of Leakesville High School's senior class of 1985. This event led me to my yearbook. I saw my picture there between two people I had long since forgotten. Somewhat predictably, I wondered what had become of them and what had become of the person I was back then.

I also realized that the silver—and rather snazzy, if I do say so myself—tie bar I was wearing in my photograph came to me by way of a man that I'd never met, a man who died in the nursing home where my mother worked. One day she brought home this orange crate that had a jacket, some dress shirts, a sweater, cuff links, three pipes, a tie pin, a money clip, and a few old style sleeveless T-shirts, the kind I hear called "wife-beater" these days. There were also some boxer shorts in there. I wish I could say I didn't wear those at least, but that would be a lie.

Since my mother's death in 2000, I can rarely think five thoughts without one of them having something to do with death. I don't mean this to sound morbid, but this sort of thing happens to a man when he reaches his late thirties and his best-loved people, one by one, begin to perish and he can no longer languish in the illusion of everlasting youthfulness. From what I can tell, you either get stuck in this phase of your life and get depressed as hell, or you let it serve as a wake-up call, and before long you begin to feel more consciously alive, more conscious of your life, than ever before.

I would have been ashamed for anyone to know where those clothes had come from when I was young, and that feeling of shame and my resistance to it and my sense of somehow having taken something that didn't belong to me led me to this draft, which in hindsight almost seems like a spell to ward away the spirit of the man whose clothes I wore without permission.

First Draft

Whatever Is Dead Stays Dead

But the chewed stem of a Meershaum pipe
can fashion air, and shoes turn to mirrors,
as when I stepped through the dew and the weeds
shined the shoes passed on to me by a man
I never knew. Did he mind? He died
a ward of the county home. I wore his blue
bow tie and his mothballed blazer
with Addlestein the Memphis Tailor stitched

to the inside pocket. Charity didn't
phase me then. I said thanks. I might have
prayed. But clearly I became the impeccably
dressed thing seated between Tammy Holder
and Quinta King in our senior class portrait.
Youth and the laid to rest worked to make
that season's best Hollywood student style.
Life is a short mile—turns—hidden drives—
certain end-stop. But death isn't an end.
It happens in the middle of other people's lives.

The first draft pretty much came out as you see it here. I liked all the proper
nouns, liked the rhyme of "drives" and "lives," and thought I'd written a real
keeper. I put it away for a week or so and when I came back to it I realized that
I had left much unresolved, too much. Where was the embarrassment of wearing the dead man's clothes? Where was the life of the speaker in the place from
which he spoke? What did it mean that a man's clothes might outlive him? What
does such an inheritance say about how the living related to the dead, or how,
if possible, the dead relate to the living?

The second draft was motivated at least partly by my need to broach these issues
from a technical viewpoint. The roughly pentameter line in the roughly sonnet length
box of a poem that was the first draft simply couldn't contain all the narrative
information without deflating the lyricism. I moved the poem into long prose lines
and looked for new places to break the lines. I kept breaking lines then moving them
back to prose lines, and thought, well, maybe it's time to write a prose poem.

Still, I didn't want to write a "story." I wanted the movement, the ability to
leap from separate moments and perspectives that the lyric allowed. I saw a program on Georgia Public Television about black holes—"Where is the Rest of the
Universe?"—and there in front of the television I wrote that title down on the back
of a napkin and put a number one in front of my first three or so lines and a number 2 after that and began what would become the basic structure of the final poem.

Second Version (Nineteenth Draft)

Whatever Is Dead Stays Dead

1 When my mother worked at the nursing home, she brought for me the
   unclaimed clothes of a man that passed away. The shoes he checked the mail
   in. The pants he jitterbugged in, one December, alive, beside himself. How I
   imagined him: whistling into a mirror, buttoning the tweed blazer.

2 Where is the rest of the universe? What the teacher asked in science class.
The answer: dark matter. Invisible luminosity. The same quarks in the pine
I leaned against that night. Familiar yard. Familiar smear of sunlight.
Beyond that? The un-named, unknown that I breathed in through the stem
of a dead man's cheroot pipe.

3 I'm wearing his bow tie between Tammy Holder and Quinta King—youth
and the laid to rest working to make that season's best senior portrait style.
My mother never told me his name. Or I've forgotten now, as I forget (left or
right?) when the barber asks on what side I'd like to part my hair.

4 Meershaum? Miller? You are born and are given a name. You are clothed.
You die. I walk through the tomato garden. I let the beaded water shine your
shoes. Your shirt is baggy and the sun is bright. I have a dollar and change in
your pants pockets. I am on my way to school.

I usually have several poems I'm working on at the same time. Maybe an essay
or story in the compost as well. My policy is to work on whatever makes me
excited about my writing that day. I spent much of my youth in a rural, agrar-
ian community and have always thought of writing different pieces at the same
time over a long period of time as working different parts of your garden, working cows one day and bailing hay the next. This way I let things take their own
shape in my absence (a piece of writing never looks the same to me after I come
back to it) and keeps me from dutifully forcing a piece toward completion, the
source of much boring writing. If I'm not excited about it, I can't very well expect
anybody else to be. So I went off and worked on something else and came back
to this a few days later.

What I liked about this draft was its imagining of the dead man, its ability to move from the narrative (sections 1 and 3) to the meditative (section 2)
to a mixture of both (section 4).

Still, the beginning felt clunky to me, expository and bland. The astronom-
ical leanings of section 2 seemed a little out of tone with the rest of the poem,
too far away from the poem's central concern, though my intention had been
to widen the center of the poem. Of course, too wide a center and the center
vanishes.

I felt that I had to make this dead man a living man somehow. I wanted him
to speak. I wanted to speak to him. I found the emotional thrust and hook of
the poem when what I most wanted to do was to thank him for this gift he never
really meant to give, and to give him an opportunity to have a say in the manner.
In short, I had to strike a deal with a dead man.

I thought about how, in societies where ancestor worship is common (in Korea,
for instance, where I'd lived for a year a few years back), people leave wine and
fruit on the graves for the dead. They light incense to attract the spirits. How
strange and wonderful to call those without bodies back to the bodily by way of
the senses. The next thing I knew, this gentleman was standing in my bedroom,
dripping wet and telling me that he wanted a tangerine. "All I want is a tangerine"

came to me in one of those strange moments of composition when all I do is serve as a scribe, a moment in which the will of my imagination succumbs to a will seemingly outside of itself, a voice outside itself.

It occurred to me that I could tie the gesture of the poem to its structure by titling the poem "Four Tangerines" instead of the somewhat bleak and overinsistent "Whatever Is Dead Stays Dead." Each section, then, is a tangerine, an offering. The scarecrow at the end was another one of those gift images, and seemed appropriate to me as a sort of mediating figure between the living and the dead, a sort of full-grown voodoo doll on the edge of a field in Leakesville, Mississippi.

Final version (Thirty-eighth Draft)*

Four Tangerines

1 In my dream an elderly man climbs through the window wearing only boxers and a threadbare tank top. His hair is dripping and it appears as though he swam a great distance. He opens the door to my closet. "Mine!" he says, touching the white shirt. The gabardine suit. The green wool sweater with leather patches on the elbows and shoulders. You can have them back, I say. I can give you some money. "Do you have a tangerine?" he asks. "All I want is a tangerine."

2 Williams? Miller? You are born and are given a name. You are clothed. One day you die in the nursing home where my mother works. I walk through the tomato garden. I let the beaded water shine your shoes. Your shirt is baggy and bright and spotless in the sun. When I wear your clothes, is there something of the living in you? Of the dead in me? Vast cities between cloth and skin? I'm with my friends, standing around in the parking lot, talking before school.

3 When given the assignment to write a poem in the style of your favorite poet, I choose Edgar Allan Poe. The best poems will be posted on the east wall of the classroom just above the desk of the lovely woman child, Annabel Lee, a.k.a. Trish. Sunday night, I stare at Poe's picture in our anthology as if it were a mirror. My poem is entitled, "The Consequences of Life" and is all about death, but with a social message: I think Trish should accompany me to the senior dance. I think that Poe would not disagree with the exact fit of a dead man's clothes.

4 I picture you watching me as if I were a small man in a small town inside a snow-globe. You see the shoes you checked the mail in. The pants you jitter-bugged in, one December, alive, beside yourself. You are so far away from me, there is no way to thank you. You do not know my name. I never hear yours.

---

*Published in *Gulf Coast*, Winter/Spring 2005, and in *My Psychic*, Sarabande Books, 2006.

I think of you as "Addlestein, the Memphis Taylor," which is stitched to the inside pocket of your black coat. The same coat that I wear, cutting a sharp figure, or so I imagine, walking home past the cornfield with its poorly attired scarecrow.

TRY THIS 6.18

The Elizabeth Bishop poem that begins these examples ends up shorter, in a tighter form, than the original draft. The Kimbrell poem ends up longer, as a prose poem, in its final form. Take a poem you have written, tighten it, and rewrite it in rhymed stanzas. Then develop it in length and scope and make it a prose poem. Which works better? What do you learn?

Or:

Identify a single sentence summary in a prose passage you have written. Lengthen it; develop it; turn it into a scene.

WORKING TOWARD A DRAFT

By now you have a pretty clear idea of what genre your first whole piece will be—creative nonfiction, fiction, poem, or play—and how long you have to complete a draft. You have a fair idea of which journal piece you will pursue. Make that choice. Make journal notes on what you think you have yet to accomplish. Freewrite a few passages where you think development is needed. Write a quick outline. Print out what you have, cut the paragraphs apart, and spread them out on a table.

What do *you* think is the next step?

Laurie Lipton, "The Self-Destructive Optimist"

Warm-up
Write, quickly, a personal memory of either: swimming, or: a time you were totally happy, or: a time you believed you could fly, or: a time you were deluded about your own power.

CHAPTER SEVEN

CREATIVE NONFICTION

The Essay and Creative Nonfiction
Memoir and the Personal Essay
Techniques of Creative Nonfiction
Fact and Truth
Creative Nonfiction Format

The essay is a pair of baggy pants into which nearly
anyone and anything can fit.

Joseph Epstein

The Essay and Creative Nonfiction

Just about anyone who goes through high school in America gets some practice in basic forms of the **essay**—expository, descriptive, persuasive, and so forth. The tradition of the essay is that it is based in fact, and that the reader has a right to expect that the facts presented will be accurate and truthful.

But the word *essay* itself comes from the French for *try*, and "A Try" captures the modest and partial nature of the form. Anything in the world is potential subject matter, and anything you say about it is an attempt to be accurate, to be interesting, to offer a perspective.

Any or all forms of the essay may be enlivened and made more meaningful through attention to imagery, voice, character, setting, and scene—the elements of imaginative writing. Such essays may be called **literary nonfiction** or **creative nonfiction,** terms to describe the kinds of essays that include the personal but don't necessarily stay there, that include the factual but search for greater range and resonance.

Lee Gutkind, an important practitioner and champion of the form, sees creative nonfiction as allowing the writer "to employ the diligence of a reporter, the shifting voices and viewpoints of a novelist, the refined wordplay of a poet, and the analytical modes of the essayist," and he sees as a requirement that the essays should "have purpose and meaning beyond the experiences related." The techniques Gutkind describes are akin to those that Tom Wolfe co-opted in the 1960s for what he termed **new journalism,** a kind of reporting in which the reporter became a character in his report, and which relied on all the techniques of a novelist including—importantly, for Wolfe—the details of dress, gesture, speech, and ownership that reveal social status.

In one sense, the rules for meaning-making are more relaxed in the essay form than in poetry, fiction, or drama, in that you may tell as well as show; you may say in so many words what the significance is for you. Often the effect of creative nonfiction rests precisely in this, that it begins in personal experience but reaches out to a larger idea or area of thought about the human condition. As authors Carol Burke and Molly Best Tinsley put it in their book *The Creative Process*, "The continuous movement back and forth from specific instance to general significance, from fact to meaning, from the sensory and emotional to the intellectual—such is the art of the essay."

Creative nonfiction is capacious, malleable, forthright, and forgiving. Unlike the conventional academic essay all students are expected to write in freshman composition, creative nonfiction does not need to follow the standard thesis–topic-sentence–conclusion outline. Instead, it can easily borrow from any form you choose: story, monologue, lesson, list, rondel, collage. The trick is to find the right shape for the idea you have to present.

Try This 7.1

At some point in your school life you were asked to write an essay that made you angry or anxious. (You needed the grade? You hated the subject? You didn't have time? You were in love?) As an exercise in showing yourself the difference between that school essay and creative nonfiction, write, in the first person, the story of writing it. See it as a chance to tell the (emotional, atmospheric, judgmental?) truths that had no place in the essay you were assigned.

Memoir and the Personal Essay

Creative nonfiction encompasses two sorts of essay that differ more in empha-sis than in kind: memoir and the personal essay. A **memoir** is a story retrieved from the writer's memory, with the writer as protagonist—the *I* remembering and commenting on the events described in the essay. Memoir tends to place the emphasis on the story, and the "point" is likely to emerge, as it does in fiction, largely from the events and characters themselves, rather than through the author's speculation or reflection.

Example: In the essay "Sundays," from his memoir *What I Can't Bear Losing*, poet Gerald Stern describes his boyhood in Pittsburgh in a Jewish neighborhood surrounded by Calvinist Christians. The emphasis is on the pattern of his Sundays: his parents' quarrels, his walks with his father, later his long walks alone through the hills of the city, the concerts of the Pittsburgh Symphony Orchestra, the ethnic clubs, an early romance. But as he recalls these days he paints a resonant picture of the ethnic, religious, and economic demarcations of the city. His overt analyses are few and light, but he evokes by implication the tensions underlying a divided society.

The *personal essay* also usually has its origin in something that has happened in the writer's life, but it may be something that happened yesterday afternoon, or it may represent an area of interest deliberately explored, and it is likely to give rise to an interpretation of or a meditation on some subject that the experience suggests.

Example: I took a photograph out of an old frame to put in a picture of my new husband and stepdaughter. Because the frame was constructed in an amazingly solid way, I thought about the man whose photo I was displacing, his assumptions about permanence, how we use frames to try to capture and hang onto moments, memories, families, selves that are in fact always in flux; how we frame our cities with roads, our shoreline with resorts, our dead with coffins— marking our territory, claiming possession. In this instance a very small task led me to write about the nature of impermanence and enclosure.

Both memoir and personal essay grow out of some degree of autobiographical experience and are usually (though there are exceptions) written in the first person. The distinction between them is not always clear, although it may be said that the memoir sets up a dialogue between the writer and his/her past, while the emphasis of the personal essay is likely to be a relationship, implied or sought, between the writer and the reader. Philip Lopate, in the brilliant introduction to his anthology *The Art of the Personal Essay*, dissects the tone in terms of its intimacy, its "drive toward candor and self-exposure," the conversational dynamic and the struggle for honesty.

The personal essay is a form that allows maximum mobility from the small, the daily, the domestic, to the universal and significant. Essayist Philip Gerard says, "The subject has to carry itself and also be an elegant vehicle for larger meanings." What makes it "creative" is that though you may take the subject matter of research or journalism, there is "an apparent subject and a deeper subject. The apparent subject . . . is only part of what we are interested in."

Example: Whereas you might write a newspaper article about the Little Miss Blue Crab Festival of Franklin County, naming the contestants, the organizers, and the judges, describing the contest, announcing the winner—if you undertook this same subject matter as a piece of creative nonfiction, your main focus would not be the event itself but the revelation of something essential about the nature of beauty contests, or children in competition, or the character of the fishing village, or coastal society, or rural festivals. In a first-person essay, the focus might be on how you personally fit or don't fit into this milieu, what memories of your own childhood it calls up, how it relates to your experience of competition in general, or other structures in your life and, by extension, life in general. You would have "distance on it," a perspective that embraces not just the immediate event but its place in a human, social, historical, even cosmic context. Because creative nonfiction has this deeper (or wider, or more universal, or significant) subject, it won't necessarily date in the manner of yesterday's newspaper.

TRY THIS 7.2

Begin with the conventional notion of titling an essay:

On _____.

- Make a list of at least six titles that represent things you might like to write about, things that interest you and that you feel confident you know something about. These may be either abstractions or specifics, *On Liberty* or *On Uncle Ernie's Saddle.*
- Then make a list of six subjects you do *not* want to write about, and wouldn't show to anybody if you did. (*On* _____).
- Make a list of six titles in which the preposition "on" could be a pun: *On Speed. On the Net. On My Feet.*
- Make a list of six titles dealing with subjects about which you know "nothing at all." For me such a list might include: *On Brain Surgery. On Refrigerator Repair. On Tasmania.*

If you choose to write an essay from the first list, you are embarking on an honorable enterprise. If you choose from the second list, you are very courageous. If you choose from list three, you'll probably have a good time—and remember that such an essay should deal with both aspects of the pun: *On My Feet* should deal with toenails, calluses, pain, or podiatry, and also with courage or persistence. The last list offers the wildest ride and may turn up something original, comic (Dave Barry makes a living in this territory), or unexpectedly true. Remember that your intent is not to deceive: signal or confess your ignorance when appropriate. Any of the four lists may, like focused freewrites, unlock subject matter that you didn't know you had in you.

Memory has its own story to tell.

Tim O'Brien

Techniques of Creative Nonfiction

Creative nonfiction tells a true story. How does it tell a story? (I'll deal with the "true" part below.)

Every writerly technique that has been discussed in these pages can be used in the essay form, and just as a character will be most richly drawn when presented by more than one method, so a variety of techniques will enrich the texture of nonfiction. As an essayist you may (and should) employ image, metaphor, voice, dialogue, point of view, character, setting, scene, conflict, human connection—and you are also free to speak your mind directly, to "tell" what you mean and what matters. The success of your essay may very well depend on whether you achieve a balance between the imaginative and the reflective. Often, the story and its drama (the showing) will fill most of the sentences—that is what keeps a reader reading—and the startling or revelatory or thoughtful nature of your insight about the story (the telling) will usually occupy less space.

Image and Voice

When writing academic research essays, you generally try for an authoritative, abstract, and impersonal voice: "Howard Dilettante was born of humble parentage . . ." or "The next four centuries were characterized by international strife . . ." But creative nonfiction calls for a conversational tone, a personal "take," and it is largely through your choice of concrete detail that you will carry the reader into the confidence of this persona.

> The park is hardly a block away, where lighted ball diamonds come into view on ducking through branches. There, too, is a fenced acre for unleashed dogs, a half dozen tennis courts with yellow balls flying and, close by, a game of summertime hoops under the lights, a scrambling, squeaking, stampede of sweat and bodies on green tarmac.
>
> *"Hoop Sex," Theodore Weesner*

Here Weesner introduces us to a persona at the same time as he declares the topic of summer night sports. The author is somebody who ducks through branches, who notices dogs and flying balls, who knows basketball as "hoops," and who is comfortable with, excited by, sweat and scramble. The same scene would come to us in a different choice of imagery from the pen of a horticuluralist or a reminiscing mother.

Scene

Like a story, creative nonfiction needs scenes. If you are working from a remembered period of your life, it may present itself as summary, and summary will have its place in your essay; but when you get to what mattered—what changed you, what moves us—it will need the immediacy of detailed action, of discovery and decision.

> Just down from the mountains, early August. Lugging my youngest child from the car, I noticed that his perfectly relaxed body was getting heavier every year. When I undressed his slack limbs, he woke up enough to mumble, "I like my own bed," then fell back down, all the way down, into sleep. The sensation of his weight was still in my arms as I shut the door.
>
> *"Images," Robert Hass*

Notice that Hass begins with a brief summary (or long shot) of the situation, then moves at once into the sensual apprehension of the action, the boy's body relaxed, heavy, slack, while the father takes care of him.

Character

Like a story, creative nonfiction depends on character, and the creation of character depends on both detail and dialogue. Dialogue is tricky because the memory does its own editing, but you can re-create a voice from memory no less than from imagination. Write, remembering as truly as you can, then test in your mind whether the other person involved would agree: *what we said was like this.*

> Whatever looks I had were hidden behind thick cat-eyed glasses and a hearing aid that was strapped to my body like a dog halter. My hallucinatory visions would sometimes lift me up and carry me through the air. When I told my mother that I was afraid of the sky, she considered it a reasonable fear, even though she said, "Well, the sky isn't something I could ever be afraid of."
>
> *"Falling in Love Again," Terry Galloway*

Setting

Like a story, creative nonfiction needs the context and texture of setting. Frequently an encounter with setting is the point and purpose of the piece, whether that encounter is with an exotic foreign country or your own backyard. If you're stuck for a way to begin, you might remember the long shot–middle shot–close-up pattern.

> It's past eleven on a Friday night in the spring of 1955. Here comes a kid down
> the length of Eighteenth Street in the Midwood section of Flatbush, in Brooklyn,
> New York. He passes the kept lawns and tidy hedges under big leafy sycamores
> and maples. The middle class is asleep, and most of the houses attached to the
> lawns are dark, though an occasional window pulses with blue-gray television
> light. Streetlamps shine benignly, and Mars is red in the sky. The kid is on his
> way home from the weekly meeting of Troop 8, Boy Scouts of America . . .
> *"For the Love of a Princess of Mars," Frederick Busch*

Interpretation

Unlike a story, creative nonfiction involves a balance of dramatization and overt reflection. This doesn't mean that the balance needs to be the same in all essays. On the contrary, a memoir that leaves us with a vivid image of an aging relative or a revelation of an error in judgment may be absolutely appropriate, whereas a piece on a walk in the woods may need half its space to analyze and elucidate the discoveries you have made. Sometimes an essay will convey its personal intensity precisely through the force of its abstractions.

> I have had with my friend Wes Jackson a number of useful conversations about
> the necessity of getting out of movements—even movements that have seemed
> necessary and dear to us—when they have lapsed into self-righteousness and
> self-betrayal, as movements seem almost invariably to do. People in movements
> too readily learn to deny to others the rights and privileges they demand for
> themselves. They too easily become unable to mean their own language, as when
> a "peace movement" becomes violent.
> *"In Distrust of Movements," Wendell Berry*

One part of the purpose of an essay will always be to inform or teach, either by presenting new knowledge or by combining old facts in a new way. Often the essay seduces the reader with a personal note into an educational enterprise. The nature essayist Barry Lopez demonstrates the technique again and again; he places himself in relation to the landscape, and later in the piece slips in the history, archeology, or biology. So a typical essay will begin, "I am standing at the margin of the sea ice called the floe edge at the mouth of Admiralty Inlet . . ." or "We left our camp on Pingok Island one morning knowing a storm was moving in from the Southwest . . ." Later in each piece, more factual or speculative paragraphs begin, "Three million colonial seabirds, mostly northern fulmars, kittiwakes, and guillemots, nest and feed here in the summer," and, "Desire for wealth, for spiritual or emotional ecstasy, for recognition—strains of all three are found in nearly every arctic expedition." Lopez immediately involves the reader in the human drama, but he also wants to teach us what he knows. He exhibits the range of the impulse toward the personal essay: involvement and intellectual enlargement, both operating at full stretch. He wants to have and to offer both the experience and the knowledge.

Research

If your essay asks for research, it may be very different, and vastly more inclusive, than what you usually mean by research. Taking a walk in your old neighborhood or getting on a surfboard for the first time, phoning or e-mailing friends and family members, reading old letters including your own, digging among photographs or mementos or recipes—any of these may be exactly what you need to research a memoir. If your subject takes you into areas you need to know more about, you may spend as much time in interview and legwork as on the Internet or in the library.

When it comes to the writing, an essay may be researched and still be "personal," either by making the research (including interview, observation, and detective work) part of the essay, or by allowing the reader to share the emotions you as writer experienced in the process. How does it *feel* to watch a kidney operation? What emotions pass among the athletes in the locker room? How did your interview of Aunt Lena change your view of your family?

TRY THIS 7.6

Write a personal essay about a building you care about. Choose one of which you have strong memories, then do at least a little research about the place itself. This research might, if it's a house or school in your hometown, consist of calling people to interview them. If it's a church or municipal building of some sort, it might be archival or library research. You will know what's appropriate. How does your memory of the place contrast with, or how is it qualified by, what you have learned? Is there an idea to be mined in the difference between them?

Although the personal essay offers an insight into the writer's life and thought, that doesn't necessarily mean that it must be written in the first person. It may be that the story you have to tell or the drama you have witnessed can be best conveyed (as in a short story) by focusing on that experience, implying rather than spelling out how it has moved you. George Plimpton wrote sports stories in the first person because his point was to expose the emotions of an amateur among the pros; whereas Roger Angell writes occasionally in the first person, and sometimes in the collective "we," but most often in the third person, focusing on the players but putting on their stories the stamp of his style. If in doubt, try a few paragraphs in first and then in third person; fool around with the perspective of fly-on-the-wall and with myself-as-participant. Usually the material will reveal its own best slant, and the experiment may help you find out what you have to say.

Transitions and Focus

Transitions are particularly important in creative nonfiction because of the needed rhythm back and forth between scene and summary, abstraction and detail. We expect a degree of direction and interpretation that in fiction would be called **authorial intrusion.** An essayist is allowed and encouraged to employ intrusion to a degree, and we expect and ask for the generalization that says, in effect: *this is what I think*. I find it useful, when I find myself getting a little wound up or mixed up in the writing, to type in "What's my point?" and try to answer the question right then. The question can come out later. Often the answer can, in some form or other, stay. Even if you end up cutting it, it may help you find your way.

In the past, when writing a critical or research essay, you've been told to pick a confined and specific subject and explore it thoroughly. The same advice holds for creative nonfiction. Don't try to write about "my family," which will overwhelm you with vagaries and contradictions, just as if your subject was "Shakespeare." Write about one afternoon when things changed. Focus on one kid in the fifth grade who didn't fit in. Write about your first encounter with language, oysters, God, hypocrisy, race, or betrayal. A memoir is a story, and like a story it will describe a journey and a change; it will be written in a scene or scenes; it will characterize through detail and dialogue. The difference is not only that it is based on the facts as your memory can dredge them up, but that you may interpret it for us as you go along or at the end or both: *this is what I learned, this is how I changed, this is how I relate my experience to the experience of the world, and of my readers*.

Try This 7.7
Interview someone at least a generation older than you are about an event that took place before you were born. Make the interview the scene of your personal essay, and let the event emerge through the conversation and your reflections on it.

I never want to discover, after reading a piece of
nonfiction, that I have not read a piece of nonfiction.

Joe Mackall

Fact and Truth

"Essays," says novelist and travel writer Edward Hoagland, "are how we speak
to one another in print—caroming thoughts not merely in order to convey a
certain packet of information but with a special edge or bounce of personal character in a kind of public letter . . . More than being instructive, as a magazine
article is, an essay has a slant . . ."

How do you balance the information against the slant? How, in that *caroming*,
do you judge when edge or bounce has overwhelmed instruction?

This is an interesting issue because in the latter half of the twentieth century readers became intensely interested in "what really happened," and memoirs,
personal experience, biography, and autobiography are now more marketable
than fiction or poetry. Television and film offer us an endless buffet of drama,
and perhaps we are tired of being overfed with formulaic dramatic plots.

But it's not always clear what is fact and what is fiction. News can be and
is manipulated; television raises the question of how much "entertainment" enters
journalistic decisions. Is a docudrama document or drama? If a memoir "remembers" dialogue from forty years ago, is it memory or fiction? If a living person
is shielded from recognition in a biography, is the piece dishonest? If you have
taken seven trips in a fishing boat and you want to write about it as personal
experience, do you have to go through seven trips, or can you conflate them
into one trip and still call it fact? How much dramatizing may be said to reveal
rather than distort the truth?

At some point every writer of memoir and personal essay has to grapple with these
issues. Luckily, they don't have to be grappled with in first draft. Having accepted
that the mere fact of putting something into words *changes* it, begin by putting into
words as clearly and vividly as you can something that you know about, care about,
or that has happened to you. Look for your particular purpose. Consider how to
raise the tension and the drama. Be scrupulously honest about the facts and, beyond
that, explore the essential truth of what you have to say. There will inevitably be
changes of emphasis and balance in the shaping of both rough draft and revisions.

The distance between "facts" and "essential truth," of course, can be troubling.
What and how much is it fair to make up? Let's say I'm writing a piece about
my mother, and I want to give an accurate image of her. When I try to remember the things she wore, what stands out are the unusual things, the embroidered
yellow wedding coat she kept for special occasions, the pink satin housecoat that
was too precious to wear often. These are in my memory precisely because they
were uncharacteristic of her, whereas the kind of housedress she wore every day
is a blur of composite images, a mnemonic generalization. As a writer I concentrate

on this vagueness and bring it into focus in my imagination *as if* it were fiction. *She wore a cap-sleeve cotton house dress, a plaid of lavender and yellow crisscrossing on faded gray.* Or: *She wore a cotton house dress with piping around the collar, sprigs of lily-of-the-valley tied with a pink bow on a pale gray ground.* I don't know whether these images came from somewhere deep in my memory, or whether I "made them up." They are true to the image of my mother I am trying to capture, and therefore they partake of "essential truth," whereas if I said she wore bikinis or Armani, I would be honoring neither fact nor truth.

Fiction writers also grapple with the level of historical or regional fact that is necessary to their truth, and like essayists, they answer it differently. James Joyce wanted every Dublin bus route and ticket price accurate in *Ulysses*; E. L. Doctorow invented the events of several famous real lives in *Ragtime*. In the only historical novel I have written, I decided that I could harmlessly put an ice house in a rural Arizona town seven years before there was actually such a thing, but that I couldn't blow off the arm of a famous Mexican general two years before, historically, it happened.

The delicacy of this issue is slightly augmented for an essayist, and I think the touchstone is: an absence of the intent to deceive. A fiction writer is in the clear to the extent that a reader understands from the beginning that the story is "made up"—yet must on whatever level of reality convince us to suspend disbelief. Since a reader of essays expects factual truth, you are under some obligation to signal its absence. It can add to both the authenticity and the interest of a piece (as long as it isn't too repetitive), to say in effect: I don't remember exactly, but I seem to see . . . Or: So-and-so says it was this way, but I think . . . Or: I am imagining that it must have been . . .

> I know nothing about how they meet. She is a schoolgirl. He is at work, probably a government clerk in a building near her school. At the hour when the school and the office are out for lunch their lives intersect at sandwich counters, soft-drink stands, traffic lights, market squares. Their eyes meet or their bodies collide at one of these food queues. He says something suggestive, complimentary. She suppresses a smile or traps one beneath her hands.
>
> *"A Son in Shadow," Fred D'Aguilar*

TRY THIS 7.8

Write a personal essay about your parents' courtship. It may be totally imaginary (in which case, that you are making it up becomes part of the subject matter and the truth of your essay); or you may write it from facts you already know (acknowledging where you fill in, leave out, or speculate); or you may "research" it by interviewing family members (in which case your research may become the subject of the essay, the family members become characters, and their interviews become dialogue). You may choose any method you like, based on whatever quantity of information you have or choose to use, but it must remain an essay; that is, with a basis in fact, so that where you invent, you acknowledge "I imagine . . . I guess . . . I'm inventing here."

"When you use memories as a source," says E. L. Doctorow, "they're no different from any other source—the composition still has to be made." Memory is imperfect; that is its nature, and you are responsible only for the honest attempt and the honest presentation. No two siblings will remember their mother, or even Christmas dinner, in the same way. One of the leaps of faith you must make to write from memory is that the process of writing itself will yield that essential truth. Sometimes clarifying a quotation, compressing several conversations or events into one, exaggerating one physical detail while omitting another, or transposing a scene from one locale to another—any of these can honor (and reveal) an essential truth when the literal truth would distort. If you get the color of your childhood wagon wrong, it will not damage that truth. If you sentimentalize an emotion, it will.

It is likely that the most troubling conflict you face as a writer of memoir and personal essay will be between your essential truth and obligation to those you know. When does honesty require that you reveal an ugly fact? Is it arrogance to suppose that anything you write is worth wounding someone else? There is no answer to this dilemma, or there are as many answers as there are works in a lifetime or paragraphs in a work. As a rough rule of thumb, I would say that the cost of honesty might be the loss of your own labor. That is: write your truth. You are under no obligation to publish it, and you may find yourself under the pressure of personal integrity not to. If you need to alter details in order to conceal a living person, let it be later. It may or may not work, but it will be easier to alter identifying details than to censor yourself as you write.

TRY THIS 7.9
Write an anonymous memoir about someone you dislike or someone you are afraid of. The surer you are that nobody is going to know who wrote it, the freer you are to write; but also, strangely! the more freely you write, the less likely anybody is to know who wrote it. You have angers and fears that nobody has ever suspected, right? Write.

More to Read

Gutkind, Lee. *The Art of Creative Nonfiction*. New York: John Wiley & Sons, 1997.

Zinsser, William. *On Writing Well*. New York: HarperCollins, 2001.

Readings

Margaret Atwood
The Female Body

> . . . entirely devoted to the subject of "The Female Body."
> Knowing how well you have written on this topic . . . this
> capacious topic . . .
>
> —*letter from Michigan Quarterly Review*

1.
I agree, it's a hot topic. But only one? Look around, there's a wide range. Take my own, for instance.

I get up in the morning. My topic feels like hell. I sprinkle it with water, brush parts of it, rub it with towels, powder it, add lubricant. I dump in the fuel and away goes my topic, my topical topic, my controversial topic, my capacious topic, my limping topic, my nearsighted topic, my topic with back problems, my badly behaved topic, my vulgar topic, my outrageous topic, my aging topic, my topic that is out of the question and anyway still can't spell, in its oversized coat and worn winter boots, scuttling along the sidewalk as if it were flesh and blood, hunting for what's out there, an avocado, an alderman, an adjective, hungry as ever.

2.
The basic Female Body comes with the following accessories: garter belt, panti-girdle, crinoline, camisole, bustle, brassiere, stomacher, chemise, virgin zone, spike heels, nose ring, veil, kid gloves, fishnet stockings, fichu, bandeau, Merry Widow, weepers, chokers, barrettes, bangles, beads, lorgnette, feather boa, basic black, compact, Lycra stretch one-piece with modesty panel, designer peignoir, flannel nightie, lace teddy, bed, head.

3.
The Female Body is made of transparent plastic that lights up when you plug it in. You press a button to illuminate the different systems. The circulatory system is red, for the heart and arteries, purple for the veins; the respiratory system is blue; the lymphatic system is yellow; the digestive

system is green, with liver and kidneys in aqua. The nerves are done in orange and the brain is pink. The skeleton, as you might expect, is white.

The reproductive system is optional, and can be removed. It comes with or without a miniature embryo. Parental judgment can thereby be exercised. We do not wish to frighten or offend.

4.

He said, I won't have one of those things in the house. It gives a young girl a false notion of beauty, not to mention anatomy. If a real woman was built like that she'd fall on her face.

She said, If we don't let her have one like all the other girls she'll feel singled out. It'll become an issue. She'll long for one and she'll long to turn into one. Repression breeds sublimation. You know that.

He said, It's not just the pointy plastic tits, it's the wardrobes. The wardrobes and that stupid male doll, what's his name, the one with the underwear glued on.

She said, Better to get it over with when she's young. He said, All right, but don't let me see it.

She came whizzing down the stairs, thrown like a dart. She was stark naked. Her hair had been chopped off, her head was turned back to front, she was missing some toes and she'd been tattooed all over her body with purple ink in a scrollwork design. She hit the potted azalea, trembled there for a moment like a botched angel, and fell.

He said, I guess we're safe.

5.

The Female Body has many uses. It's been used as a door knocker, a bottle opener, as a clock with a ticking belly, as something to hold up lampshades, as a nutcracker, just squeeze the brass legs together and out comes your nut. It bears torches, lifts victorious wreaths, grows copper wings and raises aloft a ring of neon stars; whole buildings rest on its marble heads.

It sells cars, beer, shaving lotion, cigarettes, hard liquor; it sells diet plans and diamonds, and desire in tiny crystal bottles. Is this the face that launched a thousand products? You bet it is, but don't get any funny big ideas, honey, that smile is a dime a dozen.

It does not merely sell, it is sold. Money flows into this country or that country, flies in, practically crawls in, suitful after suitful, lured by all those hairless pre-teen legs. Listen, you want to reduce the national debt, don't you? Aren't you patriotic? That's the spirit. That's my girl.

She's a natural resource, a renewable one luckily, because those things wear out so quickly. They don't make 'em like they used to. Shoddy goods.

6.

One and one equals another one. Pleasure in the female is not a requirement. Pair-bonding is stronger in geese. We're not talking about love, we're talking about biology. That's how we all got here, daughter.

Snails do it differently. They're hermaphrodites, and work in threes.

7.

Each Female Body contains a female brain. Handy. Makes things work. Stick pins in it and you get amazing results. Old popular songs. Short circuits. Bad dreams.

Anyway: each of these brains has two halves. They're joined together by a thick cord; neural pathways flow from one to the other, sparkles of electric information washing to and fro. Like light on waves. Like a conversation. How does a woman know? She listens. She listens in.

The male brain, now, that's a different matter. Only a thin connection. Space over here, time over there, music and arithmetic in their own sealed compartments. The right brain doesn't know what the left brain is doing. Good for aiming though, for hitting the target when you pull the trigger. What's the target? Who's the target? Who cares? What matters is hitting it. That's the male brain for you. Objective.

This is why men are so sad, why they feel so cut off, why they think of themselves as orphans cast adrift, footloose and stringless in the deep void. What void? she asks. What are you talking about? The void of the universe, he says, and she says Oh and looks out the window and tries to get a handle on it, but it's no use, there's too much going on, too many rustlings in the leaves, too many voices, so she says, Would you like a cheese sandwich, a piece of cake, a cup of tea? And he grinds his teeth because she doesn't understand, and wanders off, not just alone but Alone, lost in the dark, lost in the skull, searching for the other half, the twin who could complete him.

Then it comes to him: he's lost the Female Body! Look, it shines in the gloom, far ahead, a vision of wholeness, ripeness, like a giant melon, like an apple, like a metaphor for "breast" in a bad sex novel; it shines like a balloon, like a foggy noon, a watery moon, shimmering in its egg of light.

Catch it. Put it in a pumpkin, in a high tower, in a compound, in a chamber, in a house, in a room. Quick, stick a leash on it, a lock, a chain, some pain, settle it down, so it can never get away from you again.

TRY THIS 7.10
You have by this time generated a number of lists in your journal. Pick one of them and add to it. See if your list has room for a memory, a song, a metaphor, a fantasy, a machine, a sarcasm, a dream, a grand idea. Pick seven items on the list and write a paragraph about each. Do they add up to a rough draft of an essay?

Gayle Pemberton

Do He Have Your Number, Mr. Jeffrey?

During the fall of 1984 I worked for three weekends as a caterer's assistant in Southern California. Like lots of others seeking their fortunes in L.A., I was working by day as a temporary typist in a Hollywood film studio. I was moonlighting with the caterer because, like lots of others, I was going broke on my typist's wages.

Though the job was not particularly enjoyable, the caterer and her husband were congenial, interesting people who certainly would have become good friends of mine had I stayed in California. I spent my three weekends in basic scullery work—wiping and slicing mushrooms, mixing batters, peeling apples, tomatoes, and cucumbers, drying plates, glasses, and cutlery. Greater responsibilities would have come with more experience, but I had brushed off California's dust before I learned any real catering secrets or professional gourmet techniques.

One exhausting dinner party, given by a rich man for his family and friends, turned out to be among the reasons I brushed off that California dust. This dinner was such a production that our crew of five arrived the day before to start preparing. The kitchen in this house was larger than some I've seen in fine French restaurants. Our caterer was one of a new breed of gourmet cooks who do all preparation and cooking at the client's house—none of your cold-cut or warming-tray catering. As a result, her clients had a tendency to have loads of money and even more kitchen space.

Usually her staff was not expected to serve the meal, but on this occasion we did. I was directed to wear stockings and black shoes and I was given a blue-patterned apron dress, with frills here and there, to wear. Clearly, my academic lady-banker pumps were out of the question, so I invested in a pair of trendy black sneakers—which cost me five dollars less than what I earned the entire time I worked for the caterer. Buying the sneakers was plainly excessive but I told myself they were a necessary expense. I was not looking forward to wearing the little French serving-girl uniform, though. Everything about it and me were wrong, but I had signed on and it would have been unseemly and downright hostile to jump ship.

One thing I liked about the caterer was her insistence that her crew not be treated as servants—that is, we worked for her and took orders from her, not from the clients, who might find ordering us around an emboldening and socially one-upping experience. She also preferred to use crystal and china she rented, keeping her employees and herself safe from a client's rage in case a family heirloom should get broken. But on this occasion, her client insisted that we use his Baccarat crystal. We were all made particularly nervous by his tone. It was the same tone I heard from a mucky-muck at my studio typing job: cold, arrogant, a matter-of-fact "you are shit" attitude that is well known to nurses and secretaries.

I had never served a dinner before that one—that is, for strangers, formally. I had mimed serving festive meals for friends, but only in a lighthearted way. And, when I was a child, my family thought it a good exercise in etiquette—not to mention in labor savings—to have me serve at formal dinners. "It's really fun, you know," they would say. I never handled the good china, though.

I didn't mind cutting up mushrooms or stirring sauce in some foul rich man's kitchen for pennies, but I certainly didn't like the idea of serving at this one's table. I saw our host hold up one of his goblets to a guest, showing off the fine line and texture. There were too many conflicting images for me to be content with the scene. He was working hard on his image for his guests; I was bothered by the way I looked to myself and by what I might have looked like to the assembled crew, guests, and host. I couldn't get the idea of black servility to white power out of my mind.

The food was glorious. I recall serving quenelles at one point, followed by a consommé brunoise, a beef Wellington with a carrot and herb based sauce that I stirred for a short eternity, vegetables with lemon butter, and a variety of mouth-watering pastries for dessert. We worked throughout the meal, topping up wine and coffee, removing plates, bumping into each other. As long as I was doing this absurd thing I decided to make some kind of mental work attend it. I made the entire scene a movie, and as I served I created a silent voice-over. At one point, after the quenelles and the entrée and before the coffee, the table of eight sat discussing literature—a discussion of the "what'd you think of . . ." variety. My professorial ears pricked up. I discovered that one member of the party had actually read the book in question, while a few others had skimmed condensed versions in a magazine. My voice-over could have vied, I thought, with the shrillest Bolshevik propaganda ever written.

PEMBERTON (*VOICE-OVER*)

(*haughtily*)

You self-satisfied, rich, feeble-brained, idiotic, priggish, filthy maggots! You, you sit here talking literature—why, you don't even know what the word means. This is high intellectual discourse for you, isn't it? High, fine. You are proud to say, "I thought the theme honest." What, pray tell, is an honest theme? It might be better to consider the dishonesty of your disgusting lives. Why, here I am, a Ph.D in literature, listening to this garbage, making a pittance, while you illiterate pig-running-dogs consume food and non-ideas with the same relish.

Oh, I did go on. My script was melodramatic, with great soliloquies, flourishes, and, for verisimilitude, an eastern European accent. My comeuppance came as I dried the last of the Baccarat goblets. The crystal, no doubt responding to the dissonance and intensity of my sound track, shattered as I held it in my hand. The rest of the crew said they'd never seen anyone look as sick as I did at that moment. The goblet was worth more than the price of my trendy sneakers and my night's work combined. I decided to go home.

I drove slowly back to my room near Culver City; it was well past midnight. I had the distinct sense that I was the only sober driver on the Santa Monica Freeway that night, but given the weaving pattern of my driving— to avoid the other weavers—I fully expected to be picked up and jailed. Then, some alcohol residue from the broken goblet would have transported itself magically into my bloodstream to make me DWI, just as the goblet had reacted to my thoughts and sacrificed itself in the name of privilege, money, and mean-spiritedness. I made it home, feeling woozy as I left my car.

I didn't have to pay for the goblet; the caterer did. She was insured. I worked another party for her—another strange collection of people, but a more festive occasion—and I didn't have to wear the French maid's outfit. I go to stand happily behind a buffet, helping people serve themselves. I think back on my catering experience the way people do who, once something's over, say that they're glad they did it—like lassoing a bull, riding him, then busting ribs and causing permanent sacroiliac distress. The job was just one of many I've had to take to make me believe I could survive when it was obvious that I was going further and further into the hole. I never had more than ten dollars in my wallet the entire time I lived in L.A., and not much more than that in the bank. Perhaps there's something about L.A. that makes working unlikely jobs—jobs your parents send you to college to keep you from having to do—all right and reasonable, since very little makes sense there anyway, and surviving means bellying up to the illusion bar and having a taste with everyone else.

L.A. has been like that for a long time. It did not occur to me that night, as I moved from one dinner guest to another dressed in that ludicrous outfit, that I might have created some other kind of scenario—linking what I was doing to what my mother had done nearly fifty years before, probably no farther than ten miles away.

It was in the middle thirties, Los Angeles. My mother's employers supplied her with a beige uniform with a frilled bib, short puff sleeves, and a narrow, fitted waist. The skirt of the dress was narrow, stopping just below the knee. She wore seamed stockings and low pumps, black. And her job, as far as she could ascertain, was to just be, nothing else. The couple who employed her—the husband wrote screenplays—had no children, and did not require her services to either cook or clean. I suppose they thought that having a maid was a requirement of their social position. So, Mother got the job. She is fair-skinned, and at that time she wore her dark, wavy hair long, in large curls that gathered just below her neck. I've seen pictures from those days and see her most enviable figure, an old-fashioned size ten, held up by long legs that, doubtless, were enhanced by the seamed stockings and pumps. Her employers were quite proud of her and thought she looked, they said, "just like a little French girl." When I was very young and filled with important questions, Mother explained to me that she thought it "damned irritating that whites who knew full well who they were hiring and talking to went to such lengths to try to make blacks into something else. If they wanted a little French girl, why didn't they go out and get one?" Ah, the days before *au pairs*. Well, I knew the answer to that one too.

Mother had moved to L.A. with her mother. Nana had decided to leave Papa, tired of his verbal abusiveness and profligacy. There were various cousins in California, and I am sure the appeal of the West and new beginnings at the start of the Depression made the choice an easy one. Both of my parents told me that they didn't feel the Depression all that much; things had never been financially good and little changed for them after Wall Street fell. The timing seemed right to Nana. Her other daughter, my aunt, had recently married. My mother had finished her third year at the university and, I bet, got an attack of wanderlust. She went with Nana to help her—and also to get some new air. The circumstances accommodated themselves.

I remember my shock when I learned that Mother had worked as a maid. I had always known that she had lived in California, but as a child, it never occurred to me that she would have had to "do something" there. It was not so much that my middle-class feathers were ruffled by the revelation as that I found it difficult to see her in a role that, on screen at least, was so demeaning and preposterous. Mother simply did not fit the stereotype I had been fed. And, to make matters worse, Grandma had taken pains to inform my sister and me when we were little girls that we should avoid—at all costs— rooming with whites in college or working in their homes. Her own stints as a dance-hall matron had convinced her, she said, that whites were the filth- iest people on earth. The thought of my mother cleaning up after them made me want to protect her, to undo the necessity for that kind of work by some miraculous feat of time travel, to rescue her from the demeaning and the dirty.

Mother's attitude about her past employment was more pragmatic, of course. She explained to me—as if I didn't know—that there were really no avenues for black women apart from "service," as it was called, prostitution, and, perhaps, schoolteaching. Nana had no higher education and Mother's was incomplete, so service was the only route they could take. Mother also assured me that she had not cleaned unimaginable filth, but rather, with nothing else to do, had sat all day long reading novels, memorably *Anthony Adverse* by Hervey Allen, a big best-seller of 1934. My image of Mother became brighter, but in some ways more curious: there she was, imagined as a French maid by her employers, but really a black coed, lolling around a Los Angeles home reading *Anthony Adverse*. That's one far cry from Butterfly McQueen as Prissy in *Gone with the Wind*.

All good things must come to an end, as they say, and Mother's job did one day. She had been dating a man, she says, "who was very hand- some, looked Latin, like Cesar Romero, but he was black too." Talk about images. He arrived to pick her up for a date as she got off work. He inquired after her at the front door—oops—and there went the job. Seems the little French maid's Spanish-looking boyfriend should have realized that no mat- ter what black might appear to be, it better not act other than what it was. A slip in racial protocol, a lost novel-reading employ. "So it went," Mother said. After that incident she decided to look for a different kind of work and she began selling stockings for the Real Silk Hosiery Company, door-to-door.

Mother was lucky. I suspect that she and Nana might have had a tougher time if they had been brown skinned, for contrary to many images from movies, white employers—if they were going to hire blacks at all—preferred the lighter-skinned variety. This was true of professions as diverse as chorus girls, maids, schoolteachers, waitresses, and shop clerks, an implied greater worth as blackness disappears drop by drop into ginger, to mocha, to "high yellow," to white. This scale was intraracially internalized too, making a shambles of black life from the earliest slave days to the present. These gradations also made color-line crossing a popular black sport, particularly since white America seemed to be at once so secure and satisfied in its whiteness and so ignorant of who's who and who's what. Blacks existed only as whites saw them, blackness affirming white racial self-consciousness and nothing else. This is what Ralph Ellison's invisibility is all about; it is what we have all lived.

In the evenings and on weekends, Mother and Nana used to go to the movies; they both were hooked and on location for Hollywood's Golden Age. I love movies too. It is on the gene, as I frequently remind myself as I sit watching a vintage B from the forties for the fifth time or so when I ought to be reading a book. A major chunk of my misspent youth involved watching them. When I should have been reading, or studying mathematics, or learning foreign languages—like my more successful academic friends—I was hooked on three-reelers.

During my youth Mother was my partner in all this. When I was in kindergarten and first grade on half-day shifts, I never missed a morning movie. When we watched together I would barrage her with important questions: "Who is that?" "Is he dead?" "Is she dead?" "Who was she married to?" "Is this gonna be sad?" Mother was never wrong, except once. We were watching an early Charles Bickford movie and I asked the standard heady question: "Is he dead?" Mother said, "Oh, Lord, yes. He died years ago." Several years later I came home triumphantly from a drive-in and announced that I had seen Bickford in *The Big Country* and that he looked just fine and alive to me.

Of course, hopeless romanticism is the disease that can be caught from the kind of movie-going and movie-watching my mother and I have done. There she was, with her mother, frequently a part of the crowd being held behind the barricades at Hollywood premiers, sighing and pointing with agitation as gowned and white-tied stars glided from limousines into rococo movie-houses. Both she and Nana read screen magazines—the forerunners to our evening news programs—that detailed the romantic, hedonistic public and private exploits of Hollywood's royalty. It was a time when my mother, as French maid reading *Anthony Adverse*, had to wait only a few months before the novel burst onto the screen, with glorious illusionary history and

Frederic March swashbuckling his way into the hearts of screaming fans. The stars were part of the studio system and could be counted on to appear with frequency, even if the roles appeared to be the same and only the titles, and a few plot twists, changed. (I am convinced, for example, that the 1934 *Imitation of Life* was remade as *Mildred Pierce* in 1945, the major change being that the relatively good daughter of the former becomes the monster of the latter. Louise Beavers and Fredi Washington in the black theme of *Imitation of Life* only slightly alter the major plot.)

Mother's was the perfect generation to see Hollywood movies when they were fresh, new, and perhaps more palpable than they are now—when comedies of remarriage, as Stanley Cavell calls them, and historical adventures and melodramas dominated the screen, when westerns and political dramas were self-consciously mythologizing the American past and present, and when young French maids and their mothers, along with the impoverished, the disillusioned, the lost, and even the comfortable and secure, could sit before the silver screen and see a different world projected than the one they lived in. And they could dream. Mother loves to sketch faces and clothing, using an artistic talent inherited from Papa. She marveled at the stars and their sculpted (sometimes) faces, and would draw from memory the costume designs that made the likes of Edith Head, Cecil Beaton, and Irene famous.

Hopeless romanticism was the threat, but neither Nana nor Mother— nor I completely—succumbed to it. They never confused reality with anything they saw on either the big or the small screen. And they taught me what they believed. They both warned me, in different ways and at different times, to be wary of the type of people who wake up to a new world every day (and I've met some)—people with no memory, ingenuous, incapable of seeing either the implications or the connections between one event and another, people who willingly accept what the world makes of them on a Tuesday, forget as night falls, and wake up on Wednesday ready to make the same mistakes. It might have been some of that ingenuousness that produced my feelings of discomfort when I learned that Mother had been a maid, and she understood how I felt.

My mother always deplored the depiction of blacks on screen. She saw their roles as demeaning and designed to evoke either cheap sentimentality, cheap laughter, or cheap feelings of superiority in the white audiences they were aimed at. And, although she says she didn't see many of them, Mother loathed the all-black B movies Hollywood made for the "colored" audience, where the stereotypes were broader and more offensive to her, and where the musical interludes did no justice to real talent, she said, but trivialized it. She even hated musical interludes featuring black performers in the standard white A and B movies. She was—and still is—cold to arguments that say talented black performers needed to take any work they could get, and that black audiences were encouraged and happy to see black Hollywood stars no matter what they were doing. Mother countered that Hattie McDaniel's acceptance speech, when she won an Oscar for her role as Mammy in *Gone with the Wind*, was written for her, and that McDaniel was denied the status of eating dinner with her peers that night.

We have talked about all of this many, many times, particularly when I have felt it necessary to sort out my own complex and conflicting reactions to Hollywood movies. Like Mother, I have seen as nothing but illusion the world projected on the screen. But as Michael Wood notes in *America in the Movies:* "All movies mirror reality in some way or other. There are no escapes, even in the most escapist pictures. . . . The business of films is the business of dreams . . . but then dreams are scrambled messages from waking life, and there is truth in lies, too." Mother may have recoiled from black images on screen because they affirmed a reality she did not like. She could suspend her disbelief at white characters and their predicaments, she could enter the dream worlds of aristocrats and chorus girls living happily ever after, or dying romantic, drawn-out deaths, because there was some measure of inner life given these portrayals. The audience demanded some causal foundation to acts ranging from heroism and self-sacrifice to murder, duplicity, and pure cussedness. But black characters on screen, no matter how polished their roles, were ultimately as invisible as she was in her own role as French maid—a projection only of what the white world wanted to see, robbed of the implication of inner lives, nothing but glorified surfaces that really said everything about whiteness and nothing at all about blackness. It didn't matter to Mother if the characters were maids or butlers, lawyers or doctors, simpletons or singers. I knew there was an inner life, a real person in my mother—passionate and shy, lacking self-confidence but projecting intense intelligence and style—and that she had no business being anybody's French girl. The "truth in lies" was that Hollywood rent from us our human dignity while giving us work, as it sought to defuse and deflect our real meaning—a potentially dangerous meaning—in American life.

Mother found these invisible blacks painful to watch because they were so effective as images created in white minds. These complex feelings are on the gene too. I find Shirley Temple movies abominable, notwithstanding the dancing genius of Bill "Bojangles" Robinson. In *The Little Colonel* young Shirley has just been given a birthday party; there are hats and horns and all sorts of scrubbed white children celebrating with her. At some moment— I refuse to watch the film again to be precise—she gets up and takes part of her cake to a group of dusty and dusky children who are waiting outside in the backyard of the house. The only reason for their existence is to be grateful for the crumbs and to sing a song. There can be no other motivation, no reason to exist at all, except to show the dear Little Colonel's largesse and liberal-mindedness, befitting someone not quite to the manor born but clearly on her way to the manor life.

I was watching an Alfred Hitchcock festival not long ago. Hitchcock films are some of Mother's favorites. She likes the illusions and twists of plots, the scrambling of images light and dark. I realized that I hadn't seen *Rear Window* since I was a little girl, and that at the time I hadn't understood much of what had taken place in the movie. I was very interested in it this time around. There was James Stewart, as Jeffries, in the heaviest makeup ever, with his blue eyes almost enhanced out of his face, looking at evil Raymond Burr through binoculars in the apartment across the way. I was letting the film take me where it would; I created an *explication de texte*, noting how the film raises questions about voyeurism and images. Indeed, Stewart, in looking at the world from his temporary infirmity, is only content when he places a narrative line on the lives of the people on the other side of his binoculars. He is, in a sense, reacting to images and attempting to order them—as we all do.

At a crucial moment in the movie, Stewart realizes that he is in danger. The evil wife-murderer and dismemberer, Burr, knows that Stewart has figured out the crime. Stewart hobbles to the telephone, trying to reach his friend, Wendell Corey. Corey isn't in, but Stewart gets the babysitter on the line—who speaks in a vaudevillian black accent. He asks her to have Corey call him when he returns. The babysitter asks, "Do he have your number, Mr. Jeffrey?"

I called my mother to tell her that I had an interesting bit of trivia from *Rear Window*. She became angry when she heard it, said she was appalled. "He should have been ashamed of himself," she said of Hitchcock. Into the white world of *Rear Window* and questions of imagery, it was necessary to place a familiar black image—and this time it didn't even have a face.

Mother and Nana left L.A. in 1937. Working in service and selling silk stockings could not provide enough money for them to survive. They went back to the frozen North. Mother married in 1939; Nana returned to Papa and stayed with him until he died in 1967.

Nana and Papa both moved to L.A. in 1950, Papa then a semi-retired architect. They had a beautiful home on West Fourth Avenue. It was right in the middle of a two-block area that became part of the Santa Monica Freeway. One morning, on my way to a catering job, I drove my car as far as I could, to the fence above the freeway. I got out and thought long and hard about what had been lost—beyond a house, of course, but their lives gone, part of my youth as a little girl visiting in summers, and dreams about what life could be in the semi-tropical paradise of Southern California where they made dreams that seduced the whole world.

TRY THIS 7.11
Write a memoir about a job you have held. Show (and tell) why this job did not lead to a lifelong career.

William Kittredge
Interlude

At a very proper New English sort of Thanksgiving dinner, at my grandmother's table, I was seated on a couple of books in a straight-backed chair beside my great-uncle Hank, a dim, lank old alcoholic bachelor with a whiskery beard.

Uncle Hank was munching along in his silent way when he muttered some unintelligible thing and pulled his complete set of false teeth from his mouth, setting them out to dry on the fine white linen tablecloth. Hank's teeth were inextricably tangled with long strings of bright green spinach. They sat there damp and alive, staining the linen cloth, while he went on eating. I began whimpering—what a fool of a child I must have been—and there was a scene. I wish I could remember how it came out. I wish I knew if Uncle Hank was drunk that late afternoon; I wish he was here now.

Uncle Hank used to lie on the lawn in front of the old white-painted ranch house where my grandparents lived when they came to visit their properties in Warner Valley, an aged man flat on his back, watching the birds as they nested. I like to think about Uncle Hank, and what he thought about as he gazed up into the poplars. He was the prime figure of failure in my family: a stranger, the official eccentric, a drunk, a cautionary figure to frighten boys when they were lazy. Hank, it was said, was like a turkey. "He just pecks where he pecks." Which was as much as anybody could make of him. I like to imagine that Uncle Hank was intimate with the habits of birds. I want to tell myself he led a considered life, and knew it was worthwhile to spend his time utterly absorbed in the look of light through the poplar leaves.

I value his indifference to the ambitions which drove my family. He refused to join their scramble to fence the world. I want to believe he was correct, and not just lazy or drunk all the time. I want to think Uncle Hank loved to ride the nesting-ground swamplands in Warner, and thought grid-map plans for reclamation were an abomination, a bad thing in the long run, for us and not just the muskrats and waterbirds. If someone asked, "Who was your model of conduct when you were a child?" I might lie and say Uncle Hank. His is the great-hearted tradition in my family, at least in this version of things.

Richard Selzer
The Knife

One holds the knife as one holds the bow of a cello or a tulip—by the stem. Not palmed nor gripped nor grasped, but lightly, with the tips of the fingers. The knife is not for pressing. It is for drawing across the field of skin. Like a slender fish, it waits, at the ready, then, go! It darts, followed by a fine wake of red. The flesh parts, falling away to yellow globules of fat. Even now, after so many times, I still marvel at its power—cold, gleaming, silent. More, I am still struck with a kind of dread that it is I in whose hand the blade travels, that my hand is its vehicle, that yet again this terrible steel-bellied thing and I have conspired for a most unnatural purpose, the laying open of the body of a human being.

A stillness settles in my heart and is carried to my hand. It is the quietude of resolve layered over fear. And it is this resolve that lowers us, my knife and me, deeper and deeper into the person beneath. It is an entry into the body that is nothing like a caress; still, it is among the gentlest of acts. Then stroke and stroke again, and we are joined by other instruments, hemostats and forceps, until the wound blooms with strange flowers whose looped handles fall to the sides in steely array.

There is sound, the tight click of clamps fixing teeth into severed blood vessels, the snuffle and gargle of the suction machine clearing the field of blood for the next stroke, the litany of monosyllables with which one prays his way down and in: *clamp, sponge, suture, tie, cut.* And there is color. The green of the cloth, the white of the sponges, the red and yellow of the body. Beneath the fat lies the fascia, the tough fibrous sheet encasing the muscles. It must be sliced and the red beef of the muscles separated. Now there are retractors to hold apart the wound. Hands move together, part, weave. We are fully engaged, like children absorbed in a game or the craftsman of some place like Damascus.

Deeper still. The peritoneum, pink and gleaming and membranous, bulges into the wound. It is grasped with forceps, and opened. For the first time we can see into the cavity of the abdomen. Such a primitive place. One expects to find drawings of buffalo on the walls. The sense of trespassing is keener now, heightened by the world's light illuminating the organs, their secret colors revealed—maroon and salmon and yellow. The vista is sweetly vulnerable at this moment, a kind of welcoming. An arc of the liver shines high and on the right, like a dark sun. It laps over the pink sweep of the stomach, from whose lower border the gauzy omentum is draped, and through which veil one sees, sinuous, slow as just-fed snakes, the indolent coils of the intestine.

You turn aside to wash your gloves. It is a ritual cleansing. One enters this temple doubly washed. Here is man as microcosm, representing in all his parts the earth, perhaps the universe.

I must confess that the priestliness of my profession has ever been impressed on me. In the beginning there are vows, taken with all solemnity. Then there is the endless harsh novitiate of training, much fatigue, much sacrifice. At last one emerges as celebrant, standing close to the truth lying curtained in the Ark of the body. Not surplice and cassock but mask and gown are your regalia. You hold no chalice, but a knife. There is no wine, no wafer. There are only the facts of blood and flesh.

And if the surgeon is like a poet, then the scars you have made on countless bodies are like verses into the fashioning of which you have poured your soul. I think that if years later I were to see the trace from an old incision of mine, I should know it at once, as one recognizes his pet expressions.

But mostly you are a traveler in a dangerous country, advancing into the moist and jungly cleft your hands have made. Eyes and ears are shuttered from the land you left behind; mind empties itself of all other thought. You are the root of groping fingers. It is a fine hour for the fingers, their sense of touch so enhanced. The blind must know this feeling. Oh, there is risk everywhere. One goes lightly. The spleen. No! No! Do not touch the spleen that lurks below the left leaf of the diaphragm, a manta ray in a coral cave, its bloody tongue protruding. One poke and it might rupture, exploding with sudden hemorrhage. The filmy omentum must not be torn, the intestine scraped or denuded. The hand finds the liver, palms it, fingers running along its sharp lower edge, admiring. Here are the twin mounds of the kidneys, the apron of the omentum hanging in front of the intestinal coils. One lifts it aside and the fingers dip among the loops, searching, mapping territory, establishing boundaries. Deeper still, and the womb is touched, then held like a small muscular bottle—the womb and its earlike appendages, the ovaries. How they do nestle in the cup of a man's hand, their power all dormant. They are frailty itself.

There is a hush in the room. Speech stops. The hands of the others, assistants and nurses, are still. Only the voice of the patient's respiration remains. It is the rhythm of a quiet sea, the sound of waiting. Then you speak, slowly, the terse entries of a Himalayan climber reporting back.

"The stomach is okay. Greater curvature clean. No sign of ulcer. Pylorus, duodenum fine. Now comes the gall-bladder. No stones. Right kidney, left, all right. Liver . . . uh-oh."

Your speech lowers to a whisper, falters, stops for a long, long moment, then picks up again at the end of a sigh that comes through your mask like a last exhalation.

"Three big hard ones in the left lobe, one on the right. Metastatic deposits. Bad, bad. Where's the primary? Got to be coming from somewhere."

The arm shifts direction and the fingers drop lower and lower into the pelvis—the body impaled now upon the arm of the surgeon to the hilt of the elbow.

"Here it is."

The voice goes flat, all business now.

"Tumor in the sigmoid colon, wrapped all around it, pretty tight. We'll take out a sleeve of the bowel. No colostomy. Not that, anyway. But, God, there's a lot of it down there. Here, you take a feel."

You step back from the table, and lean into a sterile basin of water, resting on stiff arms, while the others locate the cancer.

When I was a small boy, I was taken by my father, a general practioner in Troy, New York, to St. Mary's Hospital, to wait while he made his rounds. The solarium where I sat was all sunlight and large plants. It smelled of soap and starch and clean linen. In the spring, clouds of lilac billowed from the vases; and in the fall, chrysanthemums crowded the magazine tables. At one end of the great high-ceilinged, glass-walled room was a huge cage where colored finches streaked and sang. Even from the first, I sensed the nearness of that other place, the Operating Room, knew that somewhere on these premises was that secret dreadful enclosure where *surgery* was at that moment happening. I sat among the cut flowers, half drunk on the scent, listening to the robes of the nuns brush the walls of the corridor, and felt the awful presence of *surgery*.

Oh, the pageantry! I longed to go there. I feared to go there. I imagined surgeons bent like storks over the body of the patient, a circle of red painted across the abdomen. Silence and dignity and awe enveloped them, these surgeons; it was the bubble in which they bent and straightened. Ah, it was a place I would never see, a place from whose walls the hung and suffering Christ turned his affliction to highest purpose. It is thirty years since I yearned for that old Surgery. And now I merely break the beam of an electric eye, and double doors swing open to let me enter, and as I enter, always, I feel the surging of a force that I feel in no other place. It is as though I am suddenly stronger and larger, heroic. Yes, that's it!

The operating room is called a theatre. One walks onto a set where the cupboards hold tanks of oxygen and other gases. The cabinets store steel cutlery of unimagined versatility, and the refrigerators are filled with bags of blood. Bodies are stroked and penetrated here, but no love is made. Nor is it ever allowed to grow dark, but must always gleam with a grotesque brightness. For the special congress into which patient and surgeon enter, the one must have his senses deadened, the other his sensibilities restrained. One lies naked, blind, offering; the other stands masked and gloved. One yields; the other does his will.

I said no love is made here, but love happens. I have stood aside with lowered gaze while a priest, wearing the purple scarf of office, administers Last Rites to the man I shall operate upon. I try not to listen to those terrible last questions, the answers, but hear, with scorching clarity, the words that formalize the expectation of death. For a moment my resolve falters before the resignation, the *attentiveness*, of the other two. I am like an executioner who hears the cleric comforting the prisoner. For the moment I am excluded from the centrality of the event, a mere technician standing by. But it is only for the moment.

The priest leaves, and we are ready. Let it begin.

Later, I am repairing the strangulated hernia of an old man. Because of his age and frailty, I am using local anesthesia. He is awake. His name is Abe Kaufman, and he is a Russian Jew. A nurse sits by his head, murmuring to him. She wipes his forehead. I know her very well. Her name is Alexandria, and she is the daughter of Ukrainian peasants. She has a flat steppe of a face and slanting eyes. Nurse and patient are speaking of blintzes, borscht, piroshki—Russian food that they both love. I listen, and think that it may have been her grandfather who raided the shtetl where the old man lived long ago, and in his high boots and his blouse and his fury this grandfather pulled Abe by his side curls to the ground and stomped his face and kicked his groin. Perhaps it was that ancient kick that caused the hernia I am fixing. I listen to them whispering behind the screen at the head of the table. I listen with breath held before the prism of history.

"Tovarich," she says, her head bent close to his.
He smiles up at her, and forgets that his body is being laid open.
"You are an angel," the old man says.

One can count on absurdity. There, in the midst of our solemnities, appears, small and black and crawling, an insect: The Ant of the Absurd. The belly is open; one has seen and felt the catastrophe within. It seems the patient is already vaporizing into angelhood in the heat escaping therefrom. One could warm one's hands in that fever. All at once that ant is there, emerging from beneath one of the sterile towels that border the operating field. For a moment one does not really see it, or else denies the sight, so impossible it is, marching precisely, heading briskly toward the open wound.

Drawn from its linen lair, where it snuggled in the steam of the great sterilizer, and survived, it comes. Closer and closer, it hurries toward the incision. Ant, art thou in the grip of some fatal *ivresse?* Wouldst hurtle over these scarlet cliffs into the very boil of the guts? Art mad for the reek we handle? Or in some secret act of formication engaged?

The alarm is sounded. An ant! An ant! And we are unnerved. Our fear of defilement is near to frenzy. It is not the mere physical contamination that we loathe. It is the evil of the interloper, that he scurries across our holy place, and filthies our altar. He *is* disease—that for whose destruction we have gathered. Powerless to destroy the sickness before us, we turn to its incarnation with a vengeance, and pluck it from the lip of the incision in the nick of time. Who would have thought an ant could move so fast?

Between thumb and forefinger, the intruder is crushed. It dies as quietly as it lived. Ah, but now there is death in the room. It is a perversion of our purpose. Albert Schweitzer would have spared it, scooped it tenderly into his hand, and lowered it to the ground.

The corpselet is flicked into the specimen basin. The gloves are changed. New towels and sheets are placed where it walked. We are pleased to have done something, if only a small killing. The operation resumes, and we draw upon ourselves once more the sleeves of office and rank. Is our reverence for life in question?

In the room the instruments lie on trays and tables. They are arranged precisely by the scrub nurse, in an order that never changes, so that you can reach blindly for a forceps or hemostat without looking away from the operating field. The instruments lie *thus!* Even at the beginning, when all is clean and tidy and no blood has been spilled, it is the scalpel that dominates. It has a figure the others do not have, the retractors and the scissors. The scalpel is all grace and line, a fierceness. It grins. It is like a cat—to be respected, deferred to, but which returns no amiability. To hold it above a belly is to know the knife's force—as though were you to give it slightest rein, it would pursue an intent of its own, driving into the flesh, a wild energy.

In a story by Borges, a deadly knife fight between two rivals is depicted. It is not, however, the men who are fighting. It is the knives themselves that are settling their own old score. The men who hold the knives are mere adjuncts to the weapons. The unguarded knife is like the unbridled war-horse that not only carries its helpless rider to his death, but tramples all beneath its hooves. The hand of the surgeon must tame this savage thing. He is a rider reining to capture a pace.

So close is the joining of knife and surgeon that they are like the Centaur— the knife, below, all equine energy, the surgeon, above, with his delicate art. One holds the knife back as much as advances it to purpose. One is master of the scissors. One is partner, sometimes rival, to the knife. In a moment it is like the long red fingernail of the Dragon Lady. Thus does the surgeon curb in order to create, restraining the scalpel, governing it shrewdly, setting the action of the operation into a pattern, giving it form and purpose.

It is the nature of creatures to live within a tight cuirass that is both their constriction and their protection. The carapace of the turtle is his fortress and retreat, yet keeps him writhing on his back in the sand. So is the surgeon rendered impotent by his own empathy and compassion. The surgeon cannot weep. When he cuts the flesh, his own must not bleed. Here it is all work. Like an asthmatic hungering for air, longing to take just one deep breath, the surgeon struggles not to feel. It is suffocating to press the feeling out. It would be easier to weep or mourn—for you know that the lovely precise world of proportion contains, just beneath, *there*, all disaster, all disorder. In a surgical operation, a risk may flash into reality: the patient dies . . . of *complication*. The patient knows this too, in a more direct and personal way, and he is afraid.

And what of that *other*, the patient, you, who are brought to the operating room on a stretcher, having been washed and purged and dressed in a white gown? Fluid drips from a bottle into your arm, diluting you, leaching your body of its personal brine. As you wait in the corridor, you hear from behind the closed door the angry clang of steel upon steel, as though a battle were being waged. There is the odor of antiseptic and ether, and masked women hurry up and down the halls, in and out of rooms. There is the watery sound of strange machinery, the tinny beeping that is the transmitted heartbeat of yet another *human being*. And all the while the dreadful knowledge that soon you will be taken, laid beneath great lamps that will reveal the secret linings of your body. In the very act of lying down, you have made a declaration of surrender. One lies down gladly for sleep or for love. But to give over one's body and will for surgery, to *lie down* for it, is a yielding of more than we can bear.

Soon a man will stand over you, gowned and hooded. In time the man will take up a knife and crack open your flesh like a ripe melon. Fingers will rummage among your viscera. Parts of you will be cut out. Blood will run free. Your blood. All the night before you have turned with the presentiment of death upon you. You have attended your funeral, wept with your mourners. You think, "I should never have had surgery in the springtime." It is too cruel. Or on a Thursday. It is an unlucky day.

Now it is time. You are wheeled in and moved to the table. An injection is given. "Let yourself go," I say. "It's a pleasant sensation," I say. "Give in," I say.

Let go? Give in? When you know that you are being tricked into the hereafter, that you will end when consciousness ends? As the monstrous silence of anesthesia falls discourteously across your brain, you watch your soul drift off.

Later, in the recovery room, you awaken and gaze through the thickness of drugs at the world returning, and you guess, at first dimly, then surely, that you have not died. In pain and nausea you will know the exultation of death averted, of life restored.

What is it, then, this thing, the knife, whose shape is virtually the same as it was three thousand years ago, but now with its head grown detachable? Before steel, it was bronze. Before bronze, stone—then back into unremembered time. Did man invent it or did the knife precede him here, hidden under ages of vegetation and hoofprints, lying in wait to be discovered, picked up, used?

The scalpel is in two parts, the handle and the blade. Joined, it is six inches from tip to tip. At one end of the handle is a narrow notched prong upon which the blade is slid, then snapped into place. Without the blade, the handle has a blind, decapitated look. It is helpless as a trussed maniac. But slide on the blade, click it home, and the knife springs instantly to life. It is headed now, edgy, leaping to mount the fingers for the gallop to its feast.

Now is the moment from which you have turned aside, from which you have averted your gaze, yet toward which you have been hastened. Now the scalpel sings along the flesh again, its brute run unimpeded by germs or other frictions. It is a slick slide home, a barracuda spurt, a rip of embedded talon. One listens, and almost hears the whine—nasal, high, delivered through that gleaming metallic snout. The flesh splits with its own kind of moan. It is like the penetration of rape.

The breasts of women are cut off, arms and legs sliced to the bone to make ready for the saw, eyes freed from sockets, intestines lopped. The hand of the surgeon rebels. Tension boils through his pores, like sweat. The flesh of the patient retaliates with hemorrhage, and the blood chases the knife wherever it is withdrawn.

Within the belly a tumor squats, toadish, fungoid. A gray mother and her brood. The only thing it does not do is croak. It too is hacked from its bed as the carnivore knife lips the blood, turning in it in a kind of ecstasy of plenty, a gluttony after the long fast. It is just for this that the knife was created, tempered, heated, its violence beaten into paper-thin force.

At last a little thread is passed into the wound and tied. The monstrous booming fury is stilled by a tiny thread. The tempest is silenced. The operation is over. On the table, the knife lies spent, on its side, the bloody meal smear-dried upon its flanks. The knife rests.

And waits.

TRY THIS 7.12
You are probably not a surgeon, but several times in your journal you have written about something at which you are in fact an expert. Focus on that expertise—its difficulties, dangers, and rewards, but also its equipment, the look of it, the setting, how it affects the body. Write a personal essay about your experience that will also teach those who have no such skill or knowledge.

ACCOMPLISHING A DRAFT

Choose among your writings so far the piece that seems most promising as a memoir or a personal essay. Using either the outline or the quilting method described in Chapter 6, rough out a draft.

Creative Nonfiction Format

"Clean copy" is the first and very visible sign of the professional. Your manuscript should be carefully proofread, neatly printed or copied, and stapled or paper clipped in the upper left-hand corner. Your particular teacher, group leader, or editor may have format requirements. To cut copying costs, some teachers will ask you to omit a cover page, and/or to single space. Otherwise, title and author's name and address (or class identification) should appear on a cover page, and your name need appear only there. Page numbering can be done in the upper or lower center or right corner of the page.

Manuscripts should be double-spaced, with generous (approximately one inch) margins, on one side of $8^1/_2$-× 11-inch white paper. The first page of the essay should begin about one-third of the way down the page.

Copyrighting of literary manuscripts is not necessary—essays, stories, poems, and plays are, alas, rarely worth money enough to be attractive to thieves. If your work is published, the magazine or publisher will apply for copyright, and you will have a contract that specifies what rights belong to you.

Always keep a copy of your work.

ROUGHING IT
by Mark Twain

Creative Nonfiction 101
Prof. Becky Thatcher
Hannibal State University
October 15, 1872

1

My brother had just been appointed Secretary of Nevada Territory—an office of such majesty that it concentrated in itself the duties and dignities of Treasurer, Comptroller, Secretary of State and Acting Governor in the Governor's absence. A salary of eighteen hundred dollars a year and the title of "Mr. Secretary" gave to the position an air of wild and imposing grandeur.

I was young and ignorant, and I envied my brother. I coveted his distinction and his financial splendor, but particularly and especially the long, strange journey he was going to make, and the curious new world he was going to explore. He was going to travel! I never had been away from home, and that word "travel" had a seductive charm for me. Pretty soon he would be hundreds and hundreds of miles away on the great plains and deserts, and among the mountains of the Far West, and would see buffaloes and

Laurie Lipton, "Facing up to Reality"

WARM-UP

What is going on in this girl's mind? What has happened in the last two hours? What has happened in the last two years? How much of this can you let us know without leaving this room, this chair, her thoughts?

CHAPTER EIGHT

FICTION

Story and Plot
Scene and Summary
Backstory and Flashback
Text and Subtext
Fiction Format

The writer of any work . . . must decide two crucial points:
what to put in and what to leave out.

Annie Dillard

You have a story to write. You have a character in mind. The character has a desire. A situation presents itself. That the situation will lead to fulfillment of the desire is possible, but uncertain. How do you proceed?

Aristotle, the Greek philosopher who was also the first critic in Western literature, famously said that a story must have a beginning, a middle, and an end. This is less obvious than it looks. As the author, the questions you must answer are: Where shall I begin? Where will I end? What is in between? When you have made these decisions, you have made a choice between *story* and *plot*.

Story and Plot

Humphry House, in his commentaries on Aristotle, defines **story** as everything the reader needs to know to make coherent sense of the plot, and **plot** as the particular portion of the story the author chooses to present—the "present tense" of the narrative.

The story of *Oedipus Rex*, for example, begins before Oedipus's birth with the oracle predicting that he will murder his father and marry his mother. It includes his birth, his abandonment with hobbled ankles, his childhood with his foster parents, his flight from them, his murder of the stranger at the crossroads, his triumph over the Sphinx, his marriage to Jocasta and his reign in Thebes, his fatherhood, the Theban plague, his discovery of the truth, and his self-blinding and self-banishment.

When Sophocles set out to plot a play on this story, he began the action at dawn on the very last day of it. All the information about Oedipus's life is necessary to understand the plot, but the plot begins with the conflict: How can Oedipus get rid of the plague in Thebes? Because the plot is so arranged, it is the revelation of the past that makes up the action of the play, a process of discovery that gives rise to the significant theme: Who am I? Had Sophocles begun with the oracle before Oedipus's birth, no such theme and no such significance could have been explored.

E. M. Forster, in *Aspects of the Novel*, makes substantially the same distinction between plot and story. A story, he says, is:

> . . . the chopped off length of the tape worm of time . . . a narrative of events arranged in their time sequence. A plot is also a narrative of events, the emphasis falling on causality. "The king died, and then the queen died," is a story. "The king died, and then the queen died of grief," is a plot. The time sequence is preserved, but the sense of causality overshadows it. Or again: "The queen died, no one knew why, until it was discovered that it was through grief at the death of the king." This is a plot with a mystery in it, a form capable of high development. It suspends the time sequence, it moves as far away from the story as its limitations will allow. Consider the death of the queen. If it is in a story we say, "and then?" If it is in a plot we ask, "why?"

The human desire to know why is as powerful as the desire to know what happened next, and it is a desire of a higher order. Once we have the facts, we inevitably look for the links between them, and only when we find such links are we satisfied that we "understand." Rote memorization in a science bores almost everyone. Grasp and a sense of discovery begin only when we perceive *why* "a body in motion tends to remain in motion" and what an immense effect this actuality has on the phenomena of our lives.

The same is true of the events of a story. Random incidents neither move nor illuminate; we want to know why one thing leads to another and to feel the inevitability of cause and effect.

Arranging for Plot

A *story* is a series of events recorded in their chronological order. A *plot* is a series of events deliberately arranged so as to reveal their dramatic, thematic, and emotional significance.

Here, for example, is a series of uninteresting events chronologically arranged.

Ariadne had a bad dream.

She woke up tired and cross.

She ate breakfast.

She headed for class.

She saw Leroy.

She fell on the steps and broke her ankle.

Leroy offered to take notes for her.

She went to a hospital.

This series of events does not constitute a plot, and if you wish to fashion it into a plot, you can do so only by letting us know the meaningful relations among the events. We first assume that Ariadne woke in a temper because of her bad dream, and that Leroy offered to take notes for her because she broke her ankle. But why did she fall? Perhaps because she saw Leroy? Does that suggest that her bad dream was about him? Was she, then, thinking about his dream-rejection as she broke her egg irritably on the edge of the frying pan? What is the effect of his offer? Is it a triumph or just another polite form of rejection when, really, he could have missed class once to drive her to the X-ray lab? All the emotional and dramatic significance of these ordinary events emerges in the relation of cause to effect, and where such relation can be shown, a possible plot comes into existence.

Ariadne's is a story you might very well choose to tell chronologically: it needs to cover only an hour or two, and that much can be handled in the compressed form of the short story. But such a choice of plot is not inevitable even in this short compass. Might it be more gripping to begin with the wince of pain as she stumbles? Leroy comes to help her up and the yolk yellow of his T-shirt fills her field of vision. In the shock of pain she is immediately back in her dream. . . .

Choosing Where to Begin

Here is another example of a quite standard story: A girl grows up bossed by her older sister, who always tells her she's fat and a nerd. She ends up with "low self-esteem," poor grades, and a stutter. She has "social anxiety"; she stays at her computer most of the time. Her mother takes her to a series of therapists, but nothing brings her out of her shell. She's not asked to the big basketball dance, and won't go alone, but on the night of the game the computer system that runs the gym lighting system breaks down, and the coach, who knows she's a computer whiz, gives her a call. She fixes the program and catches the eye of the handsome Center (who probably takes off her glasses and lets down her hair, right?). And they live happily ever after.

This Cinderella story line shows up over and over again in film and print. The question is, how can you make it fresh and interesting? Where should your *plot* begin?

You may start, if you like, with the immigration of the heroine's grandparents from Lithuania. But if you do, it's going to be a very long story and we may close the book before she's born. You may begin it, like your childhood tale of Cinderella, with the background situation of the family, but then you must summarize, generalize, and focus on minor characters; and you may have a hard time holding our attention. Begin with the announcement of the dance? Better. If so, you'll somehow have to let us know all that has gone before, either through dialogue or through the girl's memory; but you have only a few days to cover and you have an opportunity to show the sisters in conflict. Suppose you begin with the telephone call from the coach? Is that perhaps best of all? An urgent dramatic scene, an immediate conflict that must lead to a quick and striking crisis?

Try This 8.1

By now you have from your journal entries an idea for a short story. Take fifteen minutes to list all the events of this story in their chronological order. List *everything* we will need to know in order to make sense of it. If Seth's fear of water results from the time his cruel half-brother held him under when he was five, and we will need to know this is order to understand why he won't go out in a boat at twenty—then list the bullying incident in its chronological place.

- Find the item exactly halfway down your list. Write the first paragraph of your story beginning it there.
- Take the last item on your list. Write the first paragraph of the story beginning it there.
- Pick the *right* item on your list for the beginning of the story. Try these: Begin with a line of dialogue. Begin with an action. Begin with an image of danger. Begin with the weather. Begin with the protagonist's thought. Begin with a long shot. Begin with a closeup.

It is a cliché of critical reaction—and not just for the work of beginners!—that "your story actually begins on page three." I think there is good reason that this failure of technique afflicts even professional writers. When you begin a story you are very properly feeling your way, getting to know your characters, bringing the setting into focus, testing the sorts of voice and action that will work. Since you're a little unsteady on your literary feet at this point, it's a temptation to fiddle with the dialogue, alter this phrase, perfect that image. The writing, thus polished, starts to look valuable—so it's hard to see that the reader doesn't need the same extended orientation that you did. Sometimes you need a few weeks' distance, or somebody else's insight, to recognize that you can move farther faster.

TRY THIS 8.2

Take the manuscript you worked on in Try This 8.1. Toss out page one. Try beginning with the first whole paragraph on page two. Doesn't work?

Then:

Condense the first three pages to a paragraph. How much of the lost information can, in fact, be done without?

> A child in a tantrum screams, throws toys, lies on the floor, and kicks in the air. The parents say, "You're making a scene!"
>
> *Jerome Stern*

Scene and Summary

Summary and **scene** are methods of treating time in fiction. A summary covers a relatively long period of time in relatively short compass; a scene deals at length with a relatively short period of time.

Summary is a useful and often necessary device: to give information, fill in a character's background, let us understand a motive, alter pace, create a transition, leap moments or years.

Scene is *always* necessary to fiction. Scene is to time what concrete detail is to the senses; that is, it is the crucial means of allowing your reader to experience the story with the characters. A confrontation, a turning point, or a crisis occurs at given moments that take on significance as moments and cannot be summarized. The form of a story requires confrontation and change, and therefore requires scenes. As Jerome Stern points out in *Making Shapely Fiction*, when you want everyone's full attention you "make a scene" like a child in a tantrum, using the writer's full complement of "dialogue, physical reactions, gestures, smells, sounds, and thoughts."

It is quite possible to write a short story in a single scene, without any summary at all. It is not possible to write a successful story entirely in summary. One of the most common errors beginning fiction writers make is to summarize events rather than to realize them as moments.

One quite common and effective technique in fiction is to orient us with a short summary and then move to a scene when the action begins. In the following paragraphs from Margaret Atwood's *Lady Oracle*, the narrator has been walking home from her Brownie troop with older girls who tease and terrify her with threats of a bad man.

The snow finally changed to slush and then to water, which trickled down the hill of the bridge in two rivulets, one on either side of the path; the path itself turned to mud. The bridge was damp, it smelled rotten, the willow branches turned yellow, the skipping ropes came out. It was light again in the afternoons, and on one of them, when for a change Elizabeth hadn't run off but was merely discussing the possibilities with the others, a real man actually appeared.

He was standing at the far side of the bridge, a little off the path, holding a bunch of daffodils in front of him. He was a nice-looking man, neither old nor young, wearing a good tweed coat, not at all shabby or disreputable. He didn't have a hat on, his taffy-colored hair was receding and the sunlight gleamed on his high forehead.

The first paragraph of this quotation covers the way things changed over a period of a few months and then makes a transition to one of the afternoons; the second paragraph specifies a particular moment. Notice that although summary sets us at a distance from the action, sensory details remain necessary to its life: *snow, path, bridge, willow branches, skipping ropes.* The scene is introduced when an element of conflict and confrontation occurs. That the threatened bad man does appear and that he is surprisingly innocuous promises a turn of events and a change in the relationship among the girls. We need to see the moment when this change occurs.

Throughout *Lady Oracle*, which is by no means unusual in this respect, the pattern recurs: a summary leading up to, and followed by, a scene that represents a turning point.

My own job was fairly simple. I stood at the back of the archery range, wearing a red leather change apron, and rented out the arrows. When the barrels of arrows were almost used up, I'd go down to the straw targets. The difficulty was that we couldn't make sure all the arrows had actually been shot before we went down to clear the targets. Rob would shout, Bows DOWN, please, arrows OFF the string, but occasionally someone would let an arrow go, on purpose or by accident. This was how I got shot. We'd pulled the arrows and the men were carrying the barrels back to the line; I was replacing a target face, and I'd just bent over.

The summary in the second excerpt describes the general circumstances during a period of time—this is how things were, this is what usually or frequently happened: *I'd go down to the straw targets. Rob would shout.* Again, when the narrator arrives at an event that changes her circumstance (*I got shot*), she focuses on a particular moment: *I was replacing a target face, and I'd just bent over.* Notice that the pattern summary-to-scene parallels in time the spatial pattern of long shot-to-close-up.

Since the changes in your story will take place in fully developed scenes, it's important to limit the *number* of scenes, and summary can be useful to get you from one to another. Frequently, the function of summary is precisely to heighten scene. It is in the scene, the "present" of the story, that the drama, the discovery, the decision, the potential for change, engage our attention.

TRY THIS 8.3

Look at the list of your story's events. How many of them belong in summary? Which of them involve moments of discovery or decision and should be scenes? How *few* scenes would it be possible to use and still tell the story? Those three dinners with dad—could they be conflated to one? The quarrel on the morning after—could it happen the same night? List the events of the story that represent its essential scenes.

Start writing one of these scenes with a method or a mood you've never used before. Begin with a cliché. Begin with a line of angry dialogue. Begin with a death. Begin tenderly. Begin with an action no bigger than a breadbox. Begin with the outcome of the scene and then go back to get us there.

In Chapter 5, I said that the crisis point of a story must always be manifested in an action. Another way of saying this is that the crisis is always a scene. At the moment the protagonist's situation will change, we as readers must *be there*. What is important about this crisis action is not that it be violent or even external, but that its intensity signal a turning point in the character's fortune or outlook. Often, the intensity of the moment will require that all the senses come into play.

Because the crisis action is the culmination of an entire plot, it's difficult to pick an example that will illustrate the concept out of its context. But here is a crisis scene from a short story by Tobias Wolff that does show the intensity of such a moment, achieved by exact detail. In "Coming Attractions," Jean, a fifteen-year-old in a family that has been truly "broken" by divorce, has been struggling to pull a bicycle out of a swimming pool for her little brother.

> The bike was getting heavy. Jean brought her knees up and got her feet on the lowest rung. She rested a moment. Then she moved her free hand to the rail and began to straighten her legs, pushing herself up toward the light flashing on the surface just above her. She felt her mouth start to open. *No*, she thought, but her mouth opened anyway and Jean was choking when her head broke through to air. She coughed out the water in her throat and then gagged on the chlorine aftertaste until she almost puked. Her eyes burned.
>
> Jean climbed the ladder to where she could work her hips over the edge of the pool and slide forward a bit. She let go of the rail and wiped her face. Her other arm was dead, but she knew the bike was still there because she could feel its weight in her shoulders and back. In a little while she would pull it out. No problem—just as soon as she got herself back together. But until then she couldn't do a thing but lie with her cheek on the cement, and blink her eyes, and savor the cold air that passed through her.

TRY THIS 8.4
Identify the crisis of the story you are working on. Describe that moment with details involving at least three senses.

Backstory and Flashback

Clearly, if you are going to begin *in medias res* (in the middle of the action), then parts of your story will have to be brought in later. **Backstory** is a relatively new term, which started out in film meaning a *prequel*, but has come to refer to any information about the past—whatever has occurred before the plot begins and is necessary to make the story coherent. Such information can be revealed in dialogue, or in the character's thoughts, or in the narrative itself. When the narrative actually travels back from its current action to depict the past in scenes, it is called a **flashback**—also a term borrowed from film.

There is, I think, one cardinal rule about the past in fiction: don't give us more than we need. As with opening paragraphs, so with backstory: as the author you need to know so much about your characters in order to make them real and complex that you may think we readers need to know just as much. But if your characters are interesting and credible, we probably don't. Especially in the twenty-first century—accustomed to the quick cuts of film, inundated with the lessons of psychology—we will understand causal connections, accept odd behavior, and tolerate a degree of inconsistency without needing a whole lot of psychological explanation. On the other hand, our primal desire to get on with the story is as powerful as it was around the prehistoric campfire, and we are likely to be impatient with too much background information.

When intrusive passages of childhood, motivation, and explanation tend to come early in the story, before we are caught up in the action, we wonder whether there is any story on its way. Dialogue, brief summary, a reference or detail can often tell us all we need to know, and when that is the case, a flashback becomes cumbersome and overlong. If, four pages into your story, you find there is more action happening in the character's memory than in the present action, you may not yet have found where the story lies.

TRY THIS 8.5
Find a place where you either do or could use a flashback in your story. Instead, use your journal for exploring background. Write down everything, fast. Then take a hard look at it to decide just how little of it you can use, how much of it the reader can infer, how you can sharpen an image to imply a past incident or condense an emotion into a line of dialogue.

Frequently it's best to trust the reader's experience of life to understand events from action and attitude, and to keep the present of the story moving.

That said, flashback is still one of the most magical of fiction's contrivances. Effectively used to *reveal* at the *right time*, it does not so much take us from, as contribute to, the central action of the story, so that as readers we suspend the forward motion of the narrative in our minds as our understanding of it deepens. Because the reader's mind is a swifter mechanism for getting into the past than anything that has been devised for stage or even film, all you must do is give the reader smooth passage into the past, and the force of the story will be time-warped to whenever and wherever you want it.

A connection between what's happening in the present and what happened in the past will often best transport the reader, just as it does the character. Where possible avoid blatant transitions such as "Henry thought back to the time," and "I drifted back in memory." Assume the reader's intelligence and ability to follow a leap back, as in this excerpt from Nadine Gordimer's *July's People*, where the protagonist and her husband Bamford have escaped an African uprising to hide in the village of their former servant:

> The black man looked over the three sleeping children bedded-down on seats taken from the vehicle. He smiled confirmation: "They all right."
>
> "Yes, all right." As he dipped out under the doorway: "Thank you, July, thank you very much."
>
> She had slept in round mud huts roofed in thatch like this before. In the Kruger Park, a child of the shift boss and his family on leave, an enamel basin and ewer among their supplies of orange squash and biscuits on the table coming clear as this morning light came. Rondavels, adapted by Bam's ancestors on his Boer side from the huts of the blacks. They were a rusticism true to the continent; before air-conditioning, everyone praised the natural insulation of thatch against heat. Rondavels had concrete floors, thickly shined with red polish, veined with trails of coarse ants. . .

Here both a memory from her childhood and a historical vignette, each sketched with a few details, points up the irony of her situation without impeding the flow of the narrative.

When you end a flashback, make it clear that you are catching up to the present again. Repeat an action or image that the reader will remember belongs to the basic time period of the story. Often simply beginning the paragraph with "Now . . ." will accomplish the reorientation. Gordimer accomplishes it by returning from the general to the specific hut:

> This one was a prototype from which all the others had come and to which all returned: below her, beneath the iron bed on whose rusty spring they had spread the vehicle's tarpaulin, a stamped mud and dung floor. . .

TRY THIS 8.6

Put your character in motion, on foot or in a vehicle, in urgent search of something. What does he or she need? Why so urgently? Let us know in a flashback of no more than three sentences. Avoid the words *remembered, recalled, thought back to,* and others of their ilk.

Add a character. In dialogue, let us know some important thing from the past.

Add music. Let the music trigger a memory good or bad, in thought or dialogue. Let the memory reveal something we didn't know before, in no more than two sentences.

Text and Subtext

As a writer you are always trying to mean more than you say. You want dialogue to convey information and character, you want setting to convey mood and propel the action, you want clothing to indicate politics, and gesture to betray thought.

You can do this, and your reader can understand it, because people operate this way in their daily lives. We express ourselves in many ways besides words, sometimes by choice and sometimes in self-betrayal, sometimes trying to conceal for the sake of friendship and sometimes in fear or contempt. How many times have you sat through a meal in which the dialogue was all polite, anecdotal, and bland, but everybody was *desperate* with boredom, anger, anxiety, or the need to control?

The *text* is what is stated in any situation; the *subtext* is whatever remains unstated—with the usual implication that the unstated is what's really going on.

Imagine a restaurant scene in which Bill asks his friend Lex to pass the shrimp. Lex passes them by way of his wife, Sara, who takes a handful on the way. There are none left for Bill's wife, Jane, who says she didn't want any more anyway. Imagine how the dialogue, gestures, glances, facial expressions, tones of voice differ in this scene if Lex suspects that Bill is having an affair with Sara; and/or Jane is pregnant, which Sara knows but her husband doesn't; and/or Jane feels herself to be superior to the rest of them, including her husband; and/or Sara and Lex had a quarrel just before they left home in which Lex accused her of selfishness; and/or Jane is trying to get home early to intercept a phone call from Bill's mother, who may have cancer; and/or Bill wrote a report that he suspects will get Lex fired. Any combination of these complications probably means that all four of them are sick of the friendship anyway, and looking for a way to end it. Yet they may not. Situations of this complexity occur every day.

Here is a passage from Barbara Kingsolver's *Poisonwood Bible,* in which an American Baptist minister and his family sit with a Bantu council in the Belgian Congo:

> Father tried to interrupt the proceedings by loudly explaining that Jesus is exempt from popular elections. But people were excited, having just recently got the hang of democratic elections. The citizens of Kilanga were ready to cast their stones . . .
>
> Anatole, who'd sat down in his chair a little distance from the pulpit, leaned over and said quietly to Father, "They say you thatched your roof and now you must not run out of your house if it rains."
>
> Father ignored this parable. "Matters of the spirit are not decided at the marketplace," he shouted sternly. Anatole translated.
>
> "*Á bu, kwe?* Where, then?" asked Tat Nguza, standing up boldly. In his opinion, he said, a white man who has never even killed a bushbuck for his family was not the expert on which god can protect our village.
>
> When Anatole translated that one, Father looked taken aback. Where we come from, it's hard to see the connection.
>
> Father spoke slowly, as if to a half-wit, "Elections are good, and Christianity is good. Both are good." We in his family recognized the danger in his extremely calm speech, and the rising color creeping toward his hairline.

In this passage, while a controlled form of political negotiation goes on, the participants vie for status, and we have a dozen or more clues to the political and personal subtext. The contrast between the Congolese's parables and the American's abstractions, the conflicting logic, the gestures, bodily movements and expressions, the genuine calm of the translator as opposed to the bottled-fury calm of the father—all these reveal the unspoken meanings. In addition, they are interpreted through the point of view of a daughter who, in spite of her youth and relative innocence, has reason to understand the signs.

TRY THIS 8.7
Three characters: Each finds another in some way ridiculous, unattractive, or incompetent. They must agree on a specific—the design for a brochure, tonight's dessert, what to name something or someone (choose your own area for negotiation). Give us the dialogue and the actions—and the thoughts of only one of the characters.

Subtext is a necessary result and cost of civilization—if everyone went around saying what they meant all the time there would be fewer friends and a lot more pain—but it offers a glorious opportunity for art. When your characters let us know by action, tone, thought, gesture, hesitation, slip of the tongue, contradiction, or backtracking that they are leaving an iceberg's worth of the truth submerged, the reader reads their truth as well as the words.

More to Read

Gardner, John. *The Art of Fiction*. New York: Vintage Books, 1991.

Stern, Jerome. *Making Shapely Fiction*. New York: W.W. Norton, 2000.

Readings

Charles Baxter

Snow

Twelve years old, and I was so bored I was combing my hair just for the hell of it. This particular Saturday afternoon, time was stretching out unpleasantly in front of me. I held the comb under the tap and then stared into the bathroom mirror as I raked the wave at the front of my scalp upward so that it would look casual and sharp and perfect. For inspiration I had my transistor radio, balanced on the doorknob, tuned to an AM Top Forty station. But the music was making me jumpy, and instead of looking casual my hair, soaking wet, had the metallic curve of the rear fins of a De Soto. I looked aerodynamic but not handsome. I dropped the comb into the sink and went down the hallway to my brother's room.

Ben was sitting at his desk, crumpling up papers and tossing them into a wastebasket near the window. He was a great shot, particularly when he was throwing away his homework. His stainless-steel sword, a souvenir of military school, was leaning against the bookcase, and I could see my pencil-thin reflection in it as I stood in his doorway. "Did you hear about the car?" Ben asked, not bothering to look at me. He was gazing through his window at Five Oaks Lake.

"What car?"

"The car that went through the ice two nights ago. Thursday. Look. You can see the pressure ridge near Eagle Island."

I couldn't see any pressure ridge; it was too far away. Cars belonging to ice fishermen were always breaking through the ice, but swallowing up a car was a slow process in January, though not in March or April, and the drivers usually got out safely. The clear lake ice reflected perfectly the flat gray sky this drought winter, and we could still see the spiky brown grass on our back lawn. It crackled and crunched whenever I walked on it.

"I don't see it," I said. "I can't see the hole. Where did you hear about this car? Did Pop tell you?"

"No," Ben said. "Other sources." Ben's sources, his network of friends and enemies, were always calling him on the telephone to tell him things. He basked in information. Now he gave me a quick glance. "Holy smoke," he said. "What did you do to your hair?"

"Nothing," I said. "I was just combing it."

"You look like that guy," he said. "The one in the movies."

"Which guy?"

"That Harvey guy."

"Jimmy Stewart?"

"Of course not," he said. "You know the one I mean. Everybody knows that guy. The Harvey guy." When I looked blank, he said, "Never mind. Let's go down to the lake and look at the car. You'd better tell them we're going." He gestured toward the other end of the house.

In the kitchen I informed my parents that I was headed somewhere with my brother, and my mother, chopping carrots for one of her stews, looked up at me and my hair. "Be back by five," she said. "Where did you say you were off to?"

"We're driving to Navarre," I said. "Ben has to get his skates sharpened."

My stepfather's eyebrows started to go up; he exchanged a glance with my mother—the usual pantomime of skepticism. I turned around and ran out of the kitchen before they could stop me. I put on my boots, overcoat, and gloves, and hurried outside to my brother's car, a 1952 Rocket 88. He was already inside. The motor roared.

The interior of the car smelled of gum, cigarettes, wet wool, analgesic balm, and aftershave. "What'd you tell them?" my brother asked.

"I said you were going to Navarre to get your skates sharpened."

He put the car into first gear, then sighed. "Why'd you do that? I have to explain everything to you. Number one: my skates aren't in the car. What if they ask to see them when we get home? I don't have them. That's a problem, isn't it? Number two: when you lie about being somewhere, you make sure you have a friend who's there who can say you *were* there, even if you weren't. Unfortunately, we don't have any friends in Navarre."

"Then we're safe," I said. "No one will say we *weren't* there."

He shook his head. Then he took off his glasses and examined them as if my odd ideas were visible right there on the frames. I was just doing my job, being his private fool, but I knew he liked me and liked to have me around. My unworldliness amused him; it gave him a chance to lecture me. But now, tired of wasting words on me, he turned on the radio. Pulling out onto the highway, he steered the car in his customary way. He had explained to me that only very old or very sick people actually grip steering wheels. You didn't have to hold the wheel to drive a car. Resting your arm over the top of the wheel gave a better appearance. You dangled your hand down, preferably with a cigarette in it, so that the car, the entire car, responded to the mere pressure of your wrist.

"Hey," I said. "Where are we going? This isn't the way to the lake."

"We're not going there first. We're going there second."

"Where are we going first?"

"We're going to Five Oaks. We're going to get Stephanie. Then we'll see the car."

"How come we're getting her?"

"Because she wants to see it. She's never seen a car underneath the ice before. She'll be impressed."

"Does she know we're coming?"

He gave me that look again. "What do they teach you at that school you go to? Of course she knows. We have a date."

"A date? It's three o'clock in the afternoon," I said. "You can't have a date at three in the afternoon. Besides, I'm along."

"Don't argue," Ben said. "Pay attention."

By the time we reached Five Oaks, the heater in my brother's car was blowing out warm air in tentative gusts. If we were going to get Stephanie, his current girlfriend, it was fine with me. I liked her smile—she had an overbite, the same as I did, but she didn't seem self-conscious about it—and I liked the way she shut her eyes when she laughed. She had listened to my crystal radio set and admired my collection of igneous rocks on one of her two visits to our house. My brother liked to bring his girlfriends over to our house because the house was old and large and, my brother said, they would be impressed by the empty rooms and the long hallways and the laundry chutes that dropped down into nowhere. They'd be snowed. Snowing girls was something I knew better than to ask my brother about. You had to learn about it by watching and listening. That's why he had brought me along.

Ben parked outside Stephanie's house and told me to wait in the car. I had nothing to do but look at houses and telephone poles. Stephanie's front-porch swing had rusted chains, and the paint around her house seemed to have blistered in cobweb patterns. One drab lamp with a low-wattage bulb was on near an upstairs window. I could see the lampshade: birds—I couldn't tell what kind—had been painted on it. I adjusted the dashboard clock. It didn't run, but I liked to have it seem accurate. My brother had said that anyone who invented a clock that would really work in a car would become a multimillionaire. Clocks in cars never work, he said, because the mainsprings can't stand the shock of potholes. I checked my wristwatch and yawned. The inside of the front window began to frost over with my breath. I decided that when I grew up I would invent a new kind of timepiece for cars, without springs or gears. At three-twenty I adjusted the clock again. One minute later, my brother came out of the house with Stephanie. She saw me in the car, and she smiled.

I opened the door and got out. "Hi, Steph," I said. "I'll get in the backseat."

"That's okay, Russell," she said, smiling, showing her overbite. "Sit up in front with us."

"Really?"

She nodded. "Yeah. Keep us warm."

She scuttled in next to my brother, and I squeezed in on her right side, with my shoulder against the door. As soon as the car started, she and my brother began to hold hands: he steered with his left wrist over the steering wheel, and she held his right hand. I watched all this, and Stephanie noticed me watching. "Do you want one?" she asked me.

"What?"

"A hand." She gazed at me, perfectly serious. "My other hand."

"Sure," I said.

"Well, take my glove off," she said. "I can't do it by myself." My brother started chuckling, but she stopped him with a look. I took Stephanie's wrist in my left hand and removed her glove, finger by finger. I hadn't held hands with anyone since second grade. Her hand was not much larger than mine, but holding it gave me an odd sensation, because it was a woman's hand, and where my fingers were bony, hers were soft. She was wearing a bright-green cap, and when I glanced up at it she said, "I like your hair, Russell. It's kind of slummy. You're getting to look dangerous. Is there any gum?"

I figured she meant in the car. "There's some up there on the dashboard." Ben said. His car always had gum in it. It was a museum of gum. The ashtrays were full of cigarette butts and gum, mixed together, and the floor was flecked silver from the foil wrappers.

"I can't reach it," Stephanie said. "You two have both my hands tied down."

"Okay," I said. I reached up with my free hand and took a piece of gum and unwrapped it. The gum was light pink, a sunburn color.

"Now what?" I asked.

"What do you think?" She looked down at me, smiled again, then opened her mouth. I suddenly felt shy. "Come on, Russell," she said. "Haven't you ever given gum to a girl before?" I raised my hand with the gum in it. She kept her eyes open and on me. I reached forward, and just as I got the gum close to her mouth she opened wider, and I slid the gum in over her tongue without even brushing against her lipstick. She closed and began chewing.

"Thank you," she said. Stephanie and my brother nudged each other. Then they broke out in short quick laughs—vacation laughter. I knew that what had happened hinged on my ignorance, but that I wasn't exactly the butt of the joke and could laugh, too, if I wanted. The sky had turned darker, and I wondered whether, if I was still alive fifty years from now, I would remember any of this. I saw an old house on the side of the highway with a cracked upstairs window, and I thought, that's what I'll remember from this whole day when I'm old—that one cracked window.

Stephanie was looking out at the dry winter fields and suddenly said, "The state of Michigan. You know who this state is for? You know who's really happy in this state?"

"No," I said. "Who?"

"Chickens and squirrels," she said. "They love it here."

My brother parked the car on the driveway down by our dock, and we walked out onto the ice on the bay. Stephanie was stepping awkwardly, a high-center-of-gravity shuffle. "Is it safe?" she asked.

"Sure, it's safe," my brother said. "Look." He began to jump up and down. Ben was heavy enough to be a tackle on his high-school football team, and sounds of ice cracking reverberated all through the bay and beyond into the center of the lake, a deep echo. Already, four ice fishermen's houses had been set up on the ice two hundred feet out—four brightly painted shacks, male hideaways—and I could see tire tracks over the thin layer of sprinkled snow. "Clear the snow and look down into it," he said.

After lowering herself to her knees, Stephanie dusted the snow away. She held her hands to the side of her head and looked. "It's real thick," she said. "Looks a foot thick. How come a car went through?"

"It went down in a channel." Ben said, walking ahead of us and calling backward so that his voice seemed to drift in and out of the wind. "It went over a pressure ridge, and that's all she wrote."

"Did anyone drown?"

He didn't answer. She ran ahead to catch up to him, slipping, losing her balance, then recovering it. In fact I knew that no one had drowned. My stepfather had told me that the man driving the car had somehow—I wasn't sure how a person did this—pulled himself out through the window. Apparently the front end dropped through the ice first, but the car had stayed up for a few minutes before it gradually eased itself into the lake. The last two nights had been very cold, with lows around fifteen below zero, and by now the hole the car had gone through had iced over.

Both my brother and Stephanie were quite far ahead of me, and I could see them clutching at each other, Stephanie leaning against him, and my brother trying out his military-school peacock walk. I attempted this walk for a moment, then thought better of it. The late-afternoon January light was getting very raw: the sun came out for a few seconds, lighting and coloring what there was, then disappeared again, closing up and leaving us in a kind of sour grayness. I wondered if my brother and Stephanie actually liked each other or whether they were friends because they had to be.

I ran to catch up to them. "We should have brought our skates," I said, but they weren't listening to me. Ben was pointing at some clear ice, and Stephanie was nodding.

"Quiet down," my brother said. "Quiet down and listen."

All three of us stood still. Some cloud or other was beginning to drop snow on us, and from the ice underneath our feet we heard a continual chinging and barking as the ice slowly shifted.

"This is exciting," Stephanie said.

My brother nodded, but instead of looking at her he turned slightly to glance at me. Our eyes met, and he smiled.

"It's over there," he said, after a moment. The index finger of his black leather glove pointed toward a spot in the channel between Eagle Island and Crane Island where the ice was ridged and unnaturally clear. "Come on," he said.

We walked. I was ready at any moment to throw myself flat if the ice broke beneath me. I was a good swimmer—Ben had taught me—but I wasn't sure how well I would swim wearing all my clothes. I was absorbent and would probably sink headfirst, like that car.

"Get down," my brother said.

We watched him lowering himself to his hands and knees, and we followed. This was probably something he had learned in military school, this crawling. "We're ambushing this car," Stephanie said, creeping in front of me.

"There it is," he said. He pointed down.

This new ice was so smooth that it reminded me of the thick glass in the Shedd Aquarium, in Chicago. But instead of seeing a loggerhead turtle or a barracuda I looked through the ice and saw this abandoned car, this two-door Impala. It was wonderful to see—white-painted steel filtered by ice and lake water—and I wanted to laugh out of sheer happiness at the craziness of it. Dimly lit but still visible through the murk, it sat down there, its huge trunk and the sloping fins just a bit green in the algae-colored light. This is a joke, I thought, a practical joke meant to confuse the fish. I could see the car well enough to notice its radio-antenna, and the windshield wipers halfway up the front window, and I could see the chrome of the front grille reflecting the dull light that ebbed down to it from where we were lying on our stomachs, ten feet above it.

"That is one unhappy automobile," Stephanie said. "Did anyone get caught inside?"

"No," I said, because no one had, and then my brother said, "Maybe."

I looked at him quickly. As usual, he wasn't looking back at me. "They aren't sure yet," he said. "They won't be able to tell until they bring the tow truck out here and pull it up."

Stephanie said, "Well, either they know or they don't. Someone's down there or not, right?"

Ben shook his head. "Maybe they don't know. Maybe there's a dead body in the backseat of that car. Or in the trunk."

"Oh, no," she said. She began to edge backward.

"I was just fooling you," my brother said. "There's nobody down there."

"What?" She was behind the area where the ice was smooth, and she stood up.

"I was just teasing you," Ben said. "The guy that was in the car got out. He got out through the window."

"Why did you lie to me?" Stephanie asked. Her arms were crossed in front of her chest.

"I just wanted to give you a thrill," he said. He stood up and walked over to where she was standing. He put his arm around her.

"I don't mind normal," she said. "Something could be normal and I'd like that, too." She glanced at me. Then she whispered into my brother's ear for about fifteen seconds, which is a long time if you're watching. Ben nodded and bent forward and whispered something in return, but I swiveled and looked around the bay at all the houses on the shore, and the old amusement park in the distance. Lights were beginning to go on, and, as if that weren't enough, it was snowing. As far as I was concerned, all those houses were guilty, both the houses and the people in them. The whole state of Michigan was guilty—all the adults, anyway—and I wanted to see them locked up.

"Wait here," my brother said. He turned and went quickly off toward the shore of the bay.

"Where's he going?" I asked.

"He's going to get his car," she said.

"What for?"

"He's going to bring it out on the ice. Then he's going to drive me home across the lake."

"That's really stupid!" I said. "That's really one of the dumbest things I ever heard! You'll go through the ice, just like that car down there did."

"No, we won't," she said. "I know we won't."

"How do you know?"

"Your brother understands this lake," she said. "He knows where the pressure ridges are and everything. He just *knows*, Russell. You have to trust him. And he can always get off the ice if he thinks it's not safe. He can always find a road."

"Well, I'm not going with you," I said. She nodded. I looked at her, and I wondered if she might be crazed with the bad judgment my parents had told me all teenagers had. Bad judgment of this kind was starting to interest me; it was a powerful antidote for boredom, which seemed worse.

"You don't want to come?"

"No," I said. "I'll walk home." I gazed up the hill, and in the distance I could see the lights of our house, a twenty-minute walk across the bay.

"Okay," Stephanie said. "I didn't think you'd want to come along." We waited. "Russell, do you think your brother is interested in me?"

"I guess so," I said. I wasn't sure what she meant by "interested." Anybody interested him, up to a point. "He says he likes you."

"That's funny, because I feel like something in the Lost and Found," she said, scratching her boot into the ice. "You know, one of those gloves that don't match anything." She put her hand on my shoulder. "One glove. One left-handed glove, with the thumb missing."

I could hear Ben's car starting, and then I saw it heading down Gallagher's boat landing. I was glad he was driving out toward us, because I didn't want to talk to her this way anymore.

Stephanie was now watching my brother's car. His headlights were on. It was odd to see a car with headlights on out on the ice, where there was no road. I saw my brother accelerate and fishtail the car, then slam on the brakes and do a 360-degree spin. He floored it, revving the back wheels, which made a high, whining sound on the ice, like a buzz saw working through wood. He was having a thrill and soon would give Stephanie another thrill by driving her home across ice that might break at any time. Thrills did it, whatever it was. Thrills led to other thrills.

"Would you look at that," I said.

She turned. After a moment she made a little sound in her throat. I remember that sound. When I see her now, she still makes it—a sign of impatience or worry. After all, she didn't go through the ice in my brother's car on the way home. She and my brother didn't drown, together or separately. Stephanie had two marriages and several children. Recently, she and her second husband adopted a Korean baby. She has the complex dignity of many small-town people who do not resort to alcohol until well after night has fallen. She continues to live in Five Oaks, Michigan, and she works behind the counter at the post office, where I buy stamps from her and gossip, holding up the line, trying to make her smile. She still has an overbite and she still laughs easily, despite the moody expression that comes over her when she relaxes. She has moved back to the same house she grew up in. Even now the exterior point on that house blisters in cobweb patterns. I keep track of her. She and my brother certainly didn't get married; in fact, they broke up a few weeks after seeing the Chevrolet under ice.

"What are we doing out here?" Stephanie asked. I shook my head. "In the middle of winter, out here on this stupid lake? I'll tell you, Russell, I sure don't know. But I do know that your brother doesn't notice me enough, and I can't love him unless he notices me. You know your brother. You know what he pays attention to. What do I have to do to get him to notice me?"

I was twelve years old. I said, "Take off your shoes."

She stood there, thinking about what I had said, and then, quietly, she bent down and took off her boots, and, putting her hand on my shoulder to balance herself, she took off her brown loafers and her white socks. She stood there in front of me with her bare feet on the ice. I saw in the grayish January light that her toenails were painted. Bare feet with painted toenails on the ice—this was a desperate and beautiful sight, and I shivered and felt my fingers curling inside my gloves.

"How does it feel?" I asked.

"You'll know," she said. "You'll know in a few years."

My brother drove up close to us. He rolled down his window and opened the passenger-side door. He didn't say anything. I watched Stephanie get into the car, carrying her shoes and socks and boots, and then I waved good-bye to them before turning to walk back to our house. I heard the car heading north across the ice. My brother would be looking at Stephanie's bare feet on the floor of his car. He would probably not be saying anything just now.

When I reached our front lawn, I stood out in the dark and looked in through the kitchen window. My mother and stepfather were sitting at the kitchen counter; I couldn't be sure if they were speaking to each other, but then I saw my mother raise her arm in one of her can-you-believe-this gestures. I didn't want to go inside. I wanted to feel cold, so cold that the cold itself became permanently interesting. I took off my overcoat and my gloves. Tilting my head back, I felt some snow fall onto my face. I thought of the word "exposure" and of how once or twice a year deer hunters in the Upper Peninsula died of it, and I bent down and stuck my hand into the snow and frozen grass and held it there. The cold rose from my hand to my elbow, and when I had counted to forty and couldn't stand another second of it, I picked up my coat and gloves and walked into the bright heat of the front hallway.

TRY THIS 8.9

Write a scene from the point of view of a young character in a setting that is uncomfortable, threatening, dangerous, or fearful. Create the sense of conflict with the surroundings through at least three senses. Use elements of weather, time of day, and time of year as well as place.

Lydia Davis

Story

I get home from work and there is a message from him: that he is not coming, that he is busy. He will call again. I wait to hear from him, then at nine o'clock I go to where he lives, find his car, but he's not home. I knock at his apartment door and then at all the garage doors, not knowing which garage door is his—no answer. I write a note, read it over, write a new note, and stick it in his door. At home I am restless, and all I can do, though I have a lot to do, since I'm going on a trip in the morning, is play the piano. I call again at ten-forty-five and he's home, he has been to the movies with his old girlfriend, and she's still there. He says he'll call back. I wait. Finally I sit down and write in my notebook that when he calls me either he will then come to me, or he will not and I will be angry, and so I will have either him or my own anger, and this might be all right, since anger is always a great comfort, as I found with my husband. And then I go on to write, in the third person and the past tense, that clearly she always needed to have a love even if it was a complicated love. He calls back before I have time to finish writing all this down. When he calls, it is a little after eleven-thirty. We argue until nearly twelve. Everything he says is a contradiction: for example, he says he did not want to see me because he wanted to work and even more because he wanted to be alone, but he has not worked and he has not been alone. There is no way I can get him to reconcile any of his contradictions, and when this conversation begins to sound too much like many I had with my husband I say goodbye and hang up. I finish writing down what I started to write down even though by now it no longer seems true that anger is any great comfort.

I call him back five minutes later to tell him that I am sorry about all this arguing, and that I love him, but there is no answer. I call again five minutes later, thinking he might have walked out to his garage and walked back, but again there is no answer. I think of driving to where he lives again and looking for his garage to see if he is in there working, because he keeps his desk there and his books and that is where he goes to read and write. I am in my nightgown, it is after twelve and I have to leave the next morning at five. Even so, I get dressed and drive the mile or so to his place. I am afraid that when I get there I will see other cars by his house that I did not see earlier and that one of them will belong to his old girlfriend. When I drive down the driveway I see two cars that weren't there before, and one of them is parked as close as possible to his door, and I think that she is there. I walk around the small building to the back where his apartment is, and look in the window: the light is on, but I can't see anything clearly because of the half-closed venetian blinds and the steam on the glass. But things inside the room are not the same as they were earlier in the evening, and before there was no steam. I open the outer screen door and knock. I wait. No answer. I let the screen door fall shut and I walk away to check the row of garages. Now the door opens behind me as I am walking away and he comes out. I can't see him very well because it is dark in the narrow lane beside his door and he is wearing dark clothes and whatever light there is is behind him. He comes up to me and puts his arms around me without speaking, and I think he is not speaking not because he is feeling so much but because he is preparing what he will say. He lets go of me and walks around me and ahead of me out to where the cars are parked by the garage doors.

As we walk out there he says, "Look," and my name, and I am waiting for him to say that she is here and also that it's all over between us. But he doesn't, and I have the feeling he did intend to say something like that, at least say that she was here, and that he then thought better of it for some reason. Instead, he says that everything that went wrong tonight was his fault and he's sorry. He stands with his back against a garage door and his face in the light and I stand in front of him with my back to the light. At one point he hugs me so suddenly that the fire of my cigarette crumbles against the garage door behind him. I know why we're out here and not in his room, but I don't ask him until everything is all right between us. Then he says, "She wasn't here when I called you. She came back later." He says the only reason she is there is that something is troubling her and he is the only one she can talk to about it. Then he says, "You don't understand, do you?"

I try to figure it out.

So they went to the movies and then came back to his place and then I called and then she left and he called back and we argued and then I called back twice but he had gone out to get a beer (he says) and then I drove over and in the meantime he had returned from buying beer and she had also come back and she was in his room so we talked by the garage doors. But what is the truth? Could he and she both really have come back in that short interval between my last phone call and my arrival at his place? Or is the truth really that during his call to me she waited outside or in his garage or in her car and that he then brought her in again, and that when the phone rang with my second and third calls he let it ring without answering, because he was fed up with me and with arguing? Or is the truth that she did leave and did come back later but that he remained and let the phone ring without answering? Or did he perhaps bring her in and then go out for the beer while she waited there and listened to the phone ring? The last is the least likely. I don't believe anyway that there was any trip out for beer.

The fact that he does not tell me the truth all the time makes me not sure of his truth at certain times, and then I work to figure out for myself if what he is telling me is the truth or not, and sometimes I can figure out that it's not the truth and sometimes I don't know and never know, and sometimes just because he says it to me over and over again I am convinced it is the truth because I don't believe he would repeat a lie so often. Maybe the truth does not matter, but I want to know it if only so that I can come to some conclusions about such questions as: whether he is angry at me or not; if he is, then how angry; whether he still loves her or not; if he does, then how much; whether he loves me or not; how much; how capable he is of deceiving me in the act and after the act in the telling.

TRY THIS 8.10
Choose a moment when your protagonist is feeling something intensely. Write, headlong, an "interior monologue," that is, a monologue of his or her thoughts.

Ernest Hemingway

A Clean, Well-lighted Place

It was late and every one had left the café except an old man who sat in the shadow the leaves of the tree made against the electric light. In the day time the street was dusty, but at night the dew settled the dust and the old man liked to sit late because he was deaf and now at night it was quiet and he felt the difference. The two waiters inside the café knew that the old man was a little drunk, and while he was a good client they knew that if he became too drunk he would leave without paying, so they kept watch on him.

"Last week he tried to commit suicide," one waiter said.

"Why?"

"He was in despair."

"What about?"

"Nothing."

"How do you know it was nothing?"

"He has plenty of money."

They sat together at a table that was close against the wall near the door of the café and looked at the terrace where the tables were all empty except where the old man sat in the shadow of the leaves of the tree that moved slightly in the wind. A girl and a soldier went by in the street. The street light shone on the brass number on his collar. The girl wore no head covering and hurried beside him.

"The guard will pick him up," one waiter said.

"What does it matter if he gets what he's after?"

"He had better get off the street now. The guard will get him. They went by five minutes ago."

The old man sitting in the shadow rapped on his saucer with his glass. The younger waiter went over to him.

"What do you want?"

The old man looked at him. "Another brandy," he said.

"You'll be drunk," the waiter said. The old man looked at him. The waiter went away.

"He'll stay all night," he said to his colleague. "I'm sleepy now. I never get into bed before three o'clock. He should have killed himself last week."

The waiter took the brandy bottle and another saucer from the counter inside the café and marched out to the old man's table. He put down the saucer and poured the glass full of brandy.

"You should have killed yourself last week," he said to the deaf man. The old man motioned with his finger. "A little more," he said. The waiter poured on into the glass so that the brandy slopped over and ran down the stem into the top saucer of the pile. "Thank you," the old man said. The waiter took the bottle back inside the café. He sat down at the table with his colleague again.

"He's drunk now," he said.

"He's drunk every night."

"What did he want to kill himself for?"

"How should I know."

"How did he do it?"

"He hung himself with a rope."

"Who cut him down?"

"His niece."

"Why did they do it?"

"Fear for his soul."

"How much money has he got?"

"He's got plenty."

"He must be eighty years old."

"Anyway I should say he was eighty."

"I wish he would go home. I never get to bed before three o'clock. What kind of hour is that to go to bed?"

"He stays up because he likes it."

"He's lonely. I'm not lonely. I have a wife waiting in bed for me."

"He had a wife once too."

"A wife would be no good to him now."

"You can't tell. He might be better with a wife."

"His niece looks after him. You said she cut him down."

"I know."

"I wouldn't want to be that old. An old man is a nasty thing."

"Not always. This old man is clean. He drinks without spilling. Even now, drunk. Look at him."

"I don't want to look at him. I wish he would go home. He has no regard for those who must work."

The old man looked from his glass across the square, then over at the waiters.

"Another brandy," he said, pointing to his glass. The waiter who was in a hurry came over.

"Finished," he said, speaking with that omission of syntax stupid people employ when talking to drunken people or foreigners. "No more tonight. Close now."

"Another," said the old man.

"No. Finished." The waiter wiped the edge of the table with a towel and shook his head.

The old man stood up, slowly counted the saucers, took a leather coin purse from his pocket and paid for the drinks, leaving half a peseta tip.

The waiter watched him go down the street, a very old man walking unsteadily but with dignity.

"Why didn't you let him stay and drink?" the unhurried waiter asked. They were putting up the shutters. "It is not half-past two."

"I want to go home to bed."

"What is an hour?"

"More to me than to him."

"An hour is the same."

"You talk like an old man yourself. He can buy a bottle and drink at home."

"It's not the same."

"No, it is not," agreed the waiter with a wife. He did not wish to be unjust. He was only in a hurry.

"And you? You have no fear of going home before your usual hour?"

"Are you trying to insult me?"

"No, hombre, only to make a joke."

"No," the waiter who was in a hurry said, rising from pulling down the metal shutters. "I have confidence. I am all confidence."

"You have youth, confidence, and a job," the older waiter said. "You have everything."

"And what do you lack?"

"Everything but work."

"You have everything I have."

"No. I have never had confidence and I am not young."

"Come on. Stop talking nonsense and lock up."

"I am of those who like to stay late at the café," the older waiter said. "With all those who do not want to go to bed. With all those who need a light for the night."

"I want to go home and into bed."

"We are of two different kinds," the older waiter said. He was now dressed to go home. "It is not only a question of youth and confidence although those things are very beautiful. Each night I am reluctant to close up because there may be some one who needs the café."

"Hombre, there are bodegas open all night long."

"You do not understand. This is a clean and pleasant café. It is well lighted. The light is very good and also, now, there are shadows of the leaves."

"Good night," said the younger waiter.

"Good night," the other said. Turning off the electric light he continued the conversation with himself. It is the light of course but it is necessary that the place be clean and pleasant. You do not want music. Certainly you do not want music. Nor can you stand before a bar with dignity although that is all that is provided for these hours. What did he fear? It was not fear or dread. It was a nothing that he knew too well. It was all a nothing and a man was nothing too. It was only that and light was all it needed and a certain cleanness and order. Some lived in it and never felt it but he knew it all was nada y pues nada y nada y pues nada. Our nada who art in nada, nada be thy name thy kingdom nada thy will be nada in nada as it is in nada. Give us this nada our daily nada and nada us our nada as we nada our nadas and nada us not into nada but deliver us from nada; pues nada. Hail nothing full of nothing, nothing is with thee. He smiled and stood before a bar with a shining steam pressure coffee machine.

"What's yours?" asked the barman.

"Nada."

"Otro loco mas," said the barman and turned away.

"A little cup," said the waiter.

The barman poured it for him.

"The light is very bright and pleasant but the bar is unpolished," the waiter said.

The barman looked at him but did not answer. It was too late at night for conversation.

"You want another copita?" the barman asked.

"No, thank you," said the waiter and went out. He disliked bars and bodegas. A clean, well-lighted café was a very different thing. Now, without thinking further, he would go home to his room. He would lie in the bed and finally, with daylight, he would go to sleep. After all, he said to himself, it is probably only insomnia. Many must have it.

TRY THIS 8.11

If the story you are writing is in the first person or in third person giving us the thoughts of a character, recast a few paragraphs in the objective point of view. How much is still conveyed?

Or:

If your story is already written from the objective viewpoint, write a paragraph or two of your protagonist's interior monologue.

In either case, the exercise may help you to see how successful you are in "showing" the interior reality of your character through sensory detail.

Ron Carlson
Bigfoot Stole My Wife

The problem is credibility.

The problem, as I'm finding out over the last few weeks, is basic credibility. A lot of people look at me and say, sure Rick, Bigfoot stole your wife. It makes me sad to see it, the look of disbelief in each person's eye. Trudy's disappearance makes me sad, too, and I'm sick in my heart about where she may be and how he's treating her, what they do all day, if she's getting enough to eat. I believe he's being good to her—I mean I feel it—and I'm going to keep hoping to see her again, but it is my belief that I probably won't.

In the two and a half years we were married, I often had the feeling that I would come home from the track and something would be funny. Oh, she'd say things: *One of these days I'm not going to be here when you get home*, things like that, things like everybody says. How stupid of me not to see them as omens. When I'd get out of bed in the early afternoon, I'd stand right here at this sink and I could see her working in her garden in her cut-off Levi's and bikini top, weeding, planting, watering. I mean it was obvious. I was too busy thinking about the races, weighing the odds, checking the jockey roster to see what I now know: he was watching her too. He'd probably been watching her all summer.

So, in a way it was my fault. But what could I have done? Bigfoot steals your wife. I mean: even if you're home, it's going to be a mess. He's big and not well trained.

When I came home it was about eleven-thirty. The lights were on, which really wasn't anything new, but in the ordinary mess of the place, there was a little difference, signs of a struggle. There was a spilled Dr. Pepper on the counter and the fridge was open. But there was something else, something that made me sick. The smell. The smell of Bigfoot. It was hideous. It was . . . the guy is not clean.

Half of Trudy's clothes are gone, not all of them, and there is no note. Well, I know what it is. It's just about midnight there in the kitchen which smells like some part of hell. I close the fridge door. It's the saddest thing I've ever done. There's a picture of Trudy and me leaning against her Toyota taped to the fridge door. It was taken last summer. There's Trudy in her bikini top, her belly brown as a bean. She looks like a kid. She was a kid I guess, twenty-six. The two times she went to the track with me everybody looked at me like how'd I rate her. But she didn't really care for the races. She cared about her garden and Chinese cooking and Buster, her collie, who I guess Bigfoot stole too. Or ate. Buster isn't in the picture, he was nagging my nephew Chuck who took the photo. Anyway I close the fridge door and it's like part of my life closed. Bigfoot steals your wife and you're in for some changes.

You come home from the track having missed the Daily Double by a neck, and when you enter the home you are paying for and in which you and your wife and your wife's collie live, and your wife and her collie are gone as is some of her clothing, there is nothing to believe. Bigfoot stole her. It's a fact. What should I do, ignore it? Chuck came down and said something like well if Bigfoot stole her why'd they take the Celica? Christ, what a cynic! Have you ever read anything about Bigfoot not being able to drive? He'd be cramped in there, but I'm sure he could manage.

I don't really care if people believe me or not. Would that change anything? Would that bring Trudy back here? Pull the weeds in her garden?

As I think about it, no one believes anything anymore. Give me one example of someone *believing* one thing. I dare you. After that we get into this credibility thing. No one believes me. I myself can't believe all the suspicion and cynicism there is in today's world. Even at the races, some character next to me will poke over at my tip sheet and ask me if I believe that stuff. If I believe? What is there to believe? The horse's name? What he did the last time out? And I look back at this guy, too cheap to go two bucks on the program, and I say: it's history. It is historical fact here. Believe. Huh. Here's a fact: I believe everything.

Credibility.

When I was thirteen years old, my mother's trailer was washed away in the flooding waters of the Harley River and swept thirty-one miles, ending right side up and nearly dead level just outside Mercy, in fact in the old weed-eaten parking lot for the abandoned potash plant. I know this to be true because I was inside the trailer the whole time with my pal, Nuggy Reinecker, who found the experience more life-changing than I did.

Now who's going to believe this story? I mean, besides me, because I was there. People are going to say, come on, thirty-one miles? Don't you mean thirty-one feet?

We had gone in out of the rain after school to check out a magazine that belonged to my mother's boyfriend. It was a copy of *Dude*, and there was a fold-out page I will never forget of a girl lying on the beach on her back. It was a color photograph. The girl was a little pale, I mean, this was probably her first day out in the sun, and she had no clothing on. So it was good, but what made it great was that they had made her a little bathing suit out of sand. Somebody had spilled a little sand just right, here and there, and the sand was this incredible gold color, and it made her look so absolutely naked it wanted to put your eyes out.

Nuggy and I knew there was flood danger in Griggs; we'd had a flood every year almost and it had been raining for five days on and off, but when the trailer bucked the first time, we thought it was my mother come home to catch us in the dirty book. Nuggy shoved the magazine under the bed and I ran out to check the door. It only took me a second and I hollered back *Hey no sweat, no one's here,* but by the time I returned to see what other poses they'd had this beautiful woman commit, Nuggy already had his pants to his ankles and was involved in what we knew was a sin.

If it hadn't been the timing of the first wave with this act of his, Nuggy might have gone on to live what the rest of us call a normal life. But the Harley had crested and the head wave, which they estimated to be three feet minimum, unmoored the trailer with a push that knocked me over the sofa, and threw Nuggy, already entangled in his trousers, clear across the bedroom.

I watched the village of Griggs as we sailed through. Some of the village, the Exxon Station, part of it at least, and the carwash, which folded up right away, tried to come along with us, and I saw the front of Painters' Mercantile, the old porch and signboard, on and off all day.

You can believe this: it was not a smooth ride. We'd rip along for ten seconds, dropping and growling over rocks, and rumbling over tree stumps, and then wham! the front end of the trailer would lodge against a rock or something that could stop it, and whoa! we'd wheel around sharp as a carnival ride, worse really, because the furniture would be thrown against the far side and us with it, sometimes we'd end up in a chair and sometimes the chair would sit on us. My mother had about four thousand knickknacks in five big box shelves, and they gave us trouble for the first two or three miles, flying by like artillery, left, right, some small glass snail hits you in the face, later in the back, but that stuff all finally settled in the foot and then two feet of water which we took on.

We only slowed down once and it was the worst. In the railroad flats I thought we had stopped and I let go of the door I was hugging and tried to stand up and then swish, another rush sent us right along. We rammed along all day it seemed, but when we finally washed up in Mercy and the sheriff's cousin pulled open the door and got swept back to his car by water and quite a few of those knickknacks, just over an hour had passed. We had averaged, they figured later, about thirty-two miles an hour, reaching speeds of up to fifty at Lime Falls and the Willows. I was okay and walked out bruised and well washed, but when the sheriff's cousin pulled Nuggy out, he looked genuinely hurt.

"For godsakes," I remember the sheriff's cousin saying, "The damn flood knocked this boy's pants off!" But Nuggy wasn't talking. In fact, he never hardly talked to me again in the two years he stayed at the Regional School. I heard later, and I believe it, that he joined the monastery over in Malcolm County.

My mother, because she didn't have the funds to haul our rig back to Griggs, worried for a while, but then the mayor arranged to let us stay out where we were. So after my long ride in a trailer down the flooded Harley River with my friend Nuggy Reinecker, I grew up in a parking lot outside of Mercy, and to tell you the truth, it wasn't too bad, even though our trailer never did smell straight again.

Now you can believe all that. People are always saying: don't believe everything you read, or everything you hear. And I'm here to tell you. Believe it. Everything. Everything you read. Everything you hear. Believe your eyes. Your ears. Believe the small hairs on the back of your neck. Believe all of history, and all of the versions of history, and all the predictions for the future. Believe every weather forecast. Believe in God, the afterlife, unicorns, showers on Tuesday. Everything has happened. Everything is possible.

I come home from the track to find the cupboard bare. Trudy is not home. The place smells funny: hairy. It's a fact and I know it as a fact: Bigfoot has been in my house.

Bigfoot stole *my* wife.

She's gone.

Believe it.

I gotta believe it.

TRY THIS 8.12

Take a few paragraphs of the story you are writing and substitute an animal or a monster for one of the characters. What sort of creature will it be? How will it behave? What can this teach you about your character?

ACCOMPLISHING A DRAFT

Write a quick draft of the story you are working on as a short-short. If you had to condense it into a page or two, what would you retain? This exercise may help you whenever a story seems amorphous or sprawling—when you don't, in fact, quite know what it's about.

Fiction Format

As with creative nonfiction, "clean copy" is the first and very visible sign of the professional. Your manuscript should be carefully proofread, neatly printed or copied, and stapled or paper clipped in the upper left-hand corner. Your particular teacher, group leader, or editor may have format requirements. To cut copying costs, some teachers will ask you to omit a cover page, and/or to single space. Otherwise, title and author's name and address (or class identification) should appear on a cover page, and your name need appear only there. Page numbering can be done in the upper or lower center or right corner of the page.

Manuscripts should be double-spaced, with generous (approximately one inch) margins, on one side of $8\frac{1}{2}$- × 11-inch white paper. The first page of the story should begin about one-third of the way down the page.

Copyrighting of literary manuscripts is not necessary—essays, stories, poems, and plays are, alas, rarely worth money enough to be attractive to thieves. If your work is published, the magazine or publisher will apply for copyright, and you will have a contract that specifies what rights belong to you.

Always keep a copy of your work.

THE YELLOW WALLPAPER

by Charlotte Perkins Gilman

1001 Herland Street
Pasadena, CA 91101
(626) 123-6543
cpgilman@mindspring.com
www.cpgilman.com

1

It is very seldom that mere ordinary people like John and myself secure ancestral halls for the summer. A colonial mansion, a hereditary estate, I would say a haunted house, and reach the height of romantic felicity—but that would be asking too much of fate.

Still I will proudly declare that there is something queer about it. Else why should it be let so cheaply? And why stood so long untenanted? John laughs at me, of course, but one expects that in marriage.

John is practical in the extreme. He has no patience with faith, an intense horror of superstition, and he scoffs openly at any talk of things not to be felt and seen and put down in figures. John is a physician, and perhaps (I would not say it to a living soul, of course, but this is dead paper and a great relief to my mind)—perhaps that is one reason I do not get well faster.

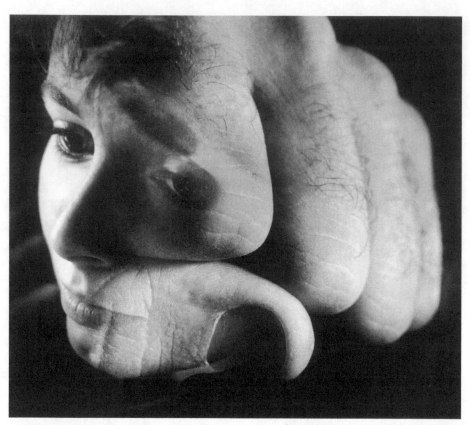

Jerry Uelsmann, "Symbolic Mutation"

WARM-UP

This photomontage is a visual metaphor—but representing what? Is the woman a victim of the fist or is she the fist? Write a poem about her. Develop the metaphor in some way.

CHAPTER NINE

POETRY

Free Verse and Formal Verse
Imagery, Connotation, and Metaphor
Density and Intensity
Prosody, Rhythm, and Rhyme
Poetry Format

Good poems are the best teachers.

Mary Oliver

There are hundreds of definitions of poetry, ranging from the religious to the flippant, from the sentimental to the psychological. Poetry is "the natural language of all worship," "devil's wine," "an imitation of an imitation," "more philosophic than history," "painting that speaks," "a criticism of life," "a way of taking life by the throat," "an escape from emotion," "the antithesis to science," "the bill and coo of sex," "a pause before death."

Unlike the essay or drama, poetry can take shapes that bear little or no resemblance to each other. Individual poems may aspire to freeze a single image like a painting or to spin off musical variations like a jazz riff. Unlike the novel or the short story, length has nothing at all to do with whether a thing may be called poetry; epics may cover many hundreds of pages or take hours to recite, while the haiku is seventeen syllables.

In *The Creative Process*, teachers Carol Burke and Molly Best Tinsley observe that poems "obey no absolute rules and serve no single purpose; rather they adapt to the distinct needs of specific times and individual poets . . . Any definition we formulate precludes others and imprisons us prematurely in a partial understanding of poetry."

Considering the difficulty, perhaps the most comprehensive and least confining definition is W. H. Auden's: *Poetry is memorable speech.*

This memorably succinct sentence contains the two essentials: Poetry is meant to be heard aloud in the human voice, and it is meant to be remembered. All of the techniques that belong to this genre aid speech or memory or both. **Rhyme,** for example, is a memory aid that pleases the ear. **Rhythm** and **meter** augment both the memory and the music of the spoken voice; so do similarities of sound such as **alliteration** (the repetition of a consonant sound) and **assonance** (the repetition of a vowel sound). Image and story are powerfully **mnemonic** (helpful to the memory), as are **figures of speech,** including simile and metaphor.

Memory is crucial because poetry predates writing. One early purpose of form—rhyme, rhythm, alliteration, and so forth—was to make it possible to remember and tell long histories of peoples, their trials, and heroic battles. Now we have print, film, tape, disk, digital recording, and other technologies for the preservation of ideas, but poetry still startles and stays in the mind through its manipulation of sound and figures of speech, which have also evolved into myriad ways of intensifying and compressing meaning.

Free Verse and Formal Verse

Learning to be a poet in the twenty-first century presents difficulties unlike any of the other genres, and the problem is this: up until the twentieth century the great bulk of poetry in English was written in **formal verse,** set patterns of rhythm and rhyme. From *Beowulf* in Old English with its lines of interlocking alliteration; through the intricate official meters of the Welsh Bards and the burgeoning verse patterns of the Renaissance; to the measured couplets of the Enlightenment, the passionate craft of the Romantics, and the sophisticated subtleties of the Victorians—all was based on formal **scansion** (the counting of stresses and syllables) and set verse pattern. But though there had been rebellions against the verse or **stanza** and experiments with looser rhythms—notably Emily Dickinson and Walt Whitman in America—it was only in the twentieth century that English poetry generally loosened its forms, set its rhymes askew, took on the rhythms of ordinary speech, and settled into **free verse.**

Poet Mary Oliver suggests that there may have been larger social forces at work, such that in an increasingly classless society, the poet's lofty traditional role was democratized. Those drawn to the looser rhythms of free verse also saw every subject, no matter how homely or mundane, as legitimate territory for their work. (Poet Caroline Kizer recounts how she once quit a workshop because she was told that pigs were not a proper subject for poetry.) A close parallel might be seen here in the way that the prescribed movements and structures of the classical ballet gave way to modern dance. In ballet, a central aspiration was to deny gravity; to extend, lift, leap, and soar beyond the limitations of the human body.

Modern dance, by contrast, accepted, celebrated, and exploited the earthbound, and gravity became a partner in the physical exploration of our condition. Just so, human limitation including the bluntness and jaggedness of ordinary speech became part of the subject matter and the mode of verse.

All the great new practitioners of free verse taught themselves the rigors of the earlier periods, but those rigors are buried deep in the speech patterns of their poetry. Although many poets in the latter part of the century returned with enthusiasm to the stricter structures of "New Formalism," you have not grown up reading formal contemporary verse. If you begin by writing in closed forms, you are likely to turn out archaic-sounding stanzas, cliché rhymes, and the singsong rhythms of greeting cards. Yet if you begin with free verse, which often disguises itself to the uninitiated ear as prose, you may develop sloppy patterns in which you fail to understand and learn the craft of sound.

Poetry is not chopped prose. The Bloomsbury poet and novelist Vita Sackville West scathingly put down people who "think they may mumble inanities which would make them blush if written in good common English, but which they think fit to print if split up into lines." Mary Oliver in *A Poetry Handbook* more gently chides that a student unschooled in verse forms "quickly, then . . . falls into a *manner* of writing, which is not a style but only a chance thing, vaguely felt and not understood . . ."

There is no easy solution to this difficulty, but since writing is learned first of all in the doing, I propose that you go about writing poems by borrowing from other genres in which you are more practiced and adept, and at the same time begin to *play* with sound and rhythm. This chapter will suggest some possibilities for such play, and the "Basic Prosody" in the Appendix will lead you to invent others of your own. Meanwhile, read widely in both formal (rhymed and metered) and **informal** (free) verse, with particular attention to metaphor and patterns of sound. Imitate what you like; imitation, which has been called the sincerest form of flattery, is also the most teaching form of play.

Begin by writing poems about the subjects that matter to you, based on patterns you have already used in your journal and other writing.

TRY THIS 9.1

Write a poem that takes advantage of your earlier exercises in one of these ways:
- That presents an image in terms of all five senses, how it looks, smells, sounds, tastes, feels
- As a dialogue between two people who see some object in very different ways
- In the form of a list
- About a memory, in the voice and from the point of view of someone other than yourself
- In the form of a letter saying good-bye

Imagery, Connotation, and Metaphor

Because poetry attempts to produce an emotional response through heightened evocation of the senses, imagery holds a central place among its techniques. John Keats famously put it, ". . . be more of an artist, and load every rift of your subject with ore," which illustrates its advice by putting it in a weighty metaphor.

But remember that not all images are metaphors. Sometimes, as Robert Hass puts it, "they do not say *this is that*, they say *this is*."

> O Western wind, when wilt thou blow,
> That the small rain down can rain?
> Christ, that my love were in my arms
> And I in my bed again!

This most famous of anonymous poems, disputedly from the thirteenth to the fifteenth centuries, contains no metaphors. Its simple images are wind, rain, lover, arms, and bed. The poem says, "I am stuck here in an ugly climate with no chance of getting out any time soon, and I'm lonely and miserable and miss my girl." But it says all that with a good deal more force partly because of the way the first line evokes the sound of the wind (all those *w*'s, the breath of *wh*, the vowel length of blow-oh-oh) and partly because it uses images rich in connotation.

Denotation and Connotation

Words have **denotation**—a literal or primary meaning (usually the first definition in the dictionary)—and also **connotation,** which refers to the layers of suggestion and implication they acquire through usage. Words can be richly encrusted with all we have heard, read, seen, felt, and experienced in their name. In the anonymous poem above, *love* implies longing, lust, romance, affection, tenderness, and, for each of us, further images of all these and more. *Bed* evokes sex, but also warmth, safety, comfort, home. *Wind* has connotations of wailing and loneliness and, in this poem, in combination with its sounds, becomes a lament, a cry of yearning. The "small rain" evokes gentleness by contrast with both the implied harshness of the climate and the force of the exclamation, "*Christ! That my love . . .*" The word *Christ* itself, its implicit gentleness and faith set against its use as a curse, offers a high tension of contradictory connotation.

Connotation is partly personal, which means that no two readers ever read exactly the same poem. Since I grew up in the desert, the first image that comes to my mind in the poet's plea for "small rain" is a parched barren landscape. Someone who grew up in New England might think of long winter and the gentler promise of spring.

Metaphor, Cliché, and Conceit

Imagery is necessary to poetry for the same picture-making reason it is necessary to all literary writing, but poetry also asks for and usually receives the special intensity of metaphor. Metaphor has a strong hold on the imagination because of its dual qualities of surprise and precision. Emily Dickinson described in a letter to a friend how she had studied the Scriptures to learn the "mode of juxtaposing elements of concrete things with equally fundamental ideas and feelings—grass, stone, heart, majesty, despair." This principle yielded Dickinson's signature style:

> "Hope" is the thing with feathers—
> That perches in the soul—
> And sings the tune without the words—
> And never stops—at all—

Metaphor (including simile) has as its central function to make concrete, so that even if one member of the comparison is an abstraction, its comparison to a thing or a sensory detail will vivify and particularize—Dickinson's "Hope" as a "thing with feathers," or "the purple terricloth robe of nobility," or "like a diver into the wretched confusion."

Most metaphors, however, compare two sensory images and let the abstraction remain unvoiced but present in the tension between them ("electric eel blink like stringlight," "a surf of blossoms," "rooms cut in half hang like flayed carcasses"). The function of comparison is not to be pretty, but to be exact, evocative, and as concrete as the sidewalk. Or as Ted Hughes's "Thistles," which:

> . . . grow grey, like men.
> Mown down, it is a feud. Their sons appear,
> Stiff with weapons, fighting back over the same ground.

Learning to recognize and flee clichés, to find metaphors that are both surprising and apt, can only be achieved through attention and a fair amount of trial and error. The ability to spot clichés, as Jerome Stern points out, is "not in the genetic code." But this is one place in your apprenticeship where the practice of brainstorming, free-associating, and freewriting can continue to help, because the attention we pay to the poetic image allows for free, extreme, even wild connection. The less you clamp down on your dreaming, the less you concede to logic, the less you allow your internal critic to shut you up, the more likely you are to produce the startling, dead-on comparison. Cut logic loose, focus on what you see, taste, touch. Freewrite, and let the strangeness in you surface.

From time to time you may even come up with a good **conceit,** which is a comparison of two things radically and startlingly unlike—in Samuel Johnson's words, "yoked by violence together." A conceit compares two things that have no evident similarity; the author must explain to us, sometimes at great length, why these things can be said to be alike. When John Donne compares a flea to marriage, the two images have no areas of reference in common, and we don't understand. He must explain to us that the flea, having bitten both the poet and his lover:

> . . . Our marriage bed, and marriage temple is;
> Though parents grudge, and you, we're met
> And cloistered in these living walls of jet.

TRY THIS 9.2

Eat a meal blindfolded. Write a poem in which you describe it literally only in terms of taste and smell. Metaphors may evoke the others senses.

Idiom and Dead Metaphor

The process of learning what's fresh and what's stale is complicated—and in no language more so than English—by the fact that not all familiar phrases are clichés. Many have settled down into the language as **idioms,** a "manner of speaking." English is so full of idioms that it is notoriously difficult for foreigners to learn. Try explaining to a non-native speaker what we mean by: *put 'em up, can you put me up? put 'er there, don't let me put you out, does she put out?, he put it off, I was put off, he put in!*

Moreover, English is full of **dead metaphors,** comparisons so familiar that they have in effect ceased to be metaphors; they have lost the force of the original comparison and acquired a new definition. Fowler's *Modern English Usage* uses the word "sift" to demonstrate the dead metaphor, one that has "been used so often that speaker and hearer have ceased to be aware that the words used are not literal."

> Thus, in *The men were sifting the meal* we have a literal use of *sift*; in *Satan hath desired to have you, that he may sift you as wheat,* sift is a live metaphor; in *the sifting of evidence,* the metaphor is so familiar that it is about equal chances whether *sifting* or *examination* will be used, and that a sieve is not present to the thought.

English abounds in dead metaphors. *Abounds* is one, where the overflowing of liquid is not present to the thought. When a person *runs* for office, legs are not present to the thought, nor is an arrow when we speak of someone's *aim*, hot stones when we go through an *ordeal*, headgear when someone *caps* a joke. Unlike clichés, dead metaphors enrich the language. There is a residual resonance from the original metaphor but no pointless effort on the part of the mind to resolve the tension of like and unlike.

Alert yourself to metaphors, idioms, and dead metaphors in your reading and in your writing; eventually the recognition will become second nature, and a powerful background awareness in your craft. Meanwhile *keep your eyes peeled* and *give it your best shot*, because *it's not whether you win or lose, it's how you play the game. Go for it; because—It's show time!*

TRY THIS 9.3
Go back to the list of clichés you made for Chapter 1. Add to it. Make a list of dead metaphors. Then choose a phrase from either list that you find particularly vivid (or detestable) and write a short poem in which you take it *literally*. Focus on, imagine, dream the images as if they were real. Some poor exhausted fellow is *running for office?* What must it feel like to have *a nose to the grindstone? Sifting the evidence? A vale of tears?*

Density and Intensity

The meaning in a poetic line is *compressed*. Whereas a journalist may treat it as a point of honor to present information objectively, and a legal writer may produce pages of jargon in an attempt to rule out any ambiguity, subjectivity and ambiguity are the literary writer's stock in trade; you are at constant pains to mean more than you say. This is why dialogue must do more than one thing at a time, why an image is better than an abstraction, and why an action needs to represent more than mere movement. Especially and to a heightened degree in poetry, this **density**, this more-than-one-thing-at-a-time, raises the **intensity** of feeling. Poet Donald Hall observes that, "In logic no two things can occupy the same point at the same time, and in poetry that happens all the time. This is almost what poetry is for, to be able to embody contrary feelings in the same motion." Notice, for example, the paradoxical effect of newspaper rhetoric in these lines from "Epithalamion":

Child-eyed among the Brooklyn cousins,
Leanne, *the bride, wore cotton lace*
Caught in a bow of peau de soie, and dozens
Of pearls of sweat adorned her face
At the upper lip. . .

Not only imagery but each of the elements discussed in this book—voice, character, setting, and story—will be relevant to achieving this compression, and each in a particular and particularly heightened way. The techniques of good prose make for good poetry—only more so. Active verbs are crucial. Nouns will do more work than adjectives. Specific details will move more than abstractions. Vocabulary, word choice, syntax, and grammar take on added importance; you will spend a good deal of time cutting vague verbiage and looking for the phrases that strike with special vividness or suggest double meaning or vibrate or *resonate* with widening significance.

The Replacement Poem

One way to demonstrate for yourself the density of poetic techniques is to write a "replacement poem." In this form of play, you take any poem you admire and replace all the nouns, verbs, adjectives, and adverbs with other words that are in each case the same part of speech. Other parts of speech—conjunctions, prepositions, articles—you may leave or change as you please. Here for an example is Gerald Stern's "Columbia The Gem":

> I know that body standing in the Low Library,
> the right shoulder lower than the left one, the lotion sea lotion—
> his hold is ended.
> Now the mouths can slash away in memory
> of his kisses and stupefying lies.
> Now the old Reds can walk with a little spring
> in and around the beloved sarcophagi.
> Now the Puerto Ricans can work up another funny America
> and the frightened Germans can open their heavy doors a little.
> Now the River can soften its huge heart
> and move, for the first time, almost like the others
> without silence

This poem is a damning portrait, made forceful by sense images and energetic verbs, compressed in its rhythm to a kind of poignant anger. If I replace all the major parts of speech (and some prepositions and conjunctions), the mood and meaning will change, but the energy will remain. Here is my replacement poem:

> They bless this mother bending in her plastic kitchen,
> the crooked knee redder than the straight one, the Clorox stink Pine Sol—
> her shine is glorious.
> Soon the peppers will leap aloft in celebration
> of her moans and hypocritical hypochondria.
> Then the fat flowers will jump to the black waters
> over and under the hysterical linoleum.
> Then the giant corporations will buy out another weeping mom-and-pop
> and the laughing Coke-folk will crank her rusted icemaker a while.
> Then the stove will burst its stinking flame
> and collapse, in its last meal, very near the drains,
> for reconciliation.

TRY THIS 9.4

Write a replacement poem. Choose any poem from anywhere in your reading, but make it one that you truly admire. You needn't worry about making sense; the poem will do it for you. You can fiddle afterward if you want to move it nearer your meaning.

Get together with three or four others and decide on a poem you will all replace. Discuss how different are your voices and your visions. What do the replacements have in common?

Poetic Voice

Voice will have a special importance in your poetry not only because of the like-lihood or inevitability that you will adopt a persona, but also because in the concentrated attention we pay to the language, diction *becomes* content, and poets reveal their way of looking at the world the moment they open their mouths. Since poetry is meant to be said and heard aloud it will have a partic-ularly close relationship to the tone of the implied speaker. Imamu Amiri Baraka says, "the first thing you look for is the stance." "Stance" is another way of saying *point of view*, in both the sense of opinion and the sense that the poem reveals who is standing where to watch the scene, which in turn reminds us of Philip Roth's statement that voice "begins around the back of the knees and reaches well above the head."

The elements of poetic voice are the same as those in prose—word choice, syntax, rhythm, pace—but because poetry is such a dense and compact form, the tone or attitude implied will be announced at once, usually in the first line. Some lines hurl themselves at the reader, some muse and meander, some put the face of calm on rage or grief. Compare the voices in these first lines from poems in this book:

> When I lay my head in my mother's lap . . .

> I drown in the drumming ploughland, I drag up . . .

> Life, friends, is boring. We must not say so . . .

> I have wanted excellence in the knife throw . . .

These are lines of roughly equal length; each has four or five accented syllables; all use language and syntax familiar to us. But in each case, we as readers have instant insight into the attitude or tone of the speaker, and could probably identify the facial expression, even the physical stance, taken by the speaker of each. Here are three further first lines all couched in the form of a command:

Remove clothes and put to one side . . .

Bulldoze the bed where we made love . . .

Don't look at his hands now . . .

Yet in this swift compass we hear the rhetoric of three very different emotions. Spoken aloud each will, literally, invite a particular tone of voice.

Poetic Action

Caroline Kizer voices the perhaps surprising requirement that "in a poem something happens." Her mentor Theodore Roethke even advised thinking of a poem "as a three-act play, where you move from one impulse to the next, and then there is a final breath, which is the summation of the whole." Kizer points out that Roethke's poem, "I Knew a Woman" (p. 117), contains the line "She taught me Turn, and Counter-turn, and Stand," which is "the essence of the dramatic structure. It's what a long poem has to do. It doesn't require physical action, but there has to be some mental or emotional movement that carries through the poem." In a poem what happens may be huge, historical, mythical, or it may be mental or microscopic. It need not involve an overt action, it may be a shift of perspective, a movement of the mind—but as in a story it will involve some discovery and also at the very least the decision to accept a new perspective. To the extent that the poem involves decision and discovery, it will also tell a story.

Doubleness

What makes for literary freshness—the combination of two things not usually combined—also makes for density. There is great poetic potential in all sorts of doubleness: not only "mixed emotions" and the larger ironies of life, but also the **pun** (a play on two meanings of the same word, as *the pun is mightier than the sword*), the **paradox** (a seeming contradiction that may nevertheless be true, as *the trap of too many options*), and the **oxymoron** (the pairing of contradictory terms, as a *deafening silence*).

Here is a poem by Sharon Olds in which image, voice, character, setting, story, and wordplay are compressed, into vivid and resonant "contrary feelings":

When I take my girl to the swimming party
I set her down among the boys. They tower and
bristle, she stands there smooth and sleek,
her math scores unfolding in the air around her.
They will strip to their suits, her body hard and
indivisible as a prime number,
they'll plunge in the deep end, she'll subtract
her height from ten feet, divide it into
hundreds of gallons of water, the numbers
bouncing in her mind like molecules of chlorine

in the bright blue pool. When they climb out,
her ponytail will hang its pencil lead
down her back, her narrow silk suit
with hamburgers and fries printed on it
will glisten in the brilliant air, and they will
see her sweet face, solemn and
sealed, a factor of one, and she will
see their eyes, two each, and the curves of their sexes,
one each, and in her head she'll be doing her
wild multiplying, as the drops
sparkle and fall to the power of a thousand from her body.

"The One Girl at the Boys Party"

This poem marries puberty and mathematics—a conceit, because we can't immediately apprehend any similarity. The strange combination begins prosaically enough, with some tension in the contrast between the boys' bristling and the girl's smoothness, and develops into an extended metaphor as the poem progresses. We are surprised by the image "her math scores unfolding in the air around her" and then the power struggle inherent in the numbers begins to unfold, the "body hard and indivisible," the "plunge in the deep end," the "pencil lead down her back," the "power of a thousand" laying out for us an absolutely generic American scene in terms that render it alive and new. As for "embodying contrary feelings in the same motion," here we have a portrait of a girl who has all the power of refusal—*smooth, sleek, indivisible, sweet, solemn, and sealed.* But what is the effect of those hamburgers and fries glistening on her suit? What of her wild multiplying?

And consider the voice. How would this poem be altered if it were in the voice of the girl herself, rather than the mother? If it were from the viewpoint of one of the boys? The poem has very much the tone of personal experience: suppose it were an essay rather than a poem. How would language have to change? What points made by the imagery would be made in explanatory or confessional prose? How *long* would it have to be?

TRY THIS 9.5
Recast "The One Girl at the Boys Party" as an essay. Untangle the syntax, supply the missing reasoning and reflection, develop the point of view of the mother.

Write the poem from the daughter's viewpoint.

Write it from a boy's viewpoint.

Write a poem, in exactly one hundred words, about a scene familiar to you, developing a metaphor or conceit.

Cut it to fifty words, leaving in all the meaning.

> Make the sound an echo to the sense.
>
> *Alexander Pope*

Prosody, Rhythm, and Rhyme

Good poets are born with innate talent, and the talent shows in the play, the rhythms, the lines, and images that "come naturally." But if a child shows talent, for example, for doodling spaceships or horses or fashion models, at some point a teacher will sit her down and say: *Draw this orange. Good. Now, this is how you make it look round; this is how you make it look rough; this is how you make it look as if the light is coming from the left; this is how you make it look as if the surface it sits on is stretching away into the distance.* The student may have no intention of painting in the style called realism; but precisely in order to master the craft that will allow successful imagination, invention, and innovation, it will be necessary to know how to produce on paper the illusion of the ordinary.

Prosody (the study of versification) is the study of drawing oranges in sound.

As a language for poetry, English has possibilities that greatly outweigh its— also considerable—disadvantages. It is a language with many thousands of different **syllables**—the unit of speech that can be uttered with a single breath. This means that it is poor in rhymes, as opposed to Italian, for example, where many words employ the same ending syllables. English poets of the Renaissance, who wanted to emulate the sonnets of Petrarch, felt a little defensive that they couldn't rhyme as densely as he could without repeating themselves. Because of the paucity of similar end-sounds, many rhymes in English have become clichés (*spoon-moon-June, why-die-I, do-blue-you,* . . .) and by the early twentieth century most poets in the language had tired of these clichés and launched into **slant rhymes,** also called **off rhymes** (*spoon-main-join, why-play-joy*), thus vastly extending the range of effects.

On the other hand, English is a language rich in **onomatopoeia.** This is true not just of words that literally imitate the sound they designate—words like *buzz, murmur, hum.* There are also a very large number in an intermediate category, which strongly echo their meaning. Try *squeal* or *crash* or *whip.* Beyond that, certain **phonemes** (the smallest unit of distinguishable sound) have an emotive or suggestive quality. *Plosives* explode, *sibilants* hiss, and *gutterals* growl. Contrast the word *stop* with the word *sprawl.* Try pretending that each word means the other. It's hard, because that plosive *p* sound *does* stop you, whereas the long lax diphthong (a double vowel with a sound separate from either of the vowels on its own) of the other really does sprawl. Beware, however: The "dingdong theory"—that individual words begin in some fundamental sensory reflex—has been thoroughly disproved. *Connotation* also determines our reaction to words and phrases. In terms of pure sound, there is nothing more inherently beautiful in *blooming goldenrod* than in *coronary thrombosis.*

Much of this you already know in a way that, if not instinctive, has come to you by a combination of imitation, context, and repetition, through nursery rhymes, songs, and jingles. But there is a sense in which things only come into existence when they are learned and can't be clearly thought without being defined. For instance, in Alexander Pope's line, "When Ajax strives some rock's vast weight to throw," you can feel the muscularity and effort. But to understand and be able to employ the effect, it helps to know that it's achieved by a combination of **spondees** and **consonant clusters.** Or again: William Butler Yeats's line, "I walk through the long schoolroom questioning." Why is this line so long? Because it uses **long vowels,** many **consonants,** and an unusual number of heavy **stresses.**

"Do you really think the poet was so deliberate as all that?" students sometimes ask. Yes. A skilled and proficient poet, if in doubt, will count the syllables. She will wait for the gift of the right words, but might purposely seek a sibilant to suggest a slithering motion, or open vowels for the emotion of awe. Poet Heather McHugh rightly says, "the poet *feels* his way toward the finishedness of the poem." On the other hand, it is reliably reported that Goethe's mistress threw him out of bed when she discovered he was tapping iambs on her bare back.

Some Prosody Terms

What follows in the next few pages is a number of prosody terms and their meanings, and some illustrations. An expanded discussion of these terms, and others related to them, will be found in the Appendix, "A Basic Prosody." As you become familiar with these concepts, set yourself short exercises in the play of prosody, but in your prosody play, *do not make sense.* Write with real words in real sentences following whatever technique you have set yourself, but *do not try to mean anything.* If you don't aim for sense, you will be free to concentrate on hearing the sound effects, and you won't write clichés or greeting card verse. If you practice long enough and playfully enough, these five-finger exercises will eventually sharpen your ear, and you will find the effects consciously and unconsciously entering your poetry.

TRY THIS 9.6
Practice in nonsense: try writing three sentences that have never been written or said before. Try writing a line that sounds like an explosion but does not describe an explosion; like a train, but does not mention a train; like a crying baby, but without the baby; like a storm, not about a storm; like tapping fingernails—but, look Ma, no hands.

> The line, when a poem is alive in its sound, measures: it is
> a proposal about listening.
>
> *Robert Hass*

The Poetic Line

The **line,** common to nearly all poetry, is a unit of verse ending in a typographical break. It visually represents a slight oral pause or hesitation, what poet Denise Levertov calls "a half-comma," so that both the word at the end of the line and the one at the beginning of the next receive a slight extra emphasis. The line operates *not as a substitute* for the sentence, but in addition to it. The line directs the breath; the rhythm of the line is played off against the rhythm of the sense, and this is one of the ways that poets alter, stress, and redirect their meaning. Here is the famous beginning of Milton's *Paradise Lost:*

> Of man's first disobedience, and the Fruit
> Of that immortal tree . . .

Notice how that fatal apple is given prominence by its position at the end of the line. In general, it may be said that the end of just about anything—line, paragraph, stanza, story—is the strongest position, and the beginning is the second strongest.

A **caesura** is a pause that occurs within the line (above, after *disobedience*), and can help manipulate the rhythm, as can **enjambment,** the running-on of the sense from one line to another (*and the Fruit / of that immortal tree . . .*). A line that is **end-stopped,** meaning that the line break coincides with a pause in the sense, ends with greater finality:

> An elegy is really about the wilting of a flower,
> the passing of the year, the falling of a stone.
>
> *"A Lecture on the Elegy," William Stafford*

Stress and Scansion

English is a **stress** language, and any sentence can be marked in a pattern of stressed and unstressed syllables, as here.

Syllabic verse employs a meter in which only the syllables are counted—for instance, in the *cinquain*, where the lines have a syllable count of 2-4-6-8-2, whatever the number of stresses:

> He yells.
> I'm going to
> Be buried in the sea
> Like a pirate and treasure
> Down deep.
>
> *"Deep," Oscar Ruiz*

But most formal English verse counts both stresses and syllables. **Scansion** is the measuring of a line into stressed (or accented) and unstressed (or unaccented) syllables and the number of repetitions of that pattern, each repetition called a **poetic foot.**

The English line is usually based on one of four poetic feet:

Iamb, unstress-stress: the ský
> They grew / their toés / and fín/gers wéll / enoúgh.
> (Note that this five-stress iambic line is the basis of, and the most common line in, English poetry.)

Trochee, stress-unstress: héaven
> Tí/ger, tí/ger, búrn/ing bríght!

Anapest, unstress-unstress-stress: in the ský
> From the dárk / to the dárk / is a slív/er of gráy

Dactyl, stress-unstress-unstress: héaven or
> Gó and ask / Sálly to / bring the bóys / óver now.

TRY THIS 9.7
Make a quick list of terms that relate to any subject you know well (you can go back and add to it at any time)—kinds of fish or shoes, baseball terms, car parts, fabrics, tools, instruments—whatever falls in your area of expertise. Try to list at least twenty or thirty words. Here, for example, is a list of some spices on my spice shelf:

ginger	turmeric	parsley
cinnamon	oregano	arrowroot
cardamom	rosemary	cayenne
pepper	cumin	fennel
peppercorns	dill weed	coriander
paprika	poppy seed	curry
cloves	sesame seed	cilantro
bay leaves	thyme	chili

Now mark the scansion of each word on your list:

> gínger   túrmeric   pársley, etc.

Can you make any general observations about the scansion of your words? I notice, for example, that a lot of spices happen to be trochees or dactyls, the stress falling on the first syllable. This might suggest that spices would be good for drumming rhythms and incantations, and if I wanted to use them in comic lyrics, I'd have to precede them with unstressed syllables: *So the gínger and sésame sáid to the sált . . .*

The **meter** of a poem is based on the number of feet in each line. A **monometer** line has only one foot, a **dimeter** line has two feet, a **trimeter** three, **tetrameter** four, **pentameter** five, and **hexameter** six.

An iambic tetrameter line, for example, would have four iambic feet:

Ă bóy / ĭs nót / ă píece / ŏf dírt.

A dactylic hexameter line would consist of six dactyls:

Whý dŏ Ĭ / wánt sŏ mŭch / pléxĭglăss / stúff ĭn mў / lúmĭnŏus / Ćadĭllăc?

TRY THIS 9.8

Add two more lines to each of the following examples. Remember not to make too much sense.

1. Iambic dimeter:
   Ĭ griéve / tŏ gó

2. Trochaic trimeter:
   Jáck bĕ / nímble, / húmblў

3. Anapestic tetrameter:
   Ĭf thĕ sún / ĭn thĕ skў / hăs ă wón/dĕr ŏf shíne

4. Iambic pentameter, the most common line in English, the meter of Shakespeare and blank verse:
   Whăt év/ĕr síl/vĕr whéel / ĭs bóund / tŏ róll

5. Dactylic hexameter:
   Béautĭfŭl / Jénnĭfĕr, / wónderfŭl / sócĭalĭte, / féll ŏn hĕr / Pókemăn

---

In addition to the **true rhymes** (*lean-green-mean*) and **slant rhymes** (*lean-mine-tone*) in English, poets manipulate sound through the use of **alliteration,** the repetition of consonants (*Peter Piper picked a peck of pickled peppers*), and **assonance,** the repetition of vowel sounds (*lady may crave a place*). Rhymes may be **internal,** rhyming within the line, or from the end of one line into the middle of another. Or they may be **end-rhymes,** the pattern that delights children for its musical quality:

Little Miss Muffet	a
Sat on a tuffet	a
Eating her curds and whey.	b
Along came a spider	c
And sat down beside her	c
And frightened Miss Muffet away.	b

The letters at right signal the traditional way of marking a rhyme pattern, each new rhyme sound assigned a succeeding letter of the alphabet.

Free verse is, of course, not free.

Mary Oliver

Free Verse

Free verse determines a pattern of sound and rhythm not at the outset but as the poem develops. The idea or meaning or pattern of imagery comes first, and the pattern of sound and rhythm comes after. It could be said that, in the case of formal verse, the meaning fills the pattern and, in the case of free verse, that the pattern fills the meaning. This would, however, seem to imply a superiority of the latter method, whereas many poets glory in the freedom that the restraints of formal verse allow. Just as the rules and equipment of a particular game, basketball or ice hockey, free an athlete to develop a particular set of excellences and stretch skills to the utmost, so the apparent arbitrariness of poetic form can free a poet to leap or flow with particular brilliance within those boundaries. Without such rules and equipment, it's harder to drive toward or develop specific strengths.

The rules of scansion briefly sketched here are reiterated and expanded on in the Appendix, "A Basic Prosody," together with some suggestions for stanza form; at the end of this chapter are some suggestions for still further study. As you become familiar and comfortable with scansion, assonance and alliteration, slant and internal rhyme, caesura, enjambment, and so forth, identify them in your poems, become aware of the possibilities they offer. When you feel skilled in using various devices, you may want to try formal verse, or you may want to employ that skill within the "free" verse that develops its rhythms and sound patterns from within.

In either case, if it is your intention, your calling, and your destiny to be a poet, then you probably drink in this technical trivia with an unslakable thirst, like a sports fan after baseball statistics or a train spotter with a schedule in hand. W. H. Auden observed that the best poets often start out with a passion, not for ideas or people, but for the possibilities of sound. It is surely true that the love of language can be practiced in the throat, the ear, the heartbeat, and the body; whatever you have or may in future have to say, the saying of it starts there.

TRY THIS 9.9

Write a dozen lines of blank verse (iambic pentameter) about the (real or imaginary) boring or marvelous things you did yesterday. When you've done that, look through your lines to find at least one example of alliteration, one example of assonance, and one internal rhyme. Find at least one end-stopped line, one run-on line, and one caesura. If you don't find any one of these things, alter the lines to put it there. Read the lines aloud and do anything you feel necessary to make them *sound* better. Don't make sense. Make music.

More to Read

Addonizio, Kim, and Dorianne Laux. *The Poet's Companion: A Guide to the Pleasures of Writing Poetry*. New York: W. W. Norton, 1997.

Bishop, Wendy. *Thirteen Ways of Looking for a Poem*. New York: Longman, 2000.

Fussell, Paul. *Poetic Meter and Poetic Form*. New York: McGraw-Hill, 1979.

Hirshfield, Jane. *Nine Gates: Entering the Mind of Poetry*. New York: Harper Perennial, 1997.

Readings

Sylvia Plath
Stillborn

These poems do not live: it's a sad diagnosis.
They grew their toes and fingers well enough,
Their little foreheads bulged with concentration.
If they missed out on walking about like people
It wasn't for any lack of mother-love.

O I cannot understand what happened to them!
They are proper in shape and number and every part.
They sit so nicely in the pickling fluid!
They smile and smile and smile and smile at me.
And still the lungs won't fill and the heart won't start.

They are not pigs, they are not even fish,
Though they have a piggy and a fishy air—
It would be better if they were alive, and that's what they were.
But they are dead, and their mother near dead with distraction,
And they stupidly stare, and do not speak of her.

Steve Kowit
The Grammar Lesson

A noun's a thing. A verb's the thing it does.
An adjective is what describes the noun.
In "The can of beets is filled with purple fuzz"

of and *with* are prepositions. *The's*
an article, a *can's* a noun,
a noun's a thing. A verb's the thing it does.

A can *can* roll—or not. What isn't was
or might be, *might* meaning not yet known.
"Our can of beets *is* filled with purple fuzz"

is present tense. While words like *our* and *us*
are pronouns—i.e., *it* is moldy, *they* are icky brown.
A noun's a thing; a verb's the thing it does.

Is is a helping verb. It helps because
filled isn't a full verb. *Can's* what *our* owns
in "*Our* can of beets is filled with purple fuzz."

See? There's almost nothing to it. Just
memorize these rules . . . or write them down!
A noun's a thing, a verb's the thing it does.
The can of beets is filled with purple fuzz.

TRY THIS 9.10

These first two poems are **self-reflexive;** they are about language and writing, one of
them in the very intricate poetic form of a **villanelle.** Write a self-reflexive poem, either
about your own poetry or about some technical point of language. If you like, try making the poem comic, choosing a formal pattern in which to do it.

Philip Larkin
Annus Mirabilis

Sexual intercourse began
In nineteen sixty-three
(Which was rather late for me)—
Between the end of the *Chatterly* ban
And the Beatles' first LP.

Up till then there'd only been
A sort of bargaining,
A wrangle for a ring,
A shame that started at sixteen
And spread to everything.

Then all at once the quarrel sank:
Everyone felt the same,
And every life became
A brilliant breaking of the bank,
A quite unlosable game.

So life was never better than
In nineteen sixty-three
(Though just too late for me)—
Between the end of the *Chatterly* ban
And the Beatles' first LP.

TRY THIS 9.11
Write four funny verses about one of these:
Sex
Religion
Birth
War

Grace Paley
Fathers

Fathers are
more fathering
these days they have
accomplished this by
being more mothering

what luck for them that
women's lib happened then
the dream of new fathering
began to shine in the eyes
for free women and was irresistible

on the New York subways
and the mass transits
of other cities one may
see fatherings of many colors

with their round babies on
their laps this may also
happen in the countryside

these scenes were brand-new
exciting for an old woman who
had watched the old fathers
gathering once again in
familiar Army camps and comfortable war rooms to consider
the necessary eradication of
the new fathering fathers
(who are their sons) as well
as the women and children who
will surely be in the way.

TRY THIS 9.12
Write four serious free-verse stanzas about one of these:
Sex
Religion
Birth
War

Dave Smith

Black Silhouettes
of Shrimpers

Grand Isle, Louisiana

Along the flat sand the cupped torsos of trash fish
arch to seek the sun, but the eyes
glaze with thick gray, death's touch
already drifting these jeweled darters.

Back and forth against the horizon slow trawlers
gulp in their bags whatever rises
here with the shrimp they come for.
Boys on deck shovel the fish off

like the clothes of their fathers out of attics.
Who knows what tides beached them,
what lives were lived to arrive just here?
I walk without stepping on any

dead, though it is hard, the sun's many blazes
spattering and blinding the way ahead
where the wildness of water coils
dark in small swamps and smells fiercely of flesh.

If a cloud shadows everything for a moment, cool,
welcome, there is still no end in sight,
body after body, stench, jewels
nothing will wear, roar and fade of engines.

TRY THIS 9.13

How many connotations do you feel or find for the word "water"? List them quickly—
a long list, as fast as you can write. Read it over *once*. Set it aside. Write a rough draft
of a poem about water.

Set it aside. Take it out in a week. What will you do with it? What will you keep? Where
is the poem in it?

Richard Wilbur
The Pardon

My dog lay dead five days without a grave
In the thick of summer, hid in a clump of pine
And a jungle of grass and honeysuckle-vine.
I who had loved him while he kept alive

Went only close enough to where he was
To sniff the heavy honeysuckle-smell
Twined with another odor heavier still
And hear the flies' intolerable buzz.

Well, I was ten and very much afraid.
In my kind world the dead were out of range
And I could not forgive the sad or strange
In beast or man. My father took the spade

And buried him. Last night I saw the grass
Slowly divide (it was the same scene
But now it glowed a fierce and mortal green)
And saw the dog emerging. I confess

I felt afraid again, but still he came
In the carnal sun, clothed in a hymn of flies,
And death was breeding in his lively eyes.
I started in to cry and call his name,

Asking forgiveness of his tongueless head.
. . . I dreamt the past was never past redeeming:
But whether this was false or honest dreaming
I beg death's pardon now. And mourn the dead.

Sharon Olds

The Language of the Brag

I have wanted excellence in the knife-throw,
I have wanted to use my exceptionally strong and accurate arms
and my straight posture and quick electric muscles
to achieve something at the center of a crowd,
the blade piercing the bark deep,
the haft slowly and heavily vibrating like the cock.

I have wanted some epic use for my excellent body,
some heroism, some American achievement
beyond the ordinary for my extraordinary self,
magnetic and tensile, I have stood by the sandlot
and watched the boys play.

I have wanted courage, I have thought about fire
and the crossing of waterfalls, I have dragged around

my belly big with cowardice and safety,
my stool black with iron pills,
my huge breasts oozing mucus,
my legs swelling, my hands swelling,
my face swelling and darkening, my hair
falling out, my inner sex
stabbed again and again with terrible pain like a knife.
I have lain down.

I have lain down and sweated and shaken
and passed blood and feces and water and
slowly alone in the center of a circle I have
passed the new person out
and they have lifted the new person free of the act
and wiped the new person free of that
language of blood like praise all over the body.

I have done what you wanted to do, Walt Whitman,
Allen Ginsberg, I have done this thing,
I and the other women this exceptional
act with the exceptional heroic body,
this giving birth, this glistening verb,
and I am putting my proud American boast
right here with the others.

> **TRY THIS 9.14**
> Write a brag. This will be a list poem. Find a refrain line (other than "I have wanted")
> to introduce each item on your list of excellences. Believe every boast.

John Berryman
Dream Song 14

Life, friends, is boring. We must not say so.
After all, the sky flashes, the great sea yearns,
we ourselves flash and yearn,
and moreover my mother told me as a boy
(repeatingly) "Ever to confess you're bored
means you have no

Inner Resources." I conclude now I have no
inner resources, because I am heavy bored.
Peoples bore me,
literature bores me, especially great literature,
Henry bores me, with his plight & gripes
as bad as achilles,

who loves people and valiant art, which bores me.
And the tranquil hills, & gin, look like a drag
and somehow a dog
has taken itself & its tail considerably away
into mountains or sea or sky, leaving
behind: me, wag.

TRY THIS 9.15

Write a poem that begins with an outrageous general pronouncement—try to make it
more outrageous than *"Life, friends, is boring."* Develop a "proof" in imagery. Try using
repetition, alliteration, assonance, and/or internal rhyme.

ACCOMPLISHING A DRAFT

Choose three rough drafts of poems that feel most promising. Spend a day with each,
reading it aloud, tinkering with the sounds and syntax. Try loosening the rhythm; try
cutting drastically. Look for internal rhymes, alliteration, puns, paradox, and doubleness of any kind. Play with the form: perhaps a prose poem? Perhaps a tighter rhythm?
Is there action or a movement of meaning within the lines?

Put each poem away for as long as you can afford; then take it out again and read as
if you had never seen it before. What will you do next?

Poetry Format

Whereas prose is always double-spaced in manuscript for ease of reading, poetry
often is not. Because the look of the poem-as-object is important to its effect, most
poets strive to produce a manuscript page that looks as much like the printed
poem as possible. Single spacing usually achieves this better.

Poems do not require a title page. Center the title above the poem and put
your name and address at the top of the page or at the end of the poem, toward
the right side of the page. If your poem spills over onto a new page and the new
page begins with a new stanza, make sure that the stanza break is clear.

Ben Johnson
123 Courtly Way
London W9 1NR
(020) 328-1563
bjohnson@cavalier.edu

Still to be Neat

Still to be neat, still to be dressed,
As you were going to a feast;
Still to be powdered, still perfumed:
Lady, it is to be presumed,
Though art's hid causes are not found,
All is not sweet, all is not sound.

Give me a look, give me a face
That makes simplicity a grace;
Robes loosely flowing, hair as free.
Such sweet neglect more taketh me
Than all the adulteries of art;
They strike my eye, but not my heart.

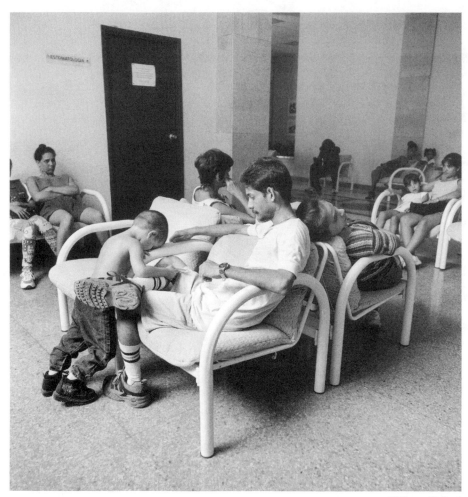

William Noland

WARM-UP
Set a scene in a hospital waiting room. Two characters talk about anything *except* illness, accident, or death.

CHAPTER TEN

DRAMA

The Difference Between Drama and Fiction
Sight: Sets, Action, Costumes, Props
Sound: Verbal and Nonverbal
Some Notes on Screenwriting
Drama Format

On the stage it is always now.

Thornton Wilder

The Difference Between Drama and Fiction

Like fiction, a play:

- tells a story of human change,
- in which a character goes on a psychic journey,
- involving a power struggle between protagonist and antagonist,
- through a process of discovery and decision,
- connection and disconnection,
- culminating in a crisis action,
- to arrive at a situation different from that in which he or she began.

As with fiction, it's important to choose the plot you will make from this story, the particular portion that will be dramatized. Why does the action begin in this place, at this particular time? In reading this chapter, then, it might be helpful to review what you have learned in Chapters 5 and 8, on Story and Fiction.

But drama is different from fiction, in fundamental ways that mean you as a writer select and arrange differently if you choose to tell your story in the form of a play. Here, for a start, is a chart detailing the differences between the two forms:

Fiction	Drama
The writer writes what the reader reads.	The script is interpreted by the stage director and cast.
Takes place in the reader's imagination.	Takes place here, now, on the stage.
Takes place in private, in solitude.	Takes place in public, communally.
All images, sensory experiences, and ideas are in words, transcribed in the brain.	Actors, props, costumes can be seen; dialogue and music can be heard.
Can go into characters' thoughts.	All thoughts must be externalized.
Author may offer direct interpretations and analysis in the course of the story.	Only characters express opinions. The author's meaning emerges indirectly.
Can go into past action.	Past must be made part of present.
Can be any length; room to digress.	Length more or less prescribed; must be focused.
Can be taken up and put down at will.	Continuous performance.
After publisher's initial cost outlay, can be reproduced indefinitely.	Theatre holds only a given number of seats; production remains expensive.

In stage drama the process of story is condensed and intensified. Usually something has happened before the curtain opens, called the **inciting incident,** which creates the situation in which the protagonist finds him/herself: *Hamlet's father has died and his mother has remarried.* The play will present this situation through **exposition:** *the watchmen reveal that the ghost of Hamlet's father has been walking near the castle at night.* Very soon, the action begins with a **point of attack:** *the ghost speaks to Hamlet, demanding revenge against Claudius.* Now the play has set up its conflict, identified the protagonist and antagonist, and it is time for the complications to begin.

All of these traditions can also be identified in a story: the inciting incident of "Cinderella" would be that her mother has died and her father has remarried; the exposition tells us that the stepmother and stepsisters mistreat her; the point of attack arrives with the invitation to the ball.

But the core fact of theater is that it takes place right now! right here! before your very eyes! Fiction is usually written in past tense, and even when it is not, there is an implied perspective of "looking back" on an action completed. The constant effort of the fiction writer must therefore be to give the imaginative past the immediacy of the present. In drama, the effort is the opposite, to present the necessary information of the past as an integral part of the present drama.

A play is *short*. It takes much longer to say words aloud than to read them silently (test it by timing yourself reading a short story, and then reading it aloud). Whereas it might take five or fifteen hours to read a novel, it's unlikely you will get an audience to sit still for more than a couple of hours (and the current tendency is toward shorter plays)—yet the substance of a short story is unlikely to be rich enough for the effort of a full evening's staging.

This means that drama is an *intense* form; the dialogue must be economical and focused. Like a short-short story, a play asks that you throw the audience immediately into the action. Like a poem, it asks for several things to be going on at once.

Whereas poetry depends for its density largely on the interplay between sound and meaning, drama depends on the interplay between sight and sound. As poetry plays the rhythm of the line in tension with the rhythm of the sentence, so drama plays the revelation of the verbal in tension with the revelation of the visual.

When you write for the stage, you lose a great deal that you may indulge as a fiction writer—the freedom not only to leap from place to place and from past to future, but also to go inside your characters' minds to tell us directly what they are thinking; to interpret for us, telling us what to believe about them or the situation; and to digress on themes or topics that may be of interest but do not add to the action.

Moreover, the trade-off between fiction and drama requires an act of faith. The audience does not receive what you wrote in the form in which you wrote it, but in an interpretation of it filtered through director, actors, and designers who may know less about it than you do. You are in effect handing them your baby to do with as they please. The theater is unforgiving, too, in terms of cost, so that practical constraints are always in the way of the imagination, demanding that you pare down the cast, presenting you with a meager version of your vision.

What you get in return is the live presence of sight and sound—movement, music, props, costumes, sound effects—to be used as inventively as you and your director can devise. You gain the immediacy and expressiveness of live actors.

You gain the thrill of an organic collaboration in which a dozen or a few dozen people are bent on a single venture, their interest vested in the success of your script, their talents laid down in tracks along your own. Because all of these tracks must work together if the project is to succeed, theater succeeds less often than prose and poetry. You need stamina for such a strong chance of failure. But because the show is alive and has the depth of all that collaboration, when it does work, it works with exhilarating immediacy. As actor Kevin Spacey puts it, "Nothing comes close to it—this living experience between the actor and the audience, sharing the same space at the same time." And nothing in a fiction author's experience matches the thrill of sitting in an audience watching the live embodiment of your words, *feeling* the emotions of the audience around you as they laugh or cry with the work of your imagination.

TRY THIS 10.1

Take any passage of fiction or memoir in your journal and play with the idea of putting it onstage. Where would it take place; what would the characters say; how would they be dressed, how would they behave?

> I take it as my principle that words do not mean everything.
>
> *Antonin Artaud*

Sight: Sets, Action, Costumes, Props

The drama begins the moment the audience sees the stage, and this first sight sets the tone for everything that follows. The set may represent the extreme of **fourth-wall realism,** the convention that we are spying on what happens through the space where the fourth wall of the room has been removed; or the opposite extreme of **theatricalism,** the convention that acknowledges the stage is a stage, the actors are actors, and the audience is an audience. It may be anywhere between or a combination of the two. In Arthur Miller's "Death of a Salesman," for example, two floors of a house are realistically represented, but when the characters move into memory or fantasy, they ignore the doors and walk through the walls.

The scenery will set the tone even if you decide on a bare stage, or "no set at all," because the less there is on the stage, the more the audience will read into what is there. Human beings are meaning-making creatures; we love to interpret and conclude. So when scenery, clothing, and objects appear onstage we will read significance at once. If the curtain opens on a maypole or a tribal mask or a backdrop of a bonfire, it's no use telling us that these are mere decoration. We will take them for clues.

This fact is full of rich possibilities for the playwright, and also for the actor. Choose clothes that characterize, objects that reveal. Remember that everything we wear and own bespeaks our desires, choices, background, gender, politics—and make your stage visually vivid with such hints.

If there are elements of familiar exterior or interior space on the stage, give them a distinct meaning. If the play takes place in a college dorm room (and you can probably make a more imaginative choice), then how do the wall hangings, clothes, objects, plants characterize the person who lives here? The playwright has no less an obligation than the poet or story writer to choose revealing specific details. How do you communicate with the readers of your play—and especially with the designer—in order to help them translate your vision either mentally or onto the stage? *"A typical college dorm room"* will *not* do it (in fact, avoid the words *normal, typical,* and *ordinary*—they are all cop-outs). A writer of stage directions is a writer and must paint the picture in the words.

It is even possible to introduce conflict before the actors enter, as in this opening stage direction from Simon Gray's *Butley:*

> An office in a College of London University. About 10 in the morning. The office is badly decorated (white walls, graying, plaster boards) with strip lighting. There are two desks opposite each other, each with a swivel chair. BEN's desk, left, is a chaos of papers, books, detritus. JOEY's desk, right, is almost bare. Behind each desk is a bookcase. Again, BEN's is chaotic with old essays and mimeographed sheets scattered among the books, while JOEY's is neat, not many books on the shelves.

Here, before a single character enters, we know a good deal about the characters of Ben and Joey, and that there will be conflict between them. When Ben enters, other props, his costume, and his way of relating to them further reveal his character, his current state of mind, the tone of the play we are going to see, and again the potential conflict:

> As the curtain rises, BEN enters, in a plastic raincoat, which he takes off and throws into the chair. He has a lump of cotton wool on his chin, from a particularly nasty shaving cut. He goes to his chair, sits down, looks around as if searching for something, shifts uncomfortably, pulls the plastic mac out from under him, searches through its pockets, takes out half a banana, a bit squashed, then throws the raincoat over to JOEY's desk. He takes a bite from the banana . . .

One important thing to notice about stage directions is that they tell us *what we see* but do not give us any information that we must learn through dialogue.

The stage direction above goes far enough to tell us that the cotton is on a bad shaving cut—which is a visual directive to the props and makeup department— but it does not say, "Ben has been quarreling with his wife." This is informa- tion that we would have to learn through dialogue, and it must wait for dia- logue to be revealed. In general, the script reveals information in the order in which it is revealed onstage. What the audience learns through sight or non- verbal sound will appear in the stage directions. What it learns through dia- logue will be revealed only when the characters say it.

Frequently, however, what the characters say is at odds with what they wear, handle, or, especially, do. They speak a text but reveal the subtext through these other means. The **stage lie** can be revealed by action, or by slips of the tongue, stumbling, exaggeration—all those verbal clues by which we learn in life that people are not telling the absolute truth. We never trust the frankness of any- one who begins, "To be frank with you . . ."

The sort of information that comes through a stage lie is a major source of understanding to the audience. The actor wears satin flounces and says, "I've always preferred the simple life." He clutches the wallet to his chest and says, "The money doesn't mean a thing to me, it's the principle." She says, "Oh, good, I was just coming to see you," and quickly slips the folder into the drawer. In all these instances, sight is at odds with sound, and we are likely to believe the evidence of our eyes. Here is Ben's first line of dialogue:

The telephone rings.

BEN: Butley, English. Hello, James, have a nice break? (*A pause—he mouths a curse.*) Sorry, James, I can't talk now—I'm right in the middle of a tutorial—'bye.

Because the truth is often revealed in the discrepancies between sight and sound, text and subtext, stage directions are important. But not *all* stage move- ment is worthy of a stage direction. Most movement is "blocking," that is, a decision on the director's part about where the actors should move and what they should do during a given passage. As playwright, you can make your stage directions count by specifying only the sights and movements that help tell a story—as "*he mouths a curse*" does above. It's fine if you see the play taking place in your mind, but "*She moves left from the chair to the couch and sits again*" is usually not going to help tell the story, and should be left up to the director.

In Chapter 4 on setting, I said that relationship to place is revealing of char- acter, and that when there is discomfort or conflict in that relationship, a story has already begun. Playwrights productively exploit this phenomenon. The cur- tain opens on a huge room dominated by a mahogany desk and leather chair. One door opens. A young woman enters clutching her handbag in front of her.

She cranes her head forward, peering at the ceiling, the walls. She reaches out gingerly and touches the desk with two fingers. She steps sideways, stops, then perches on the edge of a straight back chair. Another door opens. Another woman enters, shrugging off her coat and hooking it with one motion on the coat rack behind her. She juggles a clipboard through this process, crosses without looking at the first woman, slings herself into the leather chair, and swivels it around. How much do you know about the situation already? More important, how much do you know about the relationship between these people by their relationship to the room? Who belongs here? Who has the power? Who, so far, has your sympathy? (And remember that in literature the sympathy of the reader or the audience is very great power!)

TRY THIS 10.2

Choose a setting that seems to you both familiar and slightly dull: that dorm room, a kitchen, a restaurant, or something similar. Then write an opening stage direction of no more than a hundred words that makes it both interesting to look at and revealing of its owner.

Introduce into this setting one character who is familiar with it and comfortable with it, and one who is unfamiliar and uncomfortable. What does each want? Write a page or so of their dialogue (with stage directions as appropriate).

Sound: Verbal and Nonverbal

Dialogue is the most important element of most stage plays, but there are hundreds of nonverbal sounds that are ripe with emotional content. Make yourself aware of them and be alert to ways you can take advantage of them. A baby's cry, a scream, whistling, sobbing, laughing, a howl of pain, a sneeze, a cluck of irritation, fingers drumming, feet tapping—all of these are human sounds that are often clearer indications of mood than speech. But nonhuman sounds also often produce in us immediate reaction: a crash, splintering glass, a ringing telephone, squealing tires, a siren, a gun shot, horse's hooves . . .

TRY THIS 10.3

Make two lists, one of human nonverbal sounds, one of nonhuman sounds with emotional potential in our reaction to them. Make the lists long. Keep adding to the lists. Think about ways to use them.

Music, too, though its choice is often the province of the director, can be incorporated into the written text, as an indicator of mood, period, or character, or can even be made a part of the action by representing a conflict between two characters: the Daughter wants to practice her tryout cover for *American Idol* while Dad wants to listen to his Schubert CD. **Diegetic** sound and music, like this example, occurs realistically within the action: someone practices the violin, or the sounds of traffic come through the open window. **Nondiegetic** sound is stylized, not arising from the action but as an accompaniment or background to it: the hero bursts into song at the office water cooler, or a jazz riff covers the blackout between scenes.

In this short excerpt from "Death of a Salesman," dialogue, action, and diegetic sound come together to create a composition of meanings that is almost like the texture of music itself. The aging salesman and his wife are in the bedroom while their son Biff wanders through the house:

> **LINDA** (*timidly*):   Willy, dear, what has he got against you?
> **WILLY:**   I'm so tired. Don't talk any more.
>
> *Biff slowly returns to the kitchen. He stops, stares toward the heater.*
>
> **LINDA:**   Will you ask Howard to let you work in New York?
> **WILLY:**   First thing in the morning. Everything'll be all right.
>
> *Biff reaches behind the heater and draws out a length of rubber tubing. He is horrified and turns his head toward Willy's room, still dimly lit, from which the strains of Linda's desperate but monotonous humming rise.*

Here we have the husband and wife in "no dialogue" (*what has he got against you/Don't talk any more*); their son, in contrasting action, confirms his father's suicide attempt, while the mother hums (nonverbal) and, against Willy's reassurance—*Everything'll be all right*—the lighting symbolically fades. This very small scene, with its interlocking elements, represents **dramatic irony,** which occurs whenever the audience knows more than the characters know. In this instance, we have known for most of the act about the suicide attempt Biff has just learned about, and unlike Linda we already guess what Biff "has against" his father. We know with grim certainty that "everything" won't be all right.

TRY THIS 10.4
Rewrite the scene you did for Try This 10.2 on page 343, this time for radio. "Translate" your stage direction into sound alone, verbal, nonverbal, and musical, trying to reveal everything through the one sense.

Theatrical Dialogue

Unlike the other genres, all the dialogue in drama is direct. There is no place for indirect or summary dialogue. With the single exception of "ad lib"—which means that the actors fill in at their discretion with, for instance, greetings to each other or background mumble—you write the words any character speaks. You may not, for example, say in a stage direction, *"Joe calls in from the bathroom, still complaining."* It's the playwright's obligation to produce the words.

The most difficult dialogue to write is often the exposition, in which you must give the audience the necessary information about what has gone on before curtain rise, and what the situation is now. A useful tradition, and probably the most frequently used device, is to have a character who knows explain to a character who doesn't know. But if you don't have a character who is handily ignorant, you can have two characters talk about the situation and make it sound natural as long as they concentrate on how they feel about it, or disagree about it, so that the information comes out incidentally, sideways. If a character says, "My sister's train is due at four o'clock into Union Station," we get the facts, but if he says, "I can't talk now! I've got to make it to Union Station by four—my sister goes bananas if I'm not there to meet her train," we know something about his attitude and the relationship as well as the situation—and it sounds like talk.

A third expository device, if your play is stylized, is to have a character come forward and speak directly to the audience. Ever since film began to prove itself the best medium for realism, this **theatricalist** technique (acknowledging that the play is a play and the audience an audience) has become more and more popular in the theater.

Good dialogue will carry most of its tone as an integral part of the lines, and when this is the case, there is no need to announce the tone of voice in a stage direction—and it can in fact be insulting to the actors. An example:

> **SHE** (*slyly*):   By the way, did you get the rent money from the Smiths?
> **HE** (*suspiciously*):   What makes you ask that?
> **SHE** (*casually*):   Oh, nothing, I just wondered.
> **HE** (*angrily*):   You've had all the money you're going to get this week!

Not a single one of these tonal directions is necessary; the tone is inherent in the lines. Contrast with this version:

> **SHE:**   By the way, did you get the rent money from the Smiths?
> **HE:**   What makes you ask that?

SHE (*slipping the catalogue behind the cushion*):   Oh, nothing, I just
     wondered.

HE (*laughing*):   You've had all the money you're going to get this week!
     (*He begins to tickle her.*)

Here, actions and tone reveal a contradiction or qualification of what the
words suggest, so the stage directions are appropriate.

Here are a few further things to remember about play dialogue, to make it
natural and intense:

- The sooner you introduce the conflict, the better. A certain amount of exposition will be necessary, but if you can reveal *at the same time* the point of
  attack, it's all to the good. *Hamlet* begins with two guards discussing the fact
  that the ghost has walked (the inciting incident). But they immediately anticipate the conflict: *Will it walk again?*

- Dialogue is action when it contains both conflict and the possibility of change.
  Keep alert to the possibility that characters discover and decide through the
  medium of talk. Debate between two firmly decided people is not dramatic,
  no matter how mad they are. Disagreement between people who must stay
  in proximity to each other, especially if they care about each other, is inherently more dramatic than if they can walk away.

- Use "no" dialogue, in which people deny, contradict, refuse, qualify, or otherwise
  say no to each other.

- Dialogue has to be said, so say it aloud and make sure it flows easily, allows
  for breath, sounds like talk.

- Remember that people are not always able or willing to say just what they
  mean, and that this breaks the flow of the talk. This is especially true when
  emotions are heating up. People break off, interrupt themselves and each
  other. Use sentence fragments. Don't always finish their . . .

- Silence can be white hot. The most intense emotions are the ones you can't
  express in words. When a character spews out an eloquent paragraph of anger,
  he is probably not as angry as if he stands, breathes hard, and turns away.

- Vary short exchanges with longer ones. A change of pace, from a sharp series
  of short lines to a longer speech and back again, keeps the rhythm interesting.

- Nearly everybody tries to be funny now and again. You can often reveal character, and also what a character may be hiding, by having her try to make
  light of it. A joke that falls flat with other characters is a great tension-raiser.
  Conversely, beware of having the characters too amused by each other's wit;
  the funnier they find the jokes, the less likely the audience is to be amused.

- Similarly, avoid having the characters comment on each other's dialogue; it's self-conscious. If He says, "That's a clever way to put it!" we'll hear the author in the praise.

TRY THIS 10.5

Choose one of the characters you have written about in your journal. Write a monologue in that character's voice beginning with one of the following trigger lines:

I knew right away I'd said the wrong thing.
What is it this time?
I didn't hear the doorbell.
What took you so long?
You think you know me.
It started out fine.

Now introduce stage directions into the monologue, describing anything we can see—what the character is wearing, doing, and so forth—so as to change, contradict, or qualify the meaning of the speech.

Revealing Thought

There are also several deliberate theatrical traditions for revealing thought. In the **soliloquy** the character simply talks to himself (*To be or not to be . . .*), and the audience accepts that these words take place in the mind. In an **aside,** the character says one line to another character and another to the audience or to thin air. Traditionally, the aside is always the truth of that character's feeling. In a **voiceover,** the thoughts are recorded and play over the live scene. All of these techniques are stylized and can tend to be self-conscious. Use *very sparingly*—especially if your basic mode is realistic.

Crucial events of the past can be difficult to introduce naturally. One useful technique for doing this is the **emotional recall,** in which one character tells another about an incident from the past. But a narrated event is no more inherently dramatic than a debate, and you must not rely on the narration to hold the audience's interest. In order to keep the drama in the here! and now! the narration must hold the potential for change. The important emotion in an emotional recall is not the emotion of the teller but of the listener. Typically, a charged situation exists between one character and one or more others (it can be her mother or a mob). The first character tells a story. The listener(s) change attitude entirely. The dramatic situation is not the one in the story; it is the one on stage, where we see the change.

TRY THIS 10.6
Write a ten-minute play in which two characters must somehow divide up a quantity of goods. Is it an inheritance? A divorce? A charity sale? Leftovers? What's the conflict? What particular thing or things represent the conflict? Who wins?

Or:

Write a ten-minute play in which two characters are unfailingly polite to each other. On the last page, one of the characters turns viciously on the other, and the audience is not surprised.

Some Notes on Screenwriting

Like theater, film is a visual and audible medium in which human drama is presented directly to the senses, and in which sight can be played off against sound to heighten, reveal, and intensify.

The great difference is in the capacity of the camera to direct our attention and so create meaning. By changing angle or focus, by cutting from one sight to another, by exploiting the flexibility of technology, film can enhance both the range and the possible subtlety of the drama. Sound too can be manipulated to separate background noise from crucial dialogue, to effect a transition or signal a crisis. And of course the possibilities for special effect are now limitless.

The stage being a more or less constant area, our attention must be *taken*, by dialogue, gesture, color, or sound, so the theater tends toward simplification and exaggeration. By contrast, film actors may mumble, barely glance, merely raise a finger, and the camera will make the meaning large and clear. It is a lucky historical accident that the "Stanislavski Method" of acting, which emphasizes emotional realism rather than stylized gesture, developed and spread from its origins in the Moscow Art Theatre to Europe and America at the same time as film was developing. The combination of internalized acting and technological advance has led to a film vocabulary that is ever more visual and less verbal—and, not incidentally, to the rise of the "auteur," the director as the real creator of the film. Curiously, the three-act structure, with its pattern of conflict, crisis, and resolution, has remained the standard for the Hollywood film.

In the early days of cinema, most directors and writers naturally considered film the sister-art of the stage, since it involved actors, sets, and so forth. (A great exception was D. W. Griffith, who declared that he had learned everything about film technique from Charles Dickens.) As the cinema developed, it became ever clearer that the camera uses many of the techniques of fiction—the ability to move instantly in space and time, the advantage of point of view, close-ups and slow motion for intensity, quick cuts and juxtaposition for revealing metaphor.

At the same time, it became evident that film is a far better medium for realism than the stage, since the camera can go "on location" to depict actual city streets, aerial views, interiors, crowds, and so forth. Stage "realism," with painted flats for rooms and plywood cutouts for trees, was no match for film's ability to explore real homes and real forests. As a result, although realistic plays still abound, the general direction of the theater in the second half of the twentieth century was toward still greater stylization—theatricalism, the use of minimal stage elements and symbolic exaggeration, the incorporation of costume and set changes into the action. Since one thing the theater has over the movies is the living relationship of actor with audience, playwrights began to exploit this strength. Characters directly address or interact with the audience; the script is self-reflexive, calling attention to the fact that it's a play.

This movement toward stylization, which would appear severely limiting, has in fact been strangely freeing for the theater. Playwrights have been more inclined to borrow elements from other disciplines—dance, mime, puppetry, technology— to break the mold of "the well-made play" and display their psychological or social insights in the context of spectacle.

My advice to those who want to write for film is that, for the same reason a painter should begin with a still life, a screenwriter should begin with a stage play. It isn't easier, but it does reveal the necessary craft more clearly. Film does offer many of the freedoms of the novelist. But filmmakers who rely on these freedoms do not learn storytelling in images as well as those who grapple with the stricter discipline of the stage.

It may seem paradoxical to say that playwriting is the best first discipline toward film. But just as formal verse can teach you the possibilities of verbal music, so the limitations of this confined space can focus your efforts on the telling of a dramatic story. Many young screenwriters become so seduced by the marvels of what the camera can do, that they fail to learn what the writer must do. The delicious vocabulary—*cameo, rack focus, wipe, dolly shot, dissolve*— can mask the simple need that a film, like a story, like a memoir, like a play, must be about these people in this place with this problem. If you can put a man, a woman, a box, and a bottle, say, in a rectangular frame on a bare floor, and make us *care*—then you can *write*, and you can write a film. The imagination must come first. The machine will follow.

More to Read: On Playwriting

Spencer, Stuart. *The Playwright's Guidebook: An Insightful Primer on the Art of Dramatic Writing*. New York: Faber and Faber, 2002.

Castagno, Paul C. *New Playwriting Strategies: A Language-Based Approach to Playwriting*. New York: Taylor and Francis, 2001.

More to Read: On Screenwriting

Field, Syd. *Screenplay: The Foundations of Screenwriting, Third Edition*. New York: Dell, 1984.

Johnson, Claudia. *Crafting Short Screen Plays that Connect*. Boston: Focal Press, 2000.

READINGS

Sybil Rosen

Duet For Bear and Dog

For David

CHARACTERS

Woman
Man
Bear
Dog
She

Empty stage. A stepladder can serve as a tree. WOMAN and MAN enter.

WOMAN: (*Two-way radio noises.*) 203, this is 364. What's your 20?
MAN: 209 north above Kerhonkson. What you got?
WOMAN: Bear up a tree on Main Street in Woodstock.
MAN: I'm on my way. How'd it get there?
WOMAN: Would you believe, a little rat dog?

(*They exit. DOG chases BEAR onstage. She goes up a ladder.*)

BEAR: Oh, shit.
DOG: (*Triumphant.*) Aha! I'm a dog! I'm a dog! (*Pisses on tree.*) Take that, you rottweilers, you shepherds, you labradors! Up yours, you pachyderms and raptors and primates! You can cut off my balls, but I'm still a man! I'm a dog!
BEAR: Ah, the call of the wild. Are you finished?
DOG: (*Over.*) Cousin to the wolf, brother to the jackal, helpmate of the homo sapien—!
BEAR: Oh my God.
DOG: I'm a dog. And you—are mine!

BEAR: You're nuts! (*She growls, takes bluff swipe at him.*) I never ate a dog before, but there's always a first time. I had a pig once. It was a bad year. I'm not scared of you.

DOG: Then what are you doing up a tree?

BEAR: It's called instinct. You wouldn't know about that.

DOG: Very funny. What I lack in instinct, I make up for in finesse. They're coming for you.

BEAR: (*Panicked.*) Who? Who's they?

DOG: I don't know. Some guys got called.

BEAR: Who called them?

DOG: The one I belong to. Who belongs to me. (*Sings.*) "Fish gotta swim, birds gotta fly, I gotta love one man till I die—" She does nails. And facials.

BEAR: That explains the ribbon. (*Laughs as DOG rips ribbon from head.*) You guys have a curious thing with these humans. I bet you have a name.

DOG: (*A sore point.*) What's it to you?

BEAR: I knew it. Look, I got lost. I took a wrong turn. Just let me get down. Who knows what they'll do to me?

DOG: I don't know. Put you in a zoo maybe. (*Finds this hilarious.*)

BEAR: Don't laugh! I have a cousin that was captured by these circus people. Last thing I heard he's walking a tightrope and wearing a tutu.

DOG: You got what you deserve—plundering those garbage cans, sucking up to Dumpsters.

BEAR: Oh? I've seen your handiwork. You and your kind. You're not above delving into garbage.

DOG: I don't do garbage. I'm a lapdog. I get cashews by hand.

BEAR: (*Hungry.*) Cashews?

DOG: Yeah. And chocolates. Potato chips. Raspberries even.

BEAR: Raspberries?

DOG: I'm highly evolved.

BEAR: The little red ones? The nubbly kind you roll around on your tongue?

DOG: Whatever.

BEAR: (*Swoons.*) I love those. It was a dry year for raspberries. Blueberries too. That's why I had to go to Dumpsters. Did you ever eat a diaper?

DOG: What do I look like?

BEAR: Oh, spare me. You guys are notorious shiteaters. Me, I'm basically a herbivore.

DOG: What about the pig?

BEAR: Like I said, it was a bad year. Okay, I admit I'm not above a fish or two. When they're running. How about you? You like fish?

DOG: (*Shrugs.*) Only to roll on. (*Looks around, sees something, growls at BEAR.*)

BEAR: Hey! Quit that! What's the big idea?

DOG: (*Growling.*) She's coming, I gotta make it look good. Could be some cashews in it. (*Growls more.*)

(*SHE speaks with a thick Russian accent.*)

SHE: Good boy, Boris.

BEAR: Boris?

DOG: Shit!

SHE: Keep up there. They come soon. Good boy, Boris.

BEAR: (*Mocking.*) Good boy, Boris!

DOG: (*To BEAR.*) Shut up!

SHE: My God, that is a big bear! Look at that behind. Is big as Kremlin.

BEAR: I take that as a compliment. And this is just August. I have to put on fifty more pounds before I den and birth my babies.

SHE: Would look good, lying on floor in den, yes?

BEAR: No.

DOG: There's a thought.

BEAR: Shut up, Boris!

SHE: In Russia, we have bears. Brown bears. They drink vodka and come down chimney at Christmas time.

(*MAN and WOMAN enter.*)

BEAR: Oh God, they're here.

WOMAN: There it is.

MAN: Jesus. Nice bear.

WOMAN: What do you think? One hundred fifty pounds?

MAN: Easy.

SHE: You come for bear?

MAN: Yes ma'am. Garth McGowan. Department of Environmental Conservation. You the woman that called?

(*WOMAN walks around ladder, checking out BEAR.*)

SHE: Yes.

MAN: That the dog?

SHE: That is Boris.

BEAR: (*To WOMAN.*) What are you looking at?

MAN: What happened?

SHE: I am in shop, making motion circles on face of customer. With cucum ber facial. I make myself. And I am telling how I leave in Russia bad husband and mother of rotten heart—

MAN: Ma'am? Excuse me, we—

SHE: Wait! I tell you. So Boris is barking. Yip, yip, yip, yip, yip.

DOG: That's not how I sound.

MAN: (*Appreciatively.*) Damn dog.

WOMAN: I'll get the equipment. (*Exits.*)

SHE: I look. Oh my God. Staring in window—is bear. Standing on legs, with paws on window. Like this. (*Demonstrates.*) First I think is bad hus band from Russia, come to finish me. I am shaking in booty—

MAN: These are brown bears, ma'am. They're very docile.

SHE: What means docile?

MAN: Gentle, timid, shy.

(*WOMAN returns.*)

SHE: I should marry one. You are married?

MAN: Yes ma'am.

SHE: Why do I know that?

WOMAN: (*To MAN.*) Let's go, let's go—

MAN: Ma'am—

SHE: Let me finish story. Please. I jump. (*Demonstrates.*) Bear jumps. (*Demonstrates.*) I go to close door. Out goes Boris. Yip, yip, yip, yip, yip. Bear goes up tree. I make phone call. Customer gives big tip. End of story.

MAN: Got it.

SHE: What you do now?

MAN: First we'll dart the bear. Tranquilize it. Then when it's on the ground, we'll take some data, pull a tooth—

SHE and BEAR: A tooth?

MAN: Yes ma'am. That's how we age them.

BEAR: Ouch.

MAN: Then we'll give it some ear tags, put it in the trap we brought, take it to the mountains, and let it go.

SHE and BEAR and DOG: (*Surprised.*) Oh. That sounds nice.

MAN: Yes ma'am. It'll be a lot happier up there. So if you'll just stand back—You can call your dog off now.

DOG: (*To MAN.*) Wait a second. You don't get it.

SHE: Here, Boris.

DOG: Jeez. I treed that bear.

SHE: Boris. Come, Boris. Come to Momma.

DOG: (*Moping over.*) Times like this I wish I was a dingo.

SHE: *Sit.*

DOG: Shit. (*Sits.*)

BEAR: It's your own fault. You gave in. For the easy bone and winter hearth. For the soft bed and the cashews.

DOG: We didn't give in! It wasn't like that at all. Hell, it was our idea, we thought of it. They had scraps, for God's sake. These human beings. Just laying around. They couldn't eat everything. You know how big a mastodon is? It seemed like a good idea. It *was* a good idea. It still is. I could do without the ribbon.

BEAR: You call that evolutionary? I call it quits. Adaptation? Please. Let's not mince words. You capitulated. You should have been out there with us. In the Pleistocene. Working out the kinks of hibernation. Fine tuning the fecal plug. Learning how to give birth in our sleep.

DOG: So sue me.

(*Bam! WOMAN fires the dartgun. MAN sets a stopwatch. BEAR starts. DOG barks.*)

WOMAN: Bulls-eye.

MAN: Good shot.

WOMAN: Are you timing?

MAN: (*Nods.*) I give it sixty seconds max.

SHE: Boris. Stop. What is wrong?

BEAR: (*Beginning to slow down.*) What do you know? I have a dart in my ass.

SHE: What happen now?

MAN: It'll come down. Watch.

(*BEAR begins to get very loose and woozy. Her tongue goes in and out.*)

BEAR: I hear bees. Back and forth between nectar and hive. Follow the buzz to the succulent grubs, socked away in the waxy comb, swimming in sweet honey. Rip the hive, the paper breaks like an egg. Bees zing around my head. Sting my nose. I don't feel them. I don't feel anything. Roll the grubs on my tongue. Stinging berries dipped in sugar—

(*She falls slowly down ladder to the ground.*)

WOMAN: Bingo.

MAN: (*Stopping watch.*) Fifty-two seconds.

(*They go to BEAR. SHE and DOG go too. DOG sniffs at BEAR.*)

SHE: Is hurt?

WOMAN: No. It makes a big boom, but they're very limber. They have a lot of fat to cushion them.

SHE: It and me both. Is sleeping?

WOMAN: Not exactly. More like immobilized. Now if you could just step back, ma'am, until we're finished—

SHE: It will wake?

WOMAN: No. We just want to move as quietly as we can around the bear. If you could back up ten feet. When we're done, you'll have a chance to touch it. If you want. And the dog too, ma'am, please.

SHE: Boris. Come.

DOG: Smells like a dream I had once. One of those where your paws gallop and your jowls blow. (*Demonstrates.*) Wish I could remember what I was dreaming about. Something about savannahs, and a fire, and bones, big as a house.

SHE: (*Sharp.*) Boris! (*Then quietly.*) Boris. Come.

(*DOG and SHE go to one side.*)

WOMAN: It's a female.

MAN: Wonder if she's pregnant.

WOMAN: Hang on, honey. We're taking you home.

(*All freeze except BEAR.*)

BEAR: I follow the north side of the mountain, where the sun neither rises nor sets. Under two silver birches, below the sheltering rock, I squeeze myself into crevices an otter couldn't fill. My breath heats the den, steam rises from my fur, making weather under the earth. I sleep the long sleep, in a cradle of soil. And dream of babies, pushing out of me, cubs small as kittens, fat as flesh, eyes awake. They know the continent of my body. They find their way in the dark, to force their mouths upon me, and suck and purr and thrive. Until the unseen days lengthen and the wild crocus pushes through the snow. Then I awaken, newborn and ageless, and take my young into the still white world.

END

TRY THIS 10.7

Take a realistic scene you have written and stylize it with a major reversal of some kind: children are played by adult actors, men are played by women, the characters are animals, or something similar. What happens?

José Rivera

GAS

For Juan Carlos Rivera

CAST
Cheo

TIME: Start of the ground offensive of the Persian Gulf War.

PLACE: A gas station.

(A car at a gas station. CHEO stands next to the pump about to fill his car with gas. He is a working-class Latino. Before he pumps gas he speaks to the audience.)

CHEO: His letters were coming once a week. I could feel his fear. It was in his handwriting. He sat in a tank. In the middle of the Saudi Arabian desert. Wrote six, seven, eight hours a day. These brilliant letters of fear. This big Puerto Rican guy! What the fuck's he doing out there? What the fucking hell sense that make? He's out there, in the Saudi sand, writing letters to me about how he's gonna die from an Iraqi fucking missile. And he's got all this time on his hands to think about his own death. And there's nothing to do 'cause of these restrictions on him. No women, no magazines, 'cause the Saudis are afraid of the rev-olutionary effects of ads for women's lingerie on the population! Allah would have a cow! There's nothing he's allowed to eat even remotely reminds him of home. Nothing but the fucking time to sit and think about what it's gonna be like to have some fucking towelhead—as he calls them—run a bayonet clean through his guts. He's sitting in the tank playing target practice with the fucking camels. Shooting at the wind. The sand in all the food. Sand in his dreaming. He and his buddies got a camel one day. They shaved that motherfucker clean! Completely shaved its ass! Then they spray-painted the name of their company, in bright American spray-paint, on the side of the camel, and sent it on its way! Scorpion fights in the tents! All those scenes from fucking *Apocalypse Now* in his head. Fucking Marlon Brando decapitating that guy and Martin Sheen going fucking nuts. That's what fills my brother's daily dreams as he sits out there in the desert contemplating his own death. The Vietnam Syndrome those people are trying to eradicate. His early letters were all about that. A chronicle.

His way of laying it all down, saying it all for me, so I would know
what his last days, and months, and seconds were like. So when he got
offed by an Iraqi missile, I would at least know what it was like to be
in his soul, if just for a little while. He couldn't write to save his life at
first. Spelled everything totally, unbelievably wrong. "Enough": e-n-u-f.
"Thought": t-h-o-t. "Any": e-n-y. But with time, he started to write
beautifully. This angel started to come out of the desert. This singing
angel of words. Thoughts I honestly never knew he had. Confessions.
Ideas. We started to make plans. We start to be in sync for the first
time since I stopped telling him I loved him. I used to kick his fucking
ass! It wasn't hard or nothing. That's not bragging, just me telling you
a simple truth. He was always sick. Always the first to cry. He played
drums in a parade back home. He couldn't even play the fucking
instrument, he was so uncoordinated. Spastic. But they let him march
in the parade anyway—without drumsticks. He was the last guy in the
parade, out of step, banging make-believe drumsticks, phantom
rhythms on this snare drum—playing air drum for thousands of confused spectators! Then he got into uniforms and the scouts. But I knew
that bullshit was just a cover anyway. He didn't mean it. Though after
he joined the army and was in boot camp, he took particular delight in
coming home and demonstrating the fifty neat new ways he learned
to kill a guy. One day he forgot he weighed twice my weight and
nearly snapped my spine like a fucking cucumber! I thought, in agony,
"where's my bro? Where's that peckerhead I used to kick around? The
first one to cry when he saw something beautiful. The first one to say
'I love that' or 'I love Mom' or 'I love you.'" He never got embarrassed
by that, even after I got too old to deal with my fucking little brother
kissing me in front of other people. Even later, he always, always,
always ended every conversation with, "I love you bro," and I couldn't
say, "I love you" back, 'cause I was too hip to do that shit. But he got
deeper in it. The war thing. He wrote to say I'd never understand. He's
fighting for my right to say whatever I want. To disagree. And I just
fucking love how they tell you on the news the fucking temperature in
Riyadh, Saudi Arabia! Like I fucking care! And a couple of times the
son-of-a-bitch called me collect from Saudi! *I said collect!* And I told
him if Saddam Hussein didn't kill him, I would! He told me about
troubles with his wife back home. He'd just gotten married a month
before shipping out. He didn't really know her and was wondering if
she still loved him. My brother always loved ugly women. It was a
thing with him. Low self-esteem or something. Like he couldn't love
himself and didn't understand a woman that would. So he sought out
the absolute losers of the planet: trucker whores with prison records

who liked to tie him up and whip him, stuff like that. I honestly have trouble contemplating my little brother being whipped by some trucker whore in leather. Love! He didn't know another way. Then he met a girl who on their first date confessed she hated spiks—so my brother married her! This racist looked him in the eye, disrespected his whole race to his face, and my brother says, "I do." Last night somebody got on TV to say we shouldn't come down on rich people 'cause rich people are a minority too, and coming down on them was a form of racism! And I thought, they're fucking afraid of class warfare, and they should be! And the news showed some little white punk putting up flags all over this dipshit town in California and this little twirp's story absorbed twenty minutes of the news—this little, blond Nazi kid with a smile full of teeth—and the protests got shit. And this billboard went up in my town showing Stalin, Hitler, and Hussein, saying we stopped him twice before we have to stop him again! This billboard was put up by a local newspaper! The music, the computer graphics, the generals coming out of retirement to become media stars, public hard ons. And we gotta fight NAKED AGGRESSION—like his asshole president should come *to my fucking neighborhood* if he wants to see naked aggression! I never thought the ideas in the head of some politician would mean the death of my brother and absolutely kill my mother. I'm telling you, that woman will not survive the death of my brother no matter how much she believes in God, no matter how much praying she does. But I keep that from him. I write back about how it's not going to be another Vietnam. It's not going to be a whole country that spits on you when you come back. That we don't forget the ones we love and fight for us. Then his letters stopped. I combed the newspapers trying to figure out what's going on over there, 'cause his letters said nothing about where he was. He wasn't allowed to talk about locations, or troop size, or movement, 'cause, like, I was going to personally transmit this information to the Iraqi fucking Ministry of Defense! I thought about technology. The new shit Iraq has that was made in the United States, shit that could penetrate a tank's armour and literally travel through the guts of a tank, immolating every living human soul inside, turning human Puerto Rican flesh into hot screaming soup, the molecules of my brother's soul mixing with the metal molecules of the iron coffin he loved so much. I couldn't sleep. My mother was suicidal. Why wasn't he writing? The air war's continuing. They're bombing the shit out of that motherfucking country! And I find myself ashamed. I think, "yeah, bomb it more. Level it. Send it back to the Stone Age. Make it so every last elite Republican Guard is dead. So my brother won't get killed." For the first time in my life, I want a lot of people I don't hate to die 'cause I know one of them could kill the man I love most in this fucked up world. If my brother is killed, I will personally take a gun and blow out the brains of George Herbert Walker Bush. And I'm sick. I'm sick of rooting for the bombs. Sick of loving every day the air war continues. Sick of every air strike, every sortie. And being happy another Iraqi tank got taken out and melted, another Iraqi bunker was bombed, another bridge can't bring ammunition, can't deliver that one magic bullet that will incapacitate my brother, bring him back a vegetable, bring him back dead in his soul, or blinded, or butchered in some Iraqi concentration camp. That the Iraqi motherfucker that would torture him won't live now 'cause our smart bombs have killed that towelhead motherfucker in his sleep! They actually got me wanting this war to be bloody!

(Beat.)

Last night the ground war started. It started. The tanks are rolling. I find my gut empty now. I don't have thoughts. I don't have dreams. My mother is a shell. She has deserted herself and left behind a blathering cadaver, this pathetic creature with rosary beads in her hands looking up to Christ, and CNN, saying words like "Scud," "strategic interests," "collateral damage," "target rich environment"—words this woman from a little town in Puerto Rico has no right to know. So I fight my demons. I think of the cause. Blood for oil. I NEED MY CAR, DON'T I? I NEED MY CAR TO GET TO WORK SO I CAN PAY THE RENT AND NOT END UP A HOMELESS PERSON! DON'T I HAVE A RIGHT TO MY CAR AND MY GAS? AND WHAT ABOUT FREEING DEMOCRATIC KUWAIT?!

(Beat.)

So I wait for a sign, anything, a prayer, any sign. I'll take it. Just tell me he's okay. Tell me my brother's gonna kill well and make it through this alive. He's gonna come home and he's gonna come home the same person he left; the spastic one who couldn't spell . . . the one who couldn't play the drums.

(*CHEO starts to pump gas. As he pumps the gas, he notices something horrifying. He pulls the nozzle out of the car. Blood comes out of the gas pump. CHEO stares and stares at the bloody trickle coming out of the gas pump.*)

BLACKOUT

TRY THIS 10.8
Write a monologue in which a physical object or action functions as a symbolic comment on the words.

Josh Ben Friedman
Removing the Head

Night. Police sirens are heard in the distance. The front door opens. DEL enters into the apartment. He is dressed in a baseball mascot costume: a large bird. SPUD, his roommate, sees him.

SPUD: How many times? How many times have I told you not to wear that thing in the house?

DEL: Not tonight.

SPUD: Yes tonight. Tonight is it. This has become an issue. That bird is now most definitely an issue.

DEL: For who?

SPUD: For me, Del. In that it freaks *me* out.

(Slight pause.)

DEL: Good day?

SPUD: You don't wanna know about my day.

DEL: Sure I do.

SPUD: I was mugged. Twice. I hate this city. How was your day?

DEL: Bit bland. Had quite an interesting evening.

SPUD: How'd ya get home?

DEL: Walked.

SPUD: With the bird on?

DEL: Yes.

SPUD: And now that you've arrived at your destination it might be relaxing to . . . I don't know . . . take it off. At least your head?

DEL: I don't want to take off my head.

SPUD: Take off the damn bird head, will ya? I'm sure it's hot in there. How would you like it if I was dressed as a bird and you were dressed as a human?

DEL: You don't dress up as a human, man. You are a human. *(somber)* What if all we are is just animals dressed up as humans? I could be my real self right now, the bird, while you're in a human costume.

SPUD: I feel like I'm on acid talking to a six-foot bird.

DEL: How about Big Bird? You like Big Bird. Why don't you use your imagination?

SPUD: Talking to a bird is not fun, Del, it's sick. *Sesame Street* is sick.

DEL: People in our line of work?

SPUD: People in our line of work our sick! Everything is sick. I'm sick. I appear as pieces of giant-sized fruit for grocery store events. I'm an actor. I've done the classics. Yet to make a living I dress myself in fruit.

DEL: What classics have you done?

SPUD: Listen, I don't need to answer that question. I have done the classics, my friend. Many, many classics, many, many times. What have you done?

DEL: Excuse me? Do you have any idea how many fans I have? How many women want me? I'm a walking, talking fetish here. And the most popular bird east of the Mississippi.

SPUD: You know I've never understood why you're a bird. You're the mascot for a team called the Panthers. Last time I checked a bird is nowhere near a panther. Different ballpark all together.

DEL: Funny.

SPUD: What's that on your beak?

DEL: I . . . I wanted to talk with you about that, Spud.

SPUD: Looks red.

DEL: Pour me a drink, huh?

SPUD: That's blood on your goddamn beak.

DEL: Pour me a drink, Spud!

SPUD: You don't have to yell.

(Del stares at Spud. Spud then goes and pours Del a drink. Del removes his head and places it on a coat rack.)

DEL: I remove the head of what they call the beast and lay it to rest on a spear. The spear is dull.

(Spud watches Del. Del watches the head.)

SPUD: Here's your drink.

DEL: Thanks.

SPUD: Del?

DEL: Yes.

SPUD: Tell me how you got the blood on your beak?

DEL: Did I say it was blood?

SPUD: No. Is it blood?

DEL: Yes.

SPUD: Is it your blood?

DEL: No.

SPUD: It's somebody else's blood?

DEL: Yes.

SPUD: Dammit, Del!

DEL: Take it easy.

SPUD: Did some guy bleed on you? Is that what happened? Freakin' amateurs have no respect for the uniform I tell ya. Doesn't matter what bodily function they've got to perform, you're just livestock to them, Del. A big bird Kleenex. You know I was playing a cantaloupe for the opening of an Ozzies downtown and there was this fat little girl, fatter than a little girl should be, and I could determine as she approached me that she was oozing from every orifice with sticky water and green slime. Of course she wants a hug. Of course she does. Those are the ones that always want hugs. And that's my goddamn job.

DEL: Spud, I've had some business go down. Some important business. I need you to listen.

SPUD: I always listen, Del. It's one of my strong suits.

(*A moment passes.*)

DEL: It went down in the bottom of the fifth.

SPUD: Bring it on.

DEL: It was a cool night at the old ballpark. Plenty of people. Plenty of noise. Seemed like any other night.

SPUD: Lemme guess: it wasn't?

DEL: You know if you're gonna be a smart ass-

SPUD: Go on.

DEL: The organist was playing a Hawaiian number and I was dancing around with this lady on the top of the visitor's dugout. A little firecracker dame. Crowd was going crazy. Enjoying the hell outta it.

SPUD: Ya do know your role. Can't take that away from you.

DEL: So the Hawaiian number stops and I'd partaken in a gallon of Gator-Aid and planned to expel some electrolytes, when all of a sudden, the little firecracker dame I'd been dancing with, grabs hold of me. Like really grabs hold of me.

SPUD: You're kidding?

DEL: Now my first reaction was to throw her off but she was kinda strong. PCP strong. Had one arm yanking at my beak and the other pulling the crap out of my left wing.

SPUD: That's crazy.

DEL: The crowd saw it and started laughing, shouting, getting rowdy, throwing cans and popcorn tins at me like I wasn't human. Like I was truly some bird there for their sporting pleasure. I mean . . . god, Spud, I started to question my entire life.

SPUD: That's an odd time to start questioning one's entire life.

DEL: What the hell was I doing out on that dugout? I didn't have the strength to fight back. I was weak. Disgustingly weak. I lapsed into my childhood. My mother yelling at me for dropping a casserole. Her spittle hitting my face. Fingers pulling my ear. "You'll never get any- where in life, Del. What are we supposed to do for dinner now?!" I started to cry under that bird head.

SPUD: Oh . . . Del.

DEL: My tears mixed with my rage . . . NO MORE! No more. I flapped my wings, thrusting the hands loose, took a step back and plunged my beak into the woman.

(*A pause.*)

SPUD: Pardon?

DEL: At first I think she was startled. As if awakening from this glossy daze she looked me in the eyes. Where my eyes woulda been. She was a tired human waste just like me. I plunged my beak into her again. I was plunging my beak into all the injustice in my life. All the bullshit. The fraud. The sham. I was plunging my beak! In control. A bird by costume but a panther by nature.

(*A beat.*)

SPUD: So . . . . what...what happened?

DEL: Lady tripped off the roof of the dugout and snapped her neck. Game was stopped for five minutes to remove the body as I was politely ush- ered off the field. When I got to the snack stand I simply . . . flew away.

(*A moment then Spud begins to chuckle, frightened . . .*)

SPUD: I don't . . . I mean . . . holy shit, Del, you call that 'business'?! I mean . . . you realize you're a murderer, man. You do realize that, don't you?! That you're in deep droppings here.

DEL: Oh, I don't know.

SPUD: Well ya should know, man, ya should.

DEL: What would you've done?

SPUD: I don't know, act sensibly. I mean look, of course I would've loved to beat the snot back into that little fat girl but that isn't. . . . I mean life's gotta have order, you know. It's not how things work.

DEL: What took place tonight . . . every mascot from the Chicago Giraffe to the Houston Hippo stood up and saluted me. We are laughed at, Spud, jeered and flouted in the teeth, but not tonight. Tonight was different. My insides came out to play and nobody even knows it was Del.

SPUD: Yeah, well, God knows, man.

DEL: God? The Grand Poobah? I spoke to him tonight, too. Know what he told me? Said he was sick of being a mascot, too. You hear that, Spuddie boy, sick of being a mascot too!

SPUD: You're . . . nuts.

DEL: And you're scared. I don't blame ya. I was scared too. Until I removed my head and put on the head of truth. Once your feel it, you'll never know how you lived without it. Take a risk, Spud. Go natural. Remove your head and put on the animal.

(*Del gently, almost religiously, removes the bird head from the coat rack. Holds it out to Spud.*)

(*Black.*)

TRY THIS 10.9
In the play you are writing, introduce a striking costume or item of clothing that reveals one character and produces unease, embarrassment, or anger in another.

Lanford Wilson
Eukiah

CHARACTERS
Butch
Eukiah

TIME: The present

SETTING: An abandoned private airplane hangar.

A dark empty stage represents a long abandoned private airplane hangar. The space is vast and almost entirely dark. A streak of light from a crack in the roof stripes the floor.

   Butch walks into the light. He is a young powerful, charming man; everybody's best friend. He is also menacing. Nothing he says is introspective. Everything is for a purpose. During the indicated beats of silence he listens; for Eukiah to answer, for the sound of breathing, for the least indication of where Eukiah is. The play is a seduction.

   Voices have a slight echo in here.

BUTCH: Eukiah? (*Beat.*) Eukiah? (*Beat.*) Barry saw you run in here, so I know you're here. You're doin' it again, Eukiah, you're jumping to these weird conclusions you jump to just like some half-wit. You don't wanna be called a half-wit, you gotta stop actin' like a half-wit, don't ya? You're getting' to where nobody can joke around you, ya know that? What kind of fun is a person like that to be around, huh? One you can't joke around? We talked about that before, remember? (*Beat.*) Eukiah? What're you thinkin'? You thinkin' you heard Barry say something, you thought he meant it, didn't you? What did you think you heard? Huh? What'd you think he meant? Eukiah? (*Beat.*) You're gonna have to talk to me, I can't talk to myself here. (*Beat.*) Have you ever known me to lie to you? Eukiah? Have you ever known that? (*Pause. He might walk around some.*) Okay. Boy, this old hangar sure seen better days, hasn't it? Just like everything else on this place, huh? Been pretty much a losing proposition since I've known it, though. Probably you too, hasn't it? Hell, I don't think they have the wherewithal anymore, give even one of those ol' barns a swab a paint. You think? Might paint 'em pink, whattaya think? Or candy stripes. Red and white. Peppermint. You'd like that. (*Beat.*) This'll remind you of old Mac's heyday, though, won't it? Private airplane hangar. Talk about echoes, this is an echo of the past, huh? Ol' Mac had some winners, I guess, about twenty years ago. That must have been the life, huh? Private planes, keep 'em in your private hangar. You got your luncheons with the dukes and duchesses. Winner's Circle damn near every race. If they wasn't raised by Ol' Mac or their sire or dam one wasn't raised by Ol' Mac, I don't imagine anybody'd bother to bet on 'em, do you? Boy that's all gone, huh? Planes and limos and all, dukes and duchesses good lookin' horses, though. Damn shame we can't enter 'em in a beauty contest somewhere. I know, you're attached to 'em, but I'll tell you they make damn expensive pets.

What was you? Out by the paddock when Barry was talkin' to me? You think you overheard something, is that it? What do you think you heard? You want to talk about it? I know you'd rather talk to me than talk to Barry, huh? Eukiah? (*Pause.*) Is this where you come? When you run off all temperamental and sulking? Pretty nasty old place to play in. Echoes good though. Gotta keep awful quiet if you're trying to be secret like you always do in a place like this.

Why do you do that? You got any idea? I'm serious, now. Run off like that. They're waitin' supper on you, I guess you know. You know how happy they're gonna be about it, too. (*Beat.*) Eukiah? What was it you think you heard, honey? What? Was it about horses? 'Cause I thought I told you never trust anything anybody says if it's about horses.

EUKIAH: (*Still unseen.*) I heard what Barry said. You said you *would*, too.

BUTCH: (*Relaxes some, smiles.*) Where the dickens have you got to? There's so much echo in here I can't tell where you are. You back in those oil drums? You haven't crawled up in the rafters have you? Watch yourself. We don't want you getting' hurt. I don't think those horses would eat their oats at all, anybody gave 'em to 'em 'cept you. I think they'd flat out go on strike. Don't you figure?

EUKIAH: They wouldn't drink, you couldn't get 'em to.

BUTCH: Don't I know it. Pot-A-Gold, for sure. You're the only one to get him to do anything. I think he'd just dehydrate. He'd blow away, you wasn't leadin' him. We could lead him to water but we couldn't make him to drink, isn't that right? (*Beat.*) What are you hiding about? Nobody's gonna hurt you. Don't I always take up for you? You get the weirdest ideas. What do you think you heard Barry say?

EUKIAH: He's gonna burn the horses.

BUTCH: What? Oh, man. You are just crazy sometimes, these things you dream up. Who is? Barry? What would he wanna do something crazy like that for?

EUKIAH: I heard you talkin'.

BUTCH: Can you answer me that? Why would he even dream of doin' something like that?

EUKIAH: For the insurance.

BUTCH: No, Eukiah. Just come on to supper, now, I got a date tonight, I can't mess around with you anymore. You really are a half-wit. I'm sorry, but if you think Barry'd do something like that, I'm sorry, that's just flat out half-witted thinkin'. It's not even funny. The way you talk, you yak all day to anybody around, no idea what you're saying half the time; anybody heard something like that there wouldn't be no work for me or you or anybody else around here, 'cause they just lock us all up.

EUKIAH: You said you would.

BUTCH: *I* would? I would what?

EUKIAH: You said it was about time somebody did somethin'.

BUTCH: Eukiah, come out here. I can see you over by that old buggy, my eyes got used to the dark. There ain't no sense in hiding anymore. (*Beat.*) Come on out, damnit, so we can go to supper. I'm not going to play with you anymore. Come on. Well, just answer me one thing. How's burnin' 'em up gonna be any better than maybe splittin' a hoof or somethin' like that? Come on, crazy. The least little thing happens to make a horse not run, it's the same as if he had to be destroyed, you ought to know that. (*Eukiah is just visible now. He is maybe six-teen years old. He is slow and soft; he has the mentality of an eight-year-old.*)

EUKIAH: Yeah, but they already took Pot-A-Gold and Flashy and that gray one, the speckled one, off. They already sold 'em.

BUTCH: Which one do you call Flashy, you mean Go Carmen? The filly? And Old Ironside? Why would they do that?

EUKIAH: 'Cause they're the best ones. Then they put three no good horses in their stalls, so nobody would know. And they're gonna burn 'em and nobody can tell they ain't the horses they're supposed to be, Butchy.

BUTCH: Nobody could run Pot-A-Gold somewhere else, Euky. You know those numbers they tattoo in his mouth? That's gonna identify him no matter where he goes, anybody'll know that's Pot-A-Gold.

EUKIAH: Some other country. They wouldn't care.

BUTCH: Anywhere on earth. . .

EUKIAH: They got some plan where it'll work, 'cause I heard 'em.

BUTCH: I don't know what you think you heard, but you're really acting half-witted here.

EUKIAH: Don't call me—

BUTCH: Well, I'm sorry, but what would you call it? A person can't burn down a barn full of horses, Euky. What a horrible thing to think. No wonder you get scared, you scare yourself thinking things like that. Those horses are valued, hell I don't even know, millions of dollars probably. Insurance inspectors come around, they take a place apart. You tell me, how would somebody get away with a trick like that?

EUKIAH: What was you talkin' about then?

BUTCH: I don't even know. Where it was you heard what you thought you heard. You're too fast for me. You'll have to go into supper and ask Mac what Barry was talking about, won't you? Would that make you feel better? Instead of jumpin' to your weird conclusions. Now, can you get that out of your head? Huh? So we can go eat and I can take a bath and go on my date? Is that all right with you? Then I'll come back and tell you all about it. Got a date with Mary, you'd like to hear about that, wouldn't you?

(*Eukiah begins to grin.*)

BUTCH: Yes? That's okay with you, is it?

EUKIAH: I guess. (*He moves into the light, closer to Butch.*)

BUTCH: You guess. You're just going to have to trust me, Eukiah, nobody needs money that bad. Not even on this place. I don't even think nobody could get away tryin' to pull something like that.

(*He puts his arm around Eukiah's neck and they start to move off, but Butch has Eukiah in a head lock. He speaks with the strain of exertion.*)

BUTCH: Not unless there was some half-wit on the place that got his neck broke being kicked in the head and got burned up in the fire.

(*Eukiah goes to his knees. Butch bears down on his neck; it breaks with a dull snap. He lets Eukiah slump to the floor. Butch is breathing hard, standing over Eukiah's body.*)

BUTCH: I thought I told you. Never trust anything anybody says if it's about horses.

END

TRY THIS 10.10

Villains are most effective when they are also charming, convincing, touching, or otherwise not being villainous. Write a speech for an unsympathetic character that makes us for the moment sympathetic.

ACCOMPLISHING A DRAFT

Stuart Spencer claims that, "A play is more wrought than written. A playwright constructs a play as a wheelwright once constructed a wheel: a general shape is laid out, and then hammered, bent, nailed, reshaped, hammered again and again. . ." Take the most promising idea you have for a ten-minute play and submit it to the wheelwright's test:

- What is its general shape? Does it express a character's journey from one condition or state to another?
- Does the set help to convey the characters and their situation? Does costume reveal? Do props further the action?
- Does the protagonist deeply desire something? Is the antagonist a match in power for the protagonist? Are they both consistent and complex?
- Is the dialogue sayable? Does it further the conflict? Does it reveal more than one thing at a time?
- Does the action unfold as a series of discoveries and decisions?

Hammer, bend, reshape, and hammer again.

Drama Format

The formats for prose and poetry are relatively straightforward and easy to master. The format for plays, unfortunately, is not. It is nevertheless necessary either to learn or to achieve by software created especially for this purpose, because every peculiarity annoying to the writer is an aid to the actors, director, and designers who must interpret the script in living action. For instance, the names of characters (except when used as a form of address in dialogue), and the pronouns that refer to them, are always in capital letters and are centered before speeches because this visually helps actors spot what they say and do. Short stage directions are put in parentheses and long ones to the right of the page because that signals where the action is indicated. Pages are numbered not merely consecutively but also by act and scene because in rehearsal a director specifies "Take it from the top of scene two" rather than "Take it from page 38," which has less meaning in the structure of a play. And so forth.

The format thus designed for production is not necessarily the same one you will encounter in a printed "trade" or textbook edition of the play, where there's a higher priority on saving space than on convenience to the company. But as a playwright your goal is production and your allegiance to the theatrical troupe; your manuscript should reflect that.

Software that automatically produces a submission-ready play or screenplay is available, and is worth the investment for anyone who intends to pursue these fields. The software most often recommended by playwrights and screen writers is Final Draft.

Playwrights often feel that they *do* need to copyright their work because it may be circulated to many people, and could be produced without their knowledge; it's difficult to prove production after the fact. If you intend to send your work out to production companies and feel more comfortable with a copyright, you should write for "Form PA" to: U.S. Copyright Office, Library of Congress, Washington, DC 20559.

Plays should have a cover page with title, some sort of designation such as "A play in two scenes" or "A comedy in one act," and the author's name and address. Plays should be typed in 12-point (or "pica") font, and should be (at least for submission—probably not for class) sent in a sturdy binder.

```
              THE SCHOOL FOR SCANDAL

            A Play in Five Acts
                    by
          Richard Brinsley Sheridan




                    Eng. 4701, Drama Workshop
                     Prof. Joseph Surface
                    Drury Lane University
                        Feb. 28, 1777
```

Cast of Characters

Sir Peter Teazle
Sir Oliver Surface
Joseph Surface
Charles Surface
Crabtree
Sir Benjamin Backbite
Rowley
Trip
Moses
Snake
Careless (*and other* Companions *to* Charles
  Surface)
Servants, *etc.*
Lady Teazle
Maria
Lady Sneerwell
Mrs. Candor

SCENE
London

TIME
The present.

1 — 1 — 1

Act I

Scene 1

>LADY SNEERWELL'*s house.*
>LADY SNEERWELL *at the*
>*dressing table,* SNAKE *drinking*
>*chocolate.*

LADY SNEERWELL
The paragraphs, you say, Mr. Snake, were all
inserted?

SNAKE
They were, madam, and as I copied them myself in
a feigned hand, there can be no suspicion whence
they came.

LADY SNEERWELL
Did you circulate the reports of Lady Brittle's
intrigue with Captain Boatstall?

SNAKE
(HE *kisses his handkerchief.*) That is in as fine
a train as your ladyship could wish—in the common

1 — 1 — 2

SNAKE (Continued)

course of things, I think it must reach Mrs. Clakit's ears within four-and-twenty hours; and then, you know, the business is as good as done.

LADY SNEERWELL

Why, truly, Mrs. Clakit has a very pretty talent, and a great deal of industry.

SNAKE

True, madam, and has been tolerably successful in her day. To my knowledge, she has been the cause of six matches being broken off, and three sons being disinherited, of four forced elopements, as many close confinements, nine separate maintenances, and two divorces. Nay, I have more than once traced her causing a *tête-a-tête* in the *Town and Country Magazine*, when the parties had perhaps never seen each other's faces before in the course of their lives.

LADY SNEERWELL

She certainly has her talents, but her manner is gross.

> (SHE *dons her wig*. SNAKE, *taken aback, spills chocolate on his waistcoat*. HE *wipes at it with the handkerchief.*)

SNAKE

'Tis very true. She generally designs well, has a free tongue, and a bold invention; but

Appendix

A Basic Prosody

> In my sensory education I include my physical awareness
> of the *word*. Of a certain word, that is: the connection it
> has with what it stands for. At around age six, perhaps,
> I was standing by myself waiting for supper . . . There
> comes a moment, and I saw it then, when the moon goes
> from flat to round. For the first time it met my eyes as a
> globe. The word "moon" came into my mouth as though
> fed to me out of a silver spoon.
>
> *Eudora Welty*

Prosody is the study of versification, the metrical and auditory structure of poetry. What follows here is a very basic prosody, outlining the major units of sound and meter, the basic principles of rhyme, and a few common stanza patterns.

To begin with, these are the building blocks of poems:

- A **phoneme** is the smallest unit of sound in a language that is capable of conveying meaning. For example, the *s* in *as* conveys a different meaning in conjunction with the *a* than the *t* in *at*. A different meaning still is conveyed by adding the *b* sound in *bat*, and a different meaning still by adding the *r* sound in *brat*. Phonemes are either **vowels,** produced by relatively free passage of air through the oral cavity—for example, *a, o, e*; or **consonants,** produced by a partial obstruction of the air stream: *t, p, g*. Vowels may be pronounced as **long** sounds (ā, ē, ō, as in *place, wheat, own*) or **short** sounds (ă, ŭ, ĕ, as in *cat, up, when*). Consonants are divided into categories according to which part of the mouth obstructs the air or the manner of its obstruction, as the *labials* by the lips, the *dentals* by the teeth, the *nasals* by the nose, the *plosives* in a sudden burst, and so forth.

- A **syllable** is a unit of sound uttered in a single expulsion of breath, typically containing one or more consonants and a vowel: *mup-, done, ba-*. A syllable may be either **stressed** or **unstressed** (**accented** or **unaccented**) according to the relative force with which it is pronounced: *be-GUN, PO-e-try*. In the **scansion** or measuring of poetry, the stress is marked (avoiding the cumbersome capitals) as follows: *bĕgún, pŏĕtrý*. The double accent mark indicates a **secondary stress** (lighter than a stressed, heavier than an unstressed syllable; some prosodists hear a secondary stress in most three-syllable words).

- A **poetic foot** is a measure of syllables usually containing one stressed and one or more unstressed syllables. The poetic feet are marked by slashes:

  Í hăve / bĕgún / tŏ wríte / ă vérse.

- A **poetic line** is a unit of verse ended by a typographical break. The line may be **syllabic,** in which case its length is determined by the number of syllables without regard to how many accents it has. Or it may be **accentual,** in which case it has a given number of stressed or accented syllables and any number of unaccented syllables. It may be **metered verse,** in which both accents and syllables are counted and the lines will have a predetermined number of poetic feet or repetitions of a pattern of stressed and unstressed syllables (see "Stress and Scansion," below). Or it may be **free verse,** its length determined by the poet according to the needs of the particular poem. A **caesura** is a pause that occurs within the line. In a line that is **end-stopped,** the line break coincides with a pause; if the sense continues from the end of one line to the next, it is called a **run-on** line, or **enjambment.**

- A **stanza** is a grouping of lines within a poem, often predetermined by the chosen form, with a space break between such groupings.

TRY THIS A.1

With no attempt to make sense, write a four-line verse in which the vowel sounds are all short. (For example: *Flat on his back / the summer shop cat runs / his love and supper pot. / What fickle chumps.*) Then a four-line verse in which all the vowel sounds are long.

Time

Three terms having to do with the time element of poetry are sometimes used interchangeably, though in fact they differ in meaning.

- **Tempo** refers to the speed or slowness of a line.

- **Meter** comes from the Greek "measure," and refers to the mechanical elements of its rhythm, the number of feet, stresses and unstressed syllables; it is a relatively objective measurement.

- **Rhythm** refers to the total quality of a line's motion, affected by tempo and meter but also by emotion and sound.

Meter is something that can be measured, whereas rhythm is a feeling, a sense. It would be appropriate to say of a line or poem that the tempo is *fast* or *slow*, the meter is *iambic pentameter* or *trochaic dimeter*, and that the rhythm is *lilting, urgent, effortful,* or *sluggish.*

Stress and Scansion; the Poetic Foot

English is a stress language, the pattern of speech determined by the emphasis given to some syllables over others. This fact is so ingrained in us that it's difficult to understand a language otherwise constituted, but Greek, for example, is a language measured in vowel length, and Chinese is patterned in pitch rather than stress.

Accentual verse employs a meter in which only the stresses are counted:

When the watchman on the wall, the Shieldings' lookout
whose job it was to guard the sea-cliffs,
saw shields glittering on the gangplank
and battle-equipment being unloaded
he had to find out who and what . . .

Seamus Heaney's translation of Beowulf

(Here, each line has four stresses, but they have 12, 9, 9, 11, and 8 syllables, respectively.)

Syllabic verse employs a meter in which only the syllables are counted, as in these lines by W. H. Auden, which keep to nine syllables each although the number of stresses diminishes from five to four to three:

> Blue the sky beyond her humming sail
> As I sit today by our ship's rail
> Watching exuberant porpoises . . .

TRY THIS A.2

Write a "phone poem" as syllabic verse. Use as the title a phone number (of any length you choose) real or invented. The subject of the poem is a phone call to that number; it may be a narrative about the call, or in dialogue, or a monologue of one side of the conversation, or any combination. Each line has the number of syllables of each consecutive digit. So if the phone number is 587-9043, the first line has five syllables, the second eight syllables, the third seven, and so forth. A zero is silence.

Most formal English verse counts both stresses and syllables and is *scanned* by measuring the line into stressed (or accented) and unstressed (or unaccented) syllables.

A **poetic foot** is a unit of measurement with one stress and either one or two unstressed syllables, scanned in these basic patterns:

- An **iamb** has one unstressed syllable followed by one stressed: around.

  Iambic is the most common meter in English, probably because we tend to begin sentences with the subject, and most nouns are preceded by an article, as in: the girl, the sky, an apple.

  His house / is in / the vil/lage though.

  Note that when the scansion is marked, the feet are separated by slashes even if the foot ends between two syllables of a word.

- A **trochee** is the opposite of an iamb—a stressed syllable followed by an unstressed: heavy.

  Trochaic rhythms do tend to be heavy, hitting hard and forcefully on the stress.

  Double, / double / toil and / trouble;

- An **anapest** consists of two unstressed syllables followed by a stress: undefined.

  Notice that *anapest* is not an anapest, though it would be if I say: *You're a nuisance and a pest!* *Anapestic* rhythms tend to be rollicking frolic and light verse; it is the meter of Gilbert and Sullivan.

  From my head / to my toes / I'm all cov/ered in ros/es.

- A **dactyl** is a poetic foot that begins with a stress followed by two unstresses: cárpĕntĕr.

  Dactylic meters tend toward the mysterious or incantatory and are rare, though you are likely to have encountered a few in school:

  Thĭs ĭs thĕ / fórĕst prĭ/mévăl, thĕ / múrmŭrĭng / pínĕs ănd thĕ / hémlŏcks.

- A **spondee** is a foot with two stresses, which can be substituted for any other foot when special emphasis is wanted (you won't want to, and can't, write a whole poem in it):

  Óne, twó. / Búckle / mý shóe.

- A **pyrrhic** foot is the opposite, a substitute foot with two unstressed syllables:

  Thŏu árt / ĭndeéd / jŭst, Lórd, / ĭf Ĭ / cŏnténd
  Wĭth theé . . .

  Sometimes, as here, a spondee is balanced with a pyrrhic, so the number of stresses remains the same as in a regular line.

Those are the feet, four basic and two substitute, that you need to begin with, although infinite variations are possible, many of which have names (*chiasmus, ionic, amphibrach, anacreusis*) if your interest inclines you to seek them out.

TRY THIS A.3

Practice scanning anything at all, marking the stresses of a sentence or a cereal box, exaggerating as you pronounce the words to hear the stresses. Although scansion is not a science—people pronounce words with different emphasis according to region and habit—the more you practice the more you will hear the pattern of stressed and unstressed syllables, and the more you will be able to direct the stresses of your own poetry.

A line of poetry in a regular **meter** will be scanned according to the number of feet in that line (the following examples are in iambs):

- *Monometer*—one foot: Ĭf Í

- *Dimeter*—two feet: Ĭf Í / dŏn't gó

- *Trimeter*—three feet: Ĭf Í / dŏn't gó / ăwáy

- *Tetrameter*—four feet: Ĭf Í / dŏn't gó / ăwáy / tŏdáy

- *Pentameter*—five feet: Ĭf Í / dŏn't gó / ăwáy / tŏdáy / Ĭ wón't

- *Hexameter*—six feet: Ĭf Í / dŏn't gó / ăwáy / tŏdáy / I'll névĕr gó

- *Heptameter*—seven feet: Ĭf Í / dŏn't gó / ăwáy / tŏdáy / I'll névĕr gó / ăt áll.

You're unlikely to run into (or write) a metered line longer than this.

TRY THIS A.4

Practice meter—remember not to worry about making sense—by setting yourself more or less arbitrary rules: write three lines of iambic tetrameter, six of trochaic trimeter, and so forth. Mark the scansion of your lines; read them aloud until you're confident you hear the stresses.

Pick a favorite nursery line or lyric (country, Irish, rock, Shakespeare, hip hop, opera); write it down and mark the scansion. Then substitute other words in the same pattern of scansion.

Rhyme

Rhyme is to sound as metaphor is to imagery—that is, two things are at once alike and unlike, and our pleasure is in the tension between that likeness and unlikeness. In the case of rhyme, there are patterns of consonants and vowels that correspond to each other, usually involving the accented syllable and whatever comes after it; there also is a diminishing order of correspondence.

- In **rich rhyme,** the whole accented syllable sounds alike—any consonants before the vowel, the vowel, and any consonants after. So *tend* would be a rich rhyme with *pretend* and *contend* and *intend.* Because so many sounds in these syllables correspond, they quickly tire the ear, so whole poems in rich rhyme are rare.

- In a **true rhyme**—the sound of nursery rhymes and the first word-play in which most of us indulge—the vowel sounds of the stressed syllable are alike, as are the consonants after the vowel, but not the consonants before it. So *tend* is a true rhyme for *mend* and *lend* and *offend.* Because true rhyme also requires that the unaccented syllables after the stressed syllable correspond, *tender* rhymes with *spender* and *tendency* with *dependency.* When the accented syllable ends a rhymed line, it is called a *masculine rhyme* (out of some outdated notion of strength): *tend, send.* When it is followed by an unaccented syllable, it is called a *feminine* or *weak rhyme: tender, blender;* and when followed by two unaccented syllables, a *triple* or *treble rhyme: tenderly, slenderly.* (Perhaps these are androgynous?)

- In **slant rhyme** or **off-rhyme,** the final consonant corresponds, but not the vowel that precedes it. So *tend* is a slant rhyme for *bland,* and *tender* a slant rhyme for *grinder.* The use of slant rhyme exponentially increases the number of available rhymes in English and can introduce unexpected effects, subtle aural surprises, and interesting variations in tone.

- **Assonance** is the opposite; the vowel corresponds but not the consonant. *Tend* assonates with *spell* and *weather* and *met.* As with slant rhyme, assonance teases the ear with subtle correspondences.

- In **alliteration,** consonants (usually at the beginning of the word or stressed syllable) correspond: *tender, tickle, take, entreat.* Alliteration is often used to try to reproduce the sound or emotion of the content:

The mildest human sound can make them scatter
With a sound like seed spilled . . .

- Rhymes may be **end rhymes,** coming at the ends of lines, or **internal rhymes,** within the lines. Often the end rhyme of one line will rhyme into the middle of another:

Body my <u>house</u>
my <u>horse</u> my hound
what will I <u>do</u>
when <u>you</u> are fallen

"Question," May Swenson

In general, poetry tends toward **euphony,** the change of one quality of sound to another, from consonants to vowels and back again to facilitate pronunciation and so contribute to flow. But sometimes you will want to produce a sound that is not mellifluous or euphonic but effortful. One way of doing this is the **consonant cluster** demonstrated in the Pope line:

Whĕn Á/jăx stríves / some rock's / vast weight / tŏ thrów.

Here the consonants butt up against each other at the end of one word and the beginning of the next, so you have to stop between in order to pronounce both: *Ajax \\ strives; rock's \\ vast; weight \\ to.* At the same time, the two spondees give the line especially heavy stress: *some rock's vast weight.* A different sort of **cacophony** is achieved when vowels end one word and begin the next:

Ănd óft / thĕ eár / thĕ ó/pĕn vów/eĭs tíre.

TRY THIS A.5

Go back to the exercise on p. 323, the list of words related to your area of expertise. Are there any rich rhymes? True rhymes? Slant rhymes? Arrange a short list to form a line that alliterates: (my list of spices might yield *Cardamom, cayenne, curry, cloves*); and a line that assonates: (*Sage, bay, carraway, arrowroot*); and a line with rhymes true or slant: (*Dill weed, poppy seed, cumin seed, bay leaves, cloves*). Play around with combinations of rhyme, alliteration, and assonance: *Chili, cilantro, oregano, cinnamon, / Carraway, cardamom, gumbo, garlic, / Cinnamon, cumin, sesame, rosemary.* Can you find consonant clusters? *Nutmeg / gumbo; bay leaves / turmeric / cayenne.*

Stanzas

The most common form of English poetry is **blank verse,** unrhymed iambic pentameter—iambic probably because of our habitual arrangement of articles and nouns, pentameter probably because that length represents a comfortable expulsion of breath, unrhymed probably because it is the most free and most flexible of the formal patterns—the nearest to free verse. It is the form of Shakespeare's plays, of Milton's *Paradise Lost,* of Robert Frost's "Mending Wall," Wallace Stevens's "Sunday Morning," and innumerable modern poems. Blank verse runs to any length and is not broken into set blocks of lines. But most patterned verse is written in stanzas.

A **stanza** is a division of lines in a poem, usually linked by a pattern of meter or sound, and usually repeated more than once. It is beyond the scope of this book to enumerate the various, multifarious, loose and strict, simple and elaborate, Eastern and Western stanza forms. But here are a few that are basic to English verse, and a few from other cultures that have attracted a good deal of poetic play in the English of the twentieth century.

- **Couplet.** A two-line stanza, usually consecutively rhymed, although unrhymed couplets are also common in modern verse. A **heroic couplet** is two lines of iambic pentameter, consecutively rhymed:

The little hours: two lovers herd upstairs
two children, one of whom is one of theirs.
"Almost Aubade," Marilyn Hacker

- **Tercet,** or **triplet,** is a stanza of three lines (rhymed or unrhymed):

While mopping she muses over work undone,
Her daily chores. The blue floor tiles
Reflect where she cleans and her thoughts run . . .
"The Housekeeper," Wendy Bishop

- **Quatrain** is a stanza of four lines, of which the **ballad meter** is famous in English, usually four lines of iambic tetrameter, or alternating tetrameter and trimeter, rhymed only on the second and fourth lines (though there are many variations, of both meter and rhyme scheme). The ballad tells a story, often of betrayal and violence:

Put your hand behind the wainscot,
You have done your part;
Find the penknife there and plunge it
Into your cold heart.
W. H. Auden

- The **song** or **lyric** is often in quatrains of iambic tetrameter with a rhyme scheme of ABAB or ABBA.

- And so forth. A **quintet** has five lines, a **sestet** six, a **septet** seven, and an **octave** eight.

- The **sonnet** is a poem of fourteen lines, usually printed without a stanza break although the lines are internally grouped. The sonnet gained its popularity as an import from Italy during the Renaissance, where it was densely rhymed and usually dealt with the subject of love, especially unrequited (something like country western music today.) Because of the paucity of English rhymes, the Italian or Petrarchan rhyme scheme (ABBA ABBA CDECDE) was adapted in English to the looser scheme ABAB CDCD EFEF GG. The sonnet is a good example of the way form influences meaning. Petrarchan sonnets have a strong tendency to develop an idea in the first eight lines (or **octet**) and then to elaborate or contradict or alter it at some length in the last six lines (**sestet**). But the English sonnet, including those of Shakespeare's, developed in such a way that the three quatrains develop an idea, which must then be capped, or contradicted, or changed in a punchy couplet at the end. Here is an example from Shakespeare that is likely to be familiar:

Let me not to the marriage of true minds
Admit impediments. Love is not love
Which alters when it alteration finds,
Or bends with the remover to remove:
O no! it is an ever-fixed mark
That looks on tempests and is never shaken;
It is the star to every wandering bark,
Whose worth's unknown, although his height be taken.
Love's not Time's fool, though rosy lips and cheeks

Within his bending sickle's compass come:
Love alters not with his brief hours and weeks,
But bears it out even to the edge of doom.
    If this be error and upon me proved,
    I never writ, nor no man ever loved.

Stanzas are arranged in many set, traditional—and many more invented and original—groups, to form the poems. Like the sonnet, most of the forms that we think of as typically English were actually adapted from other languages. Terza rima, rondeau, sestina, ghazal, pantoum, villanelle—any and all of these are worth seeking out (the books recommended at the end of Chapter 9, page 326, will provide definitions and examples). Meanwhile, of the non-English forms that have become popular, none is more so than the shortest of them, the Japanese **haiku,** an unrhymed verse of seventeen syllables arranged in three lines of five, seven, and five syllables. And none of them provides better practice for encapsulating an emotion or idea in a sharply etched observation, whether *reflective:*

Escaped the nets,
escaped the ropes—
moon on the water
                    Buson

—or cynical:

a bath when you're born
a bath when you die,
how stupid.
                    Issa

—or contemporary:

These stamps are virgins—
not even licked yet. Date night
alone at my desk.
                    Devan Cook

TRY THIS A.6

Write a series of quatrains. Choose some meter and rhyme scheme in advance—iambic tetrameter in a pattern of abba rhymes, for example. This will be an "altar poem" to someone you want to honor. In the first line, name or describe a place that would be appropriate to honor this person. In subsequent lines, list or describe the objects you would bring and assemble in that place. Try slant rhymes to augment your possibilities. Play around to see if you can use and identify caesura, enjambment, alliteration, assonance.

Write a sonnet as a story: in quatrain one, introduce two characters in a setting; in quatrain two, they are in conflict; in quatrain three, a third character arrives and complicates things; in the couplet, all is resolved.

Write a haiku. Write another. One more.

Glossary

Note: Technical terms concerning **prosody** (the study of meter and sound in poetry) are also found in the Appendix on page 375.

Accent, or stress   Vocal emphasis given to a particular syllable, word, or phrase. The AC-cent or STRESS can be HEARD in the VOICE. See pp. 321–322 and 376.

Accentual verse   Poetry in which only the accented syllables in each line are counted; there may be any number of unaccented syllables. See pp. 375–376.

Alliteration   Repeated consonants, particularly at the beginning of words or stressed syllables, as in "With a sound like seed spilled . . . " See pp. 310 and 324.

Anapest (n.), **anapestic** (adj.)   A poetic foot consisting of two unaccented (unstressed) and one accented (stressed) syllables, as in: in the SKY. See **Poetic foot** and p. 377.

Antagonist   In narrative, the character who provides the major impediment or obstacle to the main character's desire. See **Protagonist.**

Aside   A theatrical convention whereby a character says something that the audience hears but the other characters do not. See p. 347.

Assonance   Repeated vowel sounds, as in "The rain in Spain stays mainly in the plain." See pp. 310 and 324.

Atmosphere   The tone and attitude, as well as the setting, period, weather, and time of day, of a story. The background to the characters' foreground. See p. 139.

Authorial interpretation; authorial intrusion   The author speaks directly to the reader, rather than through the point of view of the character. By and large, the device is interpretive any time the author tells us what we should think or feel; it is intrusive if we mind this. See pp. 90 and 245.

Backstory   Past events that are necessary to understand a narrative or its significance. See p. 280.

Ballad meter   A stanza of four lines, usually of iambic tetrameter, usually rhymed *abcb*. See p. 381.

Blank verse   Unrhymed iambic pentameter. The most common line in English poetry. See p. 380.

Brainstorm   A problem-solving technique that can also generate ideas for an imagined situation. The writer free-associates a list of ideas, connections, solutions, then uses these as prompts for writing. Often takes the form *"What if . . . ?"* See p. xxv.

Cacophony   Jarring, discordant sound. See p. 380.

Caesura   A pause within a line of poetry, often indicated by a comma or period. See p. 322.

Central Narrator   See **Narrator.**

Character   A fictional person. The basis of literary writing. See Chapter 3.

Characterization   May be direct, through describing how the character looks, acts, etc. or indirect, through summary or interpretation. See Chapter 3.

Cliché   A word, phrase, or metaphor that represents the predictable or overly familiar, and usually indicates lazy writing. See pp. 14 and 313.

Climax   See **Crisis.**

Complications   Aspects of the conflict that build the plot toward its climax. The *"nouement"* or "knotting up" of the action. See p. 167.

Conceit   A metaphor in which the connection between the two things compared is not immediately clear. In Samuel Johnson's words, "yoked by violence together," as in John Donne's comparison of a flea to the holy trinity, or Nathanael West's "love is like a vending machine." The author must explain the similarity. See p. 313.

Concrete, significant details   Specifics that address the senses in meaningful ways. The basic building blocks of imaginative writing, and what is meant by the advice: *Show, don't tell.*
- *Concrete* means that there is an image, something that can be seen, heard, smelled, tasted, or touched.
- *Detail* means that there is a degree of focus and specificity.
- *Significant* means that the specific image also suggests an abstraction, generalization, or judgment.

See p. 7.

Connotation   The complex of meanings and ideas that come to be associated with a word, as "rose" suggests not only the flower but beauty, fragrance, womanhood, perhaps ephemerality, and/or the hidden threat of thorns. See p. 312.

Conflict   The struggle between protagonist and antagonist, or between two opposing forces. Considered necessary to narrative, because it generates a desire in the reader to find out what is going to happen. See pp. 165 and 167.

Consonant   The sound produced by any obstruction of the air stream, brought about by a constriction of one or more of the organs of voice. In English, all the letters of the alphabet that are not vowels (a, e, i, o, u, sometimes y) are consonants. See p. 375 (or 321 and 375).

Consonant cluster   A poetic effect created by "back to back" consonants, so that the speaker has to stop between words in order the pronounce them, as in "The self forgets such strength." See pp. 321 and 380.

Couplet   Two lines of verse, usually rhymed, which can constitute an entire poem or stand as part of a longer stanzaic form. An example:
> "Wales, which I have never seen,
> Is gloomy, mountainous, and green . . ."

See p. 381.

Creative nonfiction   The essay, enlivened through attention to stylistic and dramatic devices, personal voice, and a search for range and resonance. Also called **literary nonfiction.** See Chapter 7, p. 237.

Crisis   The point of highest tension in a story, at which a discovery or a decision is made that decides the outcome of the conflict. See pp. 165 and 167.

Dactyl (n.), **dactylic** (adj.)   A poetic foot consisting of one accented (stressed) and two unaccented (unstressed) syllables, as in: FOR-ti-fy. See **Poetic foot** and p. 378.

Dead metaphor   A metaphor so common that it has lost the original sense of comparison and acquired a further definition, as "sifting the evidence" no longer calls a sieve to mind. See p. 314.

Denotation   The most direct or specific meaning of a word; how it is defined. See p. 312.

Denouement   The resolution at the end of a story. The return to order after the conflict, its complications, and climax have passed. See p. 167.

Density   In literature, the arrangement of words and images to pack maximum meaning into minimum space. See p. 315.

Dialogue   The characters' talk. Dialogue may be:
- **Direct,** the spoken words quoted: "No, I can't stand the little monsters and I won't herd a bunch of them to the damn park unless I'm paid."

- **Indirect,** the words related in third person: She said she couldn't stand kids and wouldn't take them to the park unless she got paid.
- **Summarized,** reported at a distance: She claimed to hate children, and irritatedly demanded payment for taking them to the park.

See pp. 83–86.

Diction   A combination of *vocabulary*, the words chosen, and *syntax*, the order in which they are used. Diction will convey not only the facts but also the tone and attitude of the person whose voice speaks to us from the page. See p. 37.

Diegetic   Musical or other effects that occur naturally as part of the dramatic narrative (a character turns on the radio and a song comes out). **Nondiegetic** effects occur when there is no such natural or realistic link (a suspenseful scene is accompanied by music to enhance the tension). See p. 344.

Dimeter   A line consisting of two poetic feet. **See Poetic foot** and p. 328.

Direct dialogue   See **Dialogue.**

Distance   The position, close or far, of the author in relation to the characters or narrator, often implying the degree to which we are intended to identify with or trust them. Distance will be affected first of all by diction and tone, and may involve a literal distance in time or space (the narrator, for example, is telling a story about himself as a child) or a psychic distance (the author is describing the exploits of a psychopath). See p. 48.

Dramatic irony   The audience (or reader) knows something that the character doesn't know. See p. 344.

Emotional recall   A theatrical convention in which one character tells another about an incident from the past, and the story changes the attitude of the second character in some dramatically significant way. See p. 347.

End rhyme   The rhyming words or syllables occur at the end of the poetic line, as in:
"Ever let the fancy roam,
Pleasure never is at home."
See p. 324.

End-stopped   The phrase, clause, or sentence punctuation occurs at the end of poetic line, as in the example just above. See p. 322.

Enjambment   The opposite of end-stopped; the sentence and its meaning carry on from one line (or stanza) to the next:
"Notwithstanding you are in your grave
These fifteen months, you are invited to apply
For a fixed-rate zero-percent American
Express . . . "
See p. 322.

Essay   From the French word meaning "a try," a prose piece with a basis in fact, on a single subject, presenting the view of the author. Kinds of essay include the expository, narrative, descriptive, persuasive, article, feature, profile, literary nonfiction, and creative nonfiction. See Chapter 7, p. 237.

Euphony   Pleasant and smooth-flowing sound, the opposite of cacophony. See p. 380.

Exposition   In narrative and especially theatre, the laying out of the situation at the opening of the action. See pp. 167 and 338.

Falling action   The portion of a plot that follows the climax and leads to the resolution. A "walking away from the fight." Also called **denouement.** See p. 167.

Figure of speech (or **trope,** or **figurative speech**)   A nonliteral use of language, such as metaphor, simile, hyperbole, personification, and so forth, to enhance or intensify meaning. See pp. 11 and 310.

First person   See **Person.**

Flashback   In narrative, film, or drama, a leap into the past. The earlier scene is inserted into the normal chronological order. See p. 280.

Foot   See **Poetic foot.**

Formal verse   Verse written in a predetermined pattern of rhythm and rhyme. See pp. 310–311 and the Appendix, "A Basic Prosody," p. 375.

Fourth-wall realism   A theatrical convention in which the stage represents a room with the fourth wall removed. Both actors and audience pretend that what is happening onstage is "really" happening at the present time. See p. 340.

Free verse or **informal verse.**   Verse that lacks a regular meter or rhyme scheme, and uses irregular line lengths according to the demands of the particular poem. See pp. 310 and 311.

Freewrite   A piece of writing undertaken without any plan or forethought whatever; writing whatever comes into your head at the moment. Gertrude Stein called this "automatic writing." A **focused freewrite** is a piece written with the same unplanned freedom, but on a chosen topic. See p. xxv.

Genre   A form of writing, such as poetry, drama, or fiction. The term is problematic because "genre fiction" and "genre writing" are terms used differently, to indicate writing in narrow, plot-driven conventions such as the western, romance, detective story, and so forth.

Haiku   A form of poetry taken from the Japanese, representing a moment of perception, in three lines with a pattern of five, seven, and five syllables, for a total of seventeen syllables. See p. 382.

Heptameter   A poetic line of seven feet. See **Poetic foot** and p. 378.

Heroic couplet   Two lines of poetry consecutively rhymed, as in:
"Suspicious, dour, morosed, perplexed,
And just a little oversexed."
See p. 381.

Hexameter   A poetic line of six feet. See **Poetic foot** and p. 378.

Hyperbole   Extreme exaggeration, as in: "You are the sun, the moon, and the stars." See **Figure of speech.**

Iamb   A poetic foot consisting of one unaccented (unstressed) and one accented (stressed) syllable: hoo-RAY. See **Poetic foot** and p. 377.

Idiom   An expression that is grammatically peculiar to itself and can't be understood by understanding its separate elements. English abounds in idioms: *put 'er there*, *keeps tabs on*, *of his own accord*, and so forth. The line between idioms, clichés, dead metaphors, and figures of speech is often not distinct. See p. 314.

Inciting incident   The event that has created the situation in which the protagonist finds him/herself at the beginning of a drama. For example, Hamlet's father has died and his mother has remarried. See p. 338.

Indirect dialogue   See **Dialogue.**

Informal verse   See **Free verse.**

Intensity   In literature, the raising of tension or emotion through character conflict, language, rhythm, situation, irony, or other artistic device. See p. 315.

Internal rhyme   A rhyme in which at least one of the rhyming words occurs within, rather than at the end of, a line, as:
Subdued, the mournful measures falling *under*
The *thunder* of this cascade . . .
See pp. 324 and 380.

Long vowel   See **Vowels.**

Line   A series of words after which there is a typographical break. In prose, the line ends because the type has arrived at a margin, and may vary from one edition or font to another. In poetry, the line implies a slight pause and is used in conjunction with or opposition to the sentence as a means of creating significance. Consequently the line is considered an integral feature of the poem, and will remain the same in each reprinting. See pp. 322 and 375.

Line editing   Careful, often final, revision of a manuscript at the level of checking punctuation, spelling, and grammar as well as the nuance of final word choice. See p. 218.

Literary nonfiction   See **Creative nonfiction.**

Lyric   A type of poem expressing subjective thoughts or feelings, often in the form of a song. See p. 381.

Memoir   A story retrieved from the writer's memory, with the writer as protagonist. See p. 238.

Metaphor   The comparison of one term with another such that a tension is created between what is alike and what is unlike between the two terms.
- A *metaphor* assumes or states the comparison, without acknowledging that it is a comparison: *My electric muscles shock the crowd; Her hair is seaweed and she is the sea.* The metaphor may come in the form of an adjective: *They have a piggy and a fishy air.* Or it may come as a verb: *The bees shouldering the grass.*
- A *simile* is a type of metaphor that acknowledges the comparison by using the words *like* or *as: His teeth rattled like dice in a box; My head is light as a balloon; I will fall like an ocean on that court.*

See p. 11.

Meter   From the Greek "measure," a relatively objective or mechanical way of measuring time in poetry, according to the number of feet and syllables in a line. See pp. 310 and 324.

Metered verse   Verse that can be so measured. See p. 376.

Metonymy   A figure of speech in which one word or phrase is used as substitute for another with which it is associated, as in *the pen is mightier than the sword*, or when *inside the beltway* is used to mean *the U.S. government in Washington.* See p. 11.

Mnemonic   Helpful to or intended to help memory. See p. 310.

Monologue   A speech of some length by a single character. See p. 41.

Monometer   A line consisting of a single poetic foot. See **Poetic foot** and p. 378.

Mood   See **Atmosphere.**

Narrative   A story; the telling of a story.

Narrator   The one who tells the story. We often speak of the author as narrator if the piece is told in the third person, although literally a story "has a narrator" only when it is told by a character. This character may be:
- The **central narrator,** the *I* writing *my* story as if it were memoir, or
- The **peripheral narrator,** someone on the edge of the action, who is nevertheless our eyes and ears in the story and therefore the person with whom we identify, and with whom we must be moved or changed.

See p. 44.

New journalism   Tom Wolfe used the term in the 1960s for a kind of reporting in which the reporter becomes a character in his report, and which relies on all the techniques of a novelist including—importantly, for Wolfe—the details of dress, gesture, speech, and ownership that reveal social status. See p. 238.

Nondiagetic   See **Diagetic.**

Octave In poetry, a group of eight lines, especially the first eight lines of a Petrarchan sonnet. See p. 381.

Off rhyme, or **slant rhyme** The final consonants correspond, but the vowels that precede them are different. Thus *stoned* is an off rhyme for *hand* and *blind*. See p. 379.

Omniscience The narrative convention by which the author knows everything—past, future, any character's thoughts, the significance of events, universal truths. It is the godlike authorial stance. See p. 46.

Onomatopoeia The use of words that sound like what they mean: *buzz, whine, murmur.* See p. 320.

Outline A preliminary plan for a piece of writing, summarizing in list form its major parts or points. See p. 210.

Oxymoron A figure of speech that combines or juxtaposes two contradictory words: *burning ice, shouting whisper, plain decoration.* The term comes from the Greek meaning "sharply foolish," which is itself an oxymoron and expresses the potential of the figure to reveal although it appears not to make sense. See pp. 12 and 318.

Paradox A seemingly contradictory statement of which both parts may nevertheless be true, as in, "A writer is someone for whom writing is more difficult than for other people." (Thomas Mann) See p. 318.

Pentameter A line of five poetic feet. See **Poetic foot** and p. 378.

Peripheral narrator See **Narrator.**

Person In grammar and narrative, any of three groups of pronouns identifying the subject. **First person:** *I look out the window.* **Second person:** *You look out the window.* **Third person:** *He looks out the window.* See p. 44.

Persona A mask adopted by the author, which may be a public manifestation of the author's self; or a distorted or partial version of that self; or a fictional, historical, or mythological character. See p. 39.

Personification The technique of giving human attributes or emotions to animals, objects, or concepts, as in, "the water lapped eagerly at the shore." See p. 11.

Phoneme The smallest sound or phonetic unit that may convey a distinction of meaning, as *cat* is distinguished from *hat*. See p. 320.

Plot A series of events arranged so as to reveal their significance. See **Story.**

Poetic foot A unit of measurement with one accented or stressed syllable, and one or two unstressed syllables. The foot may be iambic (unstress-stress), trochaic (stress-unstress), anapestic (unstress-unstress-stress), or dactylic (stress-unstress-unstress.) A line may be monometer (composed of a single foot), dimeter (two feet), and so forth: trimeter (three), tetrameter (four), pentameter (five), hexameter (six), heptameter (seven.) See p. 323 and 376.

Poetic line A unit of verse recognizable by the typographic break at the end of it, but also by general consent the basic unit of poetry. The break represents a slight pause or very brief silence. In formal poetry, it may also provide a rhyme and/or signal that a certain number of feet has been reached; in free verse, these formal elements may be absent, but the line break may still convey emphasis, suggest connotation, or imply double or even contradictory meaning. See p. 375.

Point of attack In drama, the first event that sets the plot in motion: for example, the ghost speaks to Hamlet, demanding revenge against Claudius. See p. 338.

Point of view A complex technique of narrative involving who tells the story, to whom, in what form. Importantly, the **person** in which the story is told, and the vantage point from which the story is told, contribute to the ultimate meaning of events. See p. 44.

Prose poem A poem that is not written in lines but continues to the margins of the page like prose. See p. 192.

Prosody The study of meter and sound in poetry. See p. 320 and the Appendix on p. 375.

Protagonist The main character of a narrative; usually, one with whom we identify. See p. 166.

Pun A figure of speech that plays on different meanings of the same word, or the different sense or sound of two similar words. "Hair today and gone tomorrow." See pp. 12 and 318.

Pyrrhic A substitute poetic foot with two unaccented (unstressed) syllables. See p. 378.

Quatrain A verse of four lines. See p. 381.

Quilting A (metaphor for a) method of drafting, especially a prose piece, by gathering paragraphs and physically moving them around to produce a rough structure. See p. 211.

Quintet A verse of five lines. See p. 381.

Realism A narrative or dramatic convention that aims at accuracy and verisimilitude in the presentation of period, place, speech, and behavior.

Replacement poem An exercise for reproducing the vigor of an admired poem: replace all of the verbs, nouns, adjectives, and adverbs with other words representing the same part of speech. See p. 316.

Resolution The end of conflict, usually involving the restoration of order, at the end of a plot. See pp. 165 and 167.

Rhyme A similarity or correspondence of sounds. In a true rhyme, the vowel sound of the accented syllable and everything thereafter correspond, as in *laugh* and *staff*, or *laughter* and *after*. In a rich rhyme, the consonant preceding the vowel also corresponds, (the *p* in) *pair* and *repair* and *despair*. In slant rhyme or off rhyme, the vowel sound differs and only the succeeding consonant (and everything thereafter) corresponds, so *flight* is an off rhyme for *plate* and *laughter* is an off rhyme for *softer* and *grifter*. See p. 379.

Rhythm The pattern or flow of sound created by stressed and unstressed syllables. Unlike meter, which is a mechanical measurement of such pattern, rhythm generally expresses a quality achieved by the pattern, so one may say that the rhythm is lighthearted or swaggering or effortful or numb. See p. 376.

Rich rhyme See p. 379.

Run-on line See **Enjambment.**

Scansion The measuring of verse into poetic feet, or a pattern of stressed and unstressed syllables. See p. 310, 323, and the Appendix on pp. 376–378.

Scene and summary Methods of treating time in fiction. A summary covers a relatively long period of time in relatively short compass; a scene deals at length with a relatively short period of time. See p. 277.

Secondary stress Many poets see a secondary stress—less emphasis than a stress, more than an unstress—in the scanning of English poetry. Most three- and four-syllable words offer such a secondary stress: "care-ful-ly" "in-si-di-ous". The secondary stress is marked with a double accent mark. See p. 375.

Second person See **Person.**

Self-reflexivity Referring back to the self. Generally used to indicate that the work, rather than pretending to represent a true picture of real events, acknowledges in some way that it is a fiction, an artifact, a work of imagination. See p. 327.

Septet   A group or verse of seven lines. See p. 381.

Sestet   A group or verse of six lines, especially the last six lines of a Petrarchan sonnet. See p. 381.

Setting   The place and period in which a story or drama takes place. See Chapter 4.

Short-short story   A plotted fiction of no more than 500 words, usually fewer. Also sometimes called *flash fiction* or *microfiction* See p. 164.

Short vowels   See **Vowel.**

Simile   A comparison using the terms *like* or *as*. See **Metaphor.**

Slant rhyme   See **Off rhyme.**

Soliloquy   A theatrical convention in which a character alone onstage makes a speech that we understand to represent his or her thoughts. See p. 347.

Sonnet   A poem of fourteen lines. See p. 381.

Song   May refer to any poetry or verse, but most often to a lyric or a verse meant to be set to music. See p. 381.

Spondee   A substitute foot consisting of two accented (stressed) syllables. See p. 378.

Stage lie   A theatrical convention in which the character says one thing but betrays the opposite through contradiction or visible behavior. See p. 342.

Stanza   A group of lines within a poem, usually set off by white space on the page. In formal verse, the stanzas will typically all have the same number of lines with the same rhythm and rhyme pattern. In free verse, the stanzas indicate some deliberate grouping of images or thoughts. See pp. 380–382.

Story   A sequence of fictional or remembered events, usually involving a conflict, crisis, and resolution. Humphry House, in his commentaries on Aristotle, defines story as everything the reader needs to know to make coherent sense of the plot, and plot as the particular portion of the story the author chooses to present—the "present tense" of the narrative. See Chapter 5, p. 273.

Stress   See **Accent.** See pp. 322 and 375–377.

Summary   See **Scene.**

Summarized dialogue   See **Dialogue.**

Syllable   A unit of spoken language that is a single uninterrupted sound. A syllable will always contain a vowel; it may contain one or more consonants. So *I* and *Oh* are each a single syllable, but so are *light* and *sow* and *soap*. The word LIGHT-ning thus contains two syllables, of which the first is accented or stressed and the second unaccented or unstressed. The syllable is crucial to English poetry because it is the pattern of accented and unaccented syllables that form the basis of the rhythm. See pp. 320 and 375.

Syllabic verse   Poetry in which line length is fixed by the number of syllables in the line; the number of accents is irrelevant. Some poetic forms are intrinsically syllabic, like the haiku, which consists of three lines in the pattern of five, seven, and five syllables. See p. 322.

Symbol   Something, usually an object, that stands for something larger, often an interrelated complex of ideas, values, and beliefs. For example, the flag stands for love of country. In literature, this object is particular to the work. The golden bowl in Henry James's *The Golden Bowl* stands for a situation involving deception, self-deception, betrayal, and flawed marital love. See p. 139.

Synecdoche   A figure of speech in which a part stands for the whole, as in *all hands on deck* or *I'm going to get some new wheels*. See p. 11.

Syntax The arrangement of words within a sentence. See p. 37.

Tempo The pace, speed, or slowness of a rhythm. See p. 376.

Tercet A three-line stanza. See p. 381.

Tetrameter A poetic line consisting of four feet. See **Poetic foot** and p. 378.

Theatricalism The dramatic convention by which the actors acknowledge that the stage is a stage, the play a play, and themselves players of parts. See pp. 340 and 345.

Third person See **Person.**

Trimeter A poetic line consisting of three feet. See **Poetic foot** and p. 378.

Triplet A tercet (three-line stanza) of poetry in which all the end-words rhyme. See p. 381.

Trochee (n.), **trochaic** (adj.) Poetic foot consisting of one accented or stressed and one unaccented or unstressed syllable, as in TI-ger. See **Poetic foot** and p. 377.

Trope See **Figure of speech.**

True rhyme See pp. 377–379.

Unaccented or **unstressed** A syllable that receives relatively little emphasis. See **Accent.**

Unstress See **Unaccented.**

Villanelle An intricate poem, in which the first and third lines are repeated at the end of alternating successive verses and as a couplet at the end. See pp. 222 and 327.

Vocabulary The sum total of words known and used by a writer (or a person or group of people); the choice of words in a particular work. See p. 37.

Voice The recognizable style of a particular writer or character, composed of syntax, vocabulary, attitude, and tone. See Chapter 2.

Voiceover In film and theatre, the voice of an unseen character providing narration, usually by mechanical means. See p. 347.

Vowel The speech sound created by a relatively free passage of breath through the larynx and oral cavity, in English represented by the sounds of *a, e, i, o, u* and sometimes *y*. Vowels may be either *long*, as pronounced in the words *main, feet, dine, rope,* and *cute*; or *short*, as in *cat, pet, in, hop,* and *up*. The designations *long* and *short* hark back to Greek and Latin verse, which was counted not in accented and unaccented syllables but by the length of time it took to pronounce a given syllable. See pp. 321 and 375.

Credits

Photos

Page 002   Laurie Lipton, "Leashed Passion"
Page 036   Saul Steinberg, *Untitled*, 1957
            Ink on paper Originally
            published in *The New Yorker*,
            June 1, 1957 © The Saul
            Steinberg Foundation/Artists
            Rights Society (ARS), New
            York
Page 078   John Grant
Page 130   John Coffer, "Untitled
            (Wonder Wheel)," 2002,
            Contemporary Tintype,
            Collection Akiko Nishimura,

Photo Courtesy Kerrigan
Campbell art + projects.
Page 162   © Helen Levitt, Courtesy
            Laurence Miller Gallery,
            New York
Page 206   Photos (clockwise from top left)
            Pam Valois, Reuters/Corbis,
            Pam Valois, Dirk Westphal
Page 236   Laurie Lipton, "The Self-
            Destructive Optimist"
Page 272   Laurie Lipton, "Facing up to
            Reality"
Page 308   Jerry Uelsmann, "Symbolic
            Mutation"
Page 336   William Noland

Readings

"At Navajo Monument Valley Tribal School" from The Business of Fancydancing by Sherman Alexie. Copyright © 1992 by Sherman Alexie. Used by permission of Hanging Loose Press.

From Borderlands/La Frontera: The New Mestiza. Copyright © 1987, 1999 by Gloria Anzaldúa. Reprinted by permission of Aunt Lute Books.

"The Female Body," from Good Bones and Simple Murders by Margaret Atwood. Copyright © 1983, 1992, 1994, by O. W. Toad Ltd. A Nan A. Talese Book. Used by permission of Doubleday, a division of Random House, Inc. and McClelland & Stewart Ltd.

"The School" by Donald Barthelme. Copyright © 1976 by Donald Barthelme. Reprinted with the permission of The Wylie Agency.

"Snow," from A Relative Stranger by Charles Baxter. Copyright © 1990 by Charles Baxter. Used by permission of W. W. Norton & Company, Inc.

"Dream Song #117 from The Dream Songs by John Berryman. Copyright © 1969 by John Berryman. Copyright renewed 1997 by Kate Donahue Berryman. Reprinted by permission of Farrar, Straus and Giroux, LLC.

"One Art" from The Complete Poems 1927–1979 by Elizabeth Bishop. Copyright © 1979, 1983 by Alice Helen Methfessel. Reprinted by permission of Farrar, Straus and Giroux, LLC.

From A Blind Man Can See How Much I Love You by Amy Bloom. Copyright © 2000 by Amy Bloom. Used by permission of Random House, Inc.

"Missing" from A Good Scent from a Strange Place by Robert Olen Butler. Copyright 2001. Used by permission of the author.

"A Wind from the North" by Bill Capossere from In Short: A Collection of Brief Creative Nonfiction, W. W. Norton, 1996. Used by permission of the author.

"Bigfoot Stole My Wife," from A Kind of Flying: Selected Stories by Ron Carlson. Copyright © 2003, 1997, 1992, 1987 by Ron Carlson. Used by permission of W. W. Norton & Company, Inc.

Reprinted from Writing the World by Kelly Cherry, by permission of the University of Missouri Press. Copyright © 1995 by the Curators of the University of Missouri.

"Snow Day," copyright © 2001 by Billy Collins, from Sailing Alone Around the Room by Billy Collins. Used by permission of Random House, Inc.

"Ginko Tree" from The Temple on Monday by Tom Crawford. Used by permission of Eastern Washington University Press.

"Story" by Lydia Davis from Story and Other Stories (The Figures; Great Barrington, MA). Copyright © 1983 by Lydia Davis. Reprinted by permission of the Denise Shannon Literary Agency, Inc.

"At the Dam" from The White Album by Joan Didion. Copyright © 1979 by Joan Didion. Reprinted by permission of Farrar, Straus and Giroux, LLC.

Excerpt from Chapter 1 "Heaven and Earth in Jest," pp. 5–6, from Pilgrim at Tinker Creek by

Index

Additional Titles of Interest

Note to Instructors: Any of these Penguin-Putnam, Inc. titles can be packaged with this book for a special discount of up to 60 percent off the retail price. Contact your local Allyn & Bacon/Longman sales representative for details on how to create a Penguin-Putnam, Inc. Value Package.

Albee, *Three Tall Women*
Allison, *Bastard Out of Carolina*
Alvarez, *How the Garcia Girls Lost their Accents*
Austen, *Persuasion*
Austen, *Pride & Prejudice*
Austen, *Sense & Sensibility*
Bellow, *The Adventures of Augie March*
Boyle, *Tortilla Curtain*
Cather, *My Antonia*
Cather, *O Pioneers!*
Cervantes, *Don Quixote*
Chopin, *The Awakening*
Conrad, *Nostromo*
DeLillo, *White Noise*
Desai, *Journey to Ithaca*
Douglass, *Narrative Life of Frederick Douglass*
Golding, *Lord of the Flies*
Hawthorne, *The Scarlet Letter*
Homer, *Illiad*
Homer, *Odyssey*
Hwang, *M. Butterfly*
Hulme, *Bone People*
Jen, *Typical American*
Karr, *The Liar's Club*
Kerouac, *On the Road*
Kesey, *One Flew Over the Cuckoo's Nest*
King, *Misery*
Larsen, *Passing*
Lavin, *In a Café*
Marquez, *Love in the Time of Cholera*
McBride, *The Color of Water*
Miller, *Death of a Salesman*

Morrison, *Beloved*
Morrison, *The Bluest Eye*
Morrison, *Sula*
Naylor, *Women of Brewster Place*
Orwell, *1984*
Postman, *Amusing Ourselves to Death*
Raybon, *My First White Friend*
Rose, *Lives on the Boundary*
Rose, *Possible Lives: The Promise of Public*
Rushdie, *Midnight's Children*
Shakespeare, *Four Great Comedies*
Shakespeare, *Four Great Tragedies*
Shakespeare, *Hamlet*
Shakespeare, *Four Histories*
Shakespeare, *King Lear*
Shakespeare, *Macbeth*
Shakespeare, *Othello*
Shakespeare, *Twelfth Night*
Shelley, *Frankenstein*
Silko, *Ceremony*
Solzenitsyn, *One Day in the Life of Ivan Denisovich*
Sophocles, *The Three Theban Plays*
Spence, *The Death of a Woman Wang*
Steinbeck, *The Grapes of Wrath*
Steinbeck, *The Pearl*
Stevenson, *Dr. Jekyll & Mr. Hyde*
Swift, *Gulliver's Travels*
Twain, *Adventures of Huckleberry Finn*
Wilson, *Joe Turner's Come and Gone*
Wilson, *Fences*
Woolf, *Jacob's Room*